REGULATION AND RISK

Regulation and Risk

*Occupational Health and Safety
on the Railways*

BRIDGET M. HUTTER

OXFORD
UNIVERSITY PRESS

OXFORD
UNIVERSITY PRESS

Great Clarendon Street, Oxford OX2 6DP

Oxford University Press is a department of the University of Oxford.
It furthers the University's objective of excellence in research, scholarship,
and education by publishing worldwide in

Oxford New York

Athens Auckland Bangkok Bogotá Buenos Aires Cape Town
Chennai Dar es Salaam Delhi Florence Hong Kong Istanbul Karachi
Kolkata Kuala Lumpur Madrid Melbourne Mexico City Mumbai Nairobi
Paris São Paulo Shanghai Singapore Taipei Tokyo Toronto Warsaw

with associated companies in Berlin Ibadan

Oxford is a registered trade mark of Oxford University Press
in the UK and in certain other countries

Published in the United States
by Oxford University Press Inc., New York

British Library Cataloguing in Publication Data
Data available

Library of Congress Cataloging in Publication Data
Hutter, Bridget M.
Regulation and risk: occupational health and safety on the railways/Bridget M. Hunter. p. cm
Includes bibliographical references and index.
1. Railroads—Great Britain—Safety measures 2. Railroads—Employees—
Health and hygiene—Great Britain. 3. Risk management—Great Britain.
4. Railroads—Law and legislation—Great Britain. I. Title
HE1783.G7 H86 2001 363.11'9385'0941—dc21 00-050500
ISBN 0–19–924250–X

1 3 5 7 9 10 8 6 4 2

Typeset by J&L Composition Ltd, Filey, North Yorkshire
Printed in Great Britain
on acid-free paper by
Biddles Ltd., Guildford & King's Lynn

To Richard

PREFACE

When I undertook my first research into regulation in the late 1970s/early 1980s there was very little other research on the subject.[1] Fortunately the situation is now very different. Over the past twenty years a growing and increasingly sophisticated regulation literature has emerged. This work is characterized by a number of trends, some of which reflect changes in regulation and others which are informed by broader academic considerations.

A central organizing perspective of this book is that regulation is a way of managing the risks associated with life in advanced industrial societies. While the relationship between regulation and risk has been an enduring theme in discussions of regulation it has often remained implicit in the literature. Recent regulatory and academic trends have, however, brought this relationship to the centre stage. Risk has become the focus of much academic attention, particularly within the sociological literature. Some dismiss this interest in risk as a fashion that will quickly pass, but in the case of regulation this cannot be the case as the management of risk is what regulation is all about. Moreover its relevance has been heightened by a shift in regulation itself towards the co-option of corporate risk management systems by the state regulatory effort. This in turn reflects broader trends towards a holistic view of regulation, the co-existence of public and private forms of regulation, and a mix of sources and instruments of regulation.

Academically this book shifts the gaze to a sometimes 'silent' partner in the regulation literature, namely the regulated. All too often those subject to regulation have been caricatured as the passive and sometimes recalcitrant recipients of state regulatory regimes. This is partly a result of the primary academic gaze being upon the regulatory agency. It is also a consequence of the lack of attention given in the socio-legal literature (my own earlier work included) to the nature of the economic activities subject to regulation; the main focus of attention has traditionally been on the law and government agencies rather than markets and companies. This book pursues questions about economic life, most especially the assumptions we make about the nature of corporate responses to regulation. In doing so it is part of a broader sociological trend to refocus on

[1] In particular there was very little sociologically informed or socio-legal work on regulation. Notable exceptions in Britain were Carson's documentary study of the Factory Inspectorate (1970, 1974, 1980) and the emerging literature at the Centre for Socio-Legal Studies in Oxford. This included Cranston's (1979) examination of trading standard officers and the work of Hawkins (1984), Richardson, Ogus, and Burrows (1983), and Brittan (1984) on water pollution control. In the United States the work of Kagan (1978) and Kelman (1981) and in Australia Braithwaite's research (1984; 1985), his work with Grabosky (1986), and Gunningham's studies (1974; 1984) were also important early studies. Overall, however, very little had been published during this period.

the relationship between economy and society (Granovetter and Swedberg, 1992; Smelser and Swedberg, 1994). The study also asks more conventional questions about the nature of the social control of organizational and economic activities rather than the traditional focus of the social control of individuals.

The main intellectual concern of the book is to develop the regulation and risk literature into new areas, most specifically consideration of corporate responses to regulation. This intellectual focus is explored through an in-depth empirical study of how British Railways responded to occupational health and safety legislation. British Railways was chosen as a case study because it was a major company in a risky industry and, despite its caricature, was a highly motivated industry compared to many others. It was therefore a good test for gauging how well the trend to co-opting corporate risk management capacity was understood and how it might be implemented. The case also highlights central issues of control and risk in a large organization. And more pragmatically this was an industry and a company with which I was already familiar through my earlier work on the Health and Safety Executive and the Railway Inspectorate (Hutter, 1997).

The railway industry in Britain has changed quite radically since the data for this study were collected. British Railways was then a nationalized company which ran most of the national rail network in Great Britain. Now the industry has been privatized and British Railways is one small company among over a hundred others running the national rail system. Moreover there have been some institutional changes in the regulation of health and safety. Nevertheless it is crucial to understand that the age of the data is no bar to their contemporary relevance, far from it. At one level the book contributes a detailed snapshot of the responses of a large company to a set of regulations at a particular moment in time, but this is not just an historic account. The data are of much broader value and they provide generic lessons that are of very contemporary relevance. The research period was during the early phases of the privatization of British Railways. The study maps out the pitfalls of a model of regulation that was in fact greatly extended with the privatization of the railways. It is important to appreciate that the health and safety arrangements introduced with privatization were not a complete change from before but rather a development of what was in place during the research period. Indeed, privatization actually exacerbated the very conditions identified by this research as problematic to the success of enforced self-regulation. It did so in dramatic and unfortunate circumstances. As the industry fragmented, so did the difficulties of communication. Privatization heightened the tensions between risk and regulation and productivity and safety. Trends to systematize corporate and government approaches to risk management appeared to have counterproductive side effects as they started to counter the legitimacy of regulatory objectives and hamper the ability of the industry to self-regulate. These tensions came into public focus in the late 1990s with the loss of seven people in an accident at Southall in 1997, the loss of thirty-one at Ladbroke Grove in 1999, and then again just a year later with the death of four more in an accident at Hatfield. Each of these accidents crystallized attention on the tensions between maintaining a safe railway system and satisfying commercial interests. These developments are discussed in later chapters of the book.

Occupational health and safety on the railways is obviously an emotive subject about which it would be very easy to be polemical. Some might regard the tone of this book as too temperate given the tragic consequences which may result from regulatory failure, but this is a complex subject which has serious consequences. Thus it is vital that the complexities are grasped and that we attempt to make sense of them rather than be too ready to generalize and simplify. Arguably such an approach can make a more effective contribution to policy debates and ultimately to practice. It should also be noted that the findings of this research have in fact been used to make improvements to occupational health and safety on the railways. British Railways and sub-units of the company used the findings during and after the data collection period to help them improve their systems and communication. Moreover other practitioner groups have been interested in the work and the lessons to be learned from it. More generally it is hoped that the broader lessons about different models and instruments of regulation will feed into the policy-making process and into corporate understandings of risk management, and thus effect improvements in these ways.

No research is undertaken and no book is written in isolation from other influences and comment. As always I am indebted to a number of individuals and institutions for their support in producing this work. Venetia Budgen and Gail Eaton both provided invaluable research assistance with the data collection and analysis stages of the research. Bill Bradshaw was very supportive in helping me to gain access for the study and in advising on the writing of reports to the industry and unions on the findings. Liz Fitzgerald helped prepare the final manuscript. Intellectual support was offered by colleagues at the Centre for Socio-Legal Studies in Oxford, where I worked during the data collection period, and the London School of Economics, where I worked during the writing of the book. The British Academy should also be recognized and thanked for appointing me to a post-doctoral research fellowship which funded me through the data collection, data analysis, and the early drafts of this book. These fellowships are important in establishing careers and they were particularly important in the late 1980s when the academic job market was so stagnant.

A variety of individuals have been extraordinarily generous in giving up their time to read through the manuscript. Stan Cohen and Paul Rock offered valuable comments on the first full draft of the manuscript despite being overburdened with extra teaching because of my sabbatical leave. Nigel Dodd offered comments on the final chapter and has proven a valuable colleague in discussions about economic life. Clive Briault has, as always, offered unstinting comment at all stages of the research and writing. His patience in this was not always deserved by me so I am particularly grateful to him. The anonymous reviewers who commented on the manuscript for OUP made several useful suggestions, many of which have been incorporated into the final manuscript. Mike Power should be thanked for his forbearance in commenting on drafts and redrafts of key chapters prior to the final submission of the manuscript. I am very grateful to him and to David Musson for his patience and support while this task was completed.

Thanks must go to the numerous individuals within British Railways and also the Railway Inspectorate, who supported the research and gave up their time to be interviewed. Obviously this study could not have been undertaken without the co-operation of staff across British Railways, and it could not have proved such a rich source of data without the frankness and honesty with which they approached the interviews. The Directors of British Railways and the unions should also be thanked for exposing themselves to such scrutiny. I am very grateful to them and sincerely hope that this work has already helped to improve occupational health and safety on the railways and that it will con-tribute to future improvements in this and other industries.

My children suffered (or benefited, depending upon one's point of view) as I juggled the research, this book, teaching, administration, and most of all them. Their 'price' is a book to be dedicated to each of them. This one is for Richard but Corin and Esther are not forgotten.

BMH

October 2000

CONTENTS

Part V: Postscript

Part VI: Conclusion

LIST OF FIGURES

LIST OF CHARTS

LIST OF TABLES

ABBREVIATIONS

AEU	Amalgamated Engineering Union
ASLEF	Associated Society of Locomotive Engineers and Firemen
ATP	Automatic Train Protection
BR	British Railways
BRB	British Railways Board
BTP	British Transport Police
GMB	General, Municipal, Boilermakers and Allied Trades Union
HMRI	Her Majesty's Railway Inspectorate
HSC	Health and Safety Commission
HSE	Health and Safety Executive
HSW Act	Health and Safety at Work etc. Act, 1974
ILGRA	Interdepartmental Liaison Group on Risk Assessment
IMF	International Monetary Fund
NUR	National Union of Railwaymen
OSHA	Occupational Safety and Health Administration
QRA	quantified risk assessment
RIAC	Railway Industry Advisory Committee
RMT	Railways, Maritime and Transport Workers Union
ROSPA	Royal Society for the Prevention of Accidents
RSC	Railway Safety Case
SPAD	Signals Passed at Danger
SRSC	Safety Representatives and Safety Committee
TPWS	Train Protection Warning System
TQM	total quality management
TSSA	Transport Salaried Staffs' Association
VDU	Visual Display Unit

LIST OF STATUTES

INTRODUCTION

SETTING THE SCENE

Introduction

Britain in the mid-1980s to mid-1990s was rocked by a series of disasters—health and safety disasters such as the sinking of the ferry *The Herald of Free Enterprise* at Zeebrugge in 1987; the explosion of the Piper Alpha Oil Rig in 1988; the King's Cross underground station fire in 1987; the rail collision at Clapham Junction in 1988; the collision of the *Marchioness* pleasure boat in 1989; and financial disasters such as the massive loan losses at Johnson Matthey Bank in 1984 and at BCCI in 1991; and large-scale derivative trading losses in the Far East at Barings Bank in 1995. These events were mirrored internationally, notably in the methylisocynate gas leak from the Bhopal chemical plant in India in 1984; the steam explosion and leakage of radiation across Europe from Chernobyl in the USSR in 1986; and the dramatic fall of the US stock market on 'Black Friday' in October 1987. High profile disasters such as these are the tip of an iceberg. Daily there are less dramatic failures, many of which have serious—sometimes fatal—consequences for thousands of individuals across the world. The media rarely report these, but the cumulative total in human cost is considerably greater than the sum total of those high profile events which are so widely reported by the world's media. The Labour Force Survey estimates that some 1.04 million workers suffer workplace injury in Britain every year (HSC, 2000). Meanwhile an IMF survey of bank soundness worldwide revealed that during the period 1980–96 73.5 per cent of fund member countries had experienced significant banking sector problems (Lindgren *et al.*, 1996). For example, during the period 1984–91 more than 1,400 savings and loans banks in the United States failed, with resolution costs estimated at some 3–5 per cent of gross national product (Caprio and Klingebiel, 1996). These events have a number of things in common. They are often corporate failures; and they are to varying extents regulatory failures. Moreover they are accompanied by thousands more incidents which might have happened daily but for increasingly complex risk management systems, many of which are the result of the regulation of economic activities by state and other agencies.[1] They are tangible manifestations of the risk society.

In this book I will focus on state regulation of occupational health and safety in one economic sector in Britain, namely the railway industry. More specifically I will concentrate on one major company, British Railways, which at the time of

---

[1] I am taking a broad view of the term economic life, which I take to embrace all activities which fall under the heuristic division between social regulation, which typically concerns the regulation of industrial processes, and economic (or financial) regulation, which generally refers to the regulation of financial markets, prices and profits. See Chapter 1.

the research held a monopoly position over much of the overland rail network in Britain. Occupational health and safety is not, despite its potentially devastating effects on individuals' lives, a particularly high profile area of risk management. For instance, the media rarely report worker injuries and risks unless they occur in exceptionally unusual circumstances or involve multiple deaths. Of much higher profile are train accidents involving the public (Hutter, 1992). Yet the railway industry is one of the most risky occupational settings in Britain (see Ch. 3). The main risks are fairly straightforward and tangible. Moreover they are risks which the state has sought to regulate through the law since the late nineteenth century (see Ch. 4).

Regulation, Risk, and Law

The use of the law to regulate the risks associated with economic activities is a feature of advanced industrial societies (Hancher and Moran, 1989). The use of the law to regulate rather than prohibit activities and behaviour is significant. The very use of the word regulation signals a toleration of the activity subject to control. Regulation is not an attempt to eradicate risk, crucially it is an attempt to *manage* it. Moreover it very often involves the regulation of corporate and individual behaviour.

State regulation of occupational health and safety has changed in some important respects over the past 100 years. Underlying these changes are shifting conceptions of corporate activity and changing perspectives on responsibility. The system of state regulation established in the nineteenth century was paternalistic. The 'Nanny State' set out an extensive system of detailed statutory provisions that were administered and enforced by government departments and local authorities. The legislation was precisely defined and prescriptive. It placed primary responsibility for health and safety with industry. In turn companies took a paternalistic line with their staff as occupational health and safety legislation was imposed on the workforce as a matter of hierarchy and discipline, rather than co-operation.

In 1974, however, the Health and Safety at Work etc. Act, 1974, embodied a radical new approach to workplace health and safety in Britain, important features of which are an emphasis upon self-regulation and upon employees as participatory rather than passive agents in the workplace. This legislation was the result of the Robens Committee report into *Safety and Health at Work* (1972), which represented a watershed in thinking about the legal regulation of health and safety. Underlying the changes it recommended was a corporatist philosophy which regards health and safety as the everyday concern of everyone at work. This system is communitarian to the extent that it involves everyone in regulation and emphasizes interdependencies between groups (see Ch. 7). But it also emphasizes individual responsibility and regards everyone as a stakeholder in their own and their colleagues' health and safety at work.

This shift highlights one of the distinctive features of regulatory law, namely that it attempts to constitute structures, routines, and procedures for health and safety which will be incorporated into organizational routines and also become part of everyday individual activity. Where this fails, the law can intervene through more overt forms of control, notably external regulation and sanctions. Regulatory law is thus simultaneously constitutive and constraining (Stenning *et al.*, 1990). As Stone (1975) comments, the key task is to make bureaucracies think like responsible individuals. But more than this, the law now penetrates deep into the organization in an attempt to make individuals within organizations act responsibly. It does this by attempting to constitute regulation as part of organizational life and getting the organization and those within it to take responsibility for regulation. Such an approach underlines the pervasiveness of regulation and leads us to consider different models of economic and corporate life.

According to the neo-classical model, regulation may be seen as intervention to restrain competition either to make the market operate more efficiently (i.e. remedy market failure) or to prevent undesirable outcomes (i.e. broader welfare objectives). Regulation is regarded as the natural opponent of the market (Colebatch, 1989). So without regulation it is assumed that there would be market competition and an unrestrained market. Arguably it is this model of markets and corporations which underpins state regulation of economic life (Stone, 1975). Alternative perspectives of economic life and corporate activity challenge the notion of the market being in natural antithesis to regulation and the view that firms always act solely in their own self-interest. They argue that regulation is pervasive and is part of the normal market just as regulation may be seen as part of normal social life (Novak, 1996). Some suggest that there is no such thing as an unregulated market. A corollary of this is that if the market is necessarily constituted then regulation is inevitable (Burk, 1988). These perspectives further suggest that corporations are complex, comprising different interest groups with different goals, hence they do not pursue identical and clearly specified goals. They may pursue conflicting goals and may be unable to organize to achieve agreed-upon objectives. Which model of corporate behaviour is most relevant is a research question which has implications for the way in which modern societies seek to manage risk through regulation.

The Research

The purpose of this research was to take a major company in Britain and to use it as a case study for focusing on the broader theoretical and empirical discussions of regulation, risk, and corporate activities in one advanced Western society. These broader contexts will be discussed in Chapter 1. At one level this research is an account of how workplace risks in modern societies are managed. How does risk influence lives? How is it managed by organizations? What influence does the law have in this? And what is endemic to the control of risk in large organizations that operate under performance pressure? It is also an account of corporate responses to legislation which attempts to harness the regulatory capacity of the company and penetrate deep into its risk management systems, routines, and the everyday activities of its employees.

More specifically the research sought to discover the impact of state occupational health and safety regulation on the corporate life of British Railways. Part I sets the scene for this analysis in its discussion of the railway industry in Britain and of the risks to occupational health and safety involved in the industry. Part II examines regulatory objectives through a study of regulatory legislation and also of the regulatory agency charged with enforcing occupational health and safety legislation during the research period. Whether or not it is necessary for the regulated to know and understand regulatory objectives is unclear. One argument is that it is one simple indicator of the impact of the law and regulation. It discerns whether or not the law and the regulatory apparatus are known about and if so with what level of sophistication. Some believe that this is of vital importance in a system based on self-regulation. Genn (1993), for example, argues that an awareness of legal obligations may be seen as a prerequisite of compliance. But it may be that there are other sources of regulation or that regulatory objectives are so well internalized that state regulation is automatically complied with. In such cases knowledge of the state system is arguably of less importance and significance. Regardless of these arguments we can gain some ideas of the social dimensions and distribution of knowledge within the organization by focusing on the understandings of various interest groups within it and this in turn enhances our understanding of risk management within the company.

Part III focuses on the corporate management of risk. This involves seeking to research the extent to which the risk management systems the company had in place complied with those specified in occupational health and safety legislation. This included consideration of the institutional systems and structures for health and safety. Also important was the extent to which regulatory structures within the company were participative. This necessarily involved consideration of safety representatives and the formal committees and routines incorporating them. But it also involved finding out how much different groups within the company knew about occupational health and safety risks and the systems, procedures, and practices in place to manage them. This aspect is therefore considered throughout the book as it is a cross-cutting theme. Part IV directly addresses risk and compliance. It asks a number of questions. First, what understandings of risk and uncertainty did different interest groups have of their occupational environment? Secondly, how did this relate to their propensity to take risks or, put another way, to comply with systems promoting occupational health and safety?

Part V relates the research findings to subsequent developments in the organization of the industry and the regulatory system. It focuses on the privatization of British Railways and the extension of the model of enforced self-regulation which had operated during the research period. In particular this part highlights the continuities between the research period and what happened next and the failure of an extreme version of the enforced self-regulation model. Part VI takes a broader perspective and asks what lessons can we learn about regulation through law, risk management, organizational control, and corporate behaviour. Moreover, how do these findings relate to our existing knowledge of and theories about regulation, risk, and economic life?

Data for the research were collected in the late 1980s and early 1990s. This included 134 in-depth interviews, mainly with British Railways staff but also with regional and national union representatives. More details of the research methods are provided in Chapter 3 and the Appendices. It is, however, important to emphasize here that different interest groups were included in the sample. This included staff from the four main functional departments of the railway and from different administrative (and thus geographical) regions. Different groupings of staff were also interviewed. These included directors and senior managers of the company, middle managers, supervisors who are the most junior of managers and were often recruited from the workforce, basic grade workers, and their representatives. In addition specialist health and safety staff from all departments, the sample regions, and all grades were interviewed. This study therefore maps out the social dimensions of how different groups receive and interpret knowledge about regulation and risk and, in turn, how this shaped their perceptions of risk, responsibility, and compliance.

1

Concepts and Orientations

Risk and Regulation

The past twenty years have witnessed a dramatic growth in academic discussions of two phenomena of crucial importance to advanced industrial societies, namely regulation and risk. The use of the law to regulate economic activities has become a defining characteristic of modern societies (Hancher and Moran, 1989) and arguably so has risk (Beck, 1992; Giddens, 1994). While studies of regulation have long recognized that regulation and risk are connected, the relationship between the two was assumed rather than explored. Yet it is important to appreciate that the growth of regulation is inextricably related to risk. But regulation is not an attempt to eradicate risk, crucially it is an attempt to *manage* it. And a central organizing perspective of this book is that regulation is a form of risk management.

Risk may refer to many forms of external danger (Ericson and Haggerty, 1997). Some risks are global, such as environmental degradation, whereas others are individual, for example smoking. Some risks are involuntary and some are voluntary. Some risks are natural and others are manufactured (Giddens, 1994). It is the involuntary and particularly manufactured risks that are most associated with regulation. Manufactured risks are a product of modernity, a result of enormous advances in technology, the growth of large-scale organizations and globalization—the growth and complexity of what some now term the 'risk society' (Beck, 1992). Modern societies are characterized by a paradox, namely that scientific and technological developments enhance life and also involve greater risks, sometimes catastrophic risks (Beck, 1992; Giddens, 1994; Short and Clarke, 1992). The by-products of legitimate and sometimes exciting new developments may be unintended dangers, such as pollution, threats to worker health and safety, and the capacity to upset financial markets at great speed across the globe. Governments have typically intervened to regulate these risks and to protect vulnerable groups in society and the economy. Indeed the relationship between risk and regulation is underlined by two leading policing authors who assert that 'Risk society is a regulatory society' (Ericson and Haggerty, 1997: 48). The concept of risk developed in its scope, sophistication, and academic interest in the 1990s, a period during which the concept of regulation has also been developed.

There are many definitions of *regulation* (Mitnick, 1980). Early definitions viewed regulation as state activity, in particular state intervention through the law (Kagan, 1978). This is now more commonly referred to as the 'command and control' approach to regulation. It involves the 'command' of the law and the legal authority of the state. Crucially it refers to the regulation of economic actors and economic institutions (see below).

The use of the law as a regulator of economic life first came to prominence in nineteenth-century industrial societies.[1] In the 1970s this form of regulation experienced a surge of popularity and advanced industrial societies witnessed a proliferation of laws designed to regulate economic activities across a broad economic spectrum. Sunstein (1990), writing of the US experience, refers to this as a 'rights revolution' stemming from the New Deal in 1940s America and the explosion of statutory rights in the 1970s (see also Rose-Ackerman, 1992; Sigler and Murphy, 1988). In the United Kingdom the 1970s and 1980s witnessed a similar proliferation of regulatory legislation relating, for example, to occupational health and safety, the environment, consumer protection, and finance.[2] This in part explains the awakening of academic interest in the subject, from sociologists, political scientists, and lawyers in Britain and the United States in the 1970s and 1980s (Carson, 1974; Cranston, 1978; Hawkins, 1984; Hutter, 1988; Kagan, 1978; Richardson *et al.*, 1983).

In direct contrast to this, the late 1980s witnessed a growing disillusionment with state regulation, in part stemming from criticisms of regulatory agencies (Baldwin, 1997; Dwyer, 1990, 1993; Yeager, 1991) and calls for a dismantling or 'rolling back' of the regulatory state (Rose-Ackerman, 1992; Sigler and Murphy, 1988). In the United States and the United Kingdom there was a strong deregulatory rhetoric, but whether or not this actually resulted in less regulation is highly debatable (Majone, 1989). Certainly the United Kingdom experienced a plethora of new regulatory laws in the 1990s, amounting in effect to re-regulation.[3] Academically this was reflected in greater consideration of alternative means of regulating economic activity. The term regulation became construed broadly to include an increasingly wide range of policy instruments and non-governmental activities (Baldwin, 1997; Grabosky, 1995*a*: 347). For example, the state may delegate regulation to third parties (Gilboy, 1998); there may be self-regulation;[4] or regulation may involve the exploitation

---

[1] Historically the origins of regulation can be traced much further back in time (Ogus, 1994). The reference here is to the more general and widespread use of command and control regulation in industrial societies (Novak, 1996).

[2] For instance, the Health and Safety at Work etc. Act, 1974; the Control of Pollution Act, 1974; the Consumer Credit Act, 1974; Consumer Safety Act, 1978; Consumer Protection Act, 1987; Fair Trading Act, 1985; and the Financial Services Act, 1986.

[3] For example, the Clean Air Act, 1993; Environmental Protection Act, 1990; Food and Safety Act, 1990; and the Town and Country Planning Act, 1990.

[4] This term may cover a wide range of arrangements ranging from self-regulation mandated by law to the decision of an individual firm or industry to set its own standards and enforce them. See Ogus (1994).

of commercial incentives which may already exist in the market (Grabosky, 1994).[5] More typically there has been a 'regulatory mix' in which state and other forms of regulation co-exist and where there is flexibility to adapt different methods to individual circumstances (Aalders, 1993; Ayres and Braithwaite, 1992; Bardach and Kagan, 1982; Grabosky, 1995*a*; 1995*b*; Gunningham, 1995). But despite its limitations, command and control regulation remains an important form of regulation. It is still regarded by many as an important underpinning of other regulatory methods and is particularly valued as a method which may be used as a last resort when other methods fail (Boyer and Meidinger, 1985).

Early accounts of the emergence of regulation discussed the reasons for regulation in terms of protection and intervention on behalf of consumers, the public, and the environment. The harms were seen as being associated with a rapidly changing society but the language of risk was seldom used. The ambivalent character of regulatory law was analysed in terms of the conflicting interests of business and those vulnerable to the harms created by otherwise desirable activities. The law was seen as 'tolerant'—too tolerant maybe—and reasonable—too reasonable even (Hutter, 1988). The debate centred more upon the power of different groups to have their interests represented in law than it did on the politics of risk. Discussion of the politics of risk emerged from sociological studies of science and with reference to particular domains of regulation, most notably to the environment.[6] Indeed the subject of risk tended until fairly recently to be compartmentalized into distinct academic disciplines, most notably into the areas of statistics, finance, and particularly insurance (Hood and Jones, 1996). It is only in the past decade that much broader social science approaches to risk have been developed. Likewise risk models and approaches have gained much broader currency in the commercial world (Gabe, 1995).

The massive growth in social science interest in risk has encompassed a variety of disciplinary approaches to the study of risk and a range of different focuses of interest, from the individual to cultural (see Krimsky and Golding, 1992). But as Renn (1992: 61) explains, 'All risk concepts of the social sciences have in common the principle that the causes and consequences of risks are mediated through social processes'. So it is recognized that technical, quantifiable risk calculations do not stand alone in a vacuum but they need to be interpreted. As Bernstein (1996: 206 ff.) explains, risk management is a 'practical art' since much of the information we have is incorrect or incomplete. Decisions need to be made about how much uncertainty is acceptable and what levels of risk are tolerable.

---

[5] These alternative forms of regulation are not 'new inventions'. Rather the social science and political gaze has fallen upon alternatives to 'command and control' regulation, many of which already existed in some form or another.

[6] The relationship between law, science, and risk is relatively underdeveloped. Some of the most innovative work in this area has been undertaken by Sheila Jasanoff in the United States and Brian Wynne in Britain.

What cannot be denied is that the meanings and understandings of risk are influenced by the broader social and cultural contexts within which they are situated and this is where regulation and the law emerge as significant. The law may be seen as one way of presenting an orderly account of danger, or as one way in which risk is socially constructed. The law is one way of classifying danger and setting up requirements for its recognition and management; it is also a means of communicating about risk (Ericson and Haggerty, 1997: 90).

The regulation and risk literatures have come together in a rather piecemeal way, so risk has become more incorporated into some aspects of the regulation literature than others. Discussion of risk has highlighted the importance of the relationship between expert knowledge, risk, and regulation; and as we have seen, the relationship between regulation and science has attracted some academic attention (Jasanoff *et al.*, 1995; Nelkin, 1992; Wynne, 1989). Science is of course another way of establishing and communicating about risk, but interestingly may well clash with the legal perspective on risk (Smith and Wynne, 1989). These debates have been especially important in research on policy-making (Brickman *et al.*, 1985; Jasanoff, 1991; Rayner, 1991). Indeed, policy-makers themselves have taken on board risk management and risk assessment techniques in their approach to regulation (Rimington, 1992). They have also been increasingly exposed to important distinctions which have emerged between experts and the lay public. Indeed it is in these discussions that the notion that science enables us to have greater control of risks is challenged (Giddens, 1990; Pollak, 1995). Policy-makers have very much been confronted with the reality that knowledge of risks is both a means of risk management and a producer of new risks (Ericson and Haggerty, 1997: 88).

Other aspects of regulation which have been examined with reference to risk include enforcement, which has been considered alongside risk, from a field-level perspective (Hutter and Lloyd-Bostock, 1992); and legal action, which has been examined as a form of risk-taking (Hawkins, 1989*a*). At a macro level the role of political factors in determining risk tolerance levels has been studied (Jasper, 1992), as has the relationship between global risks and regulation. The global dimension tends to concentrate on hazards, in particular ecological hazards (Turner, 1994), but the most common academic focus is on lower-level risks. These developments have thrown new light on the political, and expert—scientific—aspects of regulation and sharpened our understandings of the social, political, and economic influences on regulation. They have also underlined that regulation is itself a way of managing risks in modern societies. It is also of course a form of social control and it is to this aspect of regulation that we now turn.

Regulation, Risk, and the Social Control of Economic Life

Sociologically the study of social control has greater lineage than the study of either regulation or risk. But as Cohen (1984: 2) has argued: 'The term "social control" has become something of a Mickey Mouse concept. In sociology text-books, it appears as a neutral term to cover all social processes to induce conformity ranging from infant socialization through to public execution.' This is perhaps the fate of many academic concepts. Sociological interest in social control is part of a broader interest in how social order is maintained and how social conflict is managed and regulation is a form of social control which falls very clearly into the definition Cohen adopts: 'the organized ways in which society responds to behaviour and people it regards as deviant, problematic, worrying, threatening, troublesome or undesirable in some way or another' (1984: 1). Cohen elaborates further:

My focus is those organized responses to crime, delinquency and allied forms of deviant and/or socially problematic behaviour which are actually conceived of as such, whether in the reactive sense (after the putative act has taken place or the actor has been identified) or in the proactive sense (to prevent the act). These responses may be sponsored directly by the state or by more autonomous professional agents in, say, social work and psychiatry. Their goals may be as specific as individual punishment and treatment or as diffuse as 'crime prevention', 'public safety' and 'community public health'. (ibid. 3)

This definition is particularly helpful in this discussion because it is not so closely tied to traditional criminological perceptions which tend to focus on a fairly restricted range of 'traditional crimes'.[7] The activities subject to regulation do not fit comfortably with such a traditional focus, not least because these activities are at the core of advanced, industrialized societies. So the activities regulated are economic, typically occur in organizational settings, and are in many senses regarded as legitimate and desirable. This does not fit comfortably with traditional criminological imagery, which tends to focus on marginal, often socially excluded individuals (Hutter, 1988). Another advantage of Cohen's definition is that it is sufficiently flexible to consider sources and means of social control other than those tied to the state. Following on from this, regulation may be seen as an organized response to problems, to deviance, and in particular to risk in economic life. It is concerned with how economic order is maintained and how economic risks are managed.

But what do we mean by economic life? There is considerable general sociological confusion about this subject. Indeed if the term social control is a Mickey Mouse concept, then the term economic life has not really advanced

---

[7] The criminological and legal literature often differentiates between regulatory offences and traditional criminal offences. Some claim that regulatory offences are lesser offences which lack the gravity of traditional crime. Others differentiate between business and especially corporate offences from individual wrongdoing, especially that involving intent (*mens rea*). See Croall (1992); Hutter (1997).

sufficiently far to take on even the shape of a mouse. I will take the view that economic life includes all of the activities covered by the heuristic distinction often drawn between social and economic (or financial) regulation (Dodd and Hutter, 2000; Yeager, 1991: 24). Economic life therefore embraces the regulation of industrial processes which may cause harm to workforces, the public, and the environment, and the regulation of financial markets, prices, and profits. Issues about the market are of relevance to all studies of regulation, as are concerns about industries, businesses, firms, and the various actors within each of these.

The early social science interest in regulation was very much focused upon the law and government activity rather than upon the economic activities subject to regulation.[8] Very little thought was given to how economic life was being conceptualized and much work appeared to rely upon classic formulations of regulation and to make assumptions about the nature of economic life, in particular about the nature of markets. Regulation was construed as an attempt to intervene in markets either to correct deficiencies in the market (Olsen, 1982; Hahn, 1989) or to prevent undesirable outcomes and protect public goods (Becker, 1989; Stigler, 1971). While there was assumed to be a tension between regulation and economic and business interests, there were different views about the nature of this tension. The existence of some form of state intervention was taken to mean that business was being asked to do something it might not otherwise opt to do. But the extent to which business was assumed to be resistant to regulation was either left unquestioned or varied according to broader views about the nature of society. Some authors assumed that capitalism would never allow business interests to be restrained, while others accepted a pluralist view of society (Hutter, 1997). Certainly very little empirical data exist on the subject. Many authors simply leave the subject unquestioned and the nature of economic life uninvestigated. We can, however, throw our understandings of both regulation and corporate behaviour into sharper relief by briefly considering different models of economic behaviour.

Models of Corporate Behaviour

The model of market and corporate behaviour which is often assumed to underlie state regulation of economic life is the neo-classical one derived from economics. According to this view regulation is the natural opponent of the market. So in the absence of regulation it is assumed that there would be market competition, and that the market without regulation would be unrestrained (Abolafia, 1985: 313; Colebatch, 1989). Regulation may therefore be seen as intervention to restrain competition either to make the market operate more efficiently (i.e. remedy market failure) or to prevent undesirable outcomes (i.e. welfare objectives). This model assumes that organizations are coherent, hierarchical, and

---

[8] It is not until fairly recently that there has been much sociological interest in exploring the nature of markets (Burk, 1988).

instrumental (Colebatch, 1989: 76) . The view of business is thus that it is wealth maximizing and self-interested (Pearce and Tombs, 1990; Sigler and Murphy, 1988; Stone, 1975; see also Ch. 9 below). This model of corporate behaviour accords with the agency model found in some discussions of corporate crime: 'Agency logic . . . is underlaid by market logic. This paradigm conceptualizes organizations and the individuals within them as rational, unitary, well-informed actors' (Lofquist *et al.*, 1997: 4).

This rational view of the market and corporate behaviour has been critiqued on a number of grounds. One argument is that corporations have multiple goals. For example, the corporate responsibility model does not accept that the only reason economic enterprises regulate their activities is because of state coercion. Rather, this model argues that business may be socially responsible, concerned to do what is right and to be seen as law-abiding (Fisse and Braithwaite, 1983; Selznick, 1980; Wilthagen, 1993). A second critique is that there is variability between corporations so it cannot be accepted that they necessarily share common goals. The market comprises highly diverse organizations. It cannot be assumed that all firms are purely instrumental (Bardach and Kagan, 1982; Braithwaite, 1985). Moreover, the model may also be critiqued on the grounds that there is variability within companies, so it cannot be assumed that everyone within an organization shares the same objective, or that organizations are able to translate clearly motivation into behaviour (Ayres and Braithwaite, 1992; Lofquist *et al.*, 1997). This accords with the structural model of corporations which: 'conceptualizes organizations as complex, differentiated entities, with numerous, often competing goals, limited information, and imperfect communications' (ibid. 4).[9]

The notion of an unregulated market is the other main point of contention. The market-maintenance perspective, for example, challenges the assumption that a market free of state regulation will necessarily be an unregulated market. Abolafia (1985), for example, argues that self-regulation predates government regulation, often emerging as a response to market turbulence. Firms are seen to organize for mutual benefit in pursuit of long-term market integrity (Polanyi, 1975; Kolko, 1965).[10] Some argue that there is no such thing as an unregulated market, a corollary of this being that regulation is inevitable (Burk, 1988). According to this argument there is always regulatory space (Shearing, 1993) and this space may be occupied by a plurality of regulatory influences. This, of course, can be related back to the debates surrounding regulation, namely the

---

[9] Regulatory offences are, of course, very often corporate crimes. See Hutter (1997) for a discussion of a structural model of regulatory enforcement.

[10] The reasons for market and industry organization are the source of much controversy. Not everyone subscribes to Abolafia's explanation. Noll (1985), for example, is not convinced that Abolafia has refuted more traditional economic explanations of this type of organization being a form of cartelization. Indeed some authors have regarded co-operation as being motivated only by a desire to avert government regulation. In reality these forms of self-organization doubtless arise for a mixture of all three reasons, and possibly there are other explanations, so this for the moment must remain a research question.

recognition that there are a number of different sources of regulation of which the state is but one. The regulatory mix which occupies this space may or may not involve the state: there can be regulation without government. Moreover, some commentators now argue that far from stifling competition, regulation has the capacity to enhance it (Llewellyn, 1999; Porter, 1990).

These analyses therefore challenge the notion of the market being in natural antithesis to regulation and the view that firms always act solely in their own self-interest. They also promote the view that regulation is part of the normal market just as regulation may be seen as part of normal social life (Novak, 1996). These challenges to assumptions about economic life are important as they simultaneously confront the suppositions upon which much state regulatory activity is premised. But more importantly they offer us different models of corporate behaviour which may throw new light on regulatory activities and the way in which risk is managed.

Constitutive Regulation

It is important not to reify economic life or to take for granted that it is the passive recipient of state activity. This research takes a broad view of economic activity and it stresses the importance of paying attention to the active creation and re-creation of economic structures and activities. It is important to understand that the state has the potential to have a vital role in constituting order, including economic life (Ayres and Braithwaite, 1992: 14). Indeed regulation may itself be important in the social construction of activities as economic and legitimate. It is important to see regulation as part of a broader social process—according to Colebatch (1989: 79) as part of the 'structuration' process in which regulation structures relationships and is part of the process of ordering.

The distinguishing features of regulatory law are that it is pervasive and simultaneously constitutive and controlling. The legislation and the practices of regulatory officials suggest that regulatory law and its enforcement are often quite different from the law and enforcement associated with traditional policing. The enforcement style most often associated with regulatory officials is variously referred to as the accommodative (Richardson *et al.*, 1983; Hutter, 1988), compliance (Hawkins, 1984; Reiss, 1984), or behavioural (Stenning *et al.*, 1990) model of enforcement. In this model the enforcement task is preventative and restorative. Securing compliance through both the remedy of existing problems and, above all, the prevention of others, is its main objective. To this end the regulator may choose from a wide range of enforcement strategies encompassing informal, persuasive techniques through to criminal prosecution. In practice they tend to use sanctions selectively and the use of formal methods, especially prosecution, is regarded as a last resort, something to be avoided unless all else fails to secure compliance.

The primary objective of regulation according to this model is the shaping of motives and preferences (Shearing, 1993: 75). This mode of regulation is underpinned by a conception of order which is defined in terms of a desired state of affairs and the maintenance of order. This involves a continual process of surveillance. The rules typically associated with this type of enforcement approach are constitutive and technical. These distinctions are spelt out by Stenning *et al.* (1990) who in turn derive them from the work of Unger. Unger (1975: 68–9) explains that 'Constitutive rules define a form of conduct in such a way that the distinction between the rule and the ruled activity disappears'. These rules define what constitutes a compliant state of affairs. So, constitutive rules may define what constitutes a legitimate market. To take a simple example, registration requirements constitute the legitimate market for using certain chemicals which may result in air pollution, or constitute a market of authorized financial institutions and approved persons to work in them. But constitutive rules in the regulatory context may go much further than this. They may aim to penetrate the corporation and to define compliant systems, routines, and practices. Ideally these will be internalized by the company and individuals within it to the point that there is no longer need to refer to the law since the distinction between the rule and the ruled activity disappears. Regulatory rules are also often technical or instrumental rules which 'are guides for the choice of the most effective means to an end . . . They simply state a generalization about what means are most likely on the whole to produce the desired result' (Unger, 1975: 69).

This accommodative approach to the use of the law is significantly different from more traditional uses where order is defined as adherence to rules, where the primary concern is detecting violations and apprehending and sanctioning offenders, and where the preferred methods are penal and adversarial. This more traditional approach is termed the sanctioning strategy by Hawkins (1984), the deterrent model by Reiss (1984), and the symbolic or traditional model by Stenning *et al.* (1990). It is associated with prescriptive rules which are more closely aligned with traditional criminal law as they are 'imperatives that state what some category of persons may or may not do, ought to do, or ought not to do. Accordingly they are permissions, general commands and prohibitions' (Unger, 1975: 69). The objective of prescriptive rules is to ban and prohibit certain types of activity,[11] whereas the objectives of constitutive and technical rules are more behavioural and attempt to balance complex issues to achieve a state of affairs.

These two approaches to the law are often presented as binary models,[12] but it is important to emphasize that these broad strategies are analytical models

---

[11] Empirical studies have found that it is easier for enforcement officials to satisfy the evidential requirements of prescriptive as opposed to constitutive and technical rules which may be more broadly framed and involve more discretion in their interpretation (Hawkins, 1992*b*; Hutter and Lloyd-Bostock, 1992).

[12] The important and empirically significant middle ground between the sanctioning and compliance model is characterized by differences in rule interpretation and varying propensities to use legal coercion (Bardach and Kagan, 1982; Braithwaite *et al.*, 1987; Hutter, 1988).

which are not mutually exclusive. Both can co-exist, and both are used by most enforcement officials in a variety of settings. Authors outlining all of these models are emphatic on this point (Hawkins, 1984; Hutter, 1988; 1997; Stenning *et al.*, 1990). Moreover the compliance/accommodative/behavioural approach does not exclude the symbolic use of the law or imply that the offending is not morally problematic. The point is that there appears to be a different set of regulatory objectives when the law is used to regulate rather than to prohibit behaviour. Depending upon how regulatory objectives are construed, the effectiveness of regulation is regarded differently. For example, the effectiveness of a sanctioning enforcement strategy may be measured by the number of convictions which may be taken as a rate of success. If an accommodative strategy is adopted then prosecution may be seen as a sign of failure; indeed effectiveness may be premised on not using legal action very often (Stenning *et al.*, 1990). Where there is a failure to achieve the constitutive objectives of regulatory law then the controlling aspects of regulation provide the use of criminal, administrative, and sometimes civil sanctions. It is confusion about this dual and shifting use of the criminal law—to be simultaneously constitutive and controlling and to regulate rather than to prohibit—which has led to what Ayres and Braithwaite (1992: 20 ff.) refer to as 'a long history of barren disputation' over whether regulatory offenders are criminals and whether regulatory law is effective in controlling economic crime. These issues are barren in part because those involved are working from very different models of regulation.

Arguments over the purpose and status of regulatory law are further complicated by the fact that what is being regulated are economic activities which include corporate behaviour. These activities and organizations in themselves breed suspicion with respect to the extent of their power locally, nationally, and globally and with respect to less powerful groups who may be harmed by their activities, for example, consumers and employees. Views about economic activities, especially under capitalism, can colour perspectives and interpretations of regulatory objectives and activities. Some authors clearly believe that big business has captured the regulatory process from beginning to end and that big business has influenced the very definition of regulatory problems through to the regulatory agency's ability—even willingness—to enforce the law (Yeager, 1991). Evidence of this is taken to be their 'failure' to prosecute. While some companies are undoubtedly powerful and exploitative, the message from the research literature is that there is great variability between companies and also within companies. There is a regulatory imbalance between some large corporations and regulators in terms of resources and technical know-how but it remains the case that there are many other companies and small businesses which do not fall into this category. The problem then becomes one of ensuring that the big companies do not dominate the regulatory agenda in an anti-competitive spirit.

What cannot be ignored is that organizations pose serious problems for the law in the attribution of criminal responsibility. As Wells (1993) explains, the reliance of the criminal law on notions of individualism leads to difficulties in making corporations criminally accountable. In short, there is a difference between the company as a legal phenomenon and the corporation viewed sociologically (Stone, 1975). One form of regulation which aims to tackle the corporation at the organization and individual level is the subject of this book, namely occupational health and safety regulation in Britain. The Health and Safety at Work etc. Act, 1974, introduced a system of enforced self-regulation and constituted occupational health and safety as the responsibility of everyone in the workplace (Introduction; Ch. 3).

Ayres and Braithwaite (1992) describe the model of enforced self-regulation. As the term implies, it combines state and company regulation. So the government lays down broad standards which companies are expected to meet by, for example, developing risk management systems and rules to secure compliance. This involves worker participation. It also involves the company in monitoring whether compliance is being achieved and having procedures in place to deal with non-compliance. This form of regulation thus attempts to harness the regulatory resources of the company. But the system is not entirely self-regulatory as regulatory officials oversee this process and undertake monitoring themselves. Moreover, they have the authority to enforce the law and to sanction publicly for non-compliance. Hence the term 'enforced self-regulation' which conveys the combination of public and private regulatory resources and indicates that in this model regulation takes place in the shadow of the law. Whether the law is enforced with a light touch or heavy hand depends in part on the company's ability and willingness to manage and direct its own regulatory resources to meeting the general standards outlined by the state. Generally enforced self-regulation is most suited to large, well-informed, and well-resourced companies. The notion is that there can be in-depth monitoring by corporate inspectors and the workforce (Ayres and Braithwaite, 1992: 104). Moreover, the rules can be tailored to particular companies which it is assumed will be more committed to rules they have written themselves (ibid. 113). Ayres and Braithwaite (1992: 6, 103) describe this as a middle path between self-regulation and command and control regulation and as a form of subcontracting regulatory functions to private actors. Looked at another way it is a perspective which emphasizes the multi-dimensional nature of regulation and its interactive relationship with business. In short it is a model which underlines the pervasiveness of regulation in economic life.

Enforced self-regulation, more than many other forms of regulation, places the spotlight on corporate understandings of risk which have been hitherto assumed rather than explored. Moreover it focuses attention on one relatively under-researched area of regulation, namely corporate responses to regulation. One objective of this study is to start to explore what enforced self-regulation looks like in practice. For example, how successfully can different sources and forms of regulation be 'mixed'? What are the limits to enforced self-regulation? And more generally, is enforced self-regulation a clever solution to the control of organizations or might it be a form of risk-taking?

The Impact of Regulation

A central socio-legal concern is how influential the law is in social and economic life (Heimer, 1996). This may be approached and answered in different ways. In many respects it reflects a concern with the practical application of the law. Does it make a difference? Is it intended to make a difference? What difference does it make? And under what conditions does it make a difference?[13] Although this concern may have potentially profound policy implications, the issues raised are much broader. Questions about the influence of the law arise out of wider theoretical concerns about the nature of the law in society, the maintenance of social order, and the management of conflict.

While there are now many studies of regulation, their interest is concentrated into a number of relatively discrete areas. Much of the work done has been done in the past twenty years. Many of these studies have been of enforcement and many have been of US regulatory institutions. We still have few detailed empirical studies of regulatory policy-making. We know little about the emergence of regulation; financial regulation; and the global aspects of regulation. We know about how regulatory officials use the law but we still know remarkably little about how the law—and indeed other forms of regulation—are received by those they are intended to influence (Sitkin and Bies, 1994).

The neglect of these topics is clearly not related to their importance, since the influence of the law in society must be one of the central socio-legal questions. The dearth of material relates more to the complexity of the issues involved. Evaluating the so-called costs and benefits is extremely difficult. For example, there is no clear-cut method for isolating and measuring the improvements which may have been effected by the law and its enforcement from the complex of other factors which may have been involved. Nevertheless the enforced self-regulation model in use demands measures of 'performance'. The work which has been done has tended to focus upon the regulated, most especially at the level of the individual company, and upon the activities of the regulatory agency. This aspect of regulation draws attention to a number of important issues relating to matters such as how much those subject to regulatory laws and policies know and understand about their provisions and about the regulatory apparatus in place for their implementation; the extent to which the law might cause individuals and institutions to change their behaviour and practices; whether or not regulation influences commercial decisions about the location of industry and sites; and how these matters relate to industries' perceptions of the national and transnational risks posed by their activities. This study will focus upon corporate responses in its consideration

---

[13] Various disciplinary perspectives have their own distinct perspectives on these questions. For example, lawyers are interested in how laws may be framed to be more effective; political scientists are interested in whose interests are being represented in the political processes influencing law; economists are interested in the impact of the law on the market imperfections which provided the rationale for government intervention. This study is primarily sociological.

of the impact of health and safety legislation on the railway industry in Britain.

Regulation, as we have seen, is not the imposition of order but the enactment of a particular sort of order. More specifically, regulation is constitutive of markets and industries. Since regulation is one source of the constitution, the important question becomes how influential a source it is. Where the state is involved in regulation it may have the potential to have a vital role in constituting order. The crucial question surrounding the impact of the law is whether or not it does play such a role. More specifically, can we discern when it is likely to have an effect and when it is not? As Heimer (1996: 41) indicates, we should be wary of ignoring the potential role of the state. It may play a key role of institutionalization and it has coercive qualities. The important point to remember is that this does not necessarily lead to 'deeper social change'—it is merely capable of doing so.

The discussion above suggests that at the broadest level it is important to look at the structuring of economic life and the extent to which state institutions are significant in the ordering process. Practically, especially given the dearth of empirical research in this area, this may be tackled by focusing on one specific part/section of economic life and the role of state regulation in its ordering. Given that the law is increasingly implemented in organizational settings (Heimer, 1996), one manageable focus is the impact of legal regulation on an organization, through which the influence of the law is often mediated (Heimer, 1996). This is especially true of regulatory law, which is very much targeted at organizational behaviour.[14] From this point/baseline we need to ask a number of questions, none of which, it needs to be recognized from the start, is easy to answer.

It is initially important to try to discern regulatory objectives. Colebatch (1989: 85) warns us that we need to be cautious about applying the notion of purpose to regulation. There may be multiple interpretations of purpose. Indeed it is important to recognize that objectives are emergent from action—so an important focus is the process of social action and a consideration of how order is created and maintained, and to what extent regulation is part of that process. We need to question who is involved in the structuring of relations and what objectives appear to be embodied in regulatory law. For example, how does it attempt to constitute the area of economic life subject to examination? This involves consideration of which groups are empowered in a participative way. Ayres and Braithwaite explain (1992: 4): 'Regulations themselves can affect structure (i.e. the number of firms in the industry) and can affect motivations of the regulated.'

We need to appreciate the different groups involved in regulation and be attuned to the differing motivations of regulatory actors and to the diverse

---

[14] Note that this is not exclusively so as regulatory law is not invariably targeted at organizations and corporations. For example, regulatory law may relate to a wide range of small businesses such as corner shops, market traders, farms, and small workshops (Hutter, 1997).

objectives of regulated firms, industry associations, and individuals (Ayres and Braithwaite, 1992: 4). So it is important to consider the interpretations people apply to the world; the institutional channels through which they act and the interests served and created in the process; and to appreciate that these may differ, change, and come into conflict/harmony at different points. It is important not to reify regulation as an external mechanical construct, independent of the actions of the participants (Colebatch, 1989: 86), but rather to look at the extent to which it has become a constitutive part of everyday life.

One method of assessing the impact of legislation is outcome based. The most obvious indicator in the area of occupational health and safety, which is the substantive focus of this research, would be occupational accident statistics, since one objective of occupational health and safety legislation is surely to prevent accidents and ill health at work. But while these statistics do give us a crude measure of workplace health and safety they are a problematic measure of the impact of the law (Dawson *et al.*, 1988; Nichols, 1997). It needs to be understood, for example, that there are difficulties with the available statistics and their accuracy (see Ch. 8) and there are even greater difficulties in causally relating a change in injury figures to the law. For instance it is impossible to isolate the effects of the law from the impact of other factors such as changes in technology and labour market factors. Cost-benefit analyses encounter similar problems with the statistics. In addition there is dispute about how one assesses and computes both costs and benefits when these may look very different according to perspective. And typically costs seem to be more amenable to assessment than the benefits (Froud and Ogus, 1996). This said, these methods do offer some quantitative indication of the effects of the law. But these outcome-based assessments take a narrow view of the impact of regulatory law, in particular they give little indication of the constitutive effects of the law. This involves consideration of the institutional impact of regulation and for these purposes qualitative methods are most suitable.

The institutional impact of regulation involves an examination of how the law impacts on institutional structures, systems, policies, and procedures. Dawson *et al.* (1988), for example, considered, among other factors, the development of safety policies, worker safety representation, and safety committees. Rees (1988) undertook an empirical study into how US government regulation influenced the day-to-day conduct of regulated construction firms. He focused on compliance with an experiment by Occupational Safety and Health Administration (OSHA) in California which authorized labour-management committees to assume many of the regulatory agency's responsibilities. He traced the reception of the scheme and highlighted the importance of examining how regulatory messages are evaluated and processed by regulated firms. Heimer (1996: 38) also stresses the importance of discerning how the law functions in organizational life by examining, for instance, the extent to which the law is interpreted into organizational scripts and is adapted to local circumstances. This involves an examination of institutional responses to law. It may also involve interviews with the regulated. Brittan (1984), Clay (1984), and Genn (1993) all interviewed members of the regulated population about their knowledge of regulatory law, regulatory systems, and regulatory practice. Nelkin and Brown (1984) likewise interviewed workers about their understanding of risks in the workplace. Bardach and Kagan (1982) and Di Mento (1986) focused, largely through interviews, on business perspectives on regulation and the use of the criminal sanction.

The research reported in this book will concentrate on the institutional and everyday changes effected by occupational health and safety regulation. It will thus consider the extent to which regulatory law has penetrated corporate life in one major company in Britain through affecting the structure of industry; affecting the motivations of the regulated; influencing the rules of exchange; influencing training; influencing everyday conduct; and empowering the participation of other groups such as trade unions and the workforce. It will also consider the constraining influence of the law by examining understandings of the law and the reasons for compliance and non-compliance. It is important to recognize that the law may have instrumental and symbolic effects and that these effects can be direct and indirect, intended and unintended (Burk, 1988; Grabosky, 1995a). And we need to observe whether it is procedural or substantive outcomes which are affected (or neither or both) (Heimer, 1996). As Heimer (1996) indicates, the difficult task is to distinguish between when the law fundamentally shapes what is done; legitimates what would have been done anyway; modifies what is done; or is largely ignored.

Research Approach

This research takes as its substantive focus occupational health and safety regulation on the railways in Britain. The railways is a risky industry and at the time of the research was a monopoly industry with one company, British Railways, dominating the national rail network in Britain. Moreover, it was a nationalized industry but one which, at the time of the research, was clearly being prepared for privatization. It was also a large industry and an economically important one. This has crucial implications for what the research was likely to find. Researchers in the United States, Australia, and the United Kingdom (Grabosky and Braithwaite, 1986; Snider, 1987; Yeager, 1991) have all noted a tendency for formal legal enforcement action to figure less prominently in regulatory officials' dealings with larger and more powerful organizations than in their dealings with small organizations. There is a well-researched tendency for regulatory officials to believe that big business is more law abiding than small business (Grabosky and Braithwaite, 1986: 215 ff.; Snider, 1987: p49). Dawson et al. (1988, p. 261) found that the gap between standards of health and safety in large and small firms was considerable.

A union report into occupational health and safety regulation in Britain (GMB, 1986) notes that small companies find compliance problematic and often do not comply, as do studies of regulatory impact in other regulatory areas (Brittan, 1984) and in other countries (Gricar, 1983; Wilthagen, 1993). These findings are partly related to the capacity of organizations to comply (Grabosky and Braithwaite, 1986; Yeager, 1991) and their greater capacity to challenge how deviance is defined (Snider, 1987; Yeager, 1991). The important point for this research is that it focuses on a company which is likely to be one of the more compliant yet one, like any others, in which occupational health and safety competed with other factors in the ordering of the company.

This research is underpinned by the view that regulation is pervasive and that regulatory space may be filled in a variety of ways. Regulatory law is thus seen as but one source of regulation. The study primarily approaches regulation as a form of risk management, the particular focus being upon corporate responses to state regulation. This involves paying attention to how regulatory law seeks to manage risks to occupational health and safety and how British Railways as a company responded to this. It should be borne in mind that regulatory law is constitutive and controlling so it is important to consider corporate responses in terms of the organizational changes made in response to health and safety regulation. It is also important to examine understanding about the effects of regulation at an everyday level. This leads to a focus on the systems the company had in place for health and safety and also to the knowledge and views of the staff at all levels of the company, from managing director to the lowest grade worker, and crucially to consideration of both specialist staff *and* those for whom health and safety is part of their more general remit. This focus also leads to the use of qualitative research methods which are especially suited to elucidating the meanings of social situations for different people (see Ch. 2 and Apps.).

The next chapter will set the scene for the empirical research by giving an overview of the railways industry in Britain both historically and at the time of data collection.

PART I

THE RAILWAY INDUSTRY: REGULATION AND RISK

2

The Railway Industry in Britain

This chapter provides an overview of the history and structure of the railway industry in Great Britain. This will involve a brief consideration of the historical context of regulation, with a particular focus on the development of occupational health and safety regulation; discussion of the structure of BR at the time of my data collection in the late 1980s and early 1990s; and consideration of the wider context within which this research took place. The intention of this chapter is to explain the research setting. More recent radical developments of the railway industry and its regulation are discussed in Part V. The research period should be regarded as a 'frozen' moment in time. This chapter will set the historical and organizational scene and the subsequent sections will explore corporate responses to occupational health and safety regulation within this context.

The History of Railway Regulation

Historically a distinguishing feature of the railways in Britain has been government control (Gourvish, 1986: 567, 1997: 3). Indeed state regulation of the railway industry is almost as old as the railways themselves, dating from the 1840 Regulation of Railways Act and continuing right through to the present day. It was during the 1840s that the railway network in Britain was created and it was one of the industries that dominated the Victorian economy and had a great impact on Victorian society (Bartrip and Burman, 1983: Gourvish, 1980). At this time the railways were privately owned and privately capitalized and the industry comprised a multitude of private companies. Yet despite its growing importance the railway network was very rudimentary. Parris (1965: 9) describes it as haphazardly run and unreliable. Internationally, however, it was pioneering and the most advanced system in the world. The early decades of the railway were dominated by their construction. Bartrip and Burman (1983: 74) estimate that in 1830 there were fewer than 100 miles of railway track open to public use, but by 1870 this had risen to 17,500. They refer to this as arguably '. . . the most spectacular engineering feat of the nineteenth century'. Gourvish (1980: 21 ff.) estimates that during the period 1831–70 an average of 60,000 men were engaged annually in building the railways; by 1856 the industry had over 100,000 permanent employees; and by the late 1860s over 200,000. But the speed and extent of this growth posed serious problems.

The growth of the railways coincided with a period of extensive government intervention in the social and economic life of the country, for example, state regulation of factories, mines, education, and the introduction of the poor law (Bartrip and Burman, 1983; Parris, 1965). During the period 1840–1914 the regulation of the railways was second only to the regulation of mining (Alderman, 1973: 25). There were several focuses of intervention in this early history of the railway industry. First was protection from monopoly and mergers. This was in response to fears of a railway monopoly of transport and also excessive rail charges. It led to the first Regulation of Railways Act and the Board of Trade's jurisdiction over the railway industry. The second main focus of attention, and the most important for the purposes of this work, was safety. The third main focus arose later in the nineteenth century and early in the twentieth century, namely impatience with railway company attitudes to labour relations, a topic which eventually threatened to disrupt the national economy (Parris, 1965: 226–7). An important point to understand here is that there were various aspects to state intervention in the railways, of which safety was but one.

In the nineteenth century safety referred very much to the safety of the travelling public rather than to the safety of railway workers (Bagwell, 1963; Bartrip and Burman, 1983). Throughout the early history of the railways there was increasing public concern about railway safety. The problems were acute, particularly in the 1870s (Alderman, 1973: 44), leading in 1884 to the establishment of a Royal Commission on Railway Accidents. Kostal (1994: 258) writes that serious and fatal injury to railway employees was commonplace and remained high in the nineteenth century but it was not this that prompted the Royal Commission but rather a concern with passenger safety (Bagwell, 1963; Bartrip and Burman, 1983: 78).[1] In 1889 safety was still very much on the political agenda. The Armagh disaster, in which over seventy people (many of them children) were killed, is credited with changing Conservative policy and leading to immediate legislation (Alderman, 1973: 132–3). The reasons for the very great impact of these accidents on the public are spelt out succinctly by Kostal: 'Working class Victorians were familiar with the dangers of mechanized work. For the first time, however, railway accidents introduced the middle and upper classes to the terror of factory accidents. Highly publicized derailments, collisions, and explosions injure railway customers of every social caste' (1994: 254). It should thus be borne in mind that railway safety in the nineteenth century typically refers to public safety, with Parliament being very slow to act on behalf of railway employees.

---

[1] Bartrip and Burman (1983: 37 ff.) explain the difficulties of getting accurate statistics of railway accidents and injuries. For example, only a restricted range of accidents need be reported, the reporting of accidents was haphazard, and the Inspectorate lacked the powers to enforce the reporting requirements.

Railway Safety and State Intervention in the Nineteenth Century

State intervention to promote the safety of the railway industry in the nineteenth century can be considered in more detail under a number of headings. First, let us consider briefly the growth of state intervention and then turn to historical explanations of these developments. Before the 1840s there was no legislative regulation of the railways beyond private Acts of incorporation (Kostal, 1994: 6) and there was no state railway policy (Parris, 1965). The period 1840 to 1867 is generally taken to be the most formative period, in particular 1840–6. 1840 saw the first regulatory legislation, the establishment of the Railway Department of the Board of Trade and the appointment of railways inspectors who were appointed from the ranks of the Royal Engineers.[2] If we consider this period in context it should be borne in mind that government activity filled a small part of the broader regulatory space of the railway industry during this period. Kostal (1994: 7) refers to this as a period of 'voluntarist' regulation and points to the regulation exercised by lawyers and judges in private litigation cases as being much more significant.[3] Gourvish (1980: 49) contrasts the lack of regulation during this early period with continental Europe, where the state's presence was keenly felt from the planning to the operating stage.

If we look more closely at the responsibilities of the early inspectors for safety we find that they relate to public safety. In particular, these inspectors had powers to inspect new railways and approve all new lines before they were opened, but these powers were limited and inspectors did not have the power to prevent problematic lines being opened. The unsatisfactory nature of the early remit led in 1841 to complaint from the five inspectors then in post. They argued that the standards of the railway companies were low and they recommended that powers be given to the Board of Trade to issue regulations in the interest of public safety (Alderman, 1973: 45). In 1842 they were given the power to postpone the opening of a railway where there was likely to be danger to the public. In 1843 they requested further powers. However during the period 1846–68 few new powers were conferred, indeed Parris (1965: 212) describes the period as a 'lull'.[4]

---

[2] The reasons for this are interesting, namely their independence from the railways companies with whom they had no links; their knowledge of the railways; and the fact that they were cheaper to employ than civil engineers (Parris, 1965: 32).

[3] This included private litigation relating to the infringement of private property rights, involved in the expropriation of land for the railway companies, and also litigation concerning railway accidents (Kostal, 1994: 144, 282).

[4] During this period there were various administrative changes. In 1844, for example, the Railway Department became the Railway Board but this lasted for just a year. In 1846 a new department, independent of the Board of Trade, was set up, namely the Commissioners of Railways. They assumed the powers of the Board of Trade but they lasted just five years when responsibility reverted to the Railway Department of the Board. These changes are referred to by Parris (1965: 114) as an 'experiment that failed'.

The regulatory approach adopted during this period was persuasive rather than legalistic. The main business of the early inspectors was the enforcement of the law, but prosecution was regarded as an extreme measure only to be used in extreme cases or where one party in a dispute was too weak to defend itself against a powerful railway company. In their first four years the inspectors did not prosecute once (Parris, 1965: 34). The reasons for this were various. They include a weak legal framework and the limited powers accorded to inspectors; the lack of technical knowledge available to the inspectors; and the weighting of technical feasibility against cost (Alderman, 1973: 46). Also of significance may have been the small staff employed to enforce the railway legislation. They may not have had time to prosecute given the amount of other work they had to do. Moreover their small numbers meant that they worked in a small informal office where informal methods of enforcement may also have been favoured (Parris, 1965: 35).

Railway historians generally regard regulation during this period as unsatisfactory. This is partly because of the imbalance in information between the railway companies and the Board of Trade (Alderman, 1973) and in particular their lack of technical information. Indeed it is significant that the inspectors were seen to become more effective as their knowledge of the railways increased (Parris, 1965: 169).[5] Despite these criticisms it should be noted that the Board of Trade inspectors took a wide view of their responsibilities and worked well beyond their legal remit. The most notable example of this is their investigation of accidents which had no legal basis until the 1871 Regulation of Railways Act. Yet inspectors undertook extensive investigation of accidents from their earliest years, with the co-operation of the railway companies (Parris, 1965: 144). Their reports were published in the familiar blue book format from 1852 and prior to this the reports were appendices to the Department's annual reports. From 1854 these, still non-statutory reports, were presented to Parliament on a regular basis. In 1858 the Department produced the first edition of the *Requirements* which were standard codes for the building of new railways. These derived from the Department's experience, particularly of accident investigation. Again they had no legal basis, although they did assume a quasi-legal status (Hutter, 1997; Parris, 1965: 182). In the period 1840 to 1870 precedents for government intervention were clearly established but as Gourvish (1980: 49) notes, 'supervision was general and exhortative rather than mandatory'.

---

[5] The inspectors had various sources of information. These included their investigation of accidents; their knowledge of the individual railway companies; and occasionally they sponsored independent research into particular technical problems.

1867 to the 1890s

Parris describes 1867 as a turning-point in the relationship between the railways and the state. During the period from 1867 to the 1890s there was much greater state intervention in the overall running of the railways, prompted in part by a high rate of accidents (Gourvish, 1980). This included safety and much else, for example, legislation was passed relating to railway rates, railway accounts, and employers' liability. By the end of this period the government, the Board of Trade, and the railways companies were described as being in almost daily contact because of the succession of Acts that had been passed.[6] This close contact appeared to bring with it a closer relationship between these parties (Parris, 1965). It should also be remembered that by the 1870s the basic railway network, organizational structure and traffic patterns of the railway had been established, leading Gourvish to refer to the 1870–1914 period as 'The Mature Stage' in the development of the early railway system in Britain.

By the turn of the century things had changed rather dramatically. In particular the railway companies had lost a lot of their power. Their position was weakened considerably because of serious economic problems and political change. In addition to this railway regulation was becoming increasingly technical and thus arguably less vulnerable to political influence.

Occupational Safety Regulation in the Nineteenth Century

Railway histories pay scant attention to the specific focus of this study, namely occupational health and safety. In part this is because accidents involving the public took priority over those affecting the workforce. But this does not mean that there was no interest in the well-being of the workforce. Bartrip and Burman (1983: 68) explain that in the mid-1840s there was concern over the general living and working conditions of railway labourers but not humanitarian concern, rather because they were seen to represent a problem for public order. Although Parris (1965: 139) notes that labour matters were of continuing interest to the Railway Department, Bartrip and Burman observe that it was not until the 1870s that the Railway Inspectorate expressed concern about accidents to railway employees. The Liberal MP Francis Channing persistently attempted to tackle the high number of worker fatalities on the railways. After a number of failed attempts Channing was eventually influential in incorporating provisions for the protection of employees into the 1889 Regulation of Railways Act. In particular these required that the railway companies had to submit regulatory returns of all employees working overtime (Alderman, 1973: 130).

The link between overtime and safety was a topic which was to demand increasing amounts of attention. The Railway Department's interest in worker

---

[6] For instance, legislation relating to railways was passed in 1888, 1889, 1893, and 1894.

hours was not entirely a result of concern about occupational health and safety, since arguably it had much to do with the dangers posed to public safety (Bagwell, 1963; Parris, 1965: 225). However, as the unions took up the case of excessive hours of work, political reasons for the resolution of the matter took prominence. The 1890s saw a series of labour disputes on the subject of railway working hours and also the safety of the workforce,[7] with the subject increasingly becoming part of the political agenda (Alderman, 1973: 134). The railway unions and Francis Channing MP persistently argued the case for limiting the hours of work and after a number of setbacks achieved what Alderman (1973: 141) describes as 'a landmark in the history of the state regulation of industry in Britain', namely the 1893 Railway Servants (Hours of Labour) Act which limited the hours of work of railway employees.[8] Following this 'breakthrough' there followed greater state regulation of conditions of work.[9]

Significant distinctions were made between the travelling public and railway employees in the government regulation of railway safety and in the determinations of the courts. Kostal (1994) explains that the railways were involved in mass litigation with passengers and some workers. He observes that the courts differentiated between the two groups with injuries to passengers leading to judgements of 'vicarious liability' and the awarding of large compensation and the reverse view being taken of worker liability. Indeed employees were generally treated much less favourably even when compensation was awarded.

Why railway employees were so ignored when the dangers they were exposed to were so grave, and the industry they were working in was one of the most regulated in Britain, is a subject which one might have expected to have raised more interest among historians. Bartrip and Burman (1983) pay most attention to this subject, contrasting the treatment of railway employees to the much greater protection offered to employees in the mines and factories. They argue that the issue of passenger safety overshadowed the railway debate and had crucial implications for the reform of worker safety. There are a number of strands to Bartrip and Burman's argument. For example, they argue that passenger accidents 'made headlines' and overshadowed the unpleasant subject of accidents among railway servants. Moreover, since employee fatalities involved no risk to the public and no damage to property, and did not lead to great expense for the railway companies, they attracted little political attention. Bagwell (1963) also addresses the subject in a history of the National Union of Railwaymen. He also argues that passenger safety was of paramount importance and that the continuous and often solitary nature of occupational accidents was significant:

---

[7] Alderman (1973: 135) cites the following figures: workers killed: 1888—377; 1891—517; workers injured: 1888—2,081; 1891—2,977. See also Bartrip and Burman (1983: 43–4).

[8] See Alderman (1973: 36 ff.) for a detailed account of the struggle to enact this legislation.

[9] Parris (1965: 226) cites the following examples: The Factory & Workshop Act, 1901, and the Railway Employment (Prevention of Accidents) Act, 1900, which gave the Board of Trade power to act to reduce the danger to employees posed by plant and appliances. Bagwell (1963: 107) argues that with union persistence this did eventually lead to increased employee safety.

When a major railway accident occurs it is often the passengers who suffer the greatest number of casualties. Among railway employees the continuous toll of fatalities in their ones, twos and threes to drivers, firemen, goods and passenger guards, shunters, permanent-way men and others is less spectacular and therefore more easily escapes public attention. (1963: 95)

But none of this explains why railway workers were ignored and subject to markedly less intervention than other workers. Bartrip and Burman (1983: 78 ff.) account for this in terms of the success of the 'railway interest' in delaying reform; the fact that the statistics suggested that things were not as serious as they actually were; that passenger safety and public interest deflected interest in employee safety; and a suggestion that the railway system was unsuited to strong government control—although as we discuss below it was to become subject to total government control. Bagwell also points to the power of the railway interest in Parliament, in particular to the issue of costs, noting tersely that 'Safety costs money' (1963: 95).

Explanations of Nineteenth-Century Railway Regulation

The regulatory context of the railways in the nineteenth century is important because it laid the foundation of railway regulation for much of the following century. The biases of this regulation remained in place despite massive shifts in government control of the industry. So safety regulation was typically less prominent than other forms of regulation, especially the financial regulation of the industry. Moreover occupational health and safety remained secondary to the safety of the travelling public.

Given its importance let us pursue a little further the general regulatory context of the railways in the nineteenth century, in particular the question of how this early regulation may be explained. Historical accounts tend to focus on the politics of railway regulation (Kostal, 1994). One view is that government regulation of the railways was a response to the failure of the railway companies to secure safe, cheap, and efficient railways (Parris, 1965). In other words regulation is a response to market failure and it serves to protect the public interest. Another view is that regulation is the result of contestation between different interest groups (Alderman, 1973). Railways are seen as the epitome of big business, ruthless in pursuit of their own interest and well organized. Alderman (ibid. 15), for example, argues that the companies had the funds, the administrative organization, and the legal and technical expertise to fight government.

There is some common ground between the different explanations of regulation. For example, all are agreed that railway safety was of paramount importance and was a serious problem. There were a great number of serious accidents and many deaths. All of this resulted in growing public concern and a need for action, demands which went alongside public concerns about the monopoly position of the railways as a form of transport in a rapidly urbanizing and industrializing country. Another area of agreement is that the railway companies were politically astute. Parris (1965: 18) refers to them as 'creatures of Parliament', pointing here to their experience of getting private Acts establishing the companies through Parliament and the fact that many railway directors were MPs—what Alderman (1973) refers to as 'the Railway Interest'. What is in dispute is the extent of their power to resist regulation and the extent to which they did resist regulation.

Railway historians certainly document the industry's attempts to avoid regulation by, for instance, limiting proposals and achieving compromise. Regulation was seen as interference and was opposed on this basis alone. Alderman explains that there was opposition to legislation even when it would do nothing to seriously affect the activities of the companies, since regulation was seen as 'part of an objectionable system of Parliamentary interference' with the rights and liberty of capital (1973: 135). There were also objections that regulation was dangerous to the safe day-to-day running of the railways. This was especially so in the early days when, as we have noted, there was an imbalance of information and expertise between the Board of Trade and the railway companies.[10]

Alderman's account of the railway industry in this period is of an industry which felt under threat and which organized to fight it. But the extent to which the railway industry was united should not be overestimated. Particularly in the pre-1867 period the companies often had conflicting aims; indeed the only issue they did appear to agree on was their opposition to regulation. But their organization was much like the legislation itself, that is, piecemeal. They did eventually become more sophisticated. In 1851, for example, the companies appointed a parliamentary agent and in 1855 a permanent committee was appointed to protect railway interests in Parliament. And in 1858–61 the Railway Companies Association was set up to fight and promote bills (it was dissolved in 1861 because it was overambitious). Gourvish (1980) disputes that the strength of the 'Railway Interest' is significant for explanations of regulation. He regards the lack of government policy before 1870 as much more important. Moreover, in the post-1870 period he regards the 'Railway Interest' as counterproductive as it appeared intransigent in the face of growing public demands for control.

There were some attempts by the industry to consider the causes and circumstances of railways accidents. In 1841, for instance, they examined the causes and circumstances of accidents and proposed their own rules, regulation, and codes. It is unclear if the intention was to avert state regulation but historians imply that this was their main intention. Alderman (1973: 45) notes that Brunel saw this as a propaganda exercise to placate the government, with a view to diverting the need for state regulation (see also Parris, 1965). This said, many of the measures which the railway inspectors advocated and which were eventually required in law were adopted 'voluntarily' by many railway companies. For example, the block

---

[10] It is interesting that two of the prominent railwaymen of the nineteenth century had opposing views on the issue of state regulation of the industry. George Stephenson was pro-supervision whereas Brunel was anti-regulation.

system, interlocking, and continuous automatic brakes were all the subject of dispute and were also matters which were largely settled by the railway companies themselves. But the emphasis here is upon the *voluntary* nature of this regulation. Kostal (1994) comments that they did not often accede to public pressure. Moreover, there were continuing problems of safety throughout the nineteenth century, problems which concerned the public and were even commented upon by Queen Victoria in her correspondence to her prime minister, Gladstone (Kostal, 1994: 311).

Explanations of the regulation of the railways in Britain contrast with the debates that characterize the regulation of the US railways in the late nineteenth century and early twentieth century. The US arguments were brought into sharp relief by Kolko (1965) who broke with traditional explanations of a strong railroad industry vigorously resisting regulation to present an account which claims that the railroads broadly welcomed regulation in the face of their own failures to voluntarily and co-operatively bring stability to a fiercely competitive market. But Kolko's account is not one of strong government regulation. The state, he argued, intervened to preserve the dominant position of the railroad business when this was endangered. So Kolko does not regard the state as a neutral arbiter. Generally he argues the government worked with the railroads but on the latter's terms. Whether or not Kolko's thesis is accurate is still subject to debate (Channon, 1996).

There certainly does not seem to be much scope in the British context for arguments that the railways demanded regulation in order to promote market stability. Bartrip and Burman (1983) comment that railway regulation was more generally necessitated by commercial rather than by humanitarian reforms.[11] For example, they argue that the 1840 Regulation of Railways Act was 'directly conceived to prevent monopolistic control of railway development' (ibid. 77).

Railway Regulation in the Twentieth Century

In many respects the regulation of occupational health and safety on the railways did not develop substantially from its nineteenth-century roots until the 1960s and most especially the 1970s. Nevertheless, the railway industry became subject to increasing government control. The two world wars saw periods of intense government intervention and for the duration of each war the railways were taken into government control as a single unified system under the Railway Executive Committee (Henshaw, 1991). In the aftermath of the Second World War the whole network was nationalized as it struggled to recover from its extensive use

---

[11] This, they believe, is symbolized by the fact the Board of Trade rather than the Home Office was responsible for railway regulation. Railway regulation, argue Bartrip and Burman, is in direct contrast to the manufacturing and mining industries where reforms did appear to be humanitarian and protective of the workforce (and where the regulation was the responsibility of the Home Office).

during the wars and the neglect to repairs and renewals it had suffered (Gourvish, 1986: 5).[12] The question of public ownership of the railways had been a long-standing one. Henshaw (1991: 17) claims that consideration was given to bringing the railways into national ownership as early as 1844. It was even mooted by Winston Churchill when he was at the Board of Trade in 1917. In the aftermath of the First World War, nationalization was considered and then rejected in favour of the amalgamation of some 120 companies into four regionally based companies. But the post-Second World War Labour government instituted a radical policy of nationalization including the railways.[13] Gourvish (1986: 23) suggests that public control of the railways may even have been inevitable.

The effects of the 1946 Transport Bill are widely discussed in the literature (see Gourvish, 1986). The important point for occupational health and safety is that from 1946 through to the research period, the responsibilities for compliance with occupational health and safety lay with one nationalized company that covered the rail network of Great Britain. The history of the nationalized rail industry is one of regular reorganizations, very different government policies, and changing economic fortunes. Government relationships with the industry varied from a Conservative government which in the early 1950s intended to create a competitive era in transport to a Labour government in the mid-1960s which aimed to integrate rail and road services and subsidize socially necessary rail passenger services (Gourvish, 1986: 137, 349). State intervention was a fact of life for the industry. Another was the increasing challenge to the rail network from road traffic, initially with respect to short distance and passenger traffic, and eventually to long-distance and freight business. Indeed Henshaw (1991) blames a highly organized road lobby for playing a major part in fostering the decline of the British railway system.

Gourvish (1986: 173) reports that in the mid-1950s the railway's economic fortunes declined dramatically paving the way in the early 1960s for the newly created BRB[14] to introduce a 'modernization' (or probably more aptly named 'rationalization') programme under Dr Richard Beeching who was to become Chair of BRB. Beeching proposed 'a smaller rail network and emphasis upon profitable traffic flows' (Gourvish, 1986: 336). His report *The Reshaping of British Railways* appeared in two parts (1963 and 1965) and led to a policy spanning Conservative and Labour governments of rail closures and a concentration on developing major routes.[15]

---

[12] One consequence of this underinvestment was a spate of serious train accidents. Gourvish (1986: 8) notes, for example, that the number killed in train accidents in 1947 was the second highest in railway history. He reports that the Chief Inspector of Railways attributed five of these accidents to track maintenance arrears.

[13] For example, this government nationalized the health services, the Bank of England, civil aviation, ports, and the coal industry.

[14] BRB replaced the British Transport Commission in January 1963 as part of a broader reorganization of the national transport system.

[15] The Beeching reforms were highly unpopular with the public and they remain controversial. Some argue that Dr Beeching destroyed the rail network, others believe that he saved it, while oth-

Gourvish (1986) comments that recurring themes of the period 1948–73 were the relationships of government and senior railways management and between the centre and the regions. But government intervention emerges as most important and the main concerns here were financial. Henshaw (1991: 228) also points to state control as a major contributory factor in the decline of the railways.[16] These authors agree that mismanagement by the British Transport Commission, the Railway Executive, and railway managers contributed to the decline of the industry.

Industrial relations regularly emerged as a source of difficulty during this period, most especially wage claims. But occupational health and safety does not figure in the index of railway histories.[17] This may be because occupational health and safety on the railways did not change significantly during this period. The Railway Inspectorate remained the main enforcing authority. It came under the auspices of the Ministry of Transport or its equivalent.[18] The Royal Engineers continued to be the main source of recruitment of Inspecting Officers of Railways and this remained so until just before the research period. The Railway Inspectorate's so-called 'historic mandate' dominated until the 1970s, namely the approval of new works and accident investigation. There were minor changes to the authorizing legislation but nothing of great significance until the 1970s when occupational health and safety became a central and new addition to the Railway Inspectorate's remit. The catalyst for this change was the Robens Committee Report into Safety and Health at Work (1972).

Robens and the Health and Safety at Work etc. Act, 1974

The Report of the Robens Committee (1972) represents a watershed in thinking about occupational health and safety in Britain. In May 1970 the then Labour Secretary of State for Employment and Productivity, Barbara Castle, appointed a Committee of Inquiry to undertake a wide-ranging review of health and safety in Great Britain. The Committee was Chaired by Lord Robens and its remit was to examine critically 'the provision made for the safety and health of persons in the course of their employment' (1972, p. xiv) and to consider whether changes were needed and, if so, of what type. Three main factors prompted this enquiry:

ers argue that he inherited a disintegrating railway system which actually suffered its most serious losses after his departure (Hardy, 1989; Henshaw, 1991).

[16] Henshaw is particularly critical of the decision of the 1945 government to burden the nationalized railway with the debts of former railway companies' shareholders.

[17] Gourvish's (1986) official business history, for example, does not mention health and safety or the Railway Inspectorate in its index. The concern of Gourvish's history is economic, financial, social, and organizational matters. There are four references to accidents in the index, and discussion of these is related to the question of investment, in particular as evidence of a lack of investment.

[18] There were a variety of administrative changes during the course of the twentieth century. For instance, in 1919 the Ministry of Transport was formed and the Railway Inspectorate Department of the Board of Trade was transferred to it. In 1970 the Ministry of Transport was absorbed into the newly formed Department of the Environment.

1. There had never been a comprehensive review of the subject as a whole (1972, para. 16);
2. There were disturbing levels of accident and disease at work which were felt to be in particular need of scrutiny (1972, paras. 17 and 18); and
3. the 'traditional regulatory approach', that is, an approach based on an extensive system of detailed statutory provisions administered and enforced by government departments and local authorities, was considered to be in need of examination.

In its report, presented to Parliament in 1972, the Committee was very critical of the then existing provisions for health and safety in the workplace and it proposed radical changes. The main criticism levelled by the Committee was that administrative jurisdictions were too fragmented (1972, para. 32). It was felt that there were too many disparate agencies, responsible to too many government departments, enforcing too much legislation. In England alone, for example, five different government departments and the local authorities were responsible for the administration and enforcement of nine separate groups of health and safety statutes (ibid). The consequence, it was argued, was confusion in the individual workplace, among the inspectorates, and in policing and lawmaking (1972, para. 34–9). It was proposed that a more unified and integrated system should be created 'to increase the effectiveness of the state's contribution to safety and health at work' (1972, para. 41). Moreover it was argued that 'Reform should be aimed at creating the conditions for more effective selfregulation by employers and workpeople jointly' (1972, para. 452), the intention being to make those involved understand that health and safety matters are their own concern and not just the remit of external agencies.

The reforms favoured by the Robens Committee were essentially unifying and centralizing. It was recommended that there should be 'A New Statutory Framework' (1972, ch. 4) and a central part of this would be the establishment of a National Authority for Safety and Health at Work (1972, para. 467). This Authority would incorporate six existing inspectorates, namely those concerned with factories, mines, agriculture, explosives, nuclear installations, and alkali works. The eventual objective would be the merger of these inspectorates and the creation of a 'unified inspectorate' (1972, para. 204 ff.).

The Committee was concerned that the members of the Managing Board of the Authority should be drawn from diverse backgrounds. The role of the Board would be to help formulate policy, make decisions, and generally direct the work of the Authority. The key point here is that members of the Board would *participate* in the work of the Authority and not just offer advice (1972, para. 17). The corporatist body proposed was thus in keeping with the desire of the Committee to create a culture in which employers and the workforce would work jointly to promote health and safety.

The legislative changes proposed by the Robens Committee were as radical as the organizational changes it had suggested. The Committee recommended that the existing legislation should be replaced as far as possible by a single 'enabling Act' which would include a statement of general principles. The aim would be to replace detailed statutory regulations with broad requirements, supported by voluntary standards and codes of practice which could be easily revised as necessary.

The aims of the organizational and legislative recommendations forwarded by the Robens Committee were essentially to simplify and streamline the administration of health and safety provisions in Great Britain. The Health and Safety at Work etc. Act, 1974 (HSW Act) adopted many of the recommendations of the Robens Committee (see Hutter, 1997). But as Manning and I have argued elsewhere (Hutter and Manning, 1990), the proposals recommended by the Committee were not always as simple once enacted as it was intended they should be.[19] The goal- rather than rule-based approach has been seriously criticized, especially for the alleged opacity of the standards (Dalton, 1998: 43; James and Walters, 1999).

The Robens Report and the HSW Act are generally regarded as a significant point in the history of occupational health and safety regulation in Britain but there is considerable debate about whether they were positive additions. Some authors regard Robens as a 'remarkable innovation' (Dawson *et al.*, 1988: 3). Others regard it as flawed (Dalton, 1998: 42; Nichols, 1997) and others, while crediting it with some benefits, question its suitability in a changing world (James and Walters, 1999). Its positive aspects are well described by Dawson *et al.* (1988), namely an attempt to foster 'a particular attitude to the improvement of safety at work'. This involved encouraging a self-regulatory approach and the necessary involvement of the workforce in this. The Robens philosophy underlined the constitutive ambitions of regulatory law. In this respect Robens and the HSW Act may be regarded as promoting ideal regulatory objectives, that is, to encourage and facilitate the promotion of regulatory objectives as a normal everyday part of economic life. So why have both the Robens Report and the HSW Act attracted so much criticism? Much of the criticism has centred on the self-regulatory objectives of these documents.

For some authors self-regulation simply means 'no regulation' (Dalton, 1998: 43). Some commentators believe that the approach relies too heavily on the willingness and capacity of employers to self-regulate and there is cynicism that either is forthcoming (James and Walters, 1999). Yet Robens did not advocate 'pure' self-regulation; the model was rather one of enforced self-regulation (Ch. 1). The primary role of the law was to encourage workplace self-regulation and where this failed, external enforcement agencies would then step in (Dawson *et al.*, 1988: 11–12). The need for the 'enforced' part of enforced self-regulation was fully recognized. Yet it may be justly argued that Robens and the

---

[19] A central problem is that a large, centralized institution such as that recommended by Robens can result in complicated bureaucratization through its attempts to achieve the co-ordination of its constituent parts.

HSW Act rested upon a number of dubious assumptions. Perhaps one of the most criticized is the assumption that there is a 'natural identity of interest' about health and safety between workers and managers. The criticisms are various but range from a belief that this assumes too much goodwill, too much information about safe ways of working, and more generally, that it fails to address the realities of the power relations of the workplace (Dawson *et al.*, 1988; Nichols, 1997). Assumptions about an identity of interest between different groups led Robens to argue for consultative rather than bargaining approaches to health and safety. This too has attracted criticism, especially during the 1980s which witnessed a move away from corporatist thinking and also witnessed substantial changes in the balance of power in the workplace (Millward *et al.*, 1992; Nichols, 1997).[20] These are issues which will be addressed more fully later in this book. Let us return now to consider more specifically the effects of the Robens Report and the HSW Act on the regulation of occupational health and safety on the railways.

1974 to 1990

Upon the enactment of the HSW Act the Department of Transport entered an Agency Agreement with the Health and Safety Commission that the Railway Inspectorate would enforce the Act on all statutory railways and tramways in Great Britain and on non-statutory passenger carrying railways and tramways having a track gauge of not less than 350 mm. This agreement took effect on 1 April 1975 and it involved the Inspectorate recruiting new staff (railway employment inspectors) to undertake the additional work.

The responsibility for occupational health and safety at work and the associated recruitment of railway employment inspectors represented a major change to the Railway Inspectorate, perhaps the most dramatic this century. Its remit was greatly extended and its numbers doubled to cope with the extra work. The new inspectors were very different from the army officers who had traditionally been recruited into the Inspectorate (see Ch. 3) and increasingly the Health and Safety Executive (HSE) competed with the Department of Transport for responsibility for the Railway Inspectorate. Indeed the Railway Inspectorate worked for HSE on an agency basis until December 1990 when it became part of the Executive.

At the time of this research the Railway Inspectorate was dealing with a monopoly employer, namely British Railways. Inspectors did spend time with other smaller railways, such as London Transport, Tyne and Wear, the Glasgow Underground, and the numerous minor railways, such as the Severn Valley Railway

---

[20] It is acknowledged, however, that despite these changes the corporatist structures of HSC have remained, as has the system of safety representation resulting from the HSW Act and associated regulations. See Chapter 7.

and the Dart Valley Railway, but these were relatively small demands when compared to the national network under the control of British Railways.

British Rail: The Research Period

During the research period British Railways was a large and complex business (Gourvish, 1990). It was responsible for the main railway network in Britain, employed some 100,000 waged staff and over 30,000 salaried staff (see Table 2.1); was responsible for over 20,000 miles of track (see Table 2.2); and had an

TABLE 2.1. Rail staff numbers, BR, 31 March 1988

Type of Staff	Number of Employees
Salaried (administrative, technical, clerical staff)	37,369
Waged	
Drivers and other footplate staff	18,184
Guards and other train staff	9,562
Signalling staff	6,108
Staff employed in stations, yards, and depots	18,034
Staff employed on carriage and wagon examination	632
Permanent way, signal, and telecommunication staff	22,666
Workshop staff	17,370
Miscellaneous staff	2,123
	94,679
Total	132,048

Source: BRB (1988).

TABLE 2.2. Rail assets, BR, 31 March 1988

Assets	
Number of stations	2,541
Track miles open for traffic:	
Running lines	20,297
Sidings	3,260
Total	23,557
Rolling stock:	
Locomotives	2,270
High speed trains (power units)	197
Advanced passenger trains	2
Passenger carrying vehicles	13,013
Non-passenger carrying vehicles	1,635
Freight vehicles	28,884
Containers	24

Source: BRB (1988).

annual turnover of some £3.3 billion (BRB, 1988). These resources were organized into a large, nationwide corporate structure (see Figure 2.1) managed by British Railways Board (BRB), which stood at the apex of BR's hierarchy, and derived its authority from the Transport Act 1962: '. . . to provide railways services in Great Britain . . . and to provide such other services and facilities as appear to the Board to be expedient, and to have due regard . . . to efficiency, economy and safety of operation'. There were two main areas of organizational structure of BR of relevance to this research, namely the regional organization and the functional organization. The other main elements of the organization were the five independent business sectors introduced in 1982. I will consider these below but will concentrate for the moment on those parts of the company with which this study is most concerned.

The regional organization centred on five administrative regions, geographically based, namely the Eastern, London Midland, Scotland, Southern, and Western Regions. Cross-cutting this was a functional organization, namely the civil engineering, operations, signals and telecommunications, and mechanical and electrical engineering departments. The civil engineering department was responsible for the maintenance of the infrastructure of the railway, for example, the track, bridges, tunnels, and stations. Most of the work it engaged in was construction work, much of it trackside. The operations department was responsible for the operating railway, namely drivers, shunters, station staff, and signalmen. The signals and telecommunications department was concerned with the renewal and maintenance of signals and telecommunications equipment, so they too were track based for much of the time. Mechanical and electrical engineering staff, however, were usually based in depots, their responsibilities centring on maintaining the rolling stock.

Each functional department had a headquarters organization and a regional organization (see Fig. 2.2). A director, who was also a member of the Board, was in charge of each functional department. Part of his headquarters organization included specialist safety staff (see Ch. 6). Nominally, however, health and safety came under the auspices of the director. The regional organization varied between departments. Typically they involved a regional manager who had a staff of area managers, supervisors, and workers. The precise specialists varied between departments and region. The precise job titles also varied, with the operations and mechanical and electrical engineering departments referring to regional and area/depot managers, while the civil engineering and signals and telecommunications departments emphasized that their staff were engineers (regional and area engineers). Table 2.3 gives us some idea of the number of area managers employed by three of the functional departments in 1989.

The number of staff working for each area manager varied between departments. Operations managers varied greatly, employing between 800 and 2,500 staff, civil engineering area managers typically employed some 1,500 staff, and signals and telecommunications area managers generally had less than 1,000 staff under their control. The figures for the number of mechanical and electrical

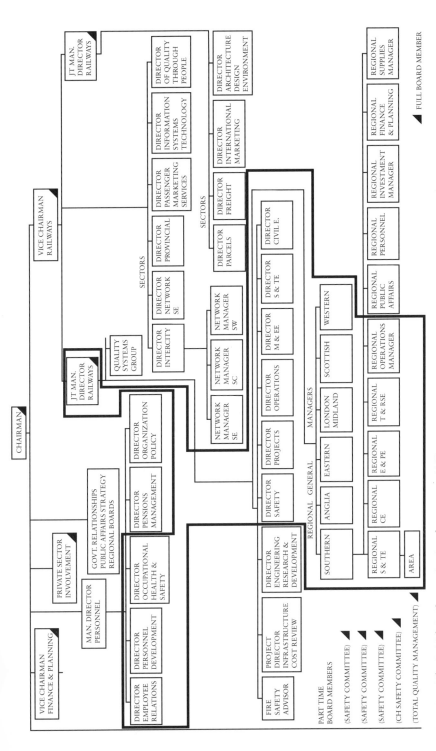

CHAIRMAN

VICE CHAIRMAN FINANCE & PLANNING

VICE CHAIRMAN RAILWAYS

JT MAN. DIRECTOR RAILWAYS

PRIVATE SECTOR INVOLVEMENT

MAN. DIRECTOR PERSONNEL

GOVT. RELATIONSHIPS PUBLIC AFFAIRS STRATEGY REGIONAL BOARDS

DIRECTOR EMPLOYEE RELATIONS

DIRECTOR PERSONNEL DEVELOPMENT

DIRECTOR OCCUPATIONAL HEALTH & SAFETY

DIRECTOR PENSIONS MANAGEMENT

DIRECTOR ORGANIZATION POLICY

FIRE SAFETY ADVISOR

PROJECT DIRECTOR INFRASTRUCTURE COST REVIEW

DIRECTOR ENGINEERING RESEARCH & DEVELOPMENT

DIRECTOR SAFETY

DIRECTOR PROJECTS

DIRECTOR OPERATIONS

DIRECTOR M & EE

DIRECTOR S & TE

DIRECTOR CIVIL E.

JT MAN. DIRECTOR RAILWAYS

QUALITY SYSTEMS GROUP

NETWORK MANAGER SE

NETWORK MANAGER SC

NETWORK MANAGER SW

DIRECTOR INTERCITY

DIRECTOR NETWORK SE

DIRECTOR PROVINCIAL

DIRECTOR PASSENGER MARKETING SERVICES

DIRECTOR INFORMATION SYSTEMS TECHNOLOGY

DIRECTOR OF QUALITY THROUGH PEOPLE

SECTORS

DIRECTOR PARCELS

DIRECTOR FREIGHT

DIRECTOR INTERNATIONAL MARKETING

DIRECTOR ARCHITECTURE DESIGN ENVIRONMENT

SECTORS

SOUTHERN

ANGLIA

EASTERN

LONDON MIDLAND

SCOTTISH

WESTERN

MANAGERS

REGIONAL GENERAL

REGIONAL S & TE

REGIONAL CE

REGIONAL E & PE

REGIONAL T & RSE

REGIONAL OPERATIONS MANAGER

REGIONAL PUBLIC AFFAIRS

REGIONAL PERSONNEL

REGIONAL INVESTMENT MANAGER

REGIONAL FINANCE & PLANNING

REGIONAL SUPPLIES MANAGER

AREA

PART TIME
BOARD MEMBERS

(SAFETY COMMITTEE)

(SAFETY COMMITTEE)

(SAFETY COMMITTEE)

(CH SAFETY COMMITTEE)

(TOTAL QUALITY MANAGEMENT)

◆ FULL BOARD MEMBER

Fig. 2.1. The British Rail organizational structure, 1988

Note: —— Part of the organization included in the research sample.

Source: Adapted from Hidden (1989).

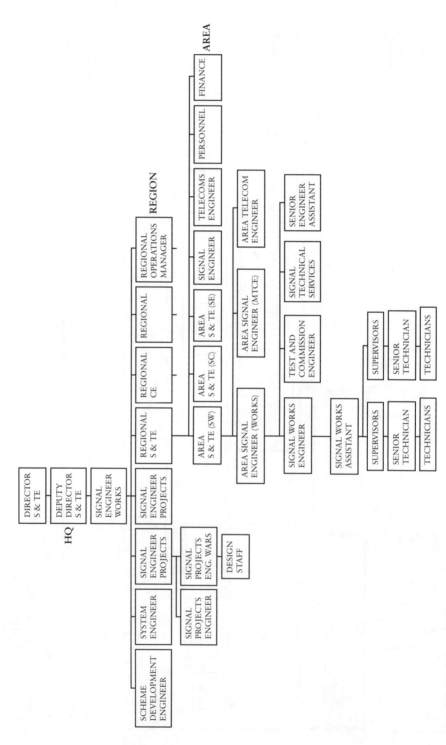

Fig. 2.2. Signals and Telecommunications Department, 1988

Source: Adapted from Hidden (1989).

TABLE 2.3. Number of area managers according to department

Region	Area managers (operations dept.)	Area civil engineers	Area signals and telecommunications engineers
Anglia	6	1	1
Eastern	9	5	2
London Midland	14	6	4
Scottish	5	4	1
Southern	11	3	3
Western	9	5	3
Total	54	24	14

Source: Private communication.

engineering depot managers were not available but the number of staff employed in each depot varied between 100 and 300 staff. These departments were hierarchically organized with distinct lines of authority from top to bottom.

The organization of work varied between departments. For example, civil engineering staff typically worked in teams which moved around the railways as required. They were managed on site by supervisors and often worked at night and through the weekends on engineering works. Signals and telecommunications staff were also required to work trackside. They tended to work in pairs or groups of three. Operations department staff varied greatly in their working practices. Some were based in offices whereas others, notably drivers, often worked alone. Mechanical and electrical engineering staff were largely depot based. The skill levels and union affiliations also varied, reflecting the different types of work. The managerial problems encountered by each department were therefore variable and from a corporate perspective a diversity of staff and working arrangements needed to be accommodated.

The regions varied geographically, in size and also with respect to railway infrastructure. Southern Region, for example, was distinguished by the presence of the third rail, an electrified third rail at track level. London Midland had more overhead electrical rails than other regions. Obviously these had specific safety risks attaching to them.

This functional and regional organization covered the large majority of employees most exposed to occupational health and safety risks. However, in some senses this structure lost its importance during the 1980s and early 1990s with the introduction of the business sectors (Dent, 1991). These were introduced in 1982 and assumed responsibility below board level for specifying to regional general managers the standards of service expected of them (Gourvish, 1990: 116). But the functional directors maintained a significant role in maintaining technical and operational performance standards.

Gourvish (1990) investigates the introduction of the business sectors in some detail and concludes that they were internally driven but in tune with government thinking. It is certainly the case that during the 1980s BR had to become more business and commercially aware. Bagwell (1996) reports that in the 1980s BR had the lowest proportion of total revenue derived from public funds of any European railways. Strict borrowing limits were imposed and led among other things to low levels of investment in the railway infrastructure and rolling stock. This was restricted to essential maintenance and renewal (Bagwell, 1996: 121) and according to some commentators this was encouraged by the 1983 Serpell Report into *Railways Finances* (Committee on the Review of Railway Finances, 1983). This recommended a reduction in levels of support for the railways from the public purse (Bagwell, 1984: 128) and also increased the pressure on BR to act as an ordinary commercial enterprise (Bagwell, 1996: 49).[21] Gourvish (1990: 130 ff.) is of the opinion that the introduction of the business sectors did help to improve BR's cost consciousness and investment appraisal; its operating and financial results; and its overall performance. But he notes that there were accompanying problems, most particularly the resistance to the introduction of the sectors.

It is also important to appreciate that during the 1980s there were significant staff cuts on BR. Gourvish (1990: 140) estimates that between 1978 and 1989 there was a reduction in BRB employees of 44.4 per cent. A substantial part of this reduction was the result of privatization, most particularly the sale of subsidiary businesses. This, coupled with increased productivity demands, low pay, and organizational changes, led to serious morale problems throughout management and the workforce. In turn this led to industrial action. In 1982 more working days were lost on BR through strikes than had been lost for the entire period from 1948 to 1981 (Bagwell, 1984: 82). But in many respects employees were not in a strong position. There was little alternative work available. Moreover, during the 1980s and early 1990s the power of the unions in Britain seriously declined (see Ch. 7).

The railways industry was heavily unionized. There were three main unions at the time of data collection, namely the National Union of Railwaymen (NUR), the Associated Society of Locomotive Engineers and Firemen (ASLEF), and the Transport Salaried Staffs' Association (TSSA). Some workers in the railway workshops were members of the Amalgamated Engineering Union (AEU).[22] The decline in the power of the unions is perhaps indicated by the amalgamation of the NUR with other transport unions in 1990, to create the Railways, Maritime and Transport Workers Union. The other significant trend was of course the beginning of the privatization process.

---

[21] Bagwell (1984: 127–8) reports that the Serpell Committee proposed the replacement rather than the modernization of signalling and cuts in the maintenance of the track.

[22] All of these unions readily co-operated with this research.

Privatization

The data collection for this research coincided with the period of privatization of nationalized industries. The privatization of BR started with the 1981 Transport Bill which provided for the sale of subsidiary BR concerns such as the company's hotels and shipping interests (Bagwell, 1996; Gourvish, 1990). There was little doubt during the fieldwork period that BR was being prepared for full privatization. Parts of the company were sold to the private sector, for example, the engineering works at Crewe, Derby, and York (British Railways Engineering Ltd.) were offered for sale as a single business in 1988. The language of the marketplace was increasingly prominent—for example, competitive tendering and the establishment of business sectors and subsidiary and divisional boards, such as British Railways Engineering Ltd., British Railways Property Board, and Freightliners. The government set BRB strict targets to reduce the public sector obligation grant. This again heightened the emphasis on costs and led to suspicion among staff whenever there was a reorganization of the company.

Full privatization did not actually come until 1993 (see Ch. 11) but the threat of it and preparation for it overshadowed the company during the fieldwork period and this should be taken into account. Meanwhile other events were throwing the spotlight onto safety. During the run-up to privatization, but completely unconnected with it, there were two major accidents, one involving a fire on the London Underground and the second a collision at Clapham Junction. These events, as we will discuss in Chapter 3, led to a major re-evaluation of safety on the railways.

The Research Sample

The research sample was selected in conjunction with railway staff. A wide cross-section of staff from the four main functional departments were interviewed across three regions. Different grades of staff were interviewed, including directors, departmental safety managers, managers, supervisors, safety representatives, and the workforce. In addition regional and national union officials were interviewed. Whereas there is a balance between the number of managerial staff and members of the workforce interviewed, there is an imbalance between departments. This is because each department differed with regard to the number of staff it felt should be interviewed so as to be representative (see App. 1). A total of 134 in-depth interviews were conducted.

Data were collected by means of in-depth interviews. The interview schedules (see App. 2) were designed to encourage open-ended discussion of questions. The objective was to avoid asking questions which would restrict interviewees in their replies and could even suggest answers to them. The emphasis was much more upon discerning how respondents interpreted issues and perceived health and safety. Interviews lasted from forty minutes to two hours, usually varying according to the grade and specialism of the staff involved. All interviews were taped and most were undertaken by the author. It should be noted that it was not always possible to ask interviewees all the questions on the schedule, usually because of limitations on the length of the interview.

The main phase of interviews was followed up in the mid-1990s with further interviews with members of the Railway Inspectorate and Railtrack. These findings are reported in Chapter 11. In addition to the interviews, documentary sources were consulted. These included official publications and internal company documents. Further details of the data collection can be found in the Appendices.

3

The Railway Industry and Risk

There are a variety of academic perspectives on risk (Krimsky and Golding, 1992) and a range of opinion about how feasible it is to establish the risks associated with any given activity or institution. These perspectives vary from a reliance on technical studies of risk identification and quantification to the view that there is no such thing as an objective measure of risk (Slovic, 1992). A less extreme position may prove more helpful, for example, the view that risks are socially constructed, so how they are perceived is a product of selection and communication (Renn, 1992: 61). This accepts that there are dangers which can be measured but also has a clear understanding that there are technical, political, and philosophical problems in establishing what the risks might be. For example, there are problems in deciding what constitutes evidence, how it might be interpreted, and so on, difficulties which relate to the paradigms and frames researchers adhere to (Nelkin, 1985: 17). On the railways risks are usually thought of in terms of potential outcomes—most prominently fatalities and injuries. So in this chapter we will consider the information available about occupational health and safety on the railways at the time of data collection. This will give us some basis for understanding the nature of the risks that regulation was aiming to manage and also what information respondents had available as a basis for understanding risk.

Indicators of Risk: Accident Statistics

This section will give a simple and brief overview of British Railways' accident statistics at the time of data collection for this research. It is important to understand that these statistics are not being taken as an indicator of the impact of the law but as the most 'objective' indicator of risk available to BR and its employees. These statistics formed the information base and communications system about 'bad news' within the industry. It is important to understand that these statistics were socially constructed. The risks derived from accident statistics are reliant on reporting systems (Rees, 1988: 110). This embraces the very definitions of recordable accidents which in England and Wales are legally defined by reporting regulations and then interpreted by the state regulatory agencies (Railway Inspectorate and HSE) and in turn the company (BR). Within the company there was a variety of influences upon the construction of these statistics, such as the propensity of staff to report accidents, how accidents were categorized, and the ease with which accidents were recorded (James, 1993). It is also important to appreciate that the very language used to describe risk is itself revealing (Nelkin, 1985). For example, some authors take issue with the term 'accident' because they consider that it suggests something unavoidable. They prefer to refer to injury (Nichols, 1997).[1]

A distinction also needs to be drawn between health and safety. The overwhelming majority of literature on health and safety on the railways refers to physical injuries, most particularly those which are immediate and tangible. Other occupational health risks, which are by comparison often less visible and have longer-term effects, are seldom discussed. The major regulatory agency publication on health and safety is entitled *Railway Safety*, with health typically forming a very minor part of the report. For instance the 1986 Railway Inspectorate *Annual Report* devoted four of 184 paragraphs to 'Health and Environment', the rest referred to safety issues. More recent reports give more prominence to occupational health, this being part of a broader HSC emphasis on health issues. The *1996/97 Annual Report*, for instance, devotes a chapter to 'Occupational Health' but this chapter is just two pages long.

It is therefore important to appreciate that there are, even now, few sources of information about occupational health and safety on the railways. In the 1980s and early 1990s there was even less information available. This is reflected in this research to the extent that it discusses corporate and individual understandings of the management of occupational health and safety risks. Overwhelmingly, as we will see, these understandings focus on safety, not health, issues. This is also reflected in this chapter and its focus on the information available to BR's staff, which again emphasizes safety risks through the medium of accident statistics. This general bias in the focus on safety risks is perhaps not entirely surprising. It partly reflects a broader tendency to concentrate on more visible and tangible happenings, such as safety, as compared with less tangible, less visible, and the more delayed, long-term effects associated with health issues. And, of course, the most compelling and immediate problems confronting workers are safety issues. Health-related factors were thus overshadowed by the very real and present safety problems associated with the industry.

A variety of sources of information about railway accidents in Britain is available. The statistics below are derived from two sources, namely Railway Inspectorate and HSE annual reports and BR data. The HSE data are probably the most accessible and simply presented data. This chapter provides a basic and summary picture of the official data. Its intention is to highlight the main

---

[1] There is a variety of disciplinary approaches to the study of accidents. For example, there are psychological, economic, organizational, technological, and sociological accounts (see e.g. Broadbent *et al.*, 1989; Viscusi, 1983; Perrow, 1984; Carson, 1982). Good critical summaries of them are to be found in Nelkin (1985) and Nichols (1997).

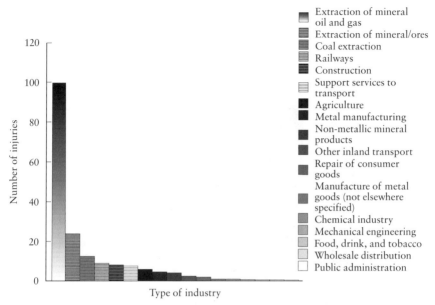

Number of injuries

Type of industry

Extraction of mineral oil and gas
Extraction of mineral/ores
Coal extraction
Railways
Construction
Support services to transport
Agriculture
Metal manufacturing
Non-metallic mineral products
Other inland transport
Repair of consumer goods
Manufacture of metal goods (not elsewhere specified)
Chemical industry
Mechanical engineering
Food, drink, and tobacco
Wholesale distribution
Public administration

FIG. 3.1. Fatal injuries per 100,000 employees: industries reporting over 30 fatal injuries to employees, 1986/7–1990/1

Source: Adapted from HSC (1991: 69).

areas of known risk and to convey some sense of the extent of the health and safety risks encountered by those working for BR during the research period.[2]

Comparative Risk: Other British Industries

Figure 3.1 details the comparative risks of injuries to employees during the period 1986/7 to 1990/1 and Figure 3.2 for 1990/1. The railway industry during this period was the fourth most dangerous industry in Britain when judged by fatal injury rates per 100,000 employees and fifth when judged by all reported injuries. It is notable that the construction industry, which is often perceived as the most dangerous industry, was ranked fifth with respect to fatal injuries and eighth when ranked according to all injuries. The explanation seems to lie in the absolute numbers of injuries where the construction industry is ranked first with respect to both fatal injuries and all injuries, while the railways appear as seventh according to fatal injury statistics and tenth according to all reported injuries (Fig. 3.2). Arguably, however, the rate per 100,000 employees gives us a clearer idea of the occupational health and safety risks involved in the industry.

---

[2] See Nichols (1997) for a more sophisticated discussion of general health and safety data in Britain. It is important to understand that the data employees saw were likely to be less simply presented (see Chs. 9 and 10).

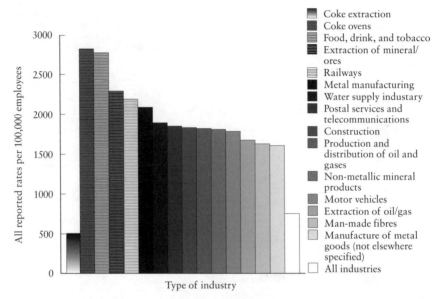

FIG. 3.2. Top fifteen industries by employee, all reported injury rates, 1990/1
Source: Adapted from HSC (1991: 69).

Comparative Risk: International data

It is not at all easy to compare the railway industry in Britain with its counter-parts in other countries. As an HSE study into comparative workplace injuries notes, 'Individual countries define and report workplace injuries in different ways' (HSE, 1997). A common problem is that railway workers are seldom iden-tified as a separate category in injury statistics. This was highlighted in a private communication from a librarian working for the International Labour Organ-ization— 'A search of our library databases revealed little which dealt specif-ically with mortality among railway workers'.[3] Eurostat data similarly cover industry sectors rather than specific industries (HSE, 1997, para. 14). We must therefore bear these distinctions in mind and work within the constraints of the data.

The Transport Sector

HSE research suggests that overall occupational fatality and injury rates in Britain are generally among the lowest in Europe and lower than the United States (HSE, 1997). Fatality rates for the general transport sector are given in Table 3.1.[4]

---

[3] I am grateful to Chryssa Kannelakis-Reimer who spent many frustrating hours trying to obtain these data. The fact that her hard work failed to produce very much data for inclusion in this chapter reveals the very real difficulties in making international comparisons of occupational health and safety performance.

[4] Data for Germany are not included as the data for this country excluded the state railways.

TABLE 3.1. Rates of fatality for the transport industry according to country (per 100,000 workers)

Great Britain		France	Spain		Italy
1993	1994	1993	1993	1994	1991
2.2	2.0	6.5	13.0	10.7	11.2

Source: Adapted from HSE (1997, table 2).

This compares with the United States where in 1990/1 the Bureau of Labor fatality statistics reveal that 'Transportation and public utilities' have 8.4 fatalities per 100,000 employees. This makes it the third highest category behind the construction industry (with a rate of 16.7) and agriculture, forestry, and fishing (with a rate of 10) (Bureau of Labor Statistics, 1993: 47).

The Australian figures for work-related traumatic fatalities for the period 1989 to 1992 reveal Transport and Storage to have the fourth highest rate of death and the highest absolute numbers of fatalities (Worksafe website, www.worksafe.gov.au, 1999). These data therefore confirm on an international basis that the transport sector is generally one of the riskier sectors to work in. Let us now turn to consider the more specific data for the railway industry.

The Railway Industry

More specific data are available for two main countries, namely the United States and Australia.[5] *Fatalities* are difficult to compare with the British figures as Federal Railroad Administration data and Australian National Occupational Health and Safety Commission data only give absolute numbers.[6] The total number of worker fatalities on American railroads was 33 in 1996 and 37 in 1997 (Federal Railroad Administration, 1998) and the absolute number of worker fatalities on Australian railways during 1996/7 was 4 (National Occupational Health and Safety Commission, 1998).

The *total injury* figures are more easily compared with Britain. The US Federal Railroad Administration report employee injuries in the railway industry as 3,310 per 100,000 employees for 1997 and 3,370 per 100,000 employees for 1998. The Australian equivalents for 1996/7 are 2,610 per 100,000 employees.[7] This

---

[5] I am grateful to Australian colleagues for helping me with the statistical data for this section. Particular thanks are due to Michelle Bunn.

[6] Strictly speaking the Australian fatality numbers are not published but it is possible to discern the number of fatalities as both the non-fatal numbers and total figures are published so presumably the difference between the two represents the number of fatalities.

[7] There is apparently notable variation between different Australian regions. Worksafe Western Australia reports on its website some of the most detailed statistics publicly available. From this site we learn that the incidence rate for lost time injuries and diseases per 100,000 employees was: 1994/5—5,900; 1995/6—4,900; 1996/7—5,000; 1997/8—5,900.

TABLE 3.2. Injuries to employees reported to the Railway Inspectorate
April 1987–March 1993

Type of injury	Year					
	1987	1988	1989	1990	1991/2	1992/3
Fatal	16	16	18	22	17	11
Major*	238	273	277	306	278	284
Minor	2,672	3,022	2,858	3,051	3,226	3,348

Note: *As defined by the Reporting of Injuries, Diseases and Dangerous Occurrences Regulations (RIDDOR), 1985.
Source: Annual Reports (Railway Safety 1991/2 (HSC, 1992); Railway Safety 1994/5 (HSE, 1995a).

compares with British figures of 2,226.2 per 100,000 employees in 1990/1. We can see that the British figures compare reasonably favourably with these two countries. So, let us return to the British railway industry and consider in more detail the nature of the risks which confronted employees.[8]

Occupational Health and Safety in the Railway Industry in Britain

Trends in Injury Rates

Table 3.2 gives some indication of the number of injuries to employees which were reported to the HSE under the reporting regulations.[9]

Figures 3.3, 3.4, and 3.5 plot the number of fatal, major, and minor injuries to railway staff and contractors over the ten-year period 1982 to 1991/2. As we can see, during the research period there was a general upward trend in the accident rate. Figure 3.3, for example, shows the accident rate for fatalities was 9 per 100,000 employees in 1986 and 14 per 100,000 employees in 1990. But in 1991/2 it had fallen again to 10.6 per 100,000 employees and it fell again in 1992/3. The rates for major and minor injuries were broadly in line with these trends. But this needs to be taken in the context of the statistics for the entire decade, which reveal a noteworthy fall in fatal accidents in the first five years of the decade and a general decline in minor injuries during the same period. This is in stark contrast to the increase in major injuries.

Type of Accident

Table 3.3 details the type of accident which led to injury, using Railway Inspectorate categories of classification and data. The basic points to glean from these

---

[8] It is important to underline that we are considering occupational health and safety risks, not the risks to passengers and the general public.

[9] HSE changed the basis of its statistical data collection from calendar years to fiscal years in 1991.

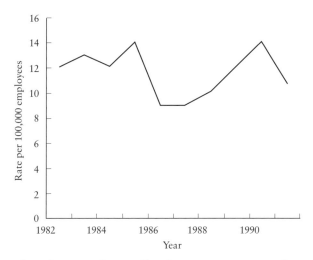

FIG. 3.3. Fatal accidents to railway staff and contractors 1982–1991/2
Source: HSE (1992: 65).

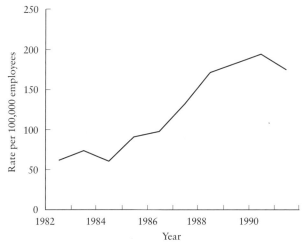

FIG. 3.4. Major injuries to railway staff and contractors, 1982–1991/2
Source: HSE (1992: 65).

data are that of the 3,000 to 4,000 accidents to railway staff (including contractors) reported each year, the majority of fatalities occurred in movement accidents and the majority of major and minor injuries were the result of non-movement accidents. *Train accidents*, involving accidents to train and rolling stock, were a cause of worker injuries but they were less important than other types of accident. It was of course train accidents that received most

TABLE 3.3. Staff casualties: type of accident

Railway casualties	Killed					Major injuries					Minor injuries				
	1991/2	1990	1989	1988	1987	1991/2	1990	1989	1988	1987	1991/2	1990	1989	1988	1987
Total	17	22	18	16	16	278	306	277	273	238	3,226	3,051	2,858	3,022	2,672
Train accidents	2	1	6	2	1	6	6	18	6	5	59	67	53	62	60
Movement	9	19	8	11	11	39	48	28	36	34	65	68	35	49	50
Non-movement	6	2	4	3	4	233	252	231	231	199	3,102	2,916	2,770	2,911	2,562

Source: Railway Safety 1991/2, appendix 2 (HSC, 1992: 68).

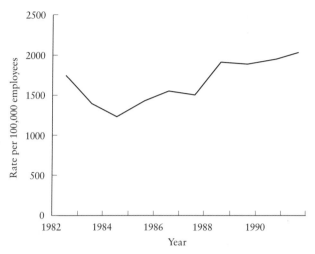

FIG. 3.5. Minor injuries to railway staff and contractors, 1982–1991/2
Source: HSE (1992: 65).

media attention and this was despite the fact that they were not the major cause of passenger deaths either, this being non-movement accidents.[10]

Movement accidents[11] are 'accidents to people caused by the movement of railway vehicles, excluding those in Train Accidents' (Department of Transport, 1987: 5). These include:

- *shunting accidents* such as getting on or off, or falling off, moving locomotives or wagons; being caught between vehicles while coupling or uncoupling; or being struck, or caught between vehicles when walking on the lines;
- *accidents during the running of trains* such as falling off moving locomotives or wagons; or coming into contact with fixed line-side objects when riding on trains;
- *accidents to staff working on or about the track*, for example, being struck by trains when acting as lookout man;[12] being struck by the trains when working on or about the track; being struck by flying objects or out-of-gauge parts of a train.

---

[10] The passenger death rate per billion passenger miles was 0.24 in 1989; 0.08 in 1991/2; and 0 in 1993/4 for train accidents compared to 1.01 in 1989; 1.16 in 1991/2; and 0.62 in 1993/4 for movement accidents; and 1.25 in 1989; 0.63 in 1991/2; and 1.30 in 1993/4 for non-movement accidents (HSE, 1995*b*: 71).

[11] These categories are the ones used by the Railway Inspectorate in their collection of accident statistics. There is an additional category, namely *failures* of rolling stock, track, and structures. These can cause train accidents or personal injury but do not necessarily do so (Department of Transport, 1987: 5).

[12] Lookouts' sole task is to look out for oncoming trains and warn the rest of the gang thus giving them time to get out of the way of the train.

The following extracts from accident reports give some idea of the sort of accident included in this category:[13]

A crane driver was crushed when he fell between the buffers of his own crane and its match wagon and another crane was used to shunt wagons onto them. (Railway Inspectorate Report)

During an unauthorised movement of a shunting locomotive along a siding at 'Y', it collided with the rear vehicle of a stationary train, killing two drivers who were in the cab and slightly injuring the Secondman. (Railway Inspectorate Report)

A man was struck when scrambling for the platform in response to a shout as the vehicles he was examining suddenly moved backwards under the impact of the attaching locomotive. The primary cause of the accident was the failure of the driver to properly control the movement of his locomotive as it set back onto the train. He was driving from the rear cab and could not see in the direction of travel due to the curvature of the line. (Railway Inspectorate Report)

A guard, attempting to board his train as it departed from the station, fell between the moving train and the platform and was killed. The train had started after the driver had seen a relief chargeman's 'Ready to start' hand signal. (Railway Inspectorate Report)

Eight track maintenance men were injured when two tamping machines were in head-on collision whilst being driven at excessive speeds in an Engineer's possession. One machine was making an unauthorised movement. (Railway Inspectorate Report)

Non-movement accidents are 'accidents to people on railway premises but not connected with the movement of railway vehicles' (Department of Transport, 1987: 5). They include:

- *being struck* by vehicles (other than rail): by suspended loads, doors, or equipment; by falling loads, doors, or equipment; by sparks, flying particles, or chippings;
- *slipping or falling* from road/rail vehicles or being thrown from road vehicles; platforms, ladders, staging etc. or into pits or holes; tripping;
- being *trapped* in or by road vehicles, by doors, equipment, goods, etc.;
- *lifting or moving* goods, equipment, couplings, signal points, levers, ground points;
- *fire, fumes*, explosions, scalding or injurious liquids;
- using *hand/manual tools*;
- contact with *live rail, electric shock,* or burns;
- using *power driven* machinery, tools.

The examples below, from accident reports, again illustrate the type of incidents which characterized non-movement railway accidents:

A man driving a battery platform tractor lost control and drove over the edge of the platform. [He suffered a] fractured pelvis, two cracked vertebrae, bruised abdomen. (Railway Inspectorate Report)

---

[13] I have removed identifying details in most cases as they are unnecessary and could cause distress to family members.

A man crossing the tracks slipped, fell on the rail and was electrocuted. (Railway Inspectorate Report)
The victim was climbing a ladder carrying a pane of glass when he fell approximately 15 feet and sustained serious head and spinal injuries from which he died. (BR Report)
An Overhead Lineman was electrocuted when attempting to attach an earth connection to the overhead line equipment . . . he failed to establish the correct overhead line to be earthed and attempted to attach an earth wire to a live wire energised at 25 kV. (Railway Inspectorate Report)

Trackside Working

The trackside was the most dangerous area of the railways for staff. Table 3.4 details Railway Inspectorate explanations of the cause of these accidents. Three main reasons emerged as significant. One centred on systemic failure, namely inadequate protection, and another on individual culpability, namely lack of vigilance. The third was potentially a mixture of the two, namely acting incorrectly after seeing or being warned of a train. This could have been the result of an individual lapse or a failure of training or supervision. A greater sense of what was involved can again be gleaned from accident reports:

[Protection inadequate] 'The victim' failed to react promptly for his own safety when warning of an approaching train was given by the lookout men. Responsibility for the accident must rest with the contractor for failing to give adequate safety training, and also allowing him to work on the line when his knowledge of English was insufficient to enable verbal warnings to be understood. (Railway Inspectorate Report)
[Lookout man at fault] A track machine man working with a tamper was struck by a train travelling on an adjacent line. An inexperienced lookout man failed to give warning of the oncoming train. (Railway Inspectorate Report)

TABLE 3.4. Fatalities to staff through being struck by trains while at work on or about the track

Cause	1991/2	1990	1989	1988	1987
Protection inadequate	3	2	2	1	1
Lookout man at fault	—	—	—	1	—
Acted incorrectly after seeing or being warned of train	1	6	1	1	—
Unaware of train owing to lack of vigilance	1	2	1	2	3
Remaining	1	1	—	1	4
Total	6	11	4	6	8

Source: Railway Safety 1991/2 (HSC, 1992: 58).

[Acted incorrectly after seeing or being warned of train] 'The deceased' and another were engaged in putting down markings in Crowborough Tunnel. The 11.41 Uckfield–Oxted train whistled as it entered the tunnel and the men inadvertently stepped into its path, the other man lost a leg. (BR Report)

A track patrolman was struck by a train from behind as he was walking alongside a bi-directional line. The locomotive's warning horn had been sounded as the train approached and the patrolman had apparently acknowledged the warning ... he appears to have been so preoccupied with his duties that he failed to assimilate the warning sounded from the train. He also failed to keep a good lookout or to keep himself in a place of safety. (Railway Inspectorate Report)

[Unaware of train owing to lack of vigilance] A permanent way supervisor, who was examining the track during tamping operations, was struck and killed by a train passing on an adjacent track. He failed to advise the lookout man he was moving on to lines open to traffic. (Railway Inspectorate Report)

A driver and guard walking to 'Y' station on an unauthorised route, were overtaken and killed by a train. Both men failed to exercise care for their own safety. (Railway Inspectorate Report)

Some accidents were a *mixture* of reasons: 'A track man was struck and seriously injured by a train as he attempted to cross a track between his trackside workplace and the station. Although the man failed to look out for his own safety before crossing, a lookout man had not been appointed' (Railway Inspectorate Report). Lookout men were also in some danger as an example cited in the *1986 Annual Report* (Department of Transport, 1987: 30) reveals. The case involved the repainting of a bridge where there were five running lines and several lookout men protecting the painters who were working on overhead gantries: 'Another of the lookout men who was closer to the approaching train sounded a warning which the deceased acknowledged and turned to pass on to the next look out man; as the train approached the deceased had his back towards it, apparently unaware of the line it was on' (Railway Inspectorate Report).

Employee Accidents 1987–1988

A more in-depth examination of the fatal accident statistics for 1987 and 1988 gives us further insight into the nature of the risks to employees on BR.[14] It is difficult to generalize on the basis of accident figures for just two years but this was the immediate information that employees would have had before them at the time of the research. It suggests that there was regional variation, and it confirms that trackside work was most dangerous. In particular trackmen who worked for the civil engineering department appeared

---

[14] It should be noted that whereas BR statistics were for calendar years, Department of Transport and HSE statistics for some of this period were for fiscal years. Moreover the BR statistics I received in early 1989 recorded one less fatality for 1987 than HSE figures. It is unclear why but there are several explanations, for example an accident may have occurred in 1987 but the death occurred in 1988, something which may have been unclear when the statistics I received were compiled.

TABLE 3.5. Staff fatality statistics according to region

Region	1987	1988
Eastern	6	5
Scottish	2	1
Southern	4	3
Western	1	2
London Midland	3	5
Anglian	0	1

TABLE 3.6. Staff fatality statistics according to job

Job	1987	1988
Trackman	10	6
Driver	2	3
Signals and telecommunications	3	1
Supervisor	0	1
Conductor	0	1
Guard	1	0
Shunter	0	2
Contractor	0	3

TABLE 3.7. Staff fatality statistics according to place of accident

Place	1987	1988
Station	0	5
Depot	0	1
Sidings/yard	3	1
Trackside	10	6
Unauthorized	0	1
Derailment/crash	1	2
Falling from train	1	1
Hit by tree	1	0

TABLE 3.8. Staff fatality statistics according to type of accident

Type	1987	1988
Hit by train	10	11
Falling	2	3
Electrocution	3	1
Derailment/crash	1	2

to be the most vulnerable.[15] But other trackside workers were also at risk, for example, signals and telecommunications staff and drivers. There was the danger of electrocution on the Southern Region where there was the third rail, and on Eastern Region where there were overhead power lines. But moving trains were without doubt the greatest danger whether they were on the running lines, in yards, or in sidings. This was underlined by the fact that mechanical and electrical engineering staff, who were almost exclusively depot based, were less often involved in fatalities. Civil engineering and contract staff were also at risk from the construction-type work they were involved in when repairing and maintaining the rail network.

The Working Environment

In attempting to understand the risks inherent in the railway industry it should be appreciated that maintenance and repair work took place at all hours in all weathers. Staff were often exposed to the elements and also to fast, heavy, and increasingly quiet trains which had long stopping distances. Typically repair and maintenance work was undertaken by gangs of workers under the guidance of supervisors who held junior management roles. Where they were working on a running line they would have possession of it, in other words the trains were stopped from using these lines. Often however they were working adjacent to a running line or between lines and needed to move when a train approached. The provision of lookout men whose sole task was to look out for oncoming trains and warn the rest of the gang was therefore essential.[16] There were temptations, however, not to appoint lookout men as the job could be finished more quickly if this member of the gang worked with the rest. Difficulties also arose where visibility was hampered by, for example, a curve in the track. As we can see from the accident reports above, lookout men could have difficulties in maintaining their vigilance and this could lead to their own death or injury. In other cases concentration on the job could result in a lack of vigilance about the immediate environment, most especially oncoming trains.

Drivers were in an altogether different situation. They were often characterized as solitary figures who were at most risk in train crashes and when they had to leave their trains and climb down onto the running track. At the time of data collection there were no cab radios and if drivers needed to communicate with anyone in the case of difficulties they would have to stop the train and walk to a trackside telephone. At these times they were at risk from other trains, especially as they had no lookout protection.

---

[15] According to department: 1987: civil engineering—11; operations—3; signals and telecommunications—2; contractor—0; 1988: civil engineering—7; operations—6; signals and telecommunications—1; contractors—3. Mechanical and electrical engineering had no fatalities in either year.

[16] There were BR rules about this. See Chapter 6 for discussion of company risk management systems.

Mechanical and electrical engineering staff spent the large majority of their time working in large locomotive sheds which resemble garage repair shops except, of course, for their scale. The dangers here were typically more low-level workshop-type dangers although the movement of trains, especially while someone was working underneath them, was an obvious danger.[17]

But it is to the trackside that we should return and below I reproduce details from a Railway Inspectorate accident report which conveys both the working conditions trackside and the circumstances of a sadly typical accident. The accident occurred at 8.30 a.m. on a fine clear day in February on Southern Region in the 1980s. It involved a man engaged on track patrol duties being struck by a train and sustaining fatal injuries. He had worked for BR for three and a half years. The accident summary reports that the accident happened because 'the victim' moved from his place of work, when warned to do so, to an unsafe place where he was struck by a train. The system of working was not defective and had he complied with the rules the accident would have been avoided. The more mundane details are relayed in the body of the Report:

'A', a track man aged 41 years, was struck by two trains while engaged in track patrol duties on the Down Main local line[18] when, on receiving a warning of an approaching train, he moved into the six-foot space between the track he was patrolling and the adjacent Up Main Local Line . . .

Earlier that day 'A' and 'B', another trackman, had patrolled a section of the Up Main Line . . . As they returned [they patrolled separate lines] . . . 'C', a leading trackman, was with them acting as lookout man . . . . All three men were walking towards oncoming traffic and this was the accepted safe system of work.

'Y' was the driver of the 8.26 passenger train from Waterloo to Hampton Court that consisted of two class 405 electric multiple units 4 car sets. He told me that . . . he saw a man standing in the six-foot space between the Up and Down Main Local lines, facing towards him, wearing a high visibility vest and carrying a spanner over his left shoulder. The driver moved his hand with the intention of sounding the train's warning horn but in fact did not do so.[19] He said he felt satisfied that the man was aware of his approach, and that he remained in the six-foot space as he passed him. He said that he heard a bang from the front of the train, but nothing very unusual although he decided to examine his train at Wimbledon. He then found nothing wrong. A closer examination on arrival at Hampton Court, however, revealed traces of blood on the fifth coach which convinced him that an accident had occurred and he advised the traffic control accordingly.

'Z' was the driver of the 8.01 passenger train from Hampton Court to Waterloo that also consisted of two class 405 electric multiple-unit sets. He told me that shortly after leaving Clapham Junction on the Up Main Local Lines he saw a man in the six-foot space between the Up Main Lines and sounded his warning horn. He estimated his train was travelling about 50 mph. The man remained in the six-foot space facing an oncoming

---

[17] Again, there were elaborate rules and procedures for all of these working environments, many of which had been developed as a result of previous accidents.

[18] Down main lines run out of London and up main lines into London.

[19] Drivers conventionally sounded the horn if they were in any doubt that those on the track had registered the presence of the train.

train on the Down Main Line and with his back to 'Z' but raised his hand which 'Z' thought was an acknowledgement of a warning.[20] 'Z' told me that he heard a bang and realised that his train had struck the man and reported the incident. He then completed the journey to Waterloo. Subsequent examination showed traces of human tissues on the fourth coach and at various other places rearward along the train with some scuff marks on the seventh coach.

'C' told me that when he saw the train approaching along the line which 'A' was patrolling he blew his whistle and shouted 'Ron' to identify the warning to 'A'. 'A' acknowledged by raising his arm . . . 'C' did not know which way 'A' moved but he together with 'A' and 'B' had patrolled this section of track three times a week for some three years . . .

The spanner that 'A' was carrying was 2ft 10in long . . . It was found later in the six-foot space and established the site of the accident. It is probable that both trains made contact with the spanner . . .

The report concludes that 'A' did not follow correct procedures, that there was no evidence that he did not know these procedures, and that he did not see the train approaching on the up main line.

Accidents such as the one described above were the most typical risk to railway industry employees, but often these accidents remained hidden from the public gaze as they were rarely reported by the media. The media gaze tended to be reserved for major train accidents, most especially those affecting the travelling public. Employee injuries were usually only reported by the media when multiple deaths were involved or in the event of a train accident.

During the period of data collection there were two main accidents which warrant discussion because of the impact they subsequently had on health and safety on the railways in general and indeed the very wide publicity they received at the time, namely the accidents at King's Cross and Clapham Junction.

King's Cross and Clapham Junction

Shortly after the evening rush hour had passed its peak on Wednesday 18 November 1987 a fire of catastrophic proportions in the King's Cross Underground station claimed the lives of 30 people and injured many more. A further person was to die in hospital making the final death toll 31. (Fennell, 1988, para. 1)

At 8.10 a.m. on the morning of Monday, 12 December 1988, a crowded commuter train ran head-on into the rear of another which was stationary in a cutting just south of Clapham Junction station. After that impact the first train veered to its right and struck a third oncoming train. As a result of the accident 35 people died and nearly 500 were injured, 69 of them seriously . . . . They were all travelling in the front two coaches of the first train. (Hidden, 1989, para. 1)

It should be appreciated that these two railway accidents took on great symbolic significance within the railway industry and caused much greater focus to

---

[20] Raising a hand was conventional acknowledgement that a train was known about.

be thrown onto health and safety issues. They attracted great media and political attention and led to the establishment of Courts of Inquiry which were in progress and reporting during the fieldwork period. This said, the changes effected as a result of the inquiries did not really affect the company as whole until after the bulk of data collection. Data collection for this research took place after the King's Cross fire, while the Clapham Junction accident occurred during the fieldwork period. The early effects of these accidents are therefore to some extent reflected in the research findings.

The King's Cross accident was in many respects an unusual one. There had been a history of fires on the London Underground but until this accident no one had died as a result of them. The reason for the high number of deaths in this accident was a flashover which engulfed the ticket hall and landing at the top of the escalator shaft some twenty minutes after the start of the fire (Fennell, 1988: 12.1). The Clapham Junction accident was much more straightforward, being the result of a simple signalling error. One of the distinguishing factors here was undoubtedly the high number of fatalities. Indeed the extent of the fatalities in both accidents partially explains the extensive and prolonged media reporting of both accidents. Also significant was the fact that both accidents occurred at busy commuter times in central London. Beyond this, however, the King's Cross and Clapham accidents need to be understood within the broader context of a number of health and safety disasters which occurred in the late 1980s—notably the sinking of the ferry *The Herald of Free Enterprise* at Zeebrugge in 1987 and the explosion on the Piper Alpha Oil Rig in 1988. Each of these had led to a public inquiry and subsequent reports recommending safety improvements. Each had led to questions about corporate failures and priorities. In the case of the King's Cross and Clapham Junction accidents the Secretary of State ordered a Court of Inquiry. These are rare and are usually reserved for cases where issues of fundamental policy are raised (Hutter, 1992).

Courts of Inquiry

King's Cross raised fundamental questions of policy regarding acceptable fire precautions and procedures on underground train systems. It is less clear that Clapham raised such policy issues but it did occur in the wake of the publication of the Fennell Report into the King's Cross Fire and at a time when a number of high profile transport accidents had caused transport to be the subject of much political and media attention. In both cases full Courts of Inquiry undertook extensive investigations and examination of the available evidence.[21] In both cases there were lengthy public hearings of evidence in which railway staff

---

[21] The causes of the Clapham Junction accident were fairly clear from the beginning. But the reasons for the King's Cross accident were not immediately understood and intensive investigations surrounded the inquiry. Apart from the Court of Inquiry and the assessors appointed to advise on technical matters, a team of consulting engineers was appointed to advise on technical matters. A scientific committee was also established.

were subject to intense public scrutiny.[22] This encompassed not just an examination of the immediate circumstances of the accident but also broader issues. The King's Cross Inquiry, for example, considered the organization, management, and ethos of London Underground. This public examination of the company was referred to by one of my BR respondents as 'washing one's dirty linen in public'. It reverberated throughout the industry and before the accident at Clapham Junction BR staff had voiced concern about being put through a similar experience. Indeed this had led to some very preliminary steps to examine safety matters. When Clapham Junction did happen, BR was quick to admit responsibility.

The most important purpose of a Public Inquiry is to discover the cause of the accident and to make recommendations to prevent the recurrence of an accident. In the case of King's Cross the cause of the disaster was found only after extensive scientific investigation. The initial fire was the result of a smoker dropping a lighted match which fell through the escalator and ignited an accumulation of grease and detritus beneath it (Fennell, 1988: 12.1). The subsequent flashover was discovered to be the result of a previously unknown phenomenon known as 'trench effect' (ibid. 1.14). The cause of the Clapham Junction accident was much more immediately discernible, namely faulty wiring in a new signalling system which caused a signal failure two days after its installation (Hidden, 1989: 1.1). The direct cause was wiring errors on the part of a signal and telecommunications senior technician.

Both inquiries also identified a number of indirect causes of the accidents. The Fennell Inquiry, for example, identified a lack of fire training on London Transport, the absence of evacuation plans for stations, and the fact that people were evacuated via the areas where the flashover subsequently occurred. Hidden concentrated on poor supervision of re-signalling work. Systemic failures were identified by both inquiries. Hidden referred to the 'collective liability which lies on British Railways' (1989: 16.8). In the Clapham Report this largely centred on BR's recruitment and training procedures and the organization of the signals and telecommunications department. The Fennel Inquiry criticized both London Regional Transport and London Transport for not giving sufficient priority to passenger safety at stations; for not strictly monitoring safety; for faults in the management, supervision, and training of staff; and also for poor communication within the company. Both reports criticized 'railway culture', in the case of London Transport for being too blinkered in accepting risks as 'inevitable' (Fennel, 1988: 1.12) and in the case of BR for its organization, training, and recruitment (Hidden, 1989: 16.80). Both reports also criticized other organizations. For instance the Hidden Report criticized the unions for resisting changes in working practices (ibid. 16.94) and the Fennell

---

[22] The King's Cross Inquiry public hearing lasted a record 91 days and the Clapham Junction hearing for 56 days. It should be noted that these inquiries were inquisitorial rather than accusatorial (see Hutter, 1992).

Report criticized the relationship between the Railway Inspectorate and London Transport for being 'too informal' (1988, 1.25).

The King's Cross report made 157 recommendations and the Clapham Junction Inquiry resulted in 93 recommendations. These covered a wide range of issues such as those addressing the immediate cause of the accident; recommendations to improve the response of the railway companies' staff, training, communications, and management of safety; and recommendations about the role of the Railway Inspectorate. I want to focus briefly on the Clapham recommendations as it is these which are most pertinent for this study. They are particularly interesting as they are another source of information about occupational health and safety on BR and one which was contemporaneous with this study.

The Hidden Report

Much of the Hidden Report into the Clapham Junction accident was focused on the signals and telecommunications department and Southern Region, where the accident happened. But the report undoubtedly has implications for the company as a whole. Part 3 of the Inquiry Report is devoted to broader matters, 'Management and the Underlying Causes', and part 4 considers 'The Concept of Safety'. So the recommendations of the Hidden Inquiry are certainly directed at BR as a whole.[23] In its consideration of the underlying causes of the accident signals and telecommunications came in for serious criticism. The report identified 'bad working practices', poor staff morale, management weaknesses, and serious deficiencies in communication and training. A number of the observations verify the findings of this research but much more starkly. For example, the report identified poor staff morale resulting from the constant reorganizations in response to growing commercial awareness and preparations for privatization (paras. 10.24, 16.18). It also mirrored some of the findings reported in Part III of this study about communication and training. It notes, for example, the voluminous amount of information available (para. 11.11) and laments lost opportunities to rationalize and clarify it (para. 11.49). More importantly it stresses the importance of ensuring the communication, implementation, and checking of this information. Three axiomatic principles are identified: first, the provision of information; secondly, its communication—'the message that never gets through might just as well never have been sent' (para. 11.3)—and thirdly, 'the staff must be taught how to deal with the information, how to approach it and how to put it into effect' (para. 11.4).

More broadly the report emphasized the crucial importance of safety on the railways and discussed the tensions between safety and funding. Pertinently, given this research, the report stresses the importance of safety being a constitutive part of railway life and culture:

---

[23] The remit of these inquiries is controversial. Neither inquiry considered the wider pressures upon the railway industry, in particular government policy towards the railway.

Management systems must ensure that there is in being a regime which will preserve the first place of safety in the running of the railway. It is not enough to talk in terms of 'absolute safety' and of 'zero accidents'. There must also be proper organization and a management to ensure that actions live up to words. (1989, para. 13.2)

Generally both the Fennell Report into King's Cross (1988, para. 23) and Hidden (1989, para. 14.51) shied away from discussing the funding of the railway companies they were investigating. Nevertheless Hidden does explicitly address the funding of safety (1989: ch. 14): 'These are important safeguards but more could and should be done to ensure that safety is not compromised by permitting commercial considerations to delay investment in safety-related projects' (para. 14.37). Of particular note for this research is 'the funding of safety through the workforce' (paras. 14.41 ff.). Again this stresses the importance of training and constituting 'proper working practices' at the everyday level.

These accidents and their aftermath are credited with being the catalyst for more profound changes in attitude towards health and safety. This is explicitly acknowledged in the Chairman's foreword to Railtrack's first Safety Plan (1994/5) which pays tribute to the former BR Chairman: 'After the tragic accidents at King's Cross and Clapham Junction it was he and his team who initiated profound changes in the way safety was managed on the railways' (Railtrack, 1995: 1).

It also figured in my more recent interviews with railway inspectors and industry representatives. One railway inspector regarded the coincidence of King's Cross and Clapham as having :

a multiplying effect over and above what one of them would have had I think—the effect was cumulative. Two big disasters and both on the railways but in completely diverse circumstances and characters. Everyone thought what else can go wrong? It led people to fear what else there can be about to go wrong, to happen. (railway inspector)

King's Cross made public bodies sit up and realize it could happen to them, likewise the *Herald of Free Enterprise*. (industry representative)

King's Cross, as the first of these disasters, was seen to cause 'incredible public dismay, resentment, reaction and consequently political embarrassment' (Railway Inspectorate). There was a feeling that these events 'moved the culture' and made people safety aware. In particular it caused greater attention to be paid to management structures and control. This said, not all of the recommendations resulting from the subsequent inquiries were implemented in the long term. As we will go on to discuss in Chapter 11, there were other counter-pressures to the impetus provided by these accidents.

In the immediate aftermath of the Clapham Junction accident, BR moved swiftly and publicly to demonstrate that it was reviewing health and safety. It employed a firm of consultants to help them do this.[24] One result of this was to

---

[24] A major safety conference was organized in August 1989, at which different firms of consultants presented their ideas. This was a 'brainstorming session', attended by senior personnel—but not the business managers. Academics, including myself, were also invited.

redefine safety so that it was all inclusive and embraced train, passenger, and employee safety. One industry representative remarked that 'disaster pushed a change in attitude. Suddenly we realized that there were things out there like risk assessment, human factors . . . all of a sudden there was a great push.' Interestingly a central philosophy in this 'new approach' was to get staff across the railways to be aware of health and safety issues, to demonstrate that those in the most senior positions take health and safety seriously and to assign responsibility for health and safety to particular people. These are all factors which emerged as centrally important in this research and which we will now proceed to examine and discuss.

PART II

REGULATORY
OBJECTIVES

4

The Law: Regulatory Objectives and the Social Dimensions of Knowledge

It is impossible to consider the impact of regulation without paying attention to what it was intended to achieve. But regulatory objectives are difficult to discern as they are multiple, changing, and may even be conflicting. Moreover they vary according to different perspectives. This part will examine regulatory objectives as they appeared in health and safety legislation during the research period (Ch. 4). It will then shift from the 'law in books' to the 'law in action' as the focus moves to the agency charged with implementing occupational health and safety legislation on the railways, namely the Railway Inspectorate (Ch. 5).

The other important preoccupation of this part of the book is to determine how much those in the industry understood of the law and of the state's regulatory structure. The extent to which it is expected or necessary that regulation is consciously thought about and understood by the regulated is debatable. For some an awareness of legal obligations is seen as essential, particularly in a system based on self-regulation, the argument being that knowledge of the law is a prerequisite of compliance (Genn, 1993). An alternative view is that while compliance with regulatory objectives is centrally important, it does not necessarily depend on a detailed knowledge of the law. Indeed it need not rely on any knowledge of the law. Ironically this may be a regulatory ideal, namely that a company's risk management systems stand alone without legal intervention and that individuals have internalized safe ways of working and take responsibility for their own health and safety and that of others without the backup of the law. A simple analogy would be to ask how many of us rely on a detailed knowledge and understanding of the traffic laws in order to drive safely. The honest answer is that presumably very few of us do have such a detailed understanding yet we drive safely most of the time.

There is, however, an important literature which suggests that companies in Britain are very concerned not to come into major conflict with regulatory inspectors and are especially worried about being on the receiving end of legal action (Ball and Friedman, 1965).[1] Indeed one of the assumptions underlying the classical models of regulation and corporate behaviour is that the legal

---

[1] There are cultural differences here. For example, there is a suggestion that larger companies, especially in the United States, are much more likely to challenge regulatory decisions (Yeager, 1991). On the other hand there is also the argument that they are much more likely to be subject to regulatory sanctioning (Bardach and Kagan, 1982).

sanction does have a deterrent effect. In considering varying models of regulatory and corporate behaviour it is therefore important to pose as a research question whether or not regulatory law, sanctions, and the activities of the regulatory agency are known about and, if so, with what level of sophistication. It is also important to understand the social dimensions of that knowledge so as to give us a greater understanding of corporate behaviour and in particular of how information flowed through the organization of British Railways. In turn this may help us to understand the influences upon the establishment and operation of the company's risk management systems. This is especially significant given the radical new approach to workplace health and safety in Britain introduced by the Robens Committee and its emphasis upon the participation of everyone in the workplace.

This chapter and Chapter 5 draw on the research data collected from staff across British Railways to consider how much staff knew about the general regulatory provisions for their occupational health and safety some twenty years after Robens and the enactment of the Health and Safety at Work etc. Act, 1974 (HSW Act). This chapter will focus on legal provisions, in particular whether those in the industry knew about the law and, if so, how much they knew about its objectives and provisions. Chapter 5 will concentrate on their knowledge of the regulatory structures in place to implement health and safety laws. The spotlight here will be upon their knowledge of the institutional arrangements for health and safety at work, with a particular emphasis upon their knowledge of the Railway Inspectorate's approach to work and enforcement. It is important to appreciate that this provides little information about whether or not the objectives were achieved. Later chapters will concentrate on more detailed subjects such as the risk management systems the company had in place in response to regulation; the everyday activities of staff; the participatory effects of the law; and the occupational health and safety risks of working on the railway and how these interact with legal provisions for constituting a safe workplace.

The Legal Mandate

Attributing purpose to the law may be fraught with difficulty. Regulatory objectives may not be clearly spelt out in the law, while the range of legislation regulating health and safety on the railways dates from 1840 to the 1980s. But it is possible to identify some broad trends which help us to understand what the regulation of the railway industry was attempting to achieve. It is also important to appreciate that the legal mandate did provide a broad reference point for those involved in the regulatory process, since the law was one way of classifying and communicating risk (Ericson and Haggerty, 1997) and was a means of structuring and guiding risk management.

A variety of legal sources could be consulted during the fieldwork period. Hierarchically, the most important and obvious was statute law, namely Acts of

Parliament. Also of importance were statutory instruments or supporting legislation, for example, regulations and orders, and administrative definitions such as codes of practice and guidance notes. Generally the Act incorporated the general duties and principles. The supporting legislation and most particularly the administrative definitions were more precise and tightly framed and could be periodically updated.

Statute Law

The main occupational health and safety legislation in Britain was—and remains—the HSW Act, 1974. Some sections of nineteenth century railway legislation[2] and much of the pre-1974 health and safety legislation[3] was still in force at the time of my research. The intention was that the HSW Act, 1974, would complement this earlier legislation and update it where necessary.

The HSW Act, 1974, is an 'enabling Act' which comprises, among other things, a statement of general principles such as general duties and broad statutory standards which are supplemented by regulations and other statutory instruments which tend to be more precisely framed. These are made under the authority of statutes. They have the same legal force as statute law. The Factories Act, 1961; Offices, Shops and Railway Premises Act, 1963; and HSW Act, 1974, all have provisions for ministers to make more detailed regulations if they wish. And the HSW Act, 1974, provides for yet more detail to be provided in administrative form, for examples, as codes of practice or guidance notes.

Administrative Definitions

Administrative interpretations of the law offer guidance for the implementation of statute law and occasionally cover topics about which statute is silent. Strictly speaking administrative definitions of compliance are not mandatory but they have assumed a quasi-legal status in practice and it is for this reason that I consider them under the heading of 'legal objectives'. Theoretically they hold administrative—non-statutory—status and are open to challenge in the courts. Few cases reach the courts but there seems to be a presumption that these definitions may be accepted by the court as evidence of a contravention of the law (see Baldwin, 1995; Hutter, 1997). Thus in practice breaches of these types of requirement could leave firms or individuals open to disciplinary action.

Important administrative requirements have been developed by the Railway Inspectorate in the form of the Railway Construction and Operations Requirements. These have been produced since the nineteenth century and detail the Inspectorate's requirements for new works. The first Requirements were written in 1858 and since then they have been developed as railway practice has developed. Although they are not mandatory the Inspectorate may not pass new

---

[2] For example the Regulation of Railways Act, 1871, authorizing the investigation of railway accidents.

[3] Examples here include the Factories Act, 1961, and the Offices, Shops and Railway Premises Act, 1963.

works as fit for passenger traffic if they do not comply with the Requirements. This guidance is quite specific. Likewise, so is the guidance on level-crossings (*Requirements for Level Crossings*, Dept. of Transport, 1981) which incorporates both general standards and precise standards.[4]

Administrative definitions of the law may also be found in the form of approved codes of practice and guidance notes made under the HSW Act, 1974. Codes of practice are made or approved by the HSE. Both are regarded as authoritative guidance on acceptable or good practice. In other words they are akin to Unger's (1975) 'technical' or 'instrumental' rules. These administrative definitions are not static. Their whole rationale is that they should be modified in response to changing circumstances, for example, new information or technological advances.

There are different levels of precision in the framing of occupational health and safety legislation. The HSW Act, 1974, takes the form of broad statutory standards and general duties, a notable example being the phrase 'so far as is reasonably practicable'. Much of the earlier legislation, regulations, and administrative guidance are much more closely framed and detailed. Regulation 12 of the Woodworking Machines Regulations, 1974, for instance, specifies the precise minimum temperatures for rooms or other places where woodworking machinery is used. These are matters which feature centrally in many legal discussions of regulation (Baldwin, 1995; Black, 1997). Concern is expressed that detailed rules are inflexible, unable to cope with change, and quickly outdated. But broad standards may lead to uncertainty, a greater risk of inconsistency, and concern that enforcement officials may be given too much scope for discretion (Baldwin and Hawkins, 1984; Davis, 1969).[5] The system established by the HSW Act, 1974, attempts to take advantage of broad standards in statute and benefit from a system of more precise details in regulations and administrative guidance.

The HSW Act, 1974, has not been without its critics. The term 'so far as is reasonably practicable', for example, may be regarded as falling short of the absolute or practicable standards which could have been included by the legislature. The term 'practicable' involves the determination of technical feasibility while the more contentious word is 'reasonably', which is generally taken to refer to the cost of the improvement (Dawson *et al.*, 1988: 15). The term 'reasonably practicable' therefore involves 'a weighing of the risks against the measures necessary to eliminate risk' (notes to Sect. 2, HSW Act, 1974). This phrase, like so much regulatory legislation in Great Britain, follows the long tradition

---

[4] These requirements have since been replaced by *Railway Safety Principles and Guidance*, published by HSE. This coincided with the transfer in 1997 of the approval of new works from the Secretary of State for Transport to HSE.

[5] If officials create their own discretion or do not enforce the law legalistically then these arguments are of course of secondary importance (Hawkins, 1984; Hutter, 1988; 1997). Alternatively time may be spent exploiting the ambiguities of law. In short, there is a real socio-legal argument that rules are as much resources as rules which are slavishly complied with and to this extent their precise form is of less importance than might be anticipated by some legal commentators.

of accommodation between competing interest groups (Carson, 1974; Gunningham, 1974, 1984; Hutter, 1988; Paulus, 1974). From the point of view of industry it is only 'fair' to take account of the cost of any duties imposed, but from the workers' perspective it is unjust to expect them to bear the health costs of any lack of provision for their health and safety at work. Whether or not the HSW Act, 1974, leads to greater clarity of legal objectives is far from certain. Arguably the growing number of administrative guidelines proves very confusing and this, as we will see later, may have influenced the impact of occupational health and safety laws upon the railways.[6]

Constitution and Control

Regulatory law has a dual purpose. Its primary objective appears to be constitutive. In other words, it aims to provide the architecture for managing risks at the level of the marketplace and at the corporate level. More ambitiously, it aims to penetrate the organization, harness the regulatory resources of the company and constitute risk management as part of everyday individual activity. Where these constitutive objectives are not realized then regulatory law falls into much more familiar legal territory through the provision of criminal sanctions. Thus regulatory law also has the capacity to control.

Constitutive Regulation

The constitutive effects of the law are various. The key areas emerging from the railway's legal mandate were the constitution of the market; the empowerment of participants; the definition of structures and procedures to promote health and safety and manage risk; and the definition of forms of everyday conduct.

Constitutive Law: Constituting the Market
Historically a key role for railways legislation has been to safeguard entry to the market through the requirements surrounding the inspection of new works. This was one of the objectives of the earliest Regulation of Railways Acts, that of 1840, which mandated the then newly created Railways Inspectorate to inspect new works. Once inspectors were given the powers to prevent the opening of lines which did not meet their standards then market entry and participation were effectively limited through law. The 1840 legislation was eventually replaced by the Road and Rail Traffic Act, 1933, the legislation under which the Railway Inspectorate was inspecting new works at the time of this research. This Act requires the railways to inform the Inspectorate of any major new

---

[6] Neither case law nor European law figured prominently at the time of this research. EU legislation has been more significant since January 1993 which saw the introduction of the so-called 'six pack' of health and safety regulations which implemented previously agreed European directives.

works, such as new stations, signalling, or level-crossings. More specific legislation, namely the British Transport Commission Act, 1957, and the Transport
Act, 1968, pertains to level-crossings, whether they be new or changes to existing crossings. Section 66 of the British Transport Commission Act, 1957,
requires the Secretary of State's approval before British Railways can change a
level-crossing. The Railway Inspectorate undertook the investigations upon
which these decisions were taken: they examined and commented upon the
modernization proposals and examined each scheme to ensure that the terms of
the order issued by the Secretary of State had been met.

The inspection of new works relates to lines, signalling, level-crossings, tunnels, bridges, station layout: essentially the technical construction and safety of
the railway network 'hardware'. The requirement for inspection is contained in
statute law—which in Unger's terminology may be regarded as 'constitutive
rules'—while the details of what is required are found in the Railway Construction and Operations Requirements—which in effect serve as 'technical' or
'instrumental' rules (Unger, 1975). The Railway Inspectorate traditionally
extended its guidance to areas not covered by statute law. Locomotives and
rolling stock have never been 'inspectable works', although the Requirements
have traditionally included details of what the Inspectorate expects. For example, the 1862 Requirements gave details of brake power requirements for passenger trains. Moreover, the railway companies have typically consulted the
Inspectorate about rolling stock standards.

Constitutive Law: Defining the Participants in Regulation
Apart from constituting the market, regulatory law delineates participants in
the regulation of health and safety at work. Pre-1974 regulation was very much
a matter confined to the railway companies and the state representatives,
namely the Railway Inspectorate. But gradually the 'net' widened. For example,
the Road and Rail Traffic Act, 1933, incorporates trade unions in looking over
plans for new railway works. Following the Court of Inquiry into the accident
at Hixon in 1968, when a heavy road transporter and a passenger train collided
on an automatic half barrier level-crossing (Ministry of Transport, 1968), there
has been increased consultation with the public when changes to level crossings
are proposed.[7]

The most dramatic change of all came with the HSW Act, 1974 which regarded
health and safety as the everyday concern of everyone at work. This was incorporated in the legislation in a variety of ways. One very central way was in the imposition of general duties upon a wide range of participants (HSW Act, 1974, sects.
2–9). The most general duty is stated in section 2 which places upon employers a
general duty 'to ensure, so far as is reasonably practicable, the health, safety

---

[7] BR must send the county and district local authorities concerned notice of their proposals.
If they consider it necessary the Railway Inspectorate can then make recommendations to the
Secretary of State.

and welfare at work of all his employees' (sect. 2(1)). This section of the Act goes on to specify some broad areas of concern in this respect, namely that attention should be paid to such matters as plant and systems of work; the handling, storage, and transport of articles and substances; and the provision of information, instructions, training, and supervision for employees. It is also the duty of employers to provide a written statement of policy regarding health and safety, including the organization and administration of this policy. This statement should be brought to the notice of employees and revised as necessary (sect. 2(3)). Duties are also imposed regarding the relations of employers with employee safety representatives, who should be both recognized and consulted (sect. 2(61)). Employers also have responsibilities towards people not in their employment 'to ensure, so far as reasonably practicable, that persons not in his employment who may be affected are not, thereby, exposed to risks to their health and safety' (sect. 3).

Although employers and management carry the overall responsibility for health and safety, the Act also places duties upon employees. For example, employees are obliged to 'take reasonable care' for the health and safety of themselves and others and to co-operate with employers in the discharge of their duties (sect. 7); and they have a duty not to interfere intentionally or recklessly with anything provided for their health, safety, or welfare (sect. 8). In addition, the legislation places duties upon 'persons in control of certain premises in relation to harmful emissions into the atmosphere' (sect. 5) and manufacturers, designers, importers, and suppliers 'as regards articles and substances for use at work' (sect. 6). Section 6, for instance, imposes the duty 'to ensure, so far as is reasonably practicable, that the article is . . . safe and without risks to health when properly used'; to carry out testing and examinations; to provide information about safe use; and to undertake research to eliminate or minimize risks to health and safety. The legislation thus constituted a very wide range of people as participants in the regulation of health and safety at work.

A second way in which legislation constituted participation was through involving and empowering different groups in the regulatory process. The HSW Act, 1974, had a clear corporatist ethos. Indeed one author describes the Health and Safety Commission (HSC) as 'the most corporatist body in Britain' (Wilson, 1985: 113). HSC, for example, comprises a full-time chairperson, elected by the Secretary of State for Employment, and representatives from the employers' association, the trade unions, and the local authorities.[8] Also, in accordance with the ethos of the Act, regulations and approved codes of practice are all the result of a consultation process between the inspectorates, industry, and unions (Baldwin, 1995).

---

[8] The Commission reports to the Secretary of State and is responsible among other things for formulating health and safety policies and promoting health and safety. HSC's duties are outlined in section 11, HSW Act, 1974.

Employees are also empowered. The HSW Act, 1974, provides for regulations to appoint safety representatives from among employees (sect. 2(4)); requires employers to consult with safety representatives (sect. 2(6)); and establishes safety committees where this is requested by safety representatives (sect. 2(7)). These provisions led to the Safety Representatives and Safety Committees Regulations which are technical rules detailing the requirements about the appointment and role of safety representatives.[9]

A third form of empowerment and participation was constituted through rights to information. Previous occupational health and safety legislation required employers to provide limited information to employees[10] but the HSW Act, 1974 (sect. 2(2)(c)) developed employee's rights to information in the form of a general duty upon employers to provide 'information, instruction, training and supervision' to ensure health and safety at work. Again more technical rules are detailed in administrative documents prepared by Health and Safety Commission. Safety representatives have even more extensive rights to information under the Safety Representatives and Safety Committee Regulations. These include, for example, rights to inspect particular health and safety-related documents (sect. 7); information about future plans which may affect workers' health and safety; technical information about hazards to health and safety; information about health and safety collected by employers, manufacturers, or consultants; and information about accidents (sect. 6).

It should not be assumed from this discussion that all participants in the regulatory process have equal rights and equal power. Corporatism has been much criticized. Wilson (1985), for instance, points to a number of inherent biases in HSC. He argues that the Trades Union Congress and especially the Confederation of British Industry dominate HSC to the detriment of the local authorities. Moreover the Confederation of British Industry (and to some extent one might argue the Trades Union Congress) is unrepresentative, especially with reference to small firms. In other words, the regulatory resources of each constituent group of HSC varies, as does the power balance within each group. Similar arguments may be made with reference to the relationship between employers and employees. Another problem with corporatism and inclusive participation is that it tends to slow down the regulatory process. The West German experience of tripartism suggests that a major disadvantage is slow procedures (Gräbe, 1991).

Constitutive Law: Occupational Health and Safety Structures and Procedures
Having empowered the participants in the market and in regulation, occupational health and safety laws further attempt to constitute structures and procedures for promoting health and safety in the workplace and most importantly

---

[9] Further detail is offered in a Code of Practice on Safety Representatives and Safety Committees.
[10] The Factories Act 1961 (sects. 138, 139) and the Information for Employees Regulations, 1965 (made under the Offices, Shops and Railway Premises Act) detailed information which employers should provide for employees.

for managing risk in the workplace. At a national level the HSW Act, 1974, provides for HSC and HSE to undertake a range of policy-making, enforcement and educational functions. At a company level the legislation, as we have already seen, provides for safety representatives and committees. The HSW Act, 1974, section 2 duties also imply a number of regular procedures to ensure health and safety at work. These are specified in more detail in Health and Safety Commission guidance literature (*Advice to Employers*). They include regular inspections; examinations and testing of plant; and monitoring of the work environment. Also important are the establishment of systems of work; cleaning; repair and maintenance; emergency procedures; and workplace audits. Procedures also need to be put in place for the provision of safety equipment; training and retraining; and information for employees.

Section 2(3) of the HSW Act, 1974, requires employers to provide a safety policy which explains the company's health and safety policy and the organization and arrangements in place to implement the policy. This involves companies setting up a system to ensure that they fulfil their health and safety duties. In particular it is expected that health and safety responsibilities are assigned to people at all levels of an organization. So the legal mandate in effect requires companies to institute quite complex systems and procedures for promoting health and safety at work. Indeed, the constitutive effects of occupational health and safety regulation extend beyond organizational matters to an attempt to influence everyday matters.

Constitutive Law: Everyday Practice

Occupational health and safety legislation attempts to constitute everyday practice in a variety of ways. The general duties, outlined earlier, refer to a broad range of areas which should be the everyday concern of participants in the workplace. These duties are general and are intended to encompass the whole area of work. An important dimension of this is that they have continuing relevance, since they refer to states of affairs rather than to one-off discrete events. So, for example, employers have a general and continuing duty to ensure the health and safety of their employees (HSW Act, 1974, sect. 2); to maintain safe and healthy conditions of work; and to ensure the safe handling, storage, and transport of articles and substances; and supervision of employees. Likewise the duties on others named in the legislation is continuous. So employees, for instance, have to take reasonable care for themselves and others and co-operate with their employers. In these ways occupational health and safety legislation attempts to define forms of conduct at an everyday level. Moreover, it aims to constitute them as normal and unthinkingly accepted activities.

Health and safety laws are thus constitutive of the market of the railways industry; of the participants in the regulation of health and safety at work; of the structures and procedures for promoting health and safety nationally and within companies; and also of everyday forms of conduct. Statute laws may be seen in Unger's terms as constitutive rules as it is usually they that 'define a form of conduct in such a way that the distinction between the rule and the ruled activity disappears' (1975: 68–9). Statutory instruments and administrative guidance serve as 'technical' or 'instrumental' rules, but in a rather more detailed way than Unger (1975: 69) suggests. Typically they offer far more than 'a generalization about what means are most likely on the whole to produce the desired result' (ibid.). The prescriptive rules referred to by Unger are typically associated with the control aspects of regulatory law and it is to this aspect of regulatory legislation that we now turn.

Control and Constraint

A second integral objective of regulatory law relating to the railways is to maintain order and where necessary to intervene to control. It is important to understand that the aim of the legislation is to regulate the railway not to close it down, *to manage risk not eliminate it*. Moreover, the primary responsibility for health and safety on the railway lies with the railway companies. As early as 1865 a Royal Commission established that the ultimate responsibility for maintaining and designing a safe railway lies with the railways companies and not the inspectorate. The HSW Act, 1974, underlines this in its ethos of self-regulation. Following the Robens Report, the Act intended that those involved in health and safety at work understood that health and safety matters are their concern and not just the remit of external agencies. Indeed, the Robens Committee (1972, para. 219) argued that although there should be inspectorates, their resources should be concentrated on 'problem areas' and 'spot checks' rather than on regular systematic assessments which it was felt companies and their employees should be routinely undertaking themselves. It was recognized that there would be occasions when intervention would be necessary to secure compliance. The very first railway inspectors, for example, had difficulty in securing compliance with their requirements for new works until 1842 when they were given the power to postpone the opening of lines they considered unsatisfactory. Accordingly health and safety inspectors have a variety of legal powers and sanctions available for their use.

There are a number of ways in which the legal mandate provides for control and constraint. It is important to appreciate that many of the legal provisions discussed in relation to the constitutive effects of occupational health and safety laws are simultaneously controlling. So, for example, while the general duties outlined in section 2 of the HSW Act, 1974, have constitutive objectives, they may simultaneously be regarded as prescriptive rules to the extent that they represent 'permissions' and 'general commands' rather than being prohibitions. The objective is that the duties will be constitutive and part of everyday life rather than an external imposition about which participants need reminding. The legislation does, however, provide for external checks on compliance with regulatory objectives. There are provisions relating to the monitoring and maintenance of order, provisions relating to the remedy of defects, and legal sanctions which may be invoked in the event of non-compliance.

The Monitoring and Maintenance of Order

Occupational health and safety legislation should, if complied with, lead to various company efforts to manage risks through monitoring and maintaining health and safety standards. Ideally companies should self-regulate, that is, they should establish the systems and procedures specified in the legal mandate as matters of routine (see above). Moreover once these systems and procedures are in place they should monitor and maintain them. In addition, external agencies have also been given powers to monitor compliance.

Occupational health and safety legislation provides for inspectors to monitor railway companies both proactively and reactively. Proactive monitoring involves inspectors in taking the initiative and organizing the checks upon companies according to their agency schedules, which typically involves inspection (see below). Reactive monitoring is prompted by a person or event outside the agency, typically a complaint or accident that suggests that order may have broken down and a company, or area of a company, needs checking upon.

The earliest monitoring remit allocated to the Railway Inspectorate was reactive. At first inspectors were the *receivers of information* about accidents (see Ch. 2). Then the 1871 Regulation of Railways Act authorized the *investigation of* railway accidents and detailed the types of accident which should be reported to the Inspectorate. Thereafter accident investigation occupied a position of central importance in the work of the Inspectorate. The primary focus of accident investigation was passenger safety, but in 1900 the first legislation authorizing inquiries into accidents involving railway employees was introduced.[11] Accidents on all statutory railways were reportable to the Inspectorate under the Railways (Notice of Accidents) Orders which are periodically updated. In addition, accidents to contractors' employees working on the railways were reportable to the Inspectorate under the Notification of Accidents Order, 1986. Railway accidents could be investigated either under the Regulation of Railways Act, 1871 or under the HSW Act, 1974, section 20. Accident inquiries under the 1871 legislation are formally ordered by the Secretary of State for Transport. The Act requires the Inspectorate to investigate the accident, determine its causes, and submit a report to the Secretary of State stating the causes and circumstances of the accident. The Secretary of State is then required to publish the report. HSW Act, 1974, investigations, by contrast, are not automatically published. HSC can, however, direct disclosure to the public of reports on incidents. Moreover section 14 of the HSW Act, 1974, gives HSC powers to direct that incident inquiry reports be made public.

---

[11] The Railway Inspectorate had investigated accidents to employees long before this. Colonel Robertson's 'Development and Functions of the Railways Inspectorate' mimeo cites the first inquiry into employees' accidents as being held in 1858.

The legal mandate also gives inspectors powers to monitor railway companies proactively. The main powers are outlined in section 20 of the HSW Act, 1974. They empower inspectors to enter premises; to take a police officer if they feel that they will be obstructed; to take authorized people and equipment with them; to inspect any premises relating to their inspectorial duties; to require that parts of premises be left undisturbed for as long as necessary for the investigation; to take measurements, photographs, samples; to seize, render harmless, or destroy items which may cause a danger; to take possession of such articles; to require that information be produced and statements given; to inspect documentation; and to require assistance to exercise these powers. The legislation therefore gives inspectors wide-ranging powers for use in both proactive and reactive situations. In this sense it enables inspectors and gives them responsibilities rather than duties.

Remedying Defects

If the monitoring procedures adopted by the Railway Inspectorate uncover defects or instances of non-compliance with the legal mandate,[12] then the law does provide for legal remedy, namely improvement notices, prohibition notices, and prosecution.

Section 21 of the HSW Act, 1974, provides for the service of an improvement notice: 'if an inspector is of the opinion that a person—(a) is contravening one or more of the relevant statutory provisions, or (b) has contravened one or more of those provisions in circumstances that make it likely that the contravention will continue or be repeated'. The notice should specify the provisions concerned, why the inspector believes they are contravened, the remedy required, and the period within which this remedy should be effected. An improvement notice in effect sanctions a temporary state of non-compliance, hence it pertains to less serious and less risky problems. This is in contrast to the circumstances which section 22 of the HSW Act, 1974, is designed to meet. Prohibition notices are for use in those cases where inspectors are of the opinion 'that the risk of serious personal injury is or, as the case may be, will be *imminent*' (sect. 22 (4)—emphasis added). It is not necessary that there is a legal contravention before such a notice may be imposed and it is perhaps worth underlining that a prohibition notice can refer to a prospective hazard.

Section 23 of the HSW Act, 1974, permits inspectors to withdraw notices and to extend the period of a notice. If the recipient of a notice considers that it should not have been served then section 24 of the Act specifies a right of appeal to an industrial tribunal which may cancel, affirm, or modify the terms of the notice.

---

[12] It should be emphasized that there is no implication here that the determination of such matters is straightforward. See Hutter (1997) for a full discussion of the meaning of compliance in regulatory enforcement.

Legal Sanctions

The ultimate legal tool available to inspectors in the event of non-compliance is prosecution. Under the terms of the HSW Act, 1974, legal proceedings may be instituted either by inspectors or by the Director of Public Prosecutions (sect. 38). Inspectors are empowered to conduct cases in Magistrates Court proceedings in England and Wales, although this is of course not possible in cases which are taken to the Crown Court. At the time of the research (1989) penalties of £420 could be imposed for summary cases. On conviction an indictment or fine may be imposed and in some cases the penalty may be 'imprisonment for a term not exceeding two years or a fine, or both' (section 33(3)(b)).

Regulatory law provides for the sanctioning of individuals and corporations. But as Wells (1993: 30 ff.) explains, the language used in the case of corporate offending is rather different than the language used with reference to individuals. So in the case of corporations the language is of sanctioning, liability, and responsibility rather than punishment and blame. This argument could be pushed further to state that this more neutral language is also used with reference to regulatory offending. Nevertheless it remains the case that applying penalties to corporations is very different from applying the term to individuals, for example, fines are presently the only sanction which can be employed against corporate offenders for regulatory offences (Wells, 1993: 31).

Discussion

A number of themes emerge from the legal mandate. Important in the context of this research is that the mode of regulation changed from a traditional command and control model to one more closely approximating enforced self-regulation. This entailed greater responsibilities being placed on business to manage occupational health and safety risks. The HSW Act, 1974, assumes a certain amount of corporate responsibility and places great emphasis upon self-regulation. The legislation thus attempts to harness the regulatory capacity of the company. This represents a broadening definition of regulation, one which goes beyond the state and involves a regulatory mix. It is a recognition of the pervasiveness of regulation and supposition that regulatory space should be filled by a plurality of actors.

Occupational health and safety laws are simultaneously constitutive and controlling. They do not seem to be underpinned by adherence to neo-classical views that economic organizations are coherent and instrumental; rather there is an acknowledgement that the market and businesses comprise different groups. Nevertheless the Robens Report, upon which the legislation is based, did assume an identity of interest between groups, an identity which may be ill-founded (Dawson *et al.*, 1988; Genn, 1993). The scope of the mandate has changed over time leading to the greater incorporation and participation of the entire workforce in regulation. This has been done through empowering different groups and also allocating them responsibilities. But we should be cautious about assuming equality of power and responsibility; management is still assumed to be dominant and to hold primary responsibility.

The objectives of this legal mandate mirror Colebatch's (1989) notion that the law may both structure occupational health and safety on the railways and serve as part of the process of ordering. It has the potential to be a major source of influence but it need not be: order may be constituted—and most especially maintained—irrespective of the law. Where companies fail to fulfil regulatory objectives on their own then the law contains the possibility of state control and intervention.

Having identified regulatory objectives as they appear in the law, let us turn our attention to how much those within BR knew about occupational health and safety laws. The interviews were structured in such a way that simple open-ended questions were asked first to see how much information respondents could give spontaneously. If necessary these were followed by rather more specific questions (see App. 1).

Knowledge of the Legal Mandate

An open-ended question asking what health and safety laws respondents had to observe revealed that the HSW Act, 1974, was generally known about. Thirty per cent (36/121) referred spontaneously to the HSW Act, 1974, and when prompted, an additional 54 per cent (65/121) said that they had heard of this Act. The Factories Act and the Offices, Shops and Railway Premises Act were respectively mentioned by just 5 per cent (6/121) of those answering this question. Only 3 per cent (4/121) of respondents were unable to cite any legislation. Many of the responses were vague, such as the following:

I: Do you know what sort of laws you have to observe regarding health and safety?

R: Extreme laws?

I: I'm talking about laws of the land, not British Railways laws.

R: Well other than the training they send me on and all the reading and writing I have to take notice of I don't think it comes out immediately what the laws are. I get reminded of them or I can look in my folder. I can remind myself of the law. The laws of whether I am allowed to do things or tell men or others to do things and get away with it. So if I tell a man to do something and he says 'but by the law I'm not supposed to do so', then I must think again. Then I'm being reminded of the law.

I: Do you know what the law is called?

R: Not offhand, no.

I: Have you heard of the HSW Act, 1974?

R: I have got literature on it. If I need to brush up on it, if I think I'm in trouble with someone who has come back and said 'you're not supposed to do it' then I will take time out to read the law. (supervisor, interviewee 111)

Moreover while some respondents knew that there was legislation about specific activities, for example a requirement to wear goggles when using a grindstone, they were unable to name the legislation involved.

More specific questions were directed to finding out how much was known about health and safety legislation beyond a simple naming of specific laws. The question 'What do these laws require you to do?' elicited a wide variety of responses. The majority in all categories understood that the law placed responsibilities upon themselves. This said, a notable proportion of respondents was unable to give very detailed or substantive replies about the nature of this responsibility. For example, they merely stated that they were required to follow the law; or 'be an enlightened employer'; or be the place where the 'buck stops':

I: Do you know what the HSW Act, 1974, requires you do?

R: ... without looking it up I can't tell you, but broadly it is based on a level of responsibility that passes down through the system to ensure that you as a manager at whatever level are providing a safe environment for your workforce. It gives you responsibilities, it gives them responsibilities.

I: Do you know what responsibilities it gives your workforce?

R: Not offhand, not without looking it up. I would have to look all this up. . . . This is not a prime part of my work and I wouldn't carry that information round on a day-to-day basis but it is readily available if I want to look it up. (manager, interviewee 121)

Replies to these questions were socially structured. Chart 4.1, for instance, reveals that of those who spontaneously cited the HSW Act, 1974, there was a heavy bias in this answer towards managerial staff and Chart 4.2 reveals that there were also differences across departments.

Similar variations emerged in response to the more specific questions. Only half of the *managers* asked what the law required them to do were able to give any detailed response: 8 out of 20 regarded the legislation as requiring them to maintain a safe workplace, with just 2 out of 20 mentioning that they had

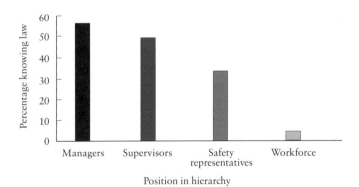

CHART 4.1. The social dimensions of knowledge: the Health and Safety at Work Act, 1974

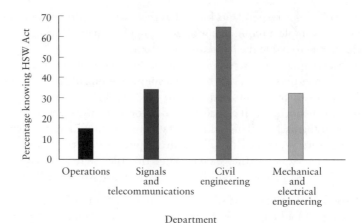

CHART 4.2. Dimensions of knowledge: department

responsibility for their own safety in addition to that of others. Half of the managers responding to this question gave evasive or vague replies. *Supervisors* also perceived their responsibilities to centre on ensuring that the working environment was safe for staff. Within the manager and supervisor categories operations staff were the least well informed of the details of the legislation, possibly because, relative to the other departments, a smaller proportion of their staff work out and about on the trackside.

All *safety representatives* had some idea of the law but they again tended to refer to the law as it affected them rather than others and with reference to specific activities[13] rather than general principles. The *workforce* were much less knowledgeable, with just under half (11/25) not knowing what the law required of them. Of those attempting to detail the requirements of the law all, except one respondent, referred to the duties they had towards themselves, only the one referred to the obligations to others:

> I believe it makes you responsible for not just your own safety but other peoples' safety. (worker, interviewee 88)
> You mustn't do anything that is dangerous, you could be held responsible for it. (worker, interviewee 103)

The social dimensions of knowledge were probed in the form of more specific questions to all respondents about what the law required of specific groups within the company, namely managers and the workforce. The answers to these questions underlined the general sentiment that the workforce should be responsible for themselves whereas managers held more general duties towards the workforce. Nevertheless, the broad principle that everyone had

[13] Nine out of 14 safety representatives referred to the obligations they had to comply; 5 out of 14 referred to their obligations to both themselves and others.

occupational health and safety responsibilities towards everyone else and towards themselves was well understood. For example:

I: Do you know what duties these laws put upon the workforce regarding health and safety?

R: They shouldn't be looking after their health and safety as much as we should be looking after theirs, it is up to everyone from the most minion of person to the most top person all to contribute to health and safety. It is no good somebody saying 'well I'm only the worker, it is not up to me what happens to my health and safety', that is not the point of it, the point of it is that everyone who takes a legal part in it which means it should work. (supervisor, interviewee 24)

R: Every employee is responsible for his own safety in work and I consider that the Act makes that absolutely clear for employees. (supervisor, interviewee 87)

Half of the workers interviewed had no clear idea of what their own responsibilities were in law, whereas managers and supervisors were most inclined to refer to the workers' responsibilities towards both themselves and others in the workplace. Half of the supervisors interviewed had no idea of managers' responsibilities which is perhaps a surprisingly high proportion given that supervisors themselves occupy junior managerial positions within the industry. Responses to questions about managerial responsibilities under occupational health and safety legislation centred on their responsibilities for their staff: the only person to refer to managers' responsibilities for their own safety was a member of the workforce. Moreover, only one manager mentioned the responsibilities they held under the HSW Act, 1974, towards members of the public.

Directors, safety officers, and union officials were asked how much they expected the staff to know about health and safety legislation. Those without a specific remit for health and safety had much more realistic expectations than did safety personnel. Safety officers expected everyone to have knowledge of the general responsibilities outlined in the legislation. One of these expected staff to be able to name a range of legislation and codes of practice, and to know the general duties outlined in the HSW Act, 1974, for example, that they have a legal responsibility to look after themselves and others. These officers expected fairly detailed knowledge because of the induction courses which all employees attended when joining the company. Managers were expected to know substantially more because they went through lengthy and detailed courses. Moreover, they were responsible for updating and implementing local safety policy statements (see Ch. 5). Those without a central health and safety remit expected that the majority of staff would have a very limited knowledge of the law and its requirements:

I would actually expect the average member of staff to have a very sketchy knowledge of what the law says because I think there is a tradition in the industry—and I hope it is a well-founded tradition—. . . managerially we have a responsibility of saying we will interpret the law and our practices and our standards and everything else will reflect the law. And therefore really saying to the average employee 'Don't worry about the niceties of the law, we are responsible employers . . . .' (director)

The argument here is that employees may not realize that they know about the legislation because their focus is upon company rules and documentation which incorporates the law's requirements. The point was reiterated by a senior union official: '"What duties does the law put upon the workforce?" Well they'd probably say that's not to do with the law but to do with the Rule Book, because the Rule Book says.' All expected that there would be a divide between managerial and workforce responses, with managers generally being expected to be much more aware than the workforce of both the HSW Act, 1974,[14] and its contents. Safety personnel and union officials thought that the workforce would have a vague knowledge but hoped that they would know that they were responsible for their own and their colleagues' health, safety, and welfare. Safety representatives were not expected to have a very wide knowledge of the law.

Comment

Overall therefore it was understood that in law everyone was regarded as participants in workplace health and safety. Beyond this there was a hazy understanding of what this involved. In particular managers did not appear to appreciate their responsibilities for their own health and safety and the workforce did not seem to understand their duties towards others, while neither group was fully aware of their duties towards the public. In essence there was evidence of a pre-Robens paternalistic attitude to health and safety, which held this to be a managerial responsibility. But there is no doubt that the HSW Act, 1974, has started to embrace the whole workforce and involve them in health and safety regulation. These findings accord with others. For example, Brittan's (1984: 75) study of water dischargers found that they had a very vague knowledge of their legal responsibilities. While most effluent dischargers claimed to know the law in general terms, none voluntarily named their titles or explained their substance. Dawson *et al.* (1988) found that even in larger firms there was often ignorance of the law at the lower levels of line management.

The significance of these findings is perhaps indicated by the fact that ignorance of regulation emerges as an important explanation of patterns of compliance. Genn (1993: 230) for instance found that ignorance of the law was widespread among managers where there was low motivation to comply, but that in highly motivated firms there were likely to be both specialized

---

[14] There seemed to be no expectation that anyone would know about any other legislation.

occupational health and safety personnel and many sources of information about occupational health and safety. This suggests that knowledge of the law is important because it offers us vital information about the extent to which there may have been even the most rudimentary knowledge of what constituted compliance with occupational health and safety regulation.

The intention of the questions discussed thus far was to discern how much information about the law respondents retained on a day-to-day basis. But it should be remembered that staff could consult various documentary sources to check up on the law's requirements (see Ch. 7). Moreover some staff went to extraordinary lengths to improve their own knowledge of health and safety issues. One safety representative could not refer to any health and safety legislation unprompted—'Laws, I don't know really. I don't know how to answer that to be honest with you' (Interviewee 90). But once the HSW Act, 1974, was referred to he correctly cited several other statutes and told the interviewer about *Redgrave's*.[15] Indeed, it transpired that he had bought several reference books himself.

Knowledge of Legal Sanctions

Knowledge of legal sanctions takes on importance according to deterrence models of corporate behaviour and law. If these models are correct then companies act to avoid sanctioning. There are a number of versions of this theory. Some suggest that the actual severity of the penalty may be significant, while others focus more heavily on the symbolic consequences of legal action.

Everyone was asked what legal action inspectors could take and managers, supervisors, and safety representatives were asked if they knew what penalties the courts could impose in the event of a guilty verdict for occupational health and safety offences. Let us consider first their knowledge of the legal action inspectors could take. Chart 4.3 reveals that the ability to respond to the question at all was very much influenced by a respondent's position in the hierarchy. Table 4.1 details the replies of those who did feel able to respond to the question.

The responses confuse the legal action that could be initiated by inspectors and the legal sanctions that could be imposed by the courts. Interestingly only one respondent referred to 'disciplinary procedures', which suggests that respondents recognized the difference between legal sanctions and disciplinary procedures.

Among those who could answer the question there was a perception of strong penalties being available:

> His powers are far reaching aren't they? He can take us to court, he can prosecute . . . he can go into anybody's house at the same time and take anything

---

[15] *Redgrave's Guides* are reference books which cover current health and safety legislation and explain it. They are among the most accessible and comprehensive guides available on the subject.

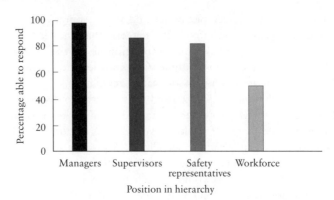

CHART 4.3. The social dimensions of knowledge: knowledge of legal action inspectors could take

> that he requires and he thinks he would require for prosecution. In fact he's got more power than the average policeman. (supervisor, interviewee 68)

While a significant proportion of respondents from all categories correctly referred to the courts or prosecution, a sizeable proportion in each category erroneously thought that the legislation gave inspectors the power to 'close down' works:

> If they carry out an examination and find that health and safety regula-tions are not being complied with then they just shut the place down. (supervisor, interviewee 99)

> I understand that they have vast powers, you know they can in fact shut a workplace down at a moment's notice. (worker: interviewee 48)

> Well, I know that they have got very strong powers and they are virtually above the law to impound anything they want. (safety representative, interviewee 33)

The social dimensions of responses reflect those of former questions. The accuracy of replies was also hierarchically structured with managers offering more precise replies than other grades of staff. For example, they were more knowledgeable about notices. Managers and safety representatives were less inclined than other staff to believe that closure of the works was a possible option.

Table 4.2 details the responses of managers, supervisors, and safety repre-sentatives to a question about the penalties which the courts could impose in the event of a guilty verdict. The interview data suggest that respondents overesti-mated the penalties which were imposed. For example, they believed that imprisonment was likely—in fact there have been no imprisonments resulting from Railway Inspectorate prosecutions although it was possible in law—or possibly the closure of the works or dismissal of staff—again these are not real-istic options:

TABLE 4.1. Knowledge of legal action inspectors can take

| | Percentage in each category identifying each action | | | |
	Managers (n=47)	Supervisors (n=28)	Safety reps. (n=18)	Workforce (n=41)
Prison	2	11	—	2
Court/ prosecution	26	28	33	22
Notices	45	11	5.5	—
Fines	—	11	5.5	—
Close down	11	18	11	27
Stop work/ impound machinery	15	3.5	28	—
Discipline	—	3.5	—	—
Don't know	2	14	17	49

TABLE 4.2. Knowledge of the penalties the courts could impose

Penalty	Number of respondents identifying each penalty
Prison	33
Fines	42
Close down	2
Dismissal	1

I understand it could be almost unlimited fines. Depending on the size or the location and of course there are individuals who could be held responsible at law. So you know it could affect myself. (manager, interviewee 13)

I know they can be hefty fines and you know it could lead to managers' dismissal but if you asked me to name a figure I wouldn't know. (manager, interviewee 44).

Heavy fines, prison sentences (manager, interviewee 74).

Comment

These data are interesting. We again find that there is a hierarchy of understanding, with those responding on the subject of sanctions tending to overestimate their severity. Yet again, however, these findings are in line with other studies of regulation which found that the regulated tended to overestimate inspectors' powers and the legal sanctions which could be imposed for a breach of the law (Brittan, 1984: 76 ff.). Indeed, some studies report that the regulated can offer support for criminal sanctions for regulatory offending (Brittan, 1984: 77; Clay, 1984: 384) but most especially for culpable offending rather than accidental offending and most particularly in the abstract rather than as something they may personally be on the receiving end of (Di Mento, 1986: 79). Indeed, there was no strong evidence in this research that many respondents fully understood that under the legislation they could be individually sanctioned.[16]

Views About the Law

Another indicator of respondents' understandings of the law was to ask them if they had views about occupational health and safety laws. Responses to this line of questioning again revealed ignorance, with half of those interviewed not holding any views about the law because they did not consider that they knew enough about it to express an opinion. Of those expressing an opinion, half (33/66) held positive views about the existing health and safety legislation; 44 per cent were mixed in their responses; and 6 per cent held negative views. Managers held the strongest views about the law whereas safety representatives tended to have more mixed responses.[17] The respondents' discussions about the law are interesting as they give us insights into what it is about the law which may help or hinder its implementation and impact.

Let us consider first positive views about occupational health and safety laws. The main advantage of the law is perceived to be the way in which it puts health and safety onto the workplace agenda:

> It's undoubtedly useful ... I think it's been very good. Maybe it hasn't stopped us as much as it ought to have done but yes, it's a good discipline ... (director)

> I think they [the rules and regulations] are very necessary to protect your workforce. One could think that health and safety can go over the top to some degree but again I think if you took that sort of approach it would be the wrong approach. I think you have got to have the well-being of staff, of the workforce as the important aspect—that is the biggest asset you have got is your workforce. If you don't have a workforce you can't produce the work or goods at the end of the day so I would have thought your biggest asset was your workforce and obviously you have got to tend that workforce and keep it running as efficiently as you can. (manager, interviewee 126)

[16] While notices are generally issued against the company, prosecutions could either be corporate or against any individual who could be held responsible within the workplace. The workforce are thus constituted as participants in regulation.

[17] Responses were again socially structured according to position in the hierarchy. For instance, the following proportions in each group had no views about occupational health and safety laws: managers—4%; supervisors—39%; workforce—60%.

> It [HSW Act, 1974] was necessary because we . . . work in a dangerous en-
> vironment and we could expose our men to all sorts of unnecessary dan-
> gers. But because the Act is there and I can be taken to court under criminal
> law . . . it forces me—it doesn't force me because I would hopefully would-
> n't condone anything dangerous anyway—but if I was not such a nice per-
> son as regards health and safety then the law could be used to force me to
> change my habits or they'd sling me in prison. (manager, interviewee 74)

> . . . it is definitely necessary . . . people talk about safety. I can remember
> going back before the Act came out—even a short time before the Act—
> safety was something that you didn't walk in front of a train and that was
> about it. But when the Act came in and because they were talking about it
> and sending people away on courses—at least the unions were—and the
> men came back and talked, you realized we could do this, and we should
> have that, you know. (supervisor, interviewee 15)

Health and safety legislation was therefore seen as a discipline on the railways, a reminder that health and safety was important and should be part of
everyday concerns. Moreover, it was regarded as an important factor in promoting and protecting the well-being of the workforce, especially in circumstances where employers and managers could be less than diligent about health
and safety. This resonates with other studies. Brittan (1984: 92) actually found
unanimous support for the control of pollution. The reasons were broadly
humanitarian, namely environmental, conservational, and recreational. But this
was qualified by concerns about the cost of control and the degree of control.
It was clear from some respondents that the HSW Act, 1974, had taken a while
to get used to:

> . . . when we first started to become actively involved I think people felt
> that it was almost an impossible task to comply with that law . . . it was
> seen in that vein, it's another series of laws that we are now required to act,
> which restricts the way we can operate. I think we've come on from that
> now and seen that you can actually get some benefits out of it in terms of
> the way you run your industry, because it's very expensive to have accidents
> anyway. And, if you want to look at it purely from a commercial point of
> view, I mean if you stop the railway because of an incident . . . where you
> could literally stop for hours then that's a lot of money down the drain. So
> we are tending to bring it into a bit more business context and say, well
> safety is good. (manager, interviewee 136)

> Now, I was rather scathing of that [HSW Act, 1974] when it first came out
> because I am not very keen on paper safety. But I must admit that it is a
> good document and there's a lot of good stuff in there and certainly, so far
> as the law is concerned, on whatever subject you look at it . . . would be
> clear what the legal requirements are. So you know, having been rather
> cynical when it first came out, I must say it is a very good document. (man-
> ager, interviewee 61)

But there was not universal praise for the HSW Act, 1974, and associated health and safety rules and regulations. One view was that the law does not give sufficient protection to the workforce. A safety representative,[18] for example, expressed the view that the laws were not tight enough and did not give sufficient protection to the workforce; the preference being for legislation which 'gives us rights and avenues to pursue things when they go wrong in a much more positive way'. A more widely held view was that the law was confusing, most especially that it could be difficult to read: 'In 1976 when I started to read them it was like ploughing through a book of Chinese proverbs, all written in Chinese . . . it is quite difficult to read, it is quite difficult to understand being honest' (supervisor, interviewee 127). This point was raised by several respondents, particularly with reference to staff whose command of basic English was not good. In this respect, the importance of simple easy to understand booklets was emphasized.

The broad framing of the HSW Act, 1974, was a particular source of concern:

> . . . it's very vague, that is, *very* vague. I know there are penalties if I don't do things . . . the law is there but it is in a written form. Unless I carry that book around all day I can't refer to it—but I know the book is somewhere. Does a solicitor or judge carry every book with him when he goes to court? (supervisor, interviewee 111)

But as staff had got used to the Act, some could see the merits of a broad approach:

> . . . the Health and Safety at Work Act, looking back upon it, remember it is 15 years old now. . . . I think the way in which they drafted that in terms of the looseness of the words, whilst very good, I think in those days we didn't see it that way. We were looking for black and white explanations because all the safety professionals were involved in the Factories Act, the Offices, Shops Act, which clearly explained that you had to do certain hard factual things, like every machine must be guarded. If you have a factory you must provide a certain number of toilets, a certain number of washbasins, the Health and Safety at Work Act, wasn't quite like that, it was a universal document. . . . I think that looking back on it now, particularly now we have some cases to judge it by. . . . I think that we are now able to advise local managers much more concisely. . . . (safety officer)

Clarity of the law and regulations has been found to be crucial to compliance. Clay (1984), for instance, cites the complexity of occupational health and safety rules as a reason for non-compliance with OSHA regulations (see also Di Mento, 1989; Genn, 1993; Hasseldine, 1993). Brittan's (1984) respondents also complained about the comprehensibility of water pollution legislation and said they would prefer simpler legislation which they could understand.

---

[18] Thirteen of the 16 safety representatives/union officials answering this question held mixed views while 3 gave positive responses. Also 45% of those giving a mixed response fell into this category of respondent.

Another concern was that the law was under-enforced:

> One, they (the laws) are only as good as the people that use them. And, two, as good as the people that administer them. (safety representative, interviewee 98)

> Well, I know in '74 it was considered, you know, a great step forward which I think it was to a certain extent ... there is a lot of backsliding gone on and I don't think it is enforced as much as it should be. (safety representative, interviewee 54)

This is a topic we will address at the end of this chapter, suffice to say here that effective enforcement of regulation emerges as centrally important from a range of studies of regulation (Barrile, 1995; Di Mento, 1989; Hasseldine, 1993; Sigler and Murphy, 1988).

Perhaps the most serious charge was that the legislation was a good point of reference rather than a living document that held any resonance for workers at ground level:

> One of the big things against the Health and Safety at Work Act is that it seems to have developed into a bit of a bureaucrat's dream which doesn't really ... suit the man on the ground who is trying to do other jobs. (manager, interviewee 75)

> In one frame of mind one just has a dumb acceptance of it [the law], in another frame of mind one has a sort of irritation and frustration by them. (director)

R: It's a necessary evil. I think you have got to have regulations like that to ensure that we have got a safe place to work.

I: Why do you think it's evil?

R: Because of all the legislation that goes with it, all the rules and regulations, all the different instructions that come out. They are so numerous so it is almost an impossibility to keep up with it and remember it. (manager, interviewee 67)

Only four managers felt that the law made no difference to health and safety in the workplace, one for instance arguing that the law is petty and another suggesting that it commanded only lip service rather than action. Whether or not this was the case may become more apparent in subsequent chapters. So far it appears that there was generally a hazy understanding of regulatory objectives but it may well be that the crucial point isn't knowing the letter of the law but the objectives of the legal mandate being absorbed and becoming part of everyday operation and perspective. So what happens in practice is potentially much more important and it is to respondents' perceptions of this that we turn in Chapter 5.

5

The Railway Inspectorate: Regulatory Objectives and the Social Dimensions of Knowledge

The main agency charged with regulating the railways at the time of data collection was the Railway Inspectorate, which decided on behalf of the state how the law and its objectives were given meaning in everyday life. They decided what constituted compliance and non-compliance and whether and when legal sanctions were invoked (Hutter, 1997). The Railway Inspectorate thus played an important role in determining how legal objectives were mediated into action. This was especially so during the research period as there was very close contact between this Inspectorate and the railway companies, especially BR.

Ascertaining an agency's regulatory objectives is no easy task. Undoubtedly there are multiple interpretations of regulatory purpose within any inspectorate according to a range of factors such as an inspector's age, experience, professional background, and position in the hierarchy (Kagan, 1994). But regulatory objectives are often left unarticulated and are tacit. One has therefore to turn to a variety of indicators of regulatory objectives, which are most obviously emergent through action, that is through the organization of the inspectorate, how it mobilizes its resources, and the enforcement approach it adopts. Regulatory objectives can also be understood through the Inspectorate's interpretative framework, for instance, their views of industry and their visions of order. Let us first consider the organization of the Railway Inspectorate at the time this research was undertaken.[1]

Organization

At the time of this research the Railway Inspectorate comprised a chief inspector and on average some six inspecting officers and fifteen railway employment inspectors.[2] Their main employer was the Department of Transport, in whose London offices the Railway Inspectorate's headquarters was located. They also

[1] The organization of the Railway Inspectorate has changed quite considerably since this research and consequently there has been a shift in objectives. This is reflected, for example, in their use of legal action (see below). The purpose of this chapter, however, is to concentrate on the research period. More recent developments are discussed in Chapter 11.

[2] There were fluctuations in the number of inspectors. During the 1980s and early 1990s Inspectorate salaries became increasingly unattractive when compared to those offered by industry. This led to recruitment difficulties.

worked for HSE on an agency basis (see Ch. 2). The chief inspector was an important symbolic figure at the top of the organization as well as someone who undertook a substantive role within the Inspectorate. The chief inspector in post in the mid-1980s estimated that HSE Agency work occupied approximately 12 per cent of his time.[3] This involved him in regular meetings with the management of the railways, in particular British Railways Board (BRB). Decisions about whether or not to inspect and approve new works were his and he also had delegated powers from the Minister to decide what type of accident inquiry to initiate. Ministerial correspondence and parliamentary questions went through his office.

There was a basic division within the Inspectorate between inspecting officers and railway employment inspectors. Inspecting officers held the more senior positions in the organization but there were also differences in training and background. Inspecting officers were traditionally ex-Royal Engineers officers but at the time of my research the Inspectorate was changing. The research period saw the appointment of the first inspecting officer with no career military background. This officer started his career in the Inspectorate as a railway employment inspector and this became a regular career route as other railway employment inspectors were promoted into senior positions within the Inspectorate.

Railway employment inspectors have been recruited since 1975 when the Agency Agreement with HSE came into effect. They were recruited almost exclusively from BR. All were chartered engineers who had ten to twenty years' experience on the railways and all had held managerial positions. Their role centred exclusively on enforcing health and safety legislation and they comprised the regional organization of the Inspectorate.

The Railway Inspectorate's organization at this time reveals a strong division between what it termed its 'traditional' activities and its newly acquired health and safety duties.[4] Railway employment inspectors who were primarily responsible for health and safety matters were numerically dominant within the Railway Inspectorate but inspecting officers, who in the main dealt with the more traditional activities, were more senior. The inspection of new works was exclusively the remit of inspecting officers; accident investigation was undertaken by all members of the Railway Inspectorate. Public inquiries were undertaken by inspecting officers whereas the less public investigations were undertaken by railway employment inspectors.

---

[3] This involved him in such activities as attending HSE Management Board meetings and chairing the Railway Industry Advisory Committee (RIAC) which included representatives from the Inspectorate, HSE, the industry, the main railway unions, and the Trades Union Congress. The majority of his time was devoted to the Inspectorate's traditional activities, notably the inspection and approval of new works and accident inquiries. He was also involved in numerous meetings with BRB and also dealing with ministerial and parliamentary queries.

[4] These duties were 'acquired' in 1975 (see Ch. 2). The research concentrated on the late 1980s and early 1990s when the Railway Inspectorate had been responsible for enforcing the HSW Act, 1974, for some ten to fifteen years.

Railway employment inspectors were headed by an inspecting officer who undertook many of the day-to-day dealings with the national or managing Executive of the Railways. He was also responsible for a district organization of inspectors who were engaged in inspecting local stations, signal boxes, and transient work sites. This district organization comprised three principal railway employment inspectors and eleven railway employment inspectors who covered England, Scotland, and Wales from eight regional offices. The majority of inspectors undertook a lot of travelling. Inspecting officers, especially those concerned with the approval of new works and the inspection of level-crossing sites, had to travel nationwide. Railway employment inspectors travelled extensively within their regional jurisdictions which were geographically large, for example there was just one railway employment inspector based in Scotland and another responsible for Southern Region of BR and the London Underground.

The research period was therefore one in which the Inspectorate had accommodated its occupational health and safety duties and was entering a period of change.

Mobilization of Resources

One indicator of regulatory objectives was the way in which the enforcement agency mobilized its resources. Proactive strategies are essentially premonitory, preventative, and driven from within the enforcement agency whereas reactive work is postmonitory and led by external events.

Proactive strategies were established as an important part of the Railway Inspectorate's remit in the nineteenth century. The approval of new works is premonitory and proactive to the extent that it is designed to prevent harm by defining the population subject to control. This is in contrast to the other major aspect of the Railway Inspectorate's historic remit, namely the reactive investigation of accidents. The HSW Act, 1974, led to a greater emphasis on proactive work. The railway employment inspectors' remit comprised a strong element of proactive organization and it is this that I want to concentrate on given our present focus upon occupational health and safety.

Routine inspections comprised the major part of the work of railway employment inspectors.[5] The Railway Inspectorate did not operate a formal inspection programme: rather railway employment inspectors were given the discretion to decide how frequently and when to visit each area in their jurisdiction. They took account of such considerations as the accident rate associated with a particular area or activity and the degree of confidence they applied to the management and workforce. In essence this was a risk-based approach, albeit an informal one which had not been systematized by the Inspectorate. Central guidance was given on particular problems that inspectors should be

---

[5] 79% of the visits on which I accompanied railway employment inspectors in the mid-1980s were routine inspections (Hutter, 1997).

alert to and, of course, to any current campaigns being run by either the Railway Inspectorate or HSE.

Railway employment inspectors typically announced visits in advance by means of a standardized letter stating the date of the proposed visit and sometimes giving some indication of the activities and areas they were interested in inspecting. The rationale for this was that most inspections on the railways required special safety arrangements to be made in advance, in the form of arranging lookout protection for the inspector. Another explanation is especially interesting in the context of this research, namely the argument that if knowledge of an impending visit by an inspector prompted the remedy of any defects, then part of the inspector's job had been completed before he arrived. Moreover, inspectors argued, those problems that were still apparent would be those not properly understood as non-compliant. There is a variety of divergent views on the subject of announcing visits beforehand[6] but these are less interesting in the context of this discussion than what these arguments tell us about Railway Inspectorate objectives. The implication of the inspectors' explanations seems to be that they were not trying to 'catch out' the regulated but to establish what they did and did not understand. Thus their concern was with the longer term, ensuring that there was both compliance and understanding of the reasons for the original requirement.

Inspections involved an assessment of both the hardware and the software of a site (Hutter, 1997). The former included the physical aspects of the site, such as buildings and equipment, whereas the software included systems of work and company procedures for ensuring health and safety compliance. Railway employment inspectors were normally accompanied by supervisors or other junior managers during their inspections, depending upon the aspects which were of particular interest to the inspector. Inspecting officers were usually accompanied by more senior managerial staff. Railway employment inspectors aimed to cover most areas of a site during a basic inspection, allowing the time spent in any one section to be dictated by what they found there. During the course of the inspection inspectors would talk with members of the workforce, stopping to check that they were happy with health and safety matters in general. Inspectors would stop and talk to anyone they saw not complying with good health and safety practice. Where they encountered a particularly difficult or unusual problem they would refer it to principal railway employment inspectors and from there to headquarters if necessary. Particularly difficult or unusual problems would be dealt with nationally by inspecting officers through negotiation with BRB. Railway employment inspectors asked to see safety representatives during their visits, although this was not always possible if the safety representative was on shift work and the shift did not coincide with the inspector's visit (Hutter, 1997).

---

[6] See the Baryugil Report (Report of the House of Representatives, 1984, para. 6.13 ff.); Di Mento (1986: 179); Hutter (1997: 113–14).

Following a visit, railway employment inspectors usually sent letters which outlined the matters requiring attention. These were sent to local managers and copied to safety representatives. When such letters were sent they could be followed by a shorter check visit to ensure that outstanding matters had been rectified.

Reactive work made variable demands on the Inspectorate. Complaints did not represent a major demand upon Railway Inspectorate time.[7] Accidents figured rather more prominently in mobilizing resources. Accident investigation was an important part of inspecting officers' workload but it figured less prominently in the work of railway employment inspectors.[8]

Accidents were reported directly to the Inspectorate. Particularly serious accidents—for example, those involving a passenger train—were reported immediately by telephone. Less serious categories of accident were reported on a monthly basis. These reports were initially processed by an assistant inspecting officer who would decide which accidents to investigate and which type of inquiry was required. Normally this inspector would decide not to investigate accidents resulting in minor injuries unless there had been a pattern or series of similar accidents. The inspector responsible for this task in the mid to late 1980s estimated that 15 per cent of accident reports were not followed through. The rest would be investigated further. The type of follow-up involved ranged from writing to the railways and requesting more information to the initiation of a public inquiry.[9]

Where an inquiry was deemed necessary the Railway Inspectorate had a strong preference to hold inquiries under the 1871 legislation.[10] This was partly a result of public expectation but principally because of the opportunities the 1871 legislation afforded for publishing the findings of the investigations and disseminating information about accidents and their causes. Three main types of inquiry were undertaken under the 1871 legislation. Most were low key investigations undertaken by railway employment inspectors. But in the case of particularly serious accidents it had become the practice for the Inspectorate to hold a public hearing of evidence, this being the Public Inquiry for which the Inspectorate is best known (see Hutter, 1992). Finally, the 1871 legislation allows for the Secretary of State for Transport to set up a formal Court of Inquiry, but this type of investigation is rarely held and is reserved for the most extreme accidents. Inquiries held under the HSW Act, 1974, were most likely where the Inspectorate was seriously considering a prosecution. Table 5.1 gives

---

[7] Railway Inspectorate 1983 and 1984 Annual Reports note that 176 and 210 complaints by railway staff were dealt with. Subsequent reports do not specify the number of complaints received.

[8] 14% of the visits I undertook with railway employment inspectors in the mid-1980s were for the purpose of accident investigation.

[9] For more information about how these decisions are made see Hutter (1997); Lloyd-Bostock (1992).

[10] This has since changed as the Inspectorate has been more influenced by HSE. The majority of accident investigations are now held under the HSW Act, 1974.

TABLE 5.1. Railway accident investigations, 1981–1991/2

Year	Courts of Inquiry	Public Inquiries	Inquiries into Fatal and Serious Accidents
1981	0	8	234
1982	0	6	241
1983	0	8	211
1984	0	10	179
1985	0	4	309
1986	0	8	264
1987	1	5	218
1988	1	17	178
1989	0	23	194
1990	0	7	330
1991/2	0	3	377

Source: Annual Reports.

some idea of the number of the differing types of accident investigation that were undertaken under the 1871 legislation during the research period.[11]

The Inspectorate's mobilization of resources therefore emphasized the importance of the objectives of prevention of non-compliance and the constitution of everyday compliance. This was especially the case for railway employment inspectors whose remit was, of course, largely concerned with occupational health and safety. Accident investigation could take up substantial amounts of time especially if there had been a high profile accident involving the public. But this tended to be the concern of inspecting officers and was, as history would suggest, very much a public safety concern and not so much a matter of occupational health and safety. Overall therefore the Railway Inspectorate's objectives, as revealed in their mobilization of resources, were in line with the apparent legal objectives.

The Railway Inspectorate's Enforcement Approach

The enforcement styles favoured by the Railway Inspectorate during the fieldwork period are very familiar to students of regulation in Britain as they are typically accommodative in style. If we return to the models of enforcement outlined in Chapter 1, then the Railway Inspectorate falls clearly within the accommodative/compliance/behavioural model. This can be demonstrated with reference to the use they make of the enforcement tools at their disposal and the theory—or 'enforcement philosophy'—they claim to adhere to.

[11] The increase in numbers of accident investigations from 1990 reflects a dramatic increase in the staff levels of the Inspectorate. In 1990, for example, their field-level staff increased from seven to fifteen.

The Inspectorate's *routine enforcement* activity typically involved the use of a wide array of informal non-legal enforcement techniques. These enforcement activities were generally long term and incremental in nature. Much of their work was educational and advisory. Railway employment inspectors were important disseminators of information within BR. They passed on information about how other sectors of the railway managed technical problems and identified sources of specialist help within the company. Where necessary they would advise on how to meet safety standards, while national or potentially difficult problems would be referred upwards for consideration by inspecting officers and senior managers within the railways. Likewise, they would when necessary explain the requirements and the reasons for them to managers and employees.

Negotiation was another enforcement tool used routinely by this Inspectorate. Typically inspectors would negotiate about what needed to be done, how to do it, and the time period within which this should be achieved. For example, railway employment inspectors and inspecting officers would both negotiate deadlines and programmes of work. A number of tactics were employed in the course of negotiation, including persuasion, bluffing, and reference to other areas where levels of compliance were higher.[12] Railway employment inspectors usually followed up visits with a letter detailing matters they expected to be remedied. In these letters they would ask for a written reply giving details of remedial action taken and often they would include a date by which they expected to have received a progress report. In case of non-compliance, more threatening letters would be sent. If this failed to secure compliance then inspectors had a number of options open to them. For example, they could refer the matter to a higher authority or threaten legal action verbally or in writing. In all of these cases it is important to emphasize that inspectors' assessment of the risk posed by any non-compliance was overriding.

If we reconsider the Railway Inspectorate's enforcement approach in light of the enforcement styles discussed earlier, there is no doubt that this Inspectorate tends to be accommodative rather than sanctioning in approach. More specifically, their enforcement approach closely resembles the persuasive approach (Hutter, 1988). Legal action was regarded as a sign of personal failure by some inspectors, who explained their objective to be making the railways regulate themselves rather than catching them out. Co-operation and flexibility were valued as effective enforcement tools. Moreover they were regarded as vital to the preventative role of inspectors. One railway employment inspector explained that he wanted the regulated to take problems to him, not to be scared that he was 'waiting around the corner ready to hammer them'. The clear implication of the rhetoric was that the Railway Inspectorate could achieve higher standards of compliance by negotiation than by more legalistic methods.

---

[12] These are typical tools in the enforcement of regulatory legislation. See Carson (1970); Hawkins (1984); Hutter (1988, 1997); Manning (1977); Richardson *et al.* (1983).

The Inspectorate's regulatory objectives were therefore to effect a long-term, compliant 'state of affairs', hence their concern to educate and advise so that the reasons for compliance were fully understood. They were concerned with the prevention of offences and the remedy of defects rather than being rule bound. Their objectives were instrumental, to constitute and maintain order, not to search out and punish offenders. Only rarely did the Railway Inspectorate use the legal tools available to them.

The Use of Legal Action

Table 5.2 details the Inspectorate's use of improvement and prohibition notices and prosecution during the period 1980 to 1992. As we can see they seldom initiated legal action. But there were some changes apparent during this period. Most notable was an increasing propensity to prosecute and most especially to use improvement notices from the mid-1980s. These changes partly reflected more fundamental changes in the Railway Inspectorate. Three changes appeared to be of particular significance; first, the appointment in 1988 of the first Chief Inspecting Officer of Railways without a railway background but with a background in the Factory Inspectorate and HSE policy branches; secondly, the increase in resources discussed above (note 11) and thirdly, the changes in 1990 which placed the Railway Inspectorate within HSE rather than the Department of Transport. The Executive, and especially the Factory Inspectorate, have traditionally adopted a more adversarial approach than the Railway Inspectorate (see Hutter, 1997). It was apparent during the mid-1980s that HSE was exerting some pressure upon the Railway Inspectorate to display a greater

TABLE 5.2. Enforcement notices issued and prosecutions made by the Railway Inspectorate, 1980–1992

Year	Notices			Prosecutions	
	Improvement	Prohibition	Total	Laid	Convictions
1980	0	0	0	0	0
1981	0	0	0	0	0
1982	0	0	0	0	0
1983	4	0	4	2	2
1984	0	7	7	3	3
1985	1	2	3	10	10
1986	1	1	2	1	1
1987	5	3	8	2	2
1988	7	3	10	4	4
1989	5	4	9	4	3
1990/1	15	7	22	5	5
1991/2	23	4	27	5	5

Source: Annual Reports.

readiness to invoke the law than they had traditionally displayed. But it is important to emphasize that there is no suggestion of any major shift in enforcement approach being implied here. The distinction is best explained with reference to the concepts of the persuasive and insistent strategies of enforcement which I first discussed in 1988 (see Ch. 1). The differences between the persuasive and insistent strategies concerning rule-interpretation in many respects mirror their varying propensities to use legal coercion: those who are most flexible in their interpretation of the law are also more inclined to be flexible in their readiness to apply legal sanctions. The Railway Inspectorate have traditionally opted for persuasive strategies whereas the Factory Inspectorate have been more characterized to a greater extent by the insistent strategy.[13] If we look more closely at those occasions when the Railway Inspectorate did decide to initiate legal action we get a clearer picture of regulatory objectives.

Choice of Legal Action

Inspectors adhered to a number of general principles when considering whether or not to initiate legal action and, if so, whether to opt for a notice or prosecution. Notices were generally considered when inspectors thought that the company or local manager was procrastinating. So notices were likely where inspectors required the purchase or installation of equipment. If immediate action was necessitated then a prohibition notice would be appropriate providing there was evidence of an imminent danger to health. Prohibition notices were also favoured when dealing with a temporary rather than permanent site, the point being that improvement notices allowed a time-limit for compliance and some sites were so temporary that they would have gone before compliance was required under an improvement notice. Hence prohibition notices were most likely on construction sites such as those typically involving the civil engineering department and contractors.

The decision to initiate various types of legal action included consideration of a range of factors. These included, for example, the severity of the non-compliance, an assessment which took account of the risk posed or harm caused by a violation. Accidents were especially likely to lead to prosecution. Indeed at the time of my fieldwork the majority of Railway Inspectorate prosecutions followed accidents (Hutter and Lloyd-Bostock, 1990). Also relevant was the local manager's attitude to the health and safety of the workforce. Culpability was also taken into account. This was indicated by blatant offending, in circumstances where inspectors perceived that non-compliance was motivated by the prospect of financial advantage and by persistent non-compliance. For example, the 1985 prosecution figures include exemplary prosecutions for overturned cranes. Following a spate of accidents involving overhead cranes the Inspectorate identified overloading of cranes to be a major problem. In this

---

[13] See Hutter (1997) for a fuller explanation of these differences and the explanations of the variations in regulatory approach. See also Kagan (1994) for a useful summary of regulatory variations and their explanation.

case a strategy of persuasion did not effect a long-term improvement in the use of cranes so the Inspectorate opted for legal action. This is reflected in Table 5.2 where we can see the high success rate of prosecutions laid by the Railway Inspectorate. A central criterion was whether or not inspectors could satisfy the evidential requirements of a legal action and the likelihood of success in any legal case. Where inspectors did not want to take the risk of losing a case they might well try and avoid legal action (Hawkins, 1989*a*). Railway Inspectorate files document a number of cases where the possibility of prosecution was fully investigated but where it was determined that the chances of a successful prosecution were negligible. These cases often went as far as seeking counsel's opinion before being dropped.

The purposes of prosecution are usually broadly defined as either retributive or utilitarian, the former being a basically punitive approach and the latter focusing on deterrence. Generally Railway Inspectorate prosecutions were motivated with both purposes in mind. Blatant offending would be most likely to prompt retributive prosecution whereas exemplary prosecutions such as those for overturned cranes in 1985 were for primarily utilitarian reasons. General deterrence was important—not between companies as BR was then a monopoly, but between different departments and regions of the company. It was assumed that news of prosecution would spread through the organization and have a salutary effect. It was also recognized that the organization was not homogeneous (see below). A prominent reason for prosecution was to 'get things done' and to remedy problems, although there were important symbolic dimensions to legal action. For instance persistent non-compliance could be perceived as an assault on the Inspectorate's credibility and this could be interpreted as a fundamental challenge to power, the state's authority, legitimacy, and even order (Garland, 1990; Hawkins, 1984; Rock, 1973). Also the symbolic effects of exemplary prosecutions were well understood and exploited by the Railway Inspectorate. But it needs to be remembered that legal action was not an option routinely considered by inspectors since their objectives centred primarily upon gaining compliance and maintaining it. Moreover they wanted compliance through understanding and education rather than pure coercion. As they were in long-term relationships with the regulated, they of course had the opportunity to try to effect this (Hutter, 1997).[14]

The Railway Inspectorate's Interpretative Framework

Consistent with its general approach to regulation the Railway Inspectorate did not have an antagonistic relationship with the railway companies. At one level this is not surprising as in the broad spectrum of economic life BR represented a company which had high regulatory capacity in terms of resources,

---

[14] Whether or not this approach was 'effective' is a separate issue, the purpose here is to understand the Railway Inspectorate's approach. See Chapter 1 for discussion of the difficulties of assessing effectiveness and efficiency.

knowledge, technical ability, and willingness to comply. In short, it was a large, well-intentioned company (see Ch. 9). But it did have a relatively high accident rate (see Ch. 3) and the Railway Inspectorate were very aware that this was not a homogeneous organization, that some parts of it were compliant and others were not. Indeed inspectors had a reflexive relationship with BR in which there was a continual process of re-adaptation by both parties in respect of each other.

There are a number of important features of the relationship between the Railway Inspectorate and BR which help us to understand the Inspectorate's interpretative framework. The population regulated by the Inspectorate was very closely defined. At the time of this research it comprised BR as the company holding the monopoly of the overwhelming majority of the railway network in Britain. Apart from this, there were a number of locally based railway systems such as the London Underground and the minor railways, many of which were run by volunteer railway enthusiasts. A very large proportion of the Inspectorate's time was therefore spent with BR officials and this had a number of significant implications for the way in which the Inspectorate approached its work and interpreted the action (or lack of action) of the regulated population. The most obvious implication is that the Inspectorate knew some members of BR very well and that this was socially structured as they tended to have most contact with those in more senior positions (Hutter, 1993).

There was close contact between regional managers and railway employment inspectors and between BRB and inspecting officers. Railway Inspectorate files revealed close and regular correspondence between inspecting officers and BRB directors, sometimes weekly. In addition there was close telephone contact and also more formal periodic liaison meetings between BRB and the chief railway inspector and inspecting officers.[15] These different forms of communication were about the full range of regulatory issues. They included, for instance, communication about accidents; recommendations arising from accident inquiries; legal developments; new proposals; programmes of action; resources for health and safety issues; and discussions of relationships between railway employment inspectors and regional staff. For example, there may have been concern that railway employment inspectors' requirements in one region had national implications which needed discussion or railway employment inspectors may have identified a series of problems which needed more national attention, for example, variation in standards across regions or non-compliance with BR rules (see Ch. 6).

Inspectors were on first-name terms with managers they were in regular contact with but their letters were quite firm; indeed the writing of a letter at all was symbolic of their increasing pressure on the railways.[16] These letters would,

---

[15] These data are derived from research I undertook during the 1980s which involved extensive observation with all members of the Railway Inspectorate and a documentary survey. See Hutter (1997). It should be observed that similar meetings were held with smaller railway companies.

[16] The notion of an enforcement pyramid is useful in understanding regulatory enforcement. See Ayres and Braithwaite (1992); Hutter (1997).

for example, request formal clarification of the company's official position towards a particular regulatory matter or ask for details of progress on an agreed programme of work. These letters sometimes cited the Inspectorate's legislative mandate. The upshot was that both parties were in a more or less continuous relationship and thus knew each other very well. This was especially so as the turnover of senior personnel in both organizations was low.[17] Railway employment inspector and especially inspecting officer interactions with less senior managers and the workforce were much more intermittent, especially given the limited numbers of Inspectorate staff covering the national rail network.

Inspectors' working theories of the motivation of different parts of BR or of different managers to comply or not to comply were often based on fairly specific knowledge. Where recalcitrance was shown then the Railway Inspectorate would be quick to use BR's hierarchy to try to effect compliance. Indeed this is an important aspect of both organizations—BR and the Railway Inspectorate were both hierarchical organizations and both exploited this fact in their relationship. Where BR's hierarchy was not prepared or was unable to comply with inspecting officers' requests then prosecution was a real possibility, although this would usually signal the breakdown of a long and persistent attempt to negotiate compliance. Typically problems were resolved prior to this stage being reached. The monopoly position of BR was useful in effecting quick, frequent and direct communication between the regulator and regulated. But BR was a huge organization and the Inspectorate were well aware that there were variations within the organization and that it was not uniformly 'good' or 'bad'; it was much more complicated than this.

Discussion

The overall message arising from this discussion of legal objectives and the Railway Inspectorate's regulatory objectives was that these objectives were broadly in line with each other. The Inspectorate attempted to gain and maintain compliance and was concerned with a general state of affairs. Very serious one-off incidents and blatant offending could prompt legal action but overall the Inspectorate were more concerned with shaping motives and preferences through education and advice than catching out and punishing offenders. In a sense they were more concerned with constitution than control, especially with constituting what was regarded as compliance in law as a matter of everyday unthinking practice. Control was thus regarded as a means to an end, as a way of effecting compliance when persistent or blatant resistance was encountered.

---

[17] It is of course recognized that the close relationship between regulators and the population they regulate is a controversial matter but again this is not a central concern for this particular study. The focus here is upon understanding how the Inspectorate saw their regulatory objectives and went about their work.

In their interactions with the company the Inspectorate appeared to be hierarchical. So although inspectors interacted with the workforce, their negotiations were, in their view necessarily, with management. They did try to talk to safety representatives but with variable success. Indeed they were vitally concerned with the everyday compliance of everyone in the company and they did place much emphasis upon the company's structures for self-regulation (see Ch. 6). What cannot be gleaned from this discussion is whether or not these objectives were understood by those in the industry and whether or not they affected health and safety in the railway industry, so let us now turn our attention to how much was known about the regulatory apparatus put in place by the state to enforce occupational health and safety laws.

The Regulated's Knowledge of the 'Law in Action': The Railway Inspectorate

The research focused on two broad areas, first on knowledge of the institutional arrangements for the enforcement of this regulation and secondly, knowledge of the Railway Inspectorate's approach to regulation both with respect to its mobilization of resources and its enforcement approach. Again these areas relate to our understandings of corporate behaviour and in particular to the role of the law in influencing this.

The questions started with very rudimentary open-ended questions about whether the interviewees knew of any government checks on health and safety matters. So the early questions were about state institutional arrangements for the regulation of occupational health and safety. When asked if they knew of any government checks on health and safety there was a variety of possibilities which could have been mentioned. The Railway Inspectorate was most central, but their institutional affiliations with the Department of Transport and HSE were also relevant. It should be borne in mind that while the Railway Inspectorate have been in existence since the last century, the relationship of HSE to the regulation of the railways at the time of the research was much more recent and indirect than it is now (Ch. 2). This was indeed reflected in the responses with 35.5 per cent (41) of the sample spontaneously referring to the Railway Inspectorate; a further 8 per cent (9) when prompted; and just 3 per cent (4) mentioned HSE.[18]

Knowledge of the institutional arrangements for health and safety at work were socially structured and most fully understood by managers across a wide range of subjects. They were very likely to know that there were governmental checks on health and safety, with 77 per cent (23/30) naming the Railway

---

[18] The Department of Transport was mentioned by 5% (6); the Factory Inspectorate by 6% (7), and a miscellany of 'other' by 21% (24). The responses in this latter group ranged from 'a government department' to BR.

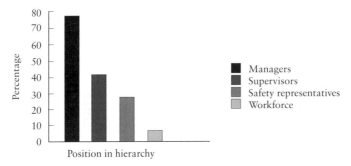

CHART 5.1. Knowledge of Railway Inspectorate

Inspectorate (see Chart 5.1) and just two giving an incorrect answer to questions about government checks. They were also most likely to cite the Railway Inspectorate by name; to know the name of their local inspector; to know what he[19] looked like; and where his local offices were (see Chart 5.2). The workforce were the least likely to know about these matters. The large majority of the workforce did not know of government checks on health and safety.[20] Supervisors and safety representatives were between the two. Amongst these groups there was a reasonable level of knowledge of the Railway Inspectorate.[21] But supervisors were more able to give a correct answer than safety representatives, where 53 per cent either gave an incorrect answer or didn't know how to respond. One worker made the point: 'there is a lot of people come round here you don't know who he is' (interviewee 130). Others know of the Railway Inspectorate because of their accident investigation work:

I: Have you ever heard of the Railway Inspectorate?
R: Only in the context of accidents like a train crash and things like this, that they show them on television, he is carrying out an investigation or something. (worker, interviewee 125)

—or because they had been reprimanded by an inspector: 'I don't know him but I have got reported by him' (supervisor, interviewee 76).

Some replies were very vague. One supervisor, in response to a question about checks on BR health and safety policies, referred to 'a government manager who sometimes walks around and checks on policy' (supervisor, interviewee 24).

---

[19] At the time of this research all members of the Railway Inspectorate were and always had been male. Hence I use the term 'he' throughout in accordance with the British Sociological Association's guidelines on sexism.

[20] 52% (22/42) could not answer at all and a further 38% attempted an answer but gave an inaccurate response. Only 7% (3/42) knew of the Railway Inspectorate.

[21] 42% of supervisors and 26% of safety representatives could cite the Railway Inspectorate immediately and a further 29% and 10% respectively when prompted.

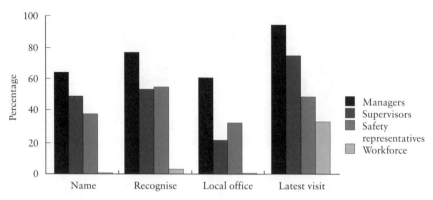

CHART 5.2. Knowledge of local railway employment inspectors

These interviews revealed confusion at all levels about the status of inspectors, with a significant minority clearly believing that they were BR personnel rather than government inspectors. One railway employment inspector in particular was repeatedly cited as the BR manager with special responsibility for health and safety within the company. One worker referred to this railway employment inspector as 'a big chap in the railway'.

In order to probe respondents' knowledge of the Inspectorate and its enforcement of health and safety legislation in greater detail, interviewees were questioned about the latest visit to their area by a railway employment inspector. They were asked when an inspector had last visited their area; if they had been visited in the previous twelve months; and how frequently their premises were inspected. Awareness of visits was again positively related to the respondents' place in the hierarchy, although the large majority of those interviewed did not know how frequently their premises/area/activities were inspected. This was the case with all grades of staff.[22]

Differences also emerged at a departmental level. Signals and telecommunications staff were the least aware of inspectors' visits while mechanical and electrical engineering staff were the most aware of these visits and were the most likely to perceive visits from inspectors as frequent. This is perhaps not surprising to the extent that signals and telecommunications staff work out and about on the track while mechanical and electrical engineering staff usually work in locomotive sheds. One might expect news about an inspector's visit to travel around a workshop rather more efficiently than among staff who are dispersed. But the interviews also reveal another reason, namely that mechanical and electrical engineering staff knew of inspectors' visits because they had been asked to tidy up the depot beforehand. When the workforce and safety

---

[22] Of those interviewed on this subject 55% of managers, 67% of supervisors, 50% of safety representatives, and 65% of workers did not know how frequently inspectors inspected their areas.

representatives were asked if they knew of inspectors' visits in advance the majority, with the exception of mechanical and electrical engineering staff, responded that they did not. Half of those members of the workforce and safety representatives who were able to respond to this question suspected (quite correctly) that their managers had known of visits in advance: 'When the inspector turns up everything gets tidied up' (worker, interviewee 95). '... the place is lovely and clean, then you could eat off the floor. Generally speaking the rest of the time you have to work through it' (worker, interviewee 104).

These statements corresponded to the Inspectorate's reasons for announcing visits in advance, namely that some matters were remedied prior to their arrival so they could concentrate on those matters which were apparently less well understood. Questions designed to discover how much respondents knew of the way the railway employment inspector's last visit had been conducted again revealed widespread ignorance amongst the workforce. Very few knew whom the inspector had spoken to during the visit. The majority of those attempting to answer this question believed that inspectors talked to managers: they were considered to have much less contact with supervisors, safety representatives, and the workforce. When *safety representatives* and the *workforce* were asked directly if the inspector had spoken to them, only one safety representative (of 18) and six (of 44) workers replied affirmatively. The majority of safety representatives and workers had no idea of how long the inspector had stayed during his visit.

Managers and *supervisors* were again the most likely to know what inspectors had done during their visits. Table 5.3, for example, shows those who were unable to answer questions about what inspectors had done during their visits. Only three of the 97 interviewed referred spontaneously to inspectors' visits in terms of their meeting the workforce. The *workforce* had very little knowledge about how long the inspector was in the area or about whether or not inspectors had found problems during their visits. The three who did know of problems knew only because they had to put things right or had been reprimanded. One worker, for example, could remember the local railway employment inspector visiting a large engineering site over the course of a weekend. He had two memories of the visit, the railway employment inspector reprimanding him for wearing trainers and the railway employment inspector sitting down to have tea with the workforce.

TABLE 5.3. Knowledge of inspectors' visits

	Proportion in each category unable to answer	
	No.	%
Managers	1	5
Supervisors	4	24
Safety representatives	8	50
Workforce	34	77

The workforce's responses contrast with the more detailed accounts offered by some managers:

I: Who does he speak to when he comes here?

R: He always speaks to me in the first instance and our usual arrangement is that he comes, he and I will have about an hour or so together, and then, whichever area he wants to look at that day—I mean he will have told us why and what he wants to go, what he wants to see, then the manager responsible for that particular activity will take him for the rest of the day, or however long he wants to be . . . I usually arrange to be sure I am about that day—it doesn't always work like that. And then he will normally call and we will have another coffee and an hour before he goes, that is the normal arrangement.

I: How long does he normally stay when he comes?

R: He normally makes a day of it.

I: What does he do while he is here?

R: . . . he and I will usually have a chat beforehand about all sorts of things and then a sort of conclusion chat afterwards. And then whichever area he wants to look at—because you know there are several depots on this site and they have their own different managers . . . he will go and do his inspection rounds and we usually fix him up with some sandwiches for lunch.

I: So he spends his day out inspecting?

R: Normally yes—going round with the guys. And he might want to do a very, very detailed inspection of the traction maintenance depot, or he might want to look at some alterations we have made in the plant and machinery workshops. And whilst he is doing that he might want to look at something that we have said we have done, whether we had done it. Yes, it tends to vary. (manager, interviewee 91)

Some supervisors also gave full accounts:

R: He spoke to the governor, myself, the safety representative, the man who looks after the safety records of course and a number of members of staff—who he spoke to on his way around on his inspection . . . . he was here for about 7 hours, 6 or 7 hours.

I: What did he do during his visit?

R: He examined all our health and safety records, policy statements, and then he did a walk around the whole depot. He examined machinery, asked questions about processes, how this was done, that was done. (supervisor, interviewee 100)

Managers were also fully aware that inspectors would follow up their visits:

'X' tends to discuss things on site and things like that. I have never known him make notes, but we certainly get letters back. And then he usually gives us a target day, well not so much a target date but he expects us to reply to his letter and quote the actual references that he lays down as to when they are complete, so there is follow up to it. (manager, interviewee 63)

All of these accounts reflect accurately the patterns of inspection I observed in an earlier study of the Railway Inspectorate (Hutter, 1997). Moreover they reinforce the socially structured nature of the relationship between the Inspectorate and the company. However, the Inspectorate did also appear to go to some effort to observe workforce practices and to interact with the workforce but it should be understood that the ratio of inspectors to BR employees necessarily meant that the probability of an employee meeting an inspector on a regular basis was extremely low (Hutter, 1993).

Safety Representatives

It is worth focusing specifically upon the responses of safety representatives since they were in a special position as the workforce representatives on health and safety. Not only might they have been expected to know more about the regulation of health and safety on the railways than the rest of the workforce—by virtue of their training (see Ch. 6)—but it might be expected that they would also have known more about inspectors' visits because of legislative provisions that they should be informed of visits.

Safety representatives knew more about the Inspectorate in terms of its name and the name, appearance and location of railway employment inspectors, than the rest of the workforce, but less than managers and about the same as supervisors. This suggests that their training and position did allow them to acquire a greater than average amount of knowledge compared to their colleagues in the workforce.

Even though safety representatives knew substantially more than the rest of the workforce about the railway employment inspector's latest visit, one might have expected them to know more than they did. For instance, it was perhaps surprising that just 45 per cent of safety representatives knew when the inspector's last visit was since inspectors let safety representatives know of their visits beforehand (as they did management) and also informed them afterwards of any problems found. Only four of the thirteen safety representatives interviewed knew in advance of the inspectors' visit and five of the fourteen received information after the visit, one verbally and the other four by letter. This may be explained by the way in which inspectors communicated with safety representatives. Their normal method was to address their letters to managers and ask them to pass an enclosed copy on to their safety representative. Their reason for doing this was that there can be a high turnover of safety representatives and this method of communication seemed to be most reliable. The evidence of this research suggests, however, that this may not be the case. Only one of eighteen safety representatives replied that they had personally spoken to inspectors during their last visit. This may be partially explained by the fact that some of these were working on a shift which did not coincide with the inspector's visit.

Also even if they did talk to railway employment inspectors, it is quite possible that they were not fully aware to whom they were talking.

It was certainly the case that national union officials expected safety representatives to know the name of their local railway employment inspector and his telephone number. Indeed, one expected them to know him personally. This was partly because information about railway employment inspectors was contained in local policy documents and partly because these officials expected railway employment inspectors to keep safety representatives informed of their visits.

There have been very few studies which have considered Inspectorate/ employee relationships. But the La Trobe/Melbourne Occupational Health and Safety project did collect valuable data on inspector/health and safety representative interaction. This study observed and assessed the operation of the Occupational Health and Safety Act, 1985, which was enacted by the State of Victoria and modelled on the Robens Report. The authors explain that the Act meant that inspectors 'now had to adjust to acknowledging the existence and powers of worker representatives' (1990: 124). Their findings and conclusions accord with those of this research. They found evidence that inspectors were not always asking to see health and safety representatives when they visited workplaces. They also discerned a concern amongst inspectors that they could be embroiled in industrial relations problems that were not strictly related to occupational health and safety. As this research into BR found, the degree of contact between inspectors and health and safety representatives seemed to be dependent upon the discretion of individual inspectors. The La Trobe study also discerned a similar reliance upon managerial prerogative to let employees know that an inspector was on site.

Reactive Work [23]

The most visible source of information about the Railway Inspectorate's reactive work was the accident reports produced following an accident inquiry under the Regulation of Railways Act, 1871. Railway staff were questioned about these reports. In response to a general question about sources of information about accidents, only six respondents (three managers and three supervisors) referred spontaneously to Railway Inspectorate inquiry reports. In response to a specific question 'Have you ever seen a Railway Inspectorate Accident Report?' 73 per cent (78/107) of respondents replied that they had seen these reports. However, when this figure is broken down according to grade of staff, we again find that the results are heavily skewed according to hierarchy, with managers and supervisors most likely to have seen these reports. There was uncertainty amongst the workforce about whose reports they see, that is, whether they were Railway Inspectorate or BR accident reports.

[23] See Chapter 7 for a more detailed discussion of accidents on the railways.

Managers, supervisors, and safety representatives were asked if they would approach inspectors for advice on health and safety matters. Of these 74 per cent (52/70) would consider this option, with 78 per cent (25/32) of managers, 52 per cent (12/23) of supervisors, and 100 per cent of safety representatives (15/15) being so inclined. One supervisor and six safety representatives said that they had approached the Railway Inspectorate with problems but just three of the safety representatives considered that an improvement had been effected as a result. The two reasons for consulting railway inspectors were for advice and where the usual internal BR channels had failed to effect a solution. Staff were more willing to consult railway employment inspectors informally: 'I'd phone "X" up—maybe 'cos I know him. I think if it was someone I didn't know and hadn't met I wouldn't do it' (manager, interviewee 110).

Unwillingness to step outside the existing grievance procedures within the company was the overwhelming reason why staff would be unwilling to consult the Railway Inspectorate. In some cases staff were under the misapprehension that they were barred from communicating directly with the Inspectorate, in other cases staff had simply never experienced a failure of the established company procedures. Alternatively they did not want to pester inspectors:

I:　Would you approach these inspectors for advice on health and safety matters?

R:　I would if it was absolutely necessary and again I think probably if I found the sources of information and advice to me were inconclusive but by and large probably not. (manager, interviewee 136)

Such an approach is within the ethos of regulatory objectives to the extent that a system of self-regulation was a primary objective, thus the company was expected to sort out problems for itself.

Respondents' Views about Railway Inspectorate Visits

Respondents were asked a variety of questions about the impact of inspectors' visits and their accident reports. Managers, supervisors, and those in more senior positions were asked how *useful* they found inspectors' visits. The majority found these visits useful, this being most particularly the case amongst more senior managers.[24] Inspections were considered to be an excellent way of keeping both employers and employees alert and sensitive to health and safety issues. In addition, managers found inspectors to be a useful source of advice and they welcomed the broader view of health and safety and the railways which inspectors could offer.

---

[24] 77% (23/30) of managers and senior personnel found Railway Inspectorate visits useful; 20% (6/30) gave a qualified response; and 1 person (3%) did not regard the visits as useful. This compares with supervisors: 39% (9/23) of whom found visits useful; 22% (5/23) gave a more qualified response; and 30% (7/23) who did not regard the visits as useful. Two (9%) did not have an opinion.

> . . . Health and safety is a very important thing but as a manager there are
> other things in life . . . and I would be sort of lying if I didn't say we aren't
> quite as up to date with the health and safety literature as you could be . . .
> I do feel that this outside help from time to time can be refreshing . . . it
> can create a space and a time . . . for you to sit back and talk to someone
> with some expertise, to bring you up to date, make you think, stimulate
> you a little bit. (manager, interviewee 126)

Negative comments about Railway Inspectorate visits centred upon their
infrequency. Individual personalities also emerged as a factor which influenced
the perceived usefulness of individual railway inspectors:

> I have to say that over ten or twelve years that a lot depends on the per-
> sonality. I find 'Y' [railway employment inspector] absolutely excellent. He
> believes that he has a positive role to play, he understands. He is not from
> the railway I don't think, but he understands what a manager's life is like.
> I find him the ideal protector of the legislation. In the past I have come
> across people who have thought they were dictators and I think that
> becomes negative, builds barriers, causes distrust between the two organ-
> izations and the staff and the environment suffer because of it, so I do
> believe that the personality is quite valuable. (manager, interviewee 43)

Some respondents felt that some inspectors could have offered more advice
during inspections. The prior announcement of inspectors' visits was also felt
to detract from their usefulness. This was a particular concern of supervisors
who felt that the areas to be inspected were 'cleaned up' and not seen in their
normal state by inspectors. '. . . they give notice don't they that they are coming
and everything is cleaned up . . . that is a bit stupid isn't it?' (workforce, interviewee 93). However, not all safety representatives and members of the workforce who suspected that management know of the visits in advance held strong
feelings about the matter. Indeed nine of the nineteen safety representatives and
union officials interviewed considered the matter irrelevant. This contrasts with
Clay's (1984) study of employers in California who complained strongly about
unannounced visits by OSHA inspectors.

Another indicator that Railway Inspectorate visits were valued are the
responses to the question 'How frequently do you think they (your
premises/area/activities) should be inspected?'. This time all categories of staff
were asked the question but very few members of the workforce felt able to
respond. The large majority wanted visits annually or more frequently, this
being especially the view of safety representatives and the workforce.[25]

> If they visited too frequently they would take over from our own responsi-
> bility, we would use them to tell us what to do. If they visit at their present
> level their role is not very useful to the men or us because there is no

---

[25] 31% (21) wanted annual visits whereas 52% (35) wanted either 6-monthly or even more frequent visits. Only 5 respondents did not want visits at all and 3 of these were managers.

return. So we want a period of visiting that's somewhere in the middle between infinity and weekly. I would guess you are going to end up with a range of period visitors, which reflect the risks in the job. I don't know if the Inspectorate have yet been out on the relaying site, which is night work, with trains flying around you, with cranes and other machinery. One might perceive that to be the most dangerous job in the railways that we do. I would expect them to visit one relaying site somewhere in the area perhaps twice annually knowing the wide range of things they have to check and I would expect them to visit the factory locations we have, the workshops, perhaps annually, and we only have two or three places like this. I expect them to visit an average work site, an average gang of men working on the track, perhaps five yearly. That's a very rough range of period visitors. (manager, interviewee 66)

Railway inspectors did prioritize their work according to risk (see Ch. 3) and railway employment inspectors did generally visit the sites referred to by this manager as frequently as he had hoped that they would. But Railway Inspectorate resources were constraining, so while it was possible to visit relaying sites twice a year it was not possible to visit the same relaying site more than once. It was partly for this reasons that railway employment inspectors spent more time with more senior regional staff as they believed that this would result in policy changes over a broader area of influence.

These responses are very interesting. They suggest that the constitutive objectives were either not fully comprehended or were regarded as unachievable, since there was a strong preference for an external review of corporate compliance. These responses certainly imply that regulation was significant in the ordering of company priorities.

Impact of Visit

Staff were asked whether or not they took notice of inspectors' comments. The overwhelming majority did take notice, for a variety of reasons. Prominent among these was that they had no choice, this being the most frequently mentioned reason amongst managers and supervisors. They also considered that inspectors gave sensible and authoritative advice:

I: Would you take a lot of notice of anything that he said?
R: Yes, for various reasons. With my lack of knowledge of the law I wouldn't know whether he was pulling the wool over my eyes or not, or whether he was going to come down heavy handed. 'X' 's [railway employment inspector] favourite statement is 'I'll close the place, I'm coming back in four weeks' time and if it is not improved I am going to close it. But it does get things done . . . he is not as heavy-handed as he sounds because he said 'I'll give you four weeks or I'm closing it'. The fact that we were back on the phone to him within two days saying it is going to take us six weeks

not four, OK I won't come until the sixth week, so he is reasonable like that. He talks sense as far as I am concerned. What he says will be an improvement, there is nothing that I have found him to do that good management wouldn't have done in the first place. (manager, interviewee 108)

Different facets of the Inspectorate's role were emphasized:

He's got the *powers* to enforce what he's saying. (emphasis added; manager, interviewee 67)

He knows the rules better than I do and he's there to *advise* you of what's going on. That's the thing he is only there to *help* you (emphasis added; supervisor, interviewee 68).

Very few members of the workforce felt able to respond to questions about the impact made by inspectors' visits, perhaps reinforcing the view that they had relatively little contact with them.

Matters which would command unambiguous compliance were so-called minor requests such as housekeeping issues, for example, cleaning up a mess room or tidying up a workshop and keeping up-to-date records. Serious matters of non-compliance would also be remedied without hesitation, for instance, the wearing of high visibility vests and adhering to the correct procedures when shunting. Only two members of the workforce could imagine ignoring Railway Inspectorate requests—an example of something that would be ignored being crossing the tracks in unauthorized places—while the rest of the sample would at most request a discussion of matters they did not fully agree with. Seven (of 22) managers would write and ask to discuss issues they disagreed with.

These responses confirm studies of enforcement which identify bluffing as a well-used regulatory enforcement technique (Hawkins, 1984; Hutter, 1997). They also suggest that the accommodative enforcement approach was very well comprehended. Indeed, some respondents clearly did not fully appreciate that there were controlling aspects of regulation. Critics of accommodative regulatory approaches do, of course, argue that these approaches favour companies as they are 'too reasonable'. When respondents were questioned about this, the overwhelming majority of staff of all categories found inspectors reasonable in their demands. This was particularly the view of safety representatives and the workforce.

Forty-two per cent of all of those holding managerial positions, from Health and Safety Officers to supervisors, considered that inspectors asked them to do unnecessary things which were perceived as 'nitpicking' or unrealistic.

There will be some things that are not necessarily . . . reasonable in terms of time-scales. And that's probably because we are conditioned to doing everything at dead slow speed on the railway when it comes to . . . getting engineering items resolved. Perhaps the fact that they set time-scales is right, that is the irritating factor in it. (manager, interviewee 5)

Certain inspectors were regarded as more reasonable than others and the key to being reasonable seemed to be a willingness to be flexible. In some cases, inspectors were regarded as being too reasonable:

I: Do you find what the Railway Inspectorate ask you is reasonable?

R: Oh yes. I mean that. In its own way it has the seeds of its own undoing— it is often that they are too reasonable, often they too appreciate that there are financial problems, or there are timescale problems.

I: You think it might be better if they weren't so sympathetic to you?

R: Well, there is a fine balance and I will just say I think there is some evidence to suggest that the balance may have just got a bit out of kilter occasionally in recent years and needs reviewing. (director)

These responses again appear to reflect an understanding of the accommodative approach and they also suggest a need for an external source of regulation to keep occupational health and safety in a prominent position in company priorities.

Senior Officials

BR directors were all in regular contact with inspecting officers, with the degree of contact between them ranging from daily to monthly (see above). Apart from biannual formal meetings between the two groups, additional formal and informal contact was generated by specific issues:

My formal interaction is two formal meetings a year when we review on a very open agenda a whole series of issues—some are progress issues, some are new issues, some are problem areas. I have informal contact with them on the basis that we do talk over problems as they arise. I talk to them about perhaps particular accidents or whatever. And frankly I expect that if I ring the chief inspecting officer of railways I will get very easy access to him personally, equally he does—and that is how we work. (director)

I: Can I ask you a bit about the Railway Inspectorate. What would be the nature of your contact with them?

R: Oh, broadly continuous. I am the main focus, so, for instance, it can quite easily be four phone calls a day. We meet formally . . . it must be three monthly. (director)

At this level there was little contact with railway employment inspectors. Health and safety officers were in regular communication with inspectorate staff locally, especially the civil engineering and mechanical and electrical engineering safety officers. Only one departmental safety officer was in regular contact with inspecting officers. There was little knowledge at these senior levels about railway employment inspectors' activities and requests unless a problem arose. So there was no central monitoring of railway employment inspectorate activities by

BR.[26] Meanwhile national union officials maintained regular contact with both Inspecting officers and railway employment inspectors.

Interestingly two directors believed that the relationship between BR and the Railway Inspectorate was 'too cosy': 'We do meet the Inspectorate as a body on occasions and there is very open contact there, perhaps too cosy, and I do accept that . . . I have tried to step back a little . . . I think my role as a Board member . . . has to be something of an arm's length with the Inspectorate' (director).[27] But not all senior personnel accepted that this was an accurate criticism of the relationship between the Railway Inspectorate and BR:

> I've never really had any problems with the Railway Inspectorate at all. I think we have a very good relationship. I mean people complain about what is thought the kind of cosy relationship between the Railway Inspectorate and the railway. I don't actually believe that to be true. I think they take their job very seriously and I think we have a very good working relationship. I actually think that contributes more towards us accepting some of their recommendations and doing something about working together . . . I might occasionally think that they are a bit over the top and occasionally we fall out with some of their details but normally we sit down and talk them through. (director).

Senior officials were divided in their views about whether the Railway Inspectorate's requests were reasonable. Seven directors and safety officers found the Railway Inspectorate generally reasonable most of the time, the other three found them 'too reasonable'. Those taking the latter position argued again that this was explained by a 'cosy relationship', but it was also relevant that there were 'too few inspectors to cover everything'. It was generally agreed, as one might expect, that they all had experience of the Railway Inspectorate either being 'too lenient' or dealing with matters which they regarded as much 'too trivial'.

Despite some criticism, there was no doubt amongst this group that railway employment inspectors' visits and the Railway Inspectorate in general were useful to the extent that they provided an outside view and external control:

> I think that any organization needs to have a policing body and if you look at living in this country of ours we have policemen who police what people do—these are no different. The Railway Inspectorate, they are policing what goes on on the railway. I think if they weren't there then I would hate to think about it but I think there would be a deterioration of standards and I think over a period of time that we would obviously have to be

---

[26] This contrasts with some other regulatory experiences. During an earlier study which also covered factory inspectors and industrial air pollution inspectors, I was told of one multinational company which kept central records of all inspectorate visits and their outcomes.

[27] The Fennel Report into the King's Cross fire was published in 1988, some 12–18 months before data collection. Interview responses suggest that BR officials were sensitized to the issue raised by the Report.

policed by somebody else and if we were policed by somebody else then they wouldn't understand the industry. After all we have got to get the trains out you know . . . we have to think to accept that the railway is a separate industry and that is why it needs a separate body to police it. (safety officer)

National Union Officials

The views of the national union officials interviewed were very similar to those expressed by senior railway personnel. For instance, they argued that the relationship between the Railway Inspectorate and BR was too close, especially the relationship between railway employment inspectors and the railways. Interestingly they also felt that the relationship between the unions and railways was too close and 'cosy'. They also argued that the Railway Inspectorate was under-resourced.

Given these views of generally reasonable Inspectorate behaviour let us now consider how much was understood about the Inspectorate's use of the sanctions available to them.

Knowledge of the Railway Inspectorate's Use of Legal Sanctions

The Railway Inspectorate adopts an accommodative approach to enforcement and seldom resorts to legal action. The regulation literature suggests that in such situations regulatory officials are able to use 'bluffing' as a resource because the regulated often overestimate their powers (Hawkins, 1983). Indeed Brittan (1984: 77) suggests that the discrepancy she discerned between dischargers' beliefs about penalties and actual penalties was the result of inspectors' bluffing. It is recognized that their ability to use bluffing may be determined by a number of factors, notably the regulatory capacity of the industries and firms they regulate. So generally one might expect the larger and more organized firms to be less susceptible to bluffing. However, we have very little knowledge of whether or not this is the case as most of the studies to date have been of regulatory enforcement from the point of view of the enforcers, not the regulated. Another suggestion in the literature is that the criminal law has great symbolic meaning and that this makes the criminal sanction an effective enforcement tool. Ball and Friedman (1965), in an early paper on the subject, contend that the criminal sanction is effective because it threatens to bring businessmen into contact with the criminal law (cf. Kadish and Kadish, 1973).

This study questioned employees across the railways about the legal sanctions available (see above) and their perceptions of the Railway Inspectorate's use of them. The most striking finding is that legal action was actually perceived as infrequent with none of the categories of respondent being able to think immediately of legal action taken by the Railway Inspectorate. Managers

TABLE 5.4. Frequency with which managers and supervisors
thought Railway Inspectorate initiated legal action

Frequency	Notices % (n=34)	Prosecution % (n=38)
Frequently	3	—
Occasionally	9	18
Probably	18	3
Threatened	9	5
Infrequently	26	34
Not heard of/never	35	40

and supervisors could seldom think of instances when the Inspectorate had
served notices, and even fewer instances of prosecutions (see Table 5.4).

I: How frequently do the Inspectorate initiate legal action?

R: I don't know, I just haven't a clue. I cannot remember them. I have been
here thirty years and I can never remember an inspector putting a notice
on anything here. (supervisor, interviewee 127)

More specific questions, also addressed to the workforce, asked if their firm
had ever been served with a notice or prosecuted. Again the large majority
(69%) had not heard of anything. Managers were most able to cite examples of
legal action against BR, with 66 per cent managers (cf. 31% workforce) claiming that they had not heard of some form of legal action against BR. Departmentally, signals and telecommunications and civil engineering staff were more
likely to have heard of prosecution than either operations or mechanical and
electrical engineering staff.[28] Generally those who could cite specific examples
of the Railway Inspectorate initiating legal action cited examples in which they
or a colleague had been involved. In addition a number of celebrated cases had
become part of recent 'folklore', including cases which had indeed been taken
for reasons of general deterrence and a case where BRB had contested prosecution and won on appeal.[29]

A number of more specific questions were asked to ascertain in more detail
the extent of respondents' knowledge of the Railway Inspectorate's use of the
legal options available to them. There were very uncertain replies in response to
questions about who is prosecuted, although the few who did feel able to answer

[28] The following had not heard of any legal action: operations staff—74%; mechanical and electrical engineering—75%; civil engineering—64.25%; signals and telecommunications—64%.

[29] Appeals were rare. This was a case where the BR department involved considered that they had
been able to do something particularly unwarranted and they invested in heavily contesting the case.
This was because they did not wish to incur the national implications if they did not win and
because they thought it unjust. This was exceptional. Typically matters never reached the courts at
all so the courts were not given the opportunity to comment on inspectors' interpretation of the law.

this referred to BRB, managers, and the individuals involved. Very few knew what would prompt prosecution, but again those who could reply to this correctly knew that a 'blatant' or 'wilful' disregard of the law would be likely to lead to prosecution.

Respondents were divided in their opinions about who *should* be held responsible in law for non-compliance with occupational health and safety regulations. Twenty-eight per cent thought that individuals involved should be; 25.5 per cent thought that BRB should be; 4 per cent thought that both should be prosecuted; and 40 per cent thought it depended upon circumstances; the remainder did not know (n = 82). This suggests that the principle that all could be held responsible for health and safety regulation may have been understood and possibly accepted by some: 'Well I suppose they should prosecute the people that's done wrong. If it is British Railways Board it is British Railways Board, if it is the lad on the shop floor he has got to go and all' (supervisor, interviewee 101). These findings reiterate those of previous studies where it is suggested that the regulated were supportive of criminal prosecution and penalties where there was evidence of culpability (see above).

Opinions among managers and supervisors were equally divided about whether or not legal action was something which concerned them and whether or not it was important that BR should try to avoid legal action. Some felt that prosecution sharpens up their awareness so is a good thing, while others feared the adverse publicity:

I: Is legal action from the Inspectorate something that worries you?

R: No because I hope I do my job in a manner where . . . I wouldn't need somebody to threaten me with legal action to do my job. (manager, interviewee 17)

I: Do you think that it is important to avoid legal action?

R: That's the goal really, that it would be far better if we regulated ourselves and use the Inspectorate as auditors only. (manager, interviewee 66)

> . . . [prosecution] is a loss of face isn't it? 'The railway's been taken to court again', I mean, it doesn't give the passengers much confidence in an organization that's always being hauled up before the court. So obviously they want to keep their nose clean. It's amazing with such a large organization they don't get done more often. (supervisor, interviewee 110)

These mixed responses again mirror those of earlier studies. Brittan, for example, found that some dischargers regarded fines as 'a joke' because of their derisory levels. Some were concerned about adverse publicity whereas others thought 'all publicity is good publicity' (Brittan, 1984: 77 ff.).

Senior Officials

All of the senior railway officials interviewed had heard of prosecutions but they were hazy about the details. They believed that notices were used infrequently. Directors thought that they were more likely to hear of prosecutions than notices but it was not automatic that they would be informed of either. Half thought that the Railway Inspectorate did prosecute, one thought that this was frequent (some twenty times a year), while others thought that the Inspectorate never prosecuted. Three had never heard of a notice being served, one again thought that they were frequent. The reason for the perception that legal action was resorted to infrequently was that initiating legal action was not the Railway Inspectorate's 'style' and because BR was sufficiently responsible for things not to reach this stage:

> In the railways, very, very rarely and that has been a long tradition and in fact I have to say to you I can't recall when they have [initiated legal action]. And that is partly because that hasn't been the style and it is also partly because we usually respond. (director)

> Improvement notices fairly frequently, prohibition—I really am digging around in the grapevine . . . I believe they may have and I think we are on the fingers of one hand if not down to one. It is conceivable that we've never had one, I don't know. (director)

These answers reveal two important things: first, that the level of ignorance among senior officials was high; secondly, that there was no central information point, no process for collating information about legal action. It was therefore not surprising that senior railway officials knew little about the circumstances which might surround a prosecution. One director admitted to not knowing what legal action inspectors could take. Two thought that imprisonment could result from a guilty verdict and one thought that someone in BR had been sentenced to six months in prison. They believed that who is prosecuted depended upon circumstances: 'The legislation is very clear isn't it? It depends on the nature of events and why it was caused and so on, and I don't think that's unreasonable' (director).

The area where senior officials gave the most accurate answers was information about what led Railway Inspectorate to initiate legal action:

> . . . the purpose of the prosecution, one is perhaps to punish and bring home to the individual, another one might be so [as] to ensure that it can be seen to be by the public and the adjacent workforce the seriousness of the situation and the way that has been adopted. I think that probably the latter is the most important. (director)

Safety officers were as well informed or uninformed as directors on the subject of legal action for occupational health and safety offences. This was perhaps surprising to the extent that they are specifically employed to focus on health and safety issues, whereas for all of the directors except one, health and safety was just one consideration to be balanced against a much broader remit.

Does all of this therefore imply that legal action was of no consequence to senior officials? In particular does it suggest that fear of the criminal sanction was sufficient to induce compliance? Questions about the impact of legal action do not suggest that these are correct interpretations. Senior officials explained that legal action was a 'sign of failure' and could prove to have a negative impact on corporate image as BR liked to be thought of as a 'responsible, caring employer':

> First of all we have a responsibility to our customers and to our workforce and as an employer I think if you are seen to be in the courts that is a very clear example that management is not fulfilling some of its basic obligations. And I think it shouts out messages to one's workforce which I wouldn't want to live with. Secondly I am very conscious of the image of BR and any prosecution and we don't want to be seen in the labour courts either so we tend to act circumspectly there, it is all to do with image. (director)

Legal action also had impact because it was so infrequent:

I: Do you think that prosecution is something that concerns the railways?

R: Oh yes.

I: Why's that?

R: Because you know, traditionally it is so unusual . . . this is a sort of circular argument . . . it's bad enough having accidents but it's much, much more painful to be punished you know, for being involved in causing one. (director)

I: What sort of impact do these prosecutions have on the railway, is it possible to say?

R: Enormous because it's inversely related to their frequency. (director)

This said, fear of legal action was not an overriding concern and not all agreed that it necessarily had adverse effects:

I: Do you think that prosecution impacts upon corporate image?

R: What prosecution on the railway? No I don't. I think we have our own very individual corporate image at the moment which is turning from a down-trodden defensive backward-looking industry into something that is dynamic and positive and making a success, a howling success, compared to five, six years ago. (director, 1989)

R: I don't think prosecuting the Board does the slightest bit of good.

I: Does it have any impact?

R: £2,000 out of a £6,00 million business?

I: Does it have a more symbolic effect?

R: Short term—it's never going to happen to me . . .

I: Do you think it affects the organization?

R: I don't think that it is much more than a pebble in a pond. I am not saying
     that the individuals concerned in the incident aren't worried, of course
     they are, and it will have more effect on them than it will on their col-
     leagues, it is a ripple effect.

I: I am wondering if prosecution is something that would worry the Board at
     all, as the corporate body—if they thought that there was going to be a
     change in prosecution policy?

R: I think that it would probably cause some concern but because the policy
     has not been to prosecute, what has happened in the past I think has had
     very little effect. (safety officer)

The impact was said to vary according to the perceived fairness of the prosecution. If it was not considered fair then there would be no black marks
against the individuals concerned, but if the prosecution was regarded as fair
then it would affect an individual's career:

> . . . it depends how the accident occurred. If we are looking at something
> relatively unforeseen and uncharted then I would say that those above him
> who invariably will have had that kind of experience themselves in the past
> will have sympathized with his position. But if he ran a very untidy shop,
> if he had generally failed to comply with health and safety problems, I
> would have thought that it would go down badly here for that guy's image.
> (safety officer)

One director made it clear that he did not consider that legal action was always
fair, but he nevertheless considered that it had a great impact 'even though the
guy who is punished often isn't responsible'.

Union officials were altogether more supportive of legal action and thought
it should be more frequent. This was because they felt that it put safety into
focus and because they felt that it had a great impact on everyone. One union
official explained that the prosecution of one of his members had 'a tremen-
dous effect' on the rest and the malpractice involved had apparently stopped for
a long time afterwards.

The Importance of the Railway Inspectorate

The overwhelming majority of managers, supervisors, safety representatives,
and workers (84% or 66/79) thought that the Inspectorate was very important
in bringing about higher standards of health and safety on the railways. The
16 per cent (n = 13) who did not agree argued that the industry could achieve
these standards without the Railway Inspectorate. Alternatively the Inspectorate was considered to be ineffective, a 'whitewash' argued one, although it
has to be said that this was a minority view.

Senior railway personnel were divided in their views about the importance of
the Railway Inspectorate. Two directors and two safety officers thought the
Inspectorate was very important while two directors and two safety officers

found this a bit strong and were more qualified in their responses. Two Directors qualified by stating there was a need for external controls to maintain high standards, BR could not do this entirely on their own. Two safety officers thought railway employment inspectors were 'too quick and superficial' to get to the root of problems and were also too lenient in their enforcement approach. The alternative view was that BR did need an outside check to maintain an ordering where heath and safety figured prominently:

> There is no doubt that for all we may see at this level of relationships being just a shade too cosy, that is not the perception down on the ground. The Inspectorate has a very high ... the Inspectorate is held in very high respect by our workforce and I have no doubt at all that for many many years they have been an enormous influence on our behaviour towards safety. (director)

> It does ensure that health and safety rather than just operational safety is probably higher up the agenda than would otherwise be the case ... I think their very existence is a very useful audit on the organization. (director)

Discussion

The general levels of knowledge about the Railway Inspectorate accord with those found by other studies. Genn (1993) found great variation: on smaller sites there was confusion about inspectors and their role, whereas larger companies used inspectors as a resource for information and advice (see also Brittan, 1984). She also found many respondents holding contradictory views of inspectors. All of this matches up with the findings of this research with the important exception that the confusion about inspectors was reflected in the lower grades of staff (Genn interviewed managerial and specialist safety staff) rather than in smaller companies (not interviewed in this research). If anything, BR respondents were better informed than those included in other studies and also more prepared to argue and negotiate with inspectors. Genn (1993) found little evidence of the regulated being prepared to engage in debate with regulators, indeed many perceived that they had no choice other than to do as inspectors requested.

The generally cordial relations between the regulated and regulated is another feature of existing studies. Authors in the United States and Great Britain have found general satisfaction in their relations with inspectors (Brittan, 1984: 87; Clay, 1984: 229; Genn, 1993; Gricar, 1983: 32). In the main inspectors were seen as co-operative, helpful, and reasonable although there were criticisms and complaints, notably centring on 'nit-picking' and impracticable demands (cf. Bardach and Kagan, 1982).

Other studies suggest that the impact of regulation on firms is variable. Clay's employers believed that OSHA inspectors had very little impact on employees (1984: 253). Gricar (1983: 32) remarks that OSHA did not pose a serious threat to business, commenting that firms 'get off easier than expected'. Indeed, her study found that OSHA regulation, frequent inspections, and the severity of enforcement action did not produce dependency on regulatory agencies, driving home the message that the primary responsibility for health and safety lies with the firm.

In this research there appeared to be a better understanding of the controlling rather than constitutive aspects of regulation. The control aspects of regulation were, not surprisingly, best understood by those who had been personally reprimanded by inspectors. Understanding of the constitutive objectives of regulatory law was positively related to the hierarchical position of respondents. There was a similar hierarchical pattern to knowledge of the regulatory structures in place for occupational health and safety and of the approach of the Railway Inspectorate. So again there was not strong evidence that everyone was participating in health and safety regulation. But there is some evidence that a significant minority across all levels of the industry had some awareness of the Railway Inspectorate and knew of inspectors' visits. Also on the subject of legal action there was a feeling among half of those questioned that all could—and even should—be held responsible for non-compliance.

What is clear from the data is that, despite attempts to constitute health and safety regulation and risk management as part of everyone's lives and everyday activities, there were still demands for some outside policing. Indeed some likened this to more general policing in society. But the purpose of this policing—like the regulatory objectives of the Railway Inspectorate—was not to 'catch out' those not complying with the law but rather with a view to ordering, that is, to keeping health and safety prominently on the industry or company's agenda. Thus inspectors' visits were generally found to be useful and respondents thought that the Railway Inspectorate was an important influence on health and safety and some wanted them to be tougher. Obviously there is a delicate balance to be maintained between self-regulation and policing by an external agency. The whole rationale of Robens and the HSW Act, 1974, was that the Inspectorate should just be a check on what industry ought to be doing for itself, and that the responsibility for health and safety lies with the regulated.[30]

The social dimensions of knowledge and understanding were striking. Senior railway personnel had the most contact with the Railway Inspectorate but this is partly an artefact of organization. Inspecting officers and senior railway officials were both in charge of policy decisions, decisions about capital expenditure, and a much wider remit than occupational health and safety, and moreover they were few in number. Railway employment inspectors, whose remit solely centred on occupational health and safety, were only fifteen in number and had to cover the entire rail network. It is therefore not surprising that they were not

---

[30] This is true of many other industrialized countries, for example, Australia, Canada, and the United States.

well known by many of the thousands of railway employees they regulated, who would only encounter them occasionally if at all. It is also the case that when staff did meet inspectors they did not fully understand who they were talking to. Perhaps of most concern for the objective of participative regulation is the finding that safety representatives did not appear to interact with inspectors very much or be very knowledgeable about the regulatory structure.[31] This said, they did generally know more than the workforce and sometimes were more knowledgeable than supervisors. This suggests that some of the participative objectives of occupational health and safety regulation were being met, but the ignorance evident among the workforce may indicate that there was still an element of paternalism evident in the system.

A significant anomaly in this social patterning was the lack of centrally held organizational knowledge. For instance, there was no centrally held record of legal action against the company for health and safety offences. Moreover there were no procedures in place to process such information; it simply was not collated. This does not seem to offer great support to models of corporate behaviour and regulation which suggest that corporations are either coherent organizations or that they so fear the criminal sanction that they will act to avoid it. Crucially there is little evidence that the legal sanction is much feared or has a great impact. Indeed, whether or not legal action was regarded as 'bad news' itself emerged as a research question. Questions about the impact of legal action suggested that this varied according to the perceived fairness of the case. If a prosecution was not considered fair then there would be no adverse consequences for the individuals concerned. But if the prosecution was regarded as fair then it would affect an individual's career.

Another aspect of the social patterning of knowledge was departmental, although this was not such a strong trend as the hierarchical one. On general issues such as an awareness of occupational health and safety laws, civil engineering staff were the most aware and operations staff the least aware. When more local issues were involved, such as knowledge of the local railway employment inspector, mechanical and electrical engineering staff were the most aware and signals and telecommunications staff the least aware. This was interesting in two main respects. The second observation suggests that the level of geographic dispersal of staff influenced their awareness, so we might have expected mechanical and electrical engineering staff to know more about local goings-on as they were workshop based whereas signals and telecommunications staff were widely dispersed and working much more on their own, typically in pairs or gangs of three. Civil engineering staff were also dispersed but they were also the most at risk, so their awareness of the more general issues may be related to this and in particular to the very great efforts their Department put into increasing their awareness of risk management issues. These are all issues which we

---

[31] See Hutter (1993) for discussion of this. See Chapter 6 for more discussion of participative regulation.

need to bear in mind when considering awareness of company risk management programmes (Ch. 6), the communication of risk (Ch. 8), and in discussing issues of compliance and risk awareness (Chs. 9 and 10).

We also need to reiterate that knowledge of regulation need not be a pre-requisite for compliance with it. This may be particularly so in a system of enforced self-regulation where the company is expected to put sophisticated risk management systems into place. In short, it may be that ignorance of the regulations may be explained by the fact that corporate risk management systems are the primary reference point for many employees. The next part will turn its attention to this and consider the impact of regulation on BR, in particular the risk management systems it instituted in response to regulation.

PART III

THE IMPACT OF REGULATION: THE MANAGEMENT OF RISK

6

Industry Enforced Self-Regulation

The Health and Safety at Work etc. Act (HSW Act), 1974, instituted a system of enforced self-regulation which placed primary responsibility for health and safety with industry. It charged companies with risk management responsibilities which ideally involved companies in developing risk management systems and rules to secure compliance and also entailed worker participation (Ch. 6). But, as Dawson *et al.* (1988: 44) warn, the creation of health and safety structures and procedures within a company is an 'imperfect measure' which does not in itself indicate an improvement in health and safety. Indeed their own case studies demonstrated that compliance with the formalities did not necessarily indicate 'a serious and established concern to improve standards of health and safety' (1988: 87). There is therefore a need to consider the impact of these structures in terms of the difference they make at an everyday level. As Stone (1975) comments, the key task is to make bureaucracies think like responsible individuals, so the systems and decision-making processes they institute are critical.

In this chapter we will consider the internal systems BR put in place in compliance with the legislation and will assess how these regulatory systems operated. The research tried to discern how much employees knew about the company's own systems, rules, and procedures for health and safety. Attention was paid to staff knowledge and perceptions of BR's written policies and to the company's systems for promoting the health and safety of the workforce. In particular it focused on the checks that existed for ensuring that the policies were implemented and on the organizational structures in place for the promotion, enforcement, and review of the health and safety of the workforce.

The Law

Section 2 of the HSW Act, 1974, outlines the general duties of employers towards employees. The most general dictate is by now familiar, namely 'It shall be the duty of every employer to ensure so far as is reasonably practicable, the health, safety and welfare at work of all his employees'. The duties outlined thereafter imply the need for internal systems and procedures to ensure corporate compliance with these duties. While there is ambiguity about what constitutes compliance, especially with the general duties specified in the legislation (Hutter, 1997), the legal mandate does give fairly clear guidance about what is required at a procedural and institutional level from corporations. As we saw in

Chapter 4, these are specified in more detail in HSC guidance literature (*Advice to Employers*). They include regular inspections; the examination and testing of plant; monitoring of the work environment; the establishment of systems of work; cleaning; repair and maintenance; emergency procedures; and workplace audits. Procedures are also required for the provision of safety equipment; training and retraining; and information for employees (see Ch. 7).

Section 2(3) of the HSW Act, 1974, requires employers to provide a safety policy which explains the company's health and safety policy and the organization and arrangements in place to implement the policy. This involves companies providing a written statement of general intent which includes details of the systems they have set up to ensure that they fulfil their health and safety duties. In particular it is expected that health and safety responsibilities are assigned to people at all levels of an organization and that the document will include the names, roles, and location of these people. It is also expected that this policy be revised and updated as necessary and brought to the attention of all employees. So the legal mandate in effect requires companies to institute basic systems and procedures for promoting health and safety at work. Section 2 also provides for the appointment of safety representatives (sect. 2 (6)) and safety committees (sect. 2(7)). These will be considered in more detail in the next chapter.

Internal Arrangements for Health and Safety on BR

BR responded to the structural and procedural requirements of occupational health and safety legislation in a variety of ways and at a number of different levels of the organization. BRB had overall responsibility for the railways and in this capacity they issued a Statement of Safety Policy for the entire network plus a Statement of General Arrangements for Health and Safety. One of the joint managing directors had a remit which included health and safety and there was also a director of safety with a specialized remit for health and safety.[1] This director had a small staff (the health and safety unit). He was responsible for BRB policy and advice which involved him in chairing health and safety committees, and membership of the Board's Safety Advisory Committee, the Railway Industry Advisory Committee, and the Safety Review Group. Health and safety was also part of the remit of the other Board members who implemented the general policy in their more specialist areas.

BRB's *Statement of Safety Policy* in 1988 read as follows:

1. The Policy of the British Railways Board in respect of safety is to conduct its affairs so as to ensure, so far as is reasonably practicable, the health, safety and welfare of

---

[1] During the period of fieldwork, responsibility for occupational health and safety moved from the remit of the Director of Employee Relations to that of the former Chief Medical Officer (who was renamed Director of Occupational Health and Safety).

employees and to protect customers, contractors and other persons who may be affected by its activities.

Safety is an essential part of management and the application of this Policy is a prime responsibility.

To this end, the Board is determined to take every step necessary to discharge the duties laid down by the HSW Act, 1974, other relevant legislation and under common law.

It shall be the duty of all employees to take reasonable care for the health and safety of themselves and other persons who may be affected by their acts of omissions at work.

Apart from this general responsibility, certain managers have specific health and safety responsibilities in the execution of their functional duties.

2. Managing Directors, General Managers and certain Directors have the responsibility for the implementation and maintenance of measures designed to achieve this Policy. This will include setting safety objectives with standards, against which performance will be monitored.

3. Managers at all levels are required to identify risks to the health and safety of employees and others and to develop and maintain safe systems of work, for which specialist advice will be available as necessary.

4. The Board's instructions defining operating, technical and engineering standards (e.g. The Rule Book, General Appendix, Working Manual and all Codes of Practice) form an integral part of this Safety Policy.

5. This Policy cannot be achieved solely by management. Therefore, regular discussions with recognised Trade Unions on health and safety matters are afforded a high priority and an essential requirement is the support and co-operation of all employees.

6. The Board is committed to the provision of such information and training as may be necessary to enable all employees to carry out their duties without risk to the health and safety of themselves or others.

7. This Policy and the arrangements for its implementation will be brought to the attention of all employees and will be kept under review.

The Statement of General Arrangements for Health and Safety explained that local Safety Statements should include detailed arrangements for the implementation of these policies. This included the specific responsibilities of individual managers. Thirteen areas were discussed in this document namely information; training; safe systems of work; design; plant and equipment; protective clothing, safety appliances and equipment; accident reporting and investigation; joint discussions on safety matters; first aid at work; safety inspection; contractors and other persons on BR's premises; accommodation and amenity standards; and monitoring safety performance.

BRB therefore provided a general mission statement about corporate commitment to occupational health and safety and it set up very broad guidance about how this intention could be translated into action. But the actual implementation was very much left to each department. Beyond this the company's rule books and manuals served as additional safety devices. Indeed these were the traditional means of incorporating health and safety into everyday routines. The lessons learnt following accidents often resulted in amendments to the rule book and non-compliance with the rule book was typically a disciplinary offence. The rule book and safety manuals were an accumulation of 'wisdom' and as a consequence they were rather voluminous. Moreover they were also a traditional device for instilling health and safety as a line-management responsibility consistent, as it turned out, with the Robens philosophy.

Departments had their own specialist safety departments nominally headed by the director but administered on a day-to-day basis by specialist safety staff under the direction of a safety officer. These departments typically had a *regional* organization but there was variation between departments. Within BR each department was left to implement the general health and safety commitment in its own way, so as a consequence there was no standardization of response across the organization. Each of the departments in my sample had a specialist safety department. Typically the safety role was combined with responsibility for training, reflected for example in the signals and telecommunications department in the title 'training and safety engineer'. These staff were all recruited from within BR, their own safety training usually amounting to a 5-week Royal Society for the Prevention of Accidents (ROSPA) course. These staff worked direct to the departmental director and each had a very small staff. Their regional organization varied. The mechanical and electrical engineering department, for example, had a safety manager based at the Railway Technical Centre in Derby and two outbased safety engineers; the civil engineering department had one training and safety officer in each region; the operations department had specialist staff in some regions and not others; and the signals and telecommunications department were in the process of changing from a sophisticated training and safety organization which encompassed headquarters staff and outbased engineers to a new organization which involved no regional specialist health and safety staff. This was intentional and derived from the director's view:

> I don't believe that with all levels in an organization you should have safety engineers because otherwise you can encourage line managers to abdicate that responsibility. If you do it that way you have got to make sure that you have got independent audits in place. This department is the only one that hasn't got safety engineers at regional level . . . but we consciously did that because of my very strong views that as long as 'X' [the technical and safety officer] is issuing very clear, simple, and precise instructions to the appropriate levels of staff we are more likely to get it embedded in everyday line management.

The primary responsibility for health and safety was not generally seen to be located with specialist departments and staff, but with line managers. The whole ethos of the BRB and departmental safety policies was to define line management responsibilities. So each *local area* had its own safety statement, running to some twenty to thirty pages, which was meant to be regularly updated by local managers, for whom health and safety was part of their more general remit. Specialist staff were there to provide general guidance and advice. Generally speaking one did not get the impression that they held high status within the organization. Their authority derived from their working direct to the departmental director, while their influence derived from their own personal zeal and commitment and the extent to which the director was prepared to take an interest in occupational health and safety. This was a reflexive relationship and one which could readily change according to circumstances or a change of personnel. For example, a change of director could prove quite influential upon the status of health and safety issues.

It should be observed that consideration of the role of specialist safety staff can help us to understand company structures for occupational health and safety more clearly. This is not a well-researched topic. Edelman *et al.* (1991), in their discussion of affirmative action officers, attribute specialist personnel a central role in forming organizational responses to law. Rees (1988: 112) likewise describes the role of the safety department as that of 'nurturing and developing' management's sense of responsibility about health and safety. But other research suggests that the influence of safety departments and safety officers is highly contingent on a variety of factors. Beaumont *et al.* (1982) note the importance of ascertaining the safety officer's status within an organization; whether or not they are full-time; whether they are part of a specialist safety department; and who they report to. Whatever their position these specialist personnel are likely to be in an ambiguous position. Edelman *et al.* (1991) explain that they are at the call of many clients and the potential sources of conflict are multiple also. Structurally they are part of management but their remit requires them to act also on behalf of particular sections of the organization, in this case all employees. In turn this may reduce the effectiveness of these departments, if indeed they were ever intended to be effective. Edelman argues that organizations may create 'symbolic structures' which 'appear attentive to law . . . and at the same time, seek to minimize law's constraints on traditional managerial prerogative' (Edelman *et al.*, 1991: 75). This, of course, is the crucial question—how effective are the structures in place to promote occupational health and safety? In the case of specialist safety staff, as with the rest of the safety approach, there was the potential for variation, something already noted in the existing literature. Leopold and Beaumont (1982) highlight the differential effects of safety policies whereas Dawson *et al.* (1988: 117) discerned wide variations in the attitudes and expectations of safety departments in large construction companies. But these other studies of course considered differences *between* companies whereas this study is focusing on differences *within* the same company.

The policies and structures were not the only BR health and safety initiatives. Running alongside the hierarchical structures for health and safety were training programmes and documentary sources of information such as videos, posters, publications, and a variety of general and local health and safety campaigns. There were also monitoring procedures. At the time of data collection this primarily involved inspections and safety audits. There was also great variability in the provision and sophistication of all of these between departments and regions.

The safety committee structure revolved around the initiatives for worker participation. At a national level there was the Railway Industry Advisory Committee (RIAC) comprising railway company directors, national union representatives, and HSE staff.[2] There were also BR health and safety committees at Board level and regional level. The regional safety committees were the committees one might except to be most well known as they were the most locally based of these committees. One regional safety committee I attended comprised ten BR staff representing the functional departments and ten union officials from the three main unions (ASLEF, NUR, and TSSA). The BR staff were regional managers and the union staff a mixture of regional and national staff. The committee was chaired by the regional employee relations manager. The meetings were held every three months and they discussed a variety of issues. For example, one of the meetings I attended discussed a number of recurring items such as the dates for safety seminars, accident statistics for the previous three months, and ongoing safety campaigns. It also discussed specific topics such as the provision and cleanliness of welfare accommodation, assaults on staff, the safety of contract staff, and visual display units (VDUs) and their safety.[3]

A Period of Change

The research period was a period of change. This was largely because of the enormous spotlight thrown onto health and safety by the Clapham Junction accident in 1988. Whereas the BRB *Annual Report and Accounts 1987/88* did not refer to health and safety at all, 1991 saw the publication of a very glossy, state of the art *Safety Plan*: 'The Safety Plan brings together all the key initiatives that are currently being pursued to improve the safety of the railway. The scale and breadth of the effort being devoted to safety is enormous. The changes required will touch every one of our staff' (Chairman's foreword, 1991: 3).

This accident plus the aftermath of the King's Cross fire on the London Underground prompted a move towards more sophisticated risk management systems and safety audits and the publication of an annually updated Safety Plan:

---

[2] See Dawson *et al.* (1988: 189 ff.) for a discussion of Advisory Committees.

[3] Walters and Gourlay (1990) noted a fall in the number of safety committees in Britain, the proportion dropping from 80% in 1980 to 70% in 1990. The loss was incurred by smaller companies so BR was, as expected, still in compliance in its provision of committees. BR also appears to contradict the more general findings of these authors to the extent that they found that meetings were more frequent in the private rather than public sectors and three-monthly visits may be regarded as frequent.

British Rail's Safety Management Programme during 1991 . . . is concerned with revising the safety management and committee structure, instituting regular safety meetings at all levels of the organization, correcting unsafe conditions and physical hazards and further development of a comprehensive safety management training programme. (ibid. 8)

Indeed the impetus of the King's Cross and Clapham accidents was acknowledged in the Plan:

A series of accidents—King's Cross, Clapham Junction, Zeebrugge and Hillsborough has resulted in a new approach to risk management and safety. On BR, the recommendations of these inquiries have been analysed in detail and have led to the formation of proposals to reduce risk. The approach to safety has been altered by these accidents and the lessons learned through the painstaking inquiries have helped to shape the strategy described in this Plan. (ibid. 4–5)

During the research period many of the initiatives were still being formulated at the most senior levels of the company and had not filtered down through the middle and lower ranks of the organization.

Knowledge of BR Health and Safety Policies

There was a cascade of safety policies filtering down through the company's organization. In accordance with the HSW Act, 1974, the policies included a written statement of general health and safety policy; a statement of the organization and arrangements for implementing the policy; procedures for revising the policy; and procedures for bringing it to the attention of employees. The research tried to discern if staff knew of any BRB official policies regarding the health and safety of the workforce and if so the extent of their knowledge.

The large majority of all staff were aware that BR had occupational health and safety policies. The greatest ignorance was among the workforce but even here 80 per cent knew that the policies existed.[4] The extent of their knowledge was more variable. Questioning tried to discern if respondents could refer to documentary sources; if they could offer details of policy content; and in the case of supervisors, workforce, and safety representatives if they knew where they could find copies of any relevant documents should they need to refer to them. *Managers* were able to refer to documentary sources but they were less clear about the contents of these policies. Sixty-two per cent were able to offer details of what was contained in the policy document but several managers said that they were vague about BR health and safety policies and volunteered that they had never read them.

---

[4] While there were no striking differences between departments there were differences between grades of staff. So all *managers* knew that BR had policies for health and safety and so, with one exception, did all *supervisors*. Eighty per cent of the workforce knew that policies existed compared to 89% of *safety representatives*.

Most *supervisors* knew where to find copies of health and safety documentation should they need them but only just over half of them could cite any relevant documents. Furthermore only 7 of the 24 (29 per cent) questioned could offer any details of policy content and all of these responses were vague:

> I haven't really looked at the policy documents but I imagine they are sort of commonsense. (supervisor, interviewee 58)

> . . . there's a health and safety document produced by management, there's a copy in the office where they can all see it. (supervisor, interviewee 87)

A similar pattern is revealed among the *workforce* although the degree and sophistication of knowledge were markedly lower than among supervisors: 49 per cent of the workforce knew where to find health and safety documents; 38 per cent were able to cite documentary sources; but only 14 per cent could offer any details, however scanty— 'I assume they're common-sense, look after yourself and don't do nothing stupid' (worker, interviewee 30). *Safety representatives* offered a more consistent set of responses—10 of the 22 interviewed could cite documentary sources; 10 of the 22 offered details of the policies; and 11 of the 22 knew where to find the policies.

A wide range of documentary sources of health and safety information were referred to by those interviewed. The most frequently mentioned were as shown in Table 6.1. In addition to these, a variety of other documents were mentioned by just a few respondents, including the legislation, departmental instructions, safety data sheets, weekly notices, and posters. Managers were the most likely to refer to Board and local policy statements whereas most members of the workforce and safety representatives who could refer to documentary sources most frequently mentioned the rule book. Supervisors referred to five main documentary sources which in descending order of frequency were local policy documents; health and safety booklets; the rule book; BRB policy; and 'policy booklets'.

TABLE 6.1. Documentary sources of health and safety mentioned by BR interviewees

Document	No. of references
BRB policy statement	17
Local policy statement	29
Generic reference to 'safety policy document/statement'	3
The rule book	20
Health and safety booklets/leaflets	12

Expectations

The overwhelming majority of respondents did not expect their staff and colleagues to know the company's health and safety policies.[5] Managers, supervisors, and safety representatives were considered the most likely to know:

> I suspect people don't know, it's [BRB safety policy] just a general statement for what is 140,000 staff. (manager, interviewee 5)

> I: Do you think that your staff know what these policies are?
>
> R: I don't think that health and safety even occurs to them. I put this document in all the mess rooms and whenever anybody books on and off and I'm sure, well I'd be very surprised, if more than one or two people have ever got it out and actually looked at it. Most people don't even think about it, they expect the management to look after them. And I think generally from our department's point of view we do, because we're a safety department anyway—we're dealing with safety of the trains. (manager, interviewee 110)

> Management should know and so should safety reps, there should be no excuse. The statements are circulated and there are the safety reps. It is a very high profile activity and it has been from the start. (manager, interviewee 121)

To a large extent these expectations were confirmed by my findings, although the extent of knowledge held by safety representatives was overestimated by respondents. It was, of course, interesting that there was an expectation that employees would *not* know the railway's policies for the health and safety of the workforce. Why this was so was partly revealed later by examining the views expressed about the existing policies. But let us now consider how the responses of BR staff compared with the hopes and expectations of the seven *directors* and four *departmental safety officers*.

This group varied in their expectations: five of the directors interviewed expected all staff to have some knowledge of the company's health and safety policies. In particular, they hoped that all staff would know the broad statement of responsibilities and overall philosophy of the policy statements. Three hoped for a much more detailed response from all levels of staff, for example, they expected reference to both the Board policy statement and local policy statements, the rule book, safety manuals, and the existence of safety representatives. The two other directors adopted a minimalist approach. Neither was very concerned about all staff having a detailed knowledge of the policies. One hoped that managers would know about the policies in some detail. But both were much more concerned that the staff knew what they should be doing and that they did it safely. Their emphasis was much more upon the rule book and line management

---

[5] Only 18% expected others to know the policies while 54% considered that most or all of the staff would not know. The remainder expected that some staff would know something about health and safety but that levels of knowledge would vary.

responsibilities for health and safety rather than reference to the formal policies: 'If the people who should be able to understand the Safety Policy Statement do understand it there's no real need for the man on the ground to know anything more than he has to do A, B and C or he has to report D, E and F'.

Five directors expected staff to know whose responsibility health and safety was but they disagreed as to the answer: three hoped that staff would understand that health and safety was the responsibility of everyone; one referred to management and union responsibility; and one perceived it as the prime responsibility of management.

Only one director believed that staff awareness of the policies would approximate to his own expectations, although he acknowledged that the health aspects of the policies were unlikely to be as well understood as those concerning safety. Of the other five directors who expressed an opinion about staff awareness, one suspected that the majority would not know the policies. Indeed, he confessed 'I don't think I am terribly clear either, sitting here cold and unprepared'. The others thought that staff awareness would vary according to the interest of individuals but in particular according to the interest of local managers and supervisors. All directors were concerned that there may be deficiencies in the knowledge and understanding of staff. In particular, there was concern that 'perceptions may be grey in slightly higher levels of management that should know'.

Departmental safety managers held fairly unanimous expectations. They hoped that staff were aware of the policies and could give a broad statement of the general principles contained in the policy documents. The documents they expected staff to refer to varied. Three expected reference to the Board's policy statement and three hoped that the local policy document would be cited. One considered the local policy document to be the most important document for all staff while another would not have been concerned if staff did not mention it at all, although he would prefer that they knew the 'spirit' of the document. This manager regarded the rule book as the major document and hoped that this would be mentioned as a 'bare minimum' by everyone.

Safety managers were divided over what they expected staff to be aware of. Two thought that staff would know the policies and rules, the other two were less confident and believed it unlikely that staff would know the policies. One thought that whereas staff might know the policies and rule book when they joined the railways, they probably did not know them any longer. He stressed the importance of refresher courses which were mentioned as important in this context by three of the four safety managers.

Views about Policies

Staff views about company health and safety policies were often detailed and extensive, especially among managers. In three of the four departments respondents were fairly well balanced in terms of the praise and criticisms offered, but in the case of the civil engineers the responses were highly critical. Generally the *aims* of the policies attracted most positive comments. Hence policies were regarded as necessary, good in their intentions, and an improvement on the past. The local policy documents were singled out for particular praise by a few respondents because it was felt that they were directed to everyday situations and made sense to the workforce.

There was, however, a high degree of cynicism about the *intentions* of the policies. The most frequently expressed view among all grades of staff was that one of the most important functions of the policy statements was to remove responsibility for the health and safety of the workforce away from the Board. Two points are important here. First is that the view was expressed quite spontaneously by nearly 25 per cent of the sample, in response to an open question about their views. Secondly, the critics did not suggest that the Board was aiming to enter into a partnership with their staff to promote health and safety but rather that they perceived the Board to be 'buck passing' (a common phrase):

> ... basically it's [the rule book] the railway's insurance if anything goes wrong, to claim that we've got, that if we haven't abided by, that Rule Book then we haven't got a leg to stand on. (worker, interviewee 23)

> I think in the majority, well many, cases they [BR policies] are unworkable and they are done to protect the Board against anything that the men might do . . . . It is the same as our rule book. The rule book is there so that when something goes wrong the blame can always be picked up at a very low level which unfortunately is something a lot of the men believe as well . . . (manager, interviewee 74)

> There is still a tendency for a 'them' and 'us' attitude. Whereas they are trying to take their responsibility and say 'it is your responsibility' and we are trying to say 'no, it's your responsibility' rather than looking at the thing as a whole and saying 'safety is everybody's responsibility'. (safety representative, interviewee 123)

The *content* of the policies was complimented by some as being reasonable and sensible. The main points of criticism related to the way in which the content was communicated and the use made of the policies. However, one person's criticism was another's compliment. For example, whereas some respondents praised the policies for being extensive and comprehensive, a major criticism of others was that they were too extensive and indigestible. Whereas a manager may find the policy documents extensive and comprehensive, the workforce (and even supervisors) may find them very difficult to comprehend:

> ... at times we go overboard . . . and seem to relieve people of their individual responsibility to use a bit of common-sense. (manager, interviewee 20)

R: They're [the policies] much too detailed really. I think there's a terrific amount of stuff that's passed down . . . have you seen the Civil Engineering Manual? It embraces all the safety work I do . . .

I: What do you think of the drawbacks of them being too detailed?

R: It is too detailed—it makes it pretty indigestible. First of all managers have got to have the time to look through all of this, you're an academic and reading all of this could be quite off-putting for you I would suggest. But from the Board, let's be frank, it looks as though they are covering themselves . . . which is a pretty human thing to do. But it all comes down in the end to some supervisor . . . I suppose if you can wade your way through it, there's references, indexes, indices, and things . . . but in the imperfect world we have there are so many other pressures on him that he's going to be a very good man indeed if he knows about it and is in strict compliance with it . . . . So what I would say about it is that on paper it's fine, it's all sorted out nicely, the problem is expecting and getting people to comply with it all. (manager, interviewee 62)

Communication emerged as a key issue. The clear majority of those interviewed felt that polices should be directed to and accessible to everyone. But difficulties in this area were identified. The accessibility of documentary sources was particularly criticized. One respondent explained 'the policies are well intentioned but not aimed at the right level for the majority of people that work on the railway' (worker, interviewee 47). Specific problems were seen to be the amount of the written material available and the way in which it was written. There was perceived to be too much paperwork which was difficult to understand, uninteresting, and unreasonable. This reiterates the literature on the law, where clarity emerges as a key factor in encouraging compliance (see Ch. 5). Directors and specialist health and safety staff were aware of the difficulties:

My own view is that displaying policies on the noticeboard is wholly insufficient. I have seen these policies over many years and if they remain and they are not torn up for something else they are illegible, grubby, maybe they've been in the sun and the sun has removed all the photocopy print. No I don't believe it's sufficient to simply display them. I think that there has to be regular safety seminars just to bring them to the highlights of the staff. (safety officer)

Clearly the first thing to consider is that when you take somebody on new you need to train them and you have got the basic instructions in these publications . . . it is not sufficient just to hand them over, they need a lot of explanation for their guidance. But there shouldn't be any doubts and of course we need to make sure that knowledge is refreshed from time to time. (safety officer)

Managers cited particular difficulties with keeping the documents up to date. These criticisms most often came from managers who had recently experienced changes in either their organizational remit or their geographical boundaries:

The local policy statement can be difficult to keep up to date. It shouldn't be difficult but it becomes another administrative call, task . . . If you aren't watching it every week you tend to suddenly find that someone's changed and you haven't issued an amendment, every year or two years we go through the whole thing, then it's fine. But that soon becomes out of date. (manager, interviewee 5)

We have a cascade of statements, we start off with a Board policy statement. We also have local policy statements that are currently being revised into a different form. Many of our local policy statements are not up to date, a lot of them were done in the late 1970s when health and safety first got through to us. We have not been rigid in updating them nor in filling in the various appendices properly. Often we have taken a standard model and just duplicated it. (manager, interviewee 66)

The availability of documents was another area of concern among some respondents and one which was most frequently mentioned as an explanation of why staff were not aware of the policies. Fifty-one per cent of respondents at workforce level did not know where they could find health and safety policy documents. A counter-argument to this was offered by a cross-section of staff who believed that staff were not aware of the policies because they were not interested. Whether or not this alleged disinterest was a result of ignorance is something we will return to later.

The use made of the policies was the final and main point of criticism. Lack of enforcement was perceived as the primary concern in this category. A quotation sums up the argument well—a manager offered the following opinion about the Rule Book: 'it's just a book that sits in a drawer or on a shelf, the use of which is quietly ignored by people on day to day operations. It has to be a living document and one that has credibility' (manager, interviewee 81). This is a strong statement and for many it may overstate the case. Nevertheless it does highlight the importance of enforcement and reveal that a failure to enforce the documentation is perceived as a signal of 'disinterest' from above. Indeed it was these problems of accessibility and enforcement that seemed to lead the critics to regard health and safety policies as a form of 'buck passing'. It is perhaps not surprising that the effectiveness of safety policies is regarded as dependent upon implementation: 'Policy statements can contain the most pious of intentions but are worthless unless an organization structure is created to implement the objectives and unless progress is systematically monitored' (Leopold and Beaumont, 1982: 24). Again this reiterates the findings of the literature on the effectiveness of the law discussed in Chapter 5, notably that enforcement is crucial.

Other less frequently expressed criticisms of the policies related to their practicality. A minority of respondents found the policies hard to implement and others believed that they increased the difficulty of the job, sometimes leading to short-cuts. A more specific problem, again cited by a minority, was that there could be problems in follow-up action when problems were identified, particularly when there was a reliance on another department to remedy the problem. There was also the view that policy documents should be regarded as secondary:

It is not simply something enshrined in documents, it is an ethos . . . there is only one way to do a job and that is safely . . . I see that it is something that is enshrined in everything we do, it is enshrined in every piece of cleaning equipment or cleaning raw material that we use, handling instructions and all that kind of thing. But the policy document is the one that is obvious . . . but I think that is simply a statement of what we believe is the way of doing a job. (manager, interviewee 25)

There is the health and safety document that came out ages ago, which is about as much use as a pound of wet tripe in terms of its principles and theory . . . Also the documents that have tried to go down to the more mundane things have ended up making themselves unreadable, that they switch anybody off and frankly you don't have the time to read them, the only time I have ever had to read these documents was when I have been on a course. (manager, interviewee 27)

The views of *directors* and *departmental safety managers* reflected very accurately the views of their staff, namely they considered that the aims of the policies were good on paper but it was felt that there were a number of deficiencies thereafter. Two in this group believed that there was a danger that the written policies made the Board look as if it was 'carrying out the letter rather than the spirit of the law'. Moreover they also recognized that it might even look as if the intention of the policies was to remove as much responsibility as possible from the Board to employees. This was partly because there was so much paperwork and partly because the original statement, at least, was written in a legalistic way. This line of reasoning was of course familiar following the discussion of staff views of the policies. Both of these criticisms related to communication and this was identified as a paramount problem by all seven directors and by the safety managers. One stated that there was a 'lack of communication downwards, upwards, and sideways'. The difficulties in communicating downwards through the hierarchy was emphasized by two directors, both of whom also referred to a dilution of policies as they were communicated through the system. One director explained:

I think the policies in themselves are reasonably soundly based. I think that statements that the Board make are not made lightly and are in fact able to be implemented given the right will of the people throughout the industry. I think occasionally we tend to forget that there is a gap, quite a wide gap, between the chappie who is relatively unskilled or the woman who is relatively unskilled and what is a fairly intellectual piece of paper. That is no excuse to chuck a piece of paper out and assume that the people receiving that piece of paper one, understand it and secondly, can run with it once they have got it. So I think that the policy is good and I think the theory of implementation is fine but I think the further it gets away from the policy to understanding how the person on the ground level actually runs with it, I think it gets diluted on the way (director).

Language difficulties were referred to by several respondents in this group. They emphasized the need to write the policies and rules in language which supervisors and the workforce could understand and communicate. Simplicity of language was perceived by one safety manager as being one way of increasing the likelihood that the documents would be readable and comprehensible. Clarity in the documentation was considered equally important. Several directors regarded this as the key to ensuring that managers and supervisors knew exactly what was required of them. They argued for clear procedures and instructions which could be readily assimilated and applied. In short, they were aiming for what one director described as 'a message that people can pick up and work with'.

Managers were identified as the other main obstacle to the successful communication and implementation of the policies. The most common worry was that managers did not perceive safety as an integral part of their job, regarding it as 'separate and almost voluntary' or at best as low on the list of priorities— 'You have got to imbibe awareness of the legislation within your line management'. Supervisors were singled out for particular criticism by several respondents. One commented that they should rediscover their role as first line management, whereas another detected a reluctance among some supervisors, especially the older ones, to hold team meetings and let their staff know what was going on. Two argued that too much reliance was placed on managers and that supervisors were unfairly apportioned responsibility. Moreover it was generally acknowledged that the documentation was not always easy to assimilate and communicate. It was also remarked that managers should recognize the worth of supervisors and should encourage them to take an interest in their staff.

Several respondents suggested that alternative or supplementary means of communication should be considered to the documentation. Suggestions here included the use of videos or more training courses. Only one director identified enforcement as a problem area.

Knowledge of Systems

Staff were asked a variety of questions about company systems for health and safety, including general questions about whether or not they knew of any checks there might be that health and safety policies were adhered to and more detailed questions about particular types of checks and about responsibility for health and safety within the company.

Awareness of checks on compliance with policies was socially structured, largely according to grade of staff. All managers were aware of checks and so were the majority of supervisors and safety representatives. But only 62 per cent of the workforce knew that there were checks that the policies and rules were adhered to. At a departmental level civil engineers were most aware of checks and mechanical and electrical engineering staff the least aware.[6] This could be a result of their differing work environments. Checks and inspections might be less in evidence in a workshop than on site. Nevertheless it was only respondents from this department who commented that they knew of inspections by railway employment inspectors in advance.

More detailed questioning tried to discern what type of checks were known about. Inspections were the most common form of check mentioned by managers from all departments. Half of the managers interviewed referred to general inspections being the only check whereas a quarter referred to specific health and safety inspections and the remaining quarter cited both. Only 4 of the 28 managers interviewed about this referred to joint inspection with safety representatives, while safety audits were mentioned by just 6 managers.

Supervisors, safety representatives, and the workforce were typically unspecific about the form of the checks. The large majority referred to proactive checks, usually inspections. Equipment and paperwork checks and examinations were also mentioned. A small minority perceived the checks to be solely reactive, taking place only once something had gone wrong.

Respondents generally believed checks to be the responsibility of managers and supervisors. The exceptions were safety representatives who typically identified a joint responsibility between management and unions. This suggests that the participative objectives of regulation were not fully comprehended and possibly not practised. This issue, as we might expect, re-emerged in response to other questions.

Workplace Inspections

Managers, supervisors, and safety representatives were asked more specific follow-up questions about workplace inspections. Managers and supervisors typically referred to daily or ad hoc general inspections. Joint union–management inspections were mentioned to a lesser extent (by 23% of managers and 13% of supervisors), with some managers explaining that they could not undertake these inspections because they had no safety representatives (see Ch. 7). Perhaps most surprising is the number of managers and supervisors who claimed that they did not undertake inspections at all:

I: How often do you undertake workplace inspections?
R: Not as often as I commit myself to in the document . . . fallen by the wayside. I do visit, have a casual glance around but nothing formal. (manager, interviewee 75)

Twenty-three per cent of the managers responding in this way claimed that they were too senior to undertake workplace inspections any more. The 35 per

---

[6] All of the civil engineers knew that checks existed as did 77% of operations staff and 72% of signals and telecommunications staff. In the mechanical and electrical engineering department 40% of supervisors and safety representatives and 62% of the workforce were unaware of any checks.

cent of supervisors not undertaking inspections were from just two depart-ments, namely the operations and signals and telecommunication depart-ments. Safety representatives referred exclusively to joint union–management inspections (see Ch. 7).

Committees

Generally there was very scanty knowledge of the committee structure. Man-agers, supervisors, and safety representatives were asked specifically about joint union–management safety committees. Those who knew anything were most likely to be in the operations department, but differences among grades of staff were the most marked.

Managers were the most likely to know that committees existed. They referred to either the regional safety committees or the local departmental committees. Forty-four per cent of supervisors and 35 per cent of safety rep-resentatives were aware of joint union–management safety committees. Not all of these could name a committee but those who could cited the regional safety committees. Beyond this basic awareness, knowledge of these commit-tees was very hazy. One-third of managers who knew about the committees received minutes of their proceedings. Managers could give details of what was discussed at the meetings but only two safety representatives and one supervisor were able to so this. Very few representatives in any category were able to give more specific details about matters such as the frequency of these meetings, who chaired them, and whether or not there was follow-up action. Very few comments were made about the committees. Those which were offered were with one exception negative, namely that these committees were just a 'talking shop' and that they were perceived by a few to be without authority.

Safety Personnel

BR employed a number of specialist health and safety staff. More generally, all staff held various health and safety responsibilities, especially managerial staff who were typically accorded health and safety responsibilities by BR. The research asked two questions to discover which people within the company were perceived to hold a health and safety remit. The first asked whether or not there was anyone working within BR with health and safety responsibilities. The sec-ond asked managers and supervisors whether or not they received health and safety queries from their staff, while the workforce were asked to whom they would actually refer health and safety problems.

Responses to the first of these questions were notable for their diversity. The only level at which there was any real awareness that there were regional and Board personnel with specific health and safety responsibilities was managerial: 'There's a safety organization which adds expert advice very helpfully when a particular problem arises and does a certain amount of monitoring as well' (manager, interviewee 61). They mentioned regional health and safety officers and Board health and safety officers. There were departmental differences in responses with no one in the operations department referring to their departmental safety officer, whereas in the signals and telecommunications department most managers could refer to the position and also name the officer responsible. This may be explained by the fact that regional signals and telecommunications safety officers had recently been abolished so all correspondence would come direct from the departmental officer, whereas in the operations department regional staff would be likely to be the point of contact.

Apart from references to Board and regional personnel, managers referred to a miscellaneous set of responses ranging from the five managers who were not aware that there was anyone within the company with special responsibility for health and safety to the three who believed that everyone was responsible. Some responses were very vague—'a director at the Board' or 'someone in personnel' or 'We have a health and safety manager I suppose' (manager, interviewee 38). A few managers referred to themselves or their area managers, while safety representatives were identified by three managers as being the responsible persons. Those managers who were aware of their safety departments clearly welcomed them and called them for advice: 'They often pointed things out to me that were so glaringly obvious that I couldn't see the wood for the trees sometimes' (manager, interviewee 86). The removal of regional health and safety staff by the signals and telecommunications department was very much regretted by the staff interviewed. Several managers commented that they had consulted their area safety engineer frequently and had appreciated knowing that there was someone local who knew what he was talking about with health and safety.

Interestingly three managers referred to railway employment inspectors as BR personnel with health and safety responsibilities. They were also mentioned by a minority of supervisors, safety representatives, and members of the workforce. Typically the responses of supervisors, safety representatives, and the workforce were localized, with references to regional personnel and Board members being rare. Supervisors were most likely to refer to safety representatives with a further 37 per cent believing that managers and supervisors held this responsibility. The majority of the workforce thought that there must be someone responsible but did not know who—'I believe that there is someone up at the top but I don't know who it is' (worker, interviewee 16). Of those who did attempt to identify the responsibility, safety representatives were again the most frequently cited group.

Nearly all *safety representatives* were aware that there were BR people with health and safety responsibilities, but specialist staff were rarely mentioned by this group and no reference was made to senior BR staff. Safety representatives were much more inclined to emphasize the responsibilities of managers and supervisors. In light of the perceptions of supervisors and the workforce, it is interesting that only one safety representative considered himself the responsible person.

Reference People within BR

So who do staff approach if they have health and safety problems? In order to answer this question managers and supervisors were asked if they were approached about health and safety matters, and if so what about. The workforce were asked who they would approach if they had a health and safety problem.

The responses of *managers* varied according to the level of their job. Generally the higher the level of the manager the fewer problems he received direct, the expectation being that problems would be resolved at a lower level. Nevertheless all managers, with just three exceptions, had received problems from staff, although just under half qualified this reply by saying that they received very few problems. Not surprisingly the overwhelming majority of *supervisors* professed to receive regular queries about health and safety matters, often from safety representatives. This is of course interesting in light of the findings in Chapter 5 where we found that supervisors were often ignorant of regulatory objectives, regulatory law, and the activities of the Railway Inspectorate. Indeed they often knew less than did safety representatives. Many in the managerial and supervisory group believed that most problems were solved through the system of line management responsibility:

> The area engineers sort their own problems out by and large but at the moment I am chairing what we call the sectional council sub-committee which can receive complaints from the staff on safety issues. So, for example, at the moment I am dealing with a particular staff complaint at 'X'. The staff are complaining about the need for safety footwear to avoid them slipping around . . . The area engineer has heard the complaint from the staff and said that in his view what they want isn't a solution to the problem. If we can talk through this as an example of how I get involved. He has had the safety rep. and they have said that because there is oil on the sleepers they want studs, studded boots, and he has said 'no, this is not going to solve the problem'. It then became an issue through the trade union branch and that has come up to me at the sub-committee and we have discussed it. We have got the regional staff reps. and me talking about it. The first thing I did was call for a site investigation and we have had that and again I've supported what the area engineer has said and said that to issue boots wouldn't solve the problem because it is oil. They are not designed to avoid slipping about on oil. What we want is to eradicate the root problem. We want to stop the oil being dropped there and if it has got to be dropped then we want to get it cleaned up, biodegraded through some process . . . We are getting the civil engineers to attack the root problem and that is how I get involved. (manager, interviewee 107)

Intriguingly the *workforce* rarely mentioned taking problems to managers and supervisors. When they did complain or have queries civil engineering and signals and telecommunications staff were most likely to approach their supervisors. Operations and mechanical and electrical engineering staff were more inclined to refer to their safety representative or union. Some managers perceived a reluctance to complain: 'Railway men have a very macho image and health and safety is mollycoddling them' (manager, interviewee 74).

A few thought that they responded quickly: 'It is important to deal with them promptly. It is important for the staff concerned that I am seen to do what I can to secure their interests' (manager, interviewee 136).

Many of the problems dealt with were described as 'minor', for example, so-called housekeeping problems, 'nuts and bolts' problems. These included hand-rail provision, accommodation problems, the provision of goggles, uneven paths, blocked walkways, slippery paths, lighting, heating, and so on. Alternatively those who might complain did not do so because they were concerned that they might be branded as 'troublemakers'. Nelkin and Brown (1984: 113) also found that whether or not problems were reported depended on the receptivity of managers to complaints.

Directors and *departmental safety officers* generally gave less detailed responses to questions about company systems for health and safety than ones about policy. They all referred to two main checks on policy, namely inspections and audits. Only two referred to joint union–management inspections, the majority thinking of inspections as a managerial task. Inspections were the most frequently cited check on policy by the rest of the sample. Audits however were mentioned by just six managers and nobody else, although as one safety officer explained, this is because their introduction was relatively recent:

> Audit is a word which is coming more and more into being in the last two months. We don't audit, we don't know how to audit, we know what a financial audit is and we have argued over a definition of what an inspection is as opposed to an audit. I am personally going on a course very shortly to find out what ROSPA suggests would be the best to meet our needs, we do need to audit. (safety officer)

Typically those in this group did not undertake *workplace inspections*. Two directors thought that they might undertake these inspections in unusual or special circumstances and one director commented that perhaps he ought to undertake them. None of the safety managers undertook workplace inspections although they expected their specialized staff to undertake some audits and inspections.

Only one director could give a detailed explanation of how he hoped his staff would respond to questions about who within the company had responsibility for health and safety. He hoped that staff would recognize that there were appointed persons within the workplace who were responsible for health and safety and he hoped that some people would be able to identify these local personnel. They should further know that the system was a joint one undertaken in partnership with the unions. He would expect first approaches to be made to safety representatives and the first line of appeal to be to local management. The other directors were less detailed in their replies. The two main groups mentioned by these directors were safety representatives and line management. Other groups such as specialized Board, departmental, or regional health and safety personnel or 'everyone' were mentioned by just one director:

> I think that every employee, whether it is the chairman or the trackman at North Berwick, every employee has a responsibility for health and safety of each of those and has a responsibility for our own health and safety. (director)

> There can't be anybody now on British Railways that hasn't seen their safety engineer or safety officer coming around . . . I suppose there are people on British Railways that don't know about safety representatives because you know in an organization as large as this you've got to have an example of just about every possibility . . . how many people don't know who is responsible for health and safety, I think it ain't more than a very, very few. They may not know the names of the person, but they must know a bit, enough about the principles to know that there is a sort of initiative on British Railways. (director)

Departmental safety managers all expected their specialized safety staff to be mentioned and recognized as significant personnel. Only one of these managers expected staff to mention them. More important to all of these safety managers was that functional line managers were held responsible for health and safety.

Directors and safety managers all received problems and queries about health and safety. They all received queries about policy issues or national issues which needed speedy resolution. They also received health and safety queries by virtue of their membership of a senior safety committee or because their functional job was so closely involved with health and safety. Three safety managers also received 'nuts and bolts' problems which should be resolved locally since sometimes all that was needed was reference to safety manuals. They were keen that this should not be their role:

I: Do many people bring health and safety problems to you?
R: Not individual problems, I am more concerned with policy. (safety officer)

Discussion

Generally BR appeared to have complied with the risk management systems demanded by occupational health and safety legislation. It had instituted the structures, procedures, and policies expected in law. Moreover the systems they had in place had been particularly scrutinized following a number of high profile accidents, two of them involving railways, one involving BR. But at the time of this research these effects were felt only at the top of the organization. The data suggest that there were some difficulties in instituting the system, most particularly in updating health and safety policy documents. But overall the structures were in place. The central question, however, was whether or not they worked.

Typically BR safety policies were known about across the railway and better known than occupational health and safety legislation. Variations did emerge, however, in individuals' understanding of the detail of these policies. Indeed these differences were reflected in the expectations of senior officials. It is interesting that directors in particular varied in their expectations, especially with regard to the extent to which they expected staff to know the policies. This said, differences were found between departments and through the hierarchy. The hopes of senior staff regarding staff awareness of the existence of health and safety policies were to a large extent met. But they were not fulfilled when it came to the amount of detail staff would know and a particular concern here was that 38 per cent of managers and 71 per cent of supervisors were not able to relate details of policy content. These findings confirmed the suspicions of directors and two safety managers that staff awareness would not be as complete as they hoped.

While the expectations of directors and departmental safety managers may have been at variance with the rest of the sample, it was notable that their views about the policies were not. Staff of all grades and departments identified common problems with the health and safety policies. Interestingly while the existing literature tends to criticize safety policies for being imprecise and vague, one of the criticisms of the BR documents was that they were too detailed. Indeed communication emerged as a key difficulty, especially where sections of the workforce were not highly educated. It is possible, for example, that accusations of 'buck passing' could be averted in part by improving the communication of health and safety problems. This would involve improvements to the formal policy statements but more particularly the rule book and other safety documents. This is a topic which will be pursued in greater depth in Chapter 8; suffice it to comment for the moment that there appears to be a tension here between producing a document which lawyers believed would satisfy the demands of the legislation and producing a document which was accessible for all levels of staff. Put another way, there is a tension between the constitutive and controlling aspects of regulation.

The second major problem identified with the policies was that of their enforcement. The interviews revealed that the checks that the policies and rules were adhered to were not universally implemented. Indeed it was very clear that knowledge of the health and safety systems in place was patchy. There was also some uncertainty about who was responsible for health and safety on the railways, especially among the workforce. Managers were much more aware of specialized health and safety personnel than the rest of the staff and obviously found their presence reassuring and helpful. Indeed, board-level and departmental-level staff were better known than they personally expected.

Possibly there was greater stress on safety representatives and less emphasis on line management than those at the top of the company expected. But the important point is that everyone identified safety representatives and line management as the main groups responsible for health and safety. However, the majority of the workforce did not know to whom they should refer if they had health and safety problems, and it might also have been expected that a greater proportion of supervisors would know that they held health and safety responsibilities. This suggests that line management responsibilities may have been better understood on BR than studies of other companies have suggested (Dawson *et al.*, 1988), albeit not at the levels of success Robens would have desired.[7]

The tension between the line management responsibilities for health and safety and the existence of a specialist health and safety department are represented by the signal and telecommunications department decision to remove specialist staff so that everyone would feel responsible. This is a familiar argument and as yet (to the best of my knowledge) is empirically untested. What can be said is that those departments which did have specialist staff on BR welcomed them and seemed to have as great an awareness as anyone else of health and safety issues.

None of the data deriving from this research suggests that BR's organizational and procedural response to occupational health and safety legislation was merely symbolic or rhetorical as some work on corporate environmental programmes suggests (Levy, 1994). But it was none the less not as effective in practice as might ideally have been expected. Let us turn next to consider whether the involvement of the workforce in this system was any more effective.

---

[7] One criticism made by other studies is that other pressures, especially production pressures, mitigate line management responsibility for health and safety. See Dawson *et al.* (1988: 47 ff.) for a good summary of these. This subject will be explored in more depth in Chapter 10.

7

Participative Regulation?

An important objective of the philosophy underlying the HSW Act, 1974, was to incorporate employees as participatory rather than passive agents in the workplace. Prior to the Act the well-being of the workplace had been largely the preserve and responsibility of employers. This chapter will consider the legislative and institutional arrangements for worker participation on the railways. In particular it will examine how much was known about the system by managers and the workforce and most important it will consider whether the objective of constituting everyone in the workplace as a participant in health and safety regulation was being met.

Worker Participation Pre-Robens

Pre-Robens arrangements for health and safety at work were paternalistic. Employees had a duty and a right to enforce statutory safety codes and typically this was a matter of discipline rather than co-operation. Howells regards paternalism as central to the common law approach to occupational safety, moreover: 'The statutory safety codes which developed from these common law principles, were from the outset equally paternalistic in concept and enforcement: while no doubt intended for the benefit and protection of the worker, they operated over his head rather than through his co-operation' (1974: 89). This approach was supplemented by a variety of voluntary rather than statutory arrangements.

The Coal Mines Regulation Act 1872 was the first legislation to give workers a right to appoint safety inspectors from among their number. These representatives monitored safety, inspected the mines on a monthly basis, investigated accidents, and reported their findings. Further legislation (Coal Mines Act, 1911; Mines and Quarries Act, 1954) strengthened the position of these inspectors (Atherley et al., 1975: 471 ff.; Howells, 1974: 91 ff.; Williams, 1960).

The rights accorded workers in coal mines were advanced and did not become general workers rights in the pre-Robens era. The 1947 Transport Act, in common with other nationalization legislation, placed a duty upon the Transport Commission to consult 'with any organization appearing to the Commission to be appropriate' and set up machinery for 'the promotion and encouragement of measures affecting the safety, health and welfare of persons employed by the Commission' (cited in Howells, 1974: 92). Howells comments, however, that the definition of 'consult' was narrow and that management had the ultimate right to decide its meaning.

In factories, worker involvement was largely voluntary and typically took the form of safety committees (Atherley *et al.*, 1975; Glendon and Booth, 1982). The Factories Act, 1961, gave the workforce no rights of inspection; to information about hazards; to see inspectors; or to see their reports (Howells, 1974). Section 138.9 of the Act required employers to display some information at the main entrance to their works, for example, an abstract of the Act and other regulations, and the name and address of the factory doctor and factory inspector. Similarly regulations made under the Offices, Shops and Railway Premises Act (Information for Employees Regulations, 1965) required the display of abstracts. The only other right of representation accorded the workforce under this legislation was the right of the unions to send representatives to formal accident inquiries.

A variety of authors document failed attempts to increase worker participation in health and safety, dating from the 1841 Select Committee on the operation of factory legislation onwards (Atherley *et al.*, 1975; Glendon and Booth, 1982; Howells, 1974). The ambiguities which seem to have surrounded the issue of worker participation are perhaps indicated by the views of the Trades Union Congress, which over time has held variable and ambivalent views on the subject (Atherley *et al.*, 1975). It was the Labour Party of the late 1960s that led the way to change and the Labour government of 1970 which, of course, set up the Robens Committee.

The Robens Report

Underlying the changes recommended by the Robens Committee report into *Safety and Health at Work* (1972) was a corporatist philosophy which regarded health and safety as the everyday concern of everyone at work and emphasized the involvement of the workforce in its own destiny and protection at work. While the Committee considered that health and safety were primarily the responsibility of management, they nevertheless emphasized that 'the full cooperation and commitment of all employees' were essential (para. 59). To this end it was suggested that the workforce should be involved in 'making and monitoring . . . arrangements for safety and health at work' and the appointment of safety representatives and joint safety committees was suggested. The role of the law in this system was carefully considered by the Committee and they eventually determined that there should be a statutory duty on employers to consult and to involve employees in the promotion of health and safety in the workplace.

Consultations between employers and employees, argued the Committee, should involve:

. . . more contacts and co-operation between inspectors and workplace and their representatives. It should be as natural to discuss safety and health problems with workpeople and their representatives as it is to discuss them with management. Sometimes it might be helpful to have joint discussions between inspectors, management and employee representatives. (para. 213)

Moreover consultations should extend to industry level, where trade unions and employers' associations should work together. The proposed national authority for safety and health at work should include, among others, representatives with union and with industrial managerial experience, one of whose functions should be collaboration with employers' organizations and the unions. Yet Robens was insistent that employers should be involved through consultation rather than collective bargaining. This emanated from the view of the Committee that there was a natural identity of interest between everyone in the workplace over health and safety. This was perceived as both self-evident and sufficient to lead to co-operation. There seems to have been no recognition of the broader conflicts and divisions which might cut across the workplace and counteract the promotion of health and safety objectives. Commentators at the time, while welcoming the proposals for greater worker participation, were nevertheless well aware of the report's limitations. Barrett (1977: 166), for example, found the recommendations of the Robens Committee 'fairly conservative' in that responsibility for safe working conditions remained with management rather than in an equal partnership between management and employees. Lewis (1974) is also critical of Robens for remaining vague about the forms of participation which may be promoted, again noting that this detracted from anything approximating equal partnership. Moreover there was widespread criticism of the Committee's assumptions that there is an 'identity of interest' between management and employees on the subject of safety which eradicates the scope for bargaining on health and safety issues (see Ch. 2).

Health and Safety at Work etc. Act, 1974 (HSW Act)

The HSW Act, 1974, followed Robens to the extent that it incorporated the workforce as participants in health and safety regulation. It placed duties on and accorded rights to workers and, of most concern to this chapter, tried to facilitate greater worker involvement through statutory provision for safety representatives and safety committees. Much of the detail of this participation was embodied in the Safety Representatives and Safety Committee (SRSC) Regulations 1977 which were made under the HSW Act, 1974, section 2(4) and came into force on 1 October 1978. Most significantly these regulations were the product of a different philosophy and political era from the HSW Act (Nichols, 1997). Contrary to Robens, the regulations provided for trade union-appointed safety representatives and according to Dawson *et al*. (1988: 19) thus facilitated a commitment to union recognition and collective bargaining.

The regulations gave broad guidance to safety representatives about how they could fulfil their statutory role and guidance to employers concerning the information to be made available to safety representatives. The regulations laid down requirements about a range of matters including the appointment of safety representatives; their functions; the inspection of the workplace; the inspection of documents and provision of information; and safety committees. These statutory requirements were further backed up by a code of practice on safety representatives and safety committees and SRSC guidance notes.

There was a flurry of publications and research into workforce participation at the time of the HSW Act, and the SRSC regulations and a revitalization of interest in the subject in the 1990s. Much of the research that has been undertaken is from an industrial relations perspective and much of this has been sponsored by either the unions or the HSE. A number of criticisms arising from this work are worth considering before discussing the findings of this research.

One important consequence of the SRSC regulations was that rights to representation were restricted to those represented by trade unions. The effect was therefore uneven representation across workplaces (Dawson *et al.*, 1988). This remained unchanged until 1990 when new legislation made provision for safety representatives to be elected from all workers (James and Walters, 1999). This particular provision did not carry implications for BR employees in so far as this was a heavily unionized workplace but it did, as we will see, lead to some controversy. More pertinent for this discussion is the experience of the 1980s when the role of trade unions in Britain was much diminished and there was a decreasing commitment to collective bargaining (Dawson *et al.*, 1988). Nichols (1997) underlines the changing balance of power in the workplace during this period and cites research by Millward *et al.* (1992) which documents a substantial decline in the extent of union recognition between 1984 and 1990. Clearly this should be borne in mind as this is the period during which the data on worker representation was collected for this research. Moreover this was also a period of reorganization and staff cuts in BR, another factor which should be remembered when reading this chapter (see Ch. 2).

Safety Representatives: Research Findings

It should be appreciated that within BR safety representatives were selected from the ranks of the unionized workforce. They received some additional health and safety training from the union and also had some extra facilities provided by the company plus time to undertake their safety representative activities.

The research sample included nineteen safety representatives. They were from a variety of railway departments and trade unions.[1] They had been safety representatives for a varying number of years—from less than a year to fourteen years: those interviewed were evenly spread across this range. This group of safety representatives was asked a series of questions about their own experiences and knowledge of health and safety in an effort to ascertain to what extent they were able to participate in the way suggested by Robens and required by the legislation. The broader workforce were also asked for their knowledge of and views about safety representatives.

---

[1] There were three main unions—RMT, ASLEF, NUR. See Chapter 2.

Appointment of Safety Representatives

All of the safety representatives interviewed were representatives of recognized trade unions (HSW Act, 1974, sect. 2(4)) so they had all become safety representatives through their membership of a local departmental council (LDC) or workshop committee. The appointment of safety representatives from those on local departmental council or workshop committees was a point of contention for some as they disapproved of safety representatives being so closely and symbolically aligned with the unions, their argument being that these two should be separate and distinct. For others this was not a problem as they saw no conflict of interest. The majority of managers, supervisors, and safety representatives knew that safety representatives were drawn from the local departmental council and workshop committees. Twenty-one per cent (15/57) of safety representatives did not know that there was such a relationship.

Managers and supervisors did not give their full support to safety representatives being selected from local departmental council members although they did recognize some advantages attaching to the situation. The reasons offered in favour of the system included the arguments that union training was particularly valuable; that as safety was negotiable then it was better to have experienced negotiators in post and to have discussions with one group, the union, rather than two; and that if safety representatives were not connected with the local departmental council then no one else could be persuaded to take the job on. Four reasons were cited in argument against the system: that union representatives were too pedantic; that the job attracted militants; that those appointed were not necessarily interested in health and safety; and that the turnover in local departmental council members led to too high a turnover of safety representatives:

> The majority of people who become local departmental council reps. are officious or perhaps even loudmouths, are very 'if you don't get that down right we will walk out' touch. Lately though that has changed a bit, the younger generation coming in, some don't seem to be quite as arrogant or quite as uptight over issues and are more sensible and can sit down and talk . . . (supervisor, interviewee 124)

Others did not mind where the safety representative came from so long as they were sensible:

> Provided the safety rep. is a good sensible person and has the health, welfare, and safety of the workforce at heart then I don't care where he comes from, provided he is the right sort of person. I think that is much more important than being a local departmental council man, I think that is totally irrelevant, far better to have somebody really interested in doing the job and will do it well. (supervisor, interviewee 100)

There was not full safety representation across industry and it was acknowledged within BR that there could be problems in appointing safety representatives (see below). This mirrors other research which has identified problems in finding people willing to take on the role (Walters *et al.*, 1993: 77) and which has also identified a decline in safety representatives since the HSW Act, 1974.[2] But it should be noted that under-representation was most associated with smaller and private sector workplaces (Dawson *et al.*, 1988; La Trobe, 1990; James and Walters, 1999). So it is likely that BR's employees were among the better represented workers in Britain.

The Role of the Safety Representative

The HSW Act, 1974, section 2(4) requires safety representatives to represent employees in consultation with employers. The regulations and code of practice outline in some detail what functions this entails. These include the investigation of accidents, potential hazards, and employee complaints; making representations to employers on behalf of the workforce; carrying out inspections; representing employees in consultations with health and safety inspectors and receiving information from them; and attending joint safety committees. The code of practice adds that safety representatives should keep themselves informed of the legal requirements relating to health and safety at work; hazards of the workplace; and workplace health and safety policies. They should also encourage co-operation between employer and employees and alert employers to any health and safety problems that come to their attention. The guidance notes expect that safety representatives will be able to take matters up without delay and they expect that a record is kept of safety representative inspections of the workplace.[3]

A wide range of responses was elicited by the question 'What do you think your main job is as a safety representative?' The three most frequent responses were to report to managers (5); to look after the safety of staff (5); and to ensure management provides safety equipment (4). Other responses were either more general—'to point out dangers', 'to keep standards up'—or more specific—'to see the equipment is in order', 'do inspections', 'ensure complaints are seen to'. One safety representative offered what some might regard as the ideal response as it combines a variety of responsibilities: 'To take care of any safety problems brought to me by the members of staff, to be aware of any problems for the staff and to liaise with management over staff matters or health matters that I find difficult or any other staff finds a problem' (interviewee 116). There is greater variety in these responses than in an earlier study by Beaumont (1981*a*). He

---

[2] Walters and Gourlay (1990) found that in 1984 80% of employees had safety representation, but this had fallen to 75% in 1990. Walters *et al.* (1993) associate this decline with a period of recession; with legislative changes which reduced trade union power; a decline in trade union membership; and a decline following an initial period of enthusiasm following the SRSC regulations.

[3] These provisions are contentious. For example there is debate about the meaning of 'consultation'—does it mean 'negotiation'? If so, should health and safety be negotiable? See Glendon (1977*a*).

reports the results of a postal questionnaire to safety representatives where respondents identified themselves as a channel of communication for workers' complaints or they emphasized the technical aspects of inspection and dealing with complaints.

Let us now turn our attention to how safety representatives responded to more specific questions about their role.

Safety Representatives' Knowledge of Joint Union–Management Systems for Health and Safety

There were a number of important ways in which occupational health and safety legislation incorporates the workforce, through its safety representatives, into the routine regulation of health and safety. Safety representatives, managers, and supervisors were asked about two of these, namely joint union–management safety committees and workplace inspections.

Joint Union–Management Safety Committees

As we saw in Chapter 6, although BR had a structure of joint union–management safety committees, there was a very scanty knowledge among respondents of this structure. Those who knew anything were again most likely to be in the operations department, but differences among grades of staff were most marked. Managers were the most likely to know that committees existed and they referred to either regional safety committees or the local departmental committees. Forty-four per cent of supervisors and 35 per cent of safety representatives were aware of joint union–management safety committees. Not all of these could name a committee, but those who could cited the regional safety committees. Beyond this basic awareness, knowledge of these committees was very hazy. One-third of the managers and safety representatives who knew of the committees received minutes of the proceedings. Managers could give details of what was discussed at the meetings but only two safety representatives and one supervisor were able to do this:

I: What kind of issues are discussed there ?
R: Well from what I've read in the minutes it doesn't seem to be anything . . .
     It is more a general policy sort of way than being on specific issues. Now
     if I thought that I could send one of our issues up there and get it resolved
     then I would do. On occasions they have certain things in but I don't think
     it, it seems to me to be divorced from the everyday health and safety sort
     of set up, especially here and I know the same in 'X'. I mean we went to a
     meeting with them once and they all sat around a table and they all had
     health and safety reps from 'Y' (the area) and to be honest it was a wasted
     day because the . . . first thing they said was we are not here to discuss spe-
     cific issues, this is just a meeting about how generally health and safety

goes on in the region. And there was a lot of people there that wanted to discuss specific issues. Now I understand why they couldn't, I mean it would have taken a week or two weeks to get through anything but most people afterwards felt let down by it. (safety representative, interviewee 54)

Very few representatives in any category were able to give more specific details about such matters as the frequency of these meetings, who chaired them, and whether or not there was follow-up action. Very few comments were offered about these committees. Those which were offered were, with one exception, negative, namely that these committees were just 'a talking shop' and that they were perceived by a few to be without authority (see also Dawson *et al.*, 1988).

These findings contrast with those of Barrett *et al.* (1985*a*), who found that most of the 33 safety representatives they interviewed regarded safety committees as beneficial. But the discrepancy is explained by other research on the topic. Rees (1988: 138), for example, observes that the few empirical studies of safety committees that do exist agree that the mere existence of safety committees makes little difference. He comments that there must be an actual improvement in occupational health and safety effected, not just a perception that these committees are effective; communication is vital so workers must feel that they are directly represented; and workers must feel confident in the committee and be willing to take complaints to it. Perhaps most important for this research was the finding that the creation of the committee was just a first step, and that there was a need to maintain involvement and reward worker contributions (Rees, 1988: 144). Also of relevance to this study is Walters and Gourlay's (1990: 121) observation that effective committees need to be compact, to meet regularly, be well organized, be regularly attended, and have good communication with the workforce (see Ch. 5).

Joint Union–Management Inspections

Joint union–management inspections were provided for by SRSC Regulations 1977, section 5. These entitled safety representatives to inspect the workplace at least once every three months. They were expected to give employers notice in writing of their intention to inspect and employers were expected to provide facilities and assist safety representatives. Thirteen of fifteen (87 per cent) safety representatives interviewed undertook joint union–management workplace inspections with either a manager or supervisor, while the other two undertook them on their own (although they should have been joint). The frequency of these joint inspections varied, from 'as requested' to six-monthly, although the most common response was quarterly. This was also the most common frequency cited by safety representatives, although lapses were mentioned, especially by signals and telecommunications staff.

There was some dissatisfaction among safety representatives about follow-up action after joint inspections. This echoes other research which found that

workplace inspections were not used as they might be (Walters *et al.*, 1993: 63).
Within BR, operations department staff were the most critical here, complaining of slowness of response or a failure to do anything. Others referred to problems occurring when other departments were responsible for correcting
problems. Cost was another delaying factor mentioned by a minority of respondents. Criticism, however, was not unanimous. A minority commented that
problems were promptly remedied and a safety representative from one
mechanical and electrical engineering depot was very satisfied as problems identified on his joint inspections were either remedied within fourteen days or he
received notification and an explanation of any delay.

Safety Representatives and Information about Health and Safety

One of the important aspects of being a safety representative is to be especially
knowledgeable about health and safety matters. This involves receiving additional health and safety training and also being a recipient of information from,
for example, the Railway Inspectorate following their inspections.

The most formal source of health and safety information available to safety
representatives was a ten-week Trade Unions Congress course on health and
safety at work. These courses were usually day-release courses funded by the
Trade Unions Congress but taken in paid time-off. The intensive courses covered a broad range of topics such as the law; the role of safety representatives;
the identification of hazards at work; accident investigation; the work of HSE;
and safety committees (Glendon, 1977*b*). This training is described by Walters
et al. (1993: 62) as among the best in Europe. All except two of the safety representatives interviewed had been on this course, the two exceptions being
recently new to the job. Everyone who had been on the course had found it helpful and all wanted to go on further courses, but there was a suspicion that management would not be keen on them attending more courses.

All except one respondent knew that the safety representative health and
safety course was Trade Unions Congress rather than BR based. The courses
attracted praise and criticism. The advantages were that it gave safety representatives knowledge and confidence. Indeed it was cited by several as one of the
attractions of the job. The criticisms were that it attempted to cover too wide a
range of topics and that sometimes it went 'above the heads' of those on the
course. Some safety representatives found it ridiculous that management did
not have similar courses available to them. This view was fully supported by
many of the managers interviewed. Other studies suggest that training is an
important factor in improving the role of safety representatives (Beaumont,
1981*b*; Walters and Gourlay, 1990: 132; Walters *et al.*, 1993: 62).

Other chapters have discussed how much safety representatives knew about
health and safety and offered comparison with other respondents. These findings confirmed that safety representatives did have a greater knowledge than the
rest of the workforce across a broad range of issues. These include knowledge

of the law and the regulatory system and knowledge of the health and safety policies and practice within the company. Generally their levels of knowledge approximated that of supervisors. This was perhaps encouraging as it suggested that safety representatives were in fact receiving the information they should have been and that they seemed to be assimilating at least some of it (see Chs. 4, 5, and 6). But they were not confident that they were kept up to date with changes in, for example, the law. Those who did hear of changes cited BR as their source of information. One senior union official mentioned that the unions sent out information about changes in the law, but he doubted that anyone read it.

As well as receiving information, safety representatives were also disseminators of information. While it was clear that safety representatives communicated some of the information they received to the workforce they were not regarded as a major source of information on health and safety. When the workforce were asked a general question about the sources of information on health and safety available to them, the unions and safety representatives were rarely mentioned. Of those who received information from their safety representative all except one found that information useful. Safety representatives communicated with the workforce in a variety of ways but most of this communication was verbal rather than written.[4] Shift working could be an obstacle to direct communication between safety representatives and their colleagues but was not necessarily so: 'I have come down on different shifts to see people or I have let them communicate to me via letter which I have received . . . or they telephone me at home' (interviewee 90).

Knowledge of Safety Representatives

I turn next to how much knowledge there was about safety representatives. Managers, supervisors, and safety representatives were asked how many unions represented their area of responsibility. They were then questioned about the number of safety representatives there were in their area. The majority knew how many unions represented their area and most, but slightly fewer, knew about safety representatives. The general view was that there were not as many safety representatives in post as there should be and that this varied between departments. The civil engineering and signals and telecommunications departments were the most likely to have no representation and respondents in these departments revealed most ignorance about how many safety representatives there were. Three managers (two of them from the signals and telecommunications department) commented that they could not get staff to become safety representatives, a subject to which we will return later.

---

[4] Eight major ways of communication were cited by safety representatives: verbal/personal communication (9); branch meetings (5); noticeboards (4); letters/notes (3); telephone (3); walkabouts (1); shift meetings (1); supervisor (1).

Workforce responses were very similar to those of managers to the extent that the majority knew that there were safety representatives[5] and approximately half knew the name of their local representative.[6] Most were in regular contact with him or her, typically on a daily basis (because they worked with him or her). This high level of contact was supported by responses to the question 'How would you contact your safety representative?'—thirteen responded that they saw him or her regularly; fourteen would contact him or her directly, either by letter or telephone; and two would make contact via an unspecified third party. Safety representatives were therefore generally well known among the workforce and this was very much what safety representatives themselves expected to be the case.[7]

Willingness to Consult Safety Representatives

Given the position of safety representatives as delegates of the workforce it is of course important that the workforce are willing to consult with them. Indeed dealing with complaints is one of their legislative functions and Rees's (1988: 145) US study suggests that acting on complaints is crucial to making workers feel represented. Ten of the sixteen safety representatives questioned about this were approached by staff with health and safety problems. The number of approaches varied between one and ten per month.[8] Most of the problems they encountered concerned housekeeping, for example, broken ladders, unclean mess rooms, and tripping hazards. The safety representatives believed that complainants expected them to refer the problems to management and most felt that complainants expected immediate responses and remedy. Evidence that safety representatives did refer problems to management was offered by supervisors who confirmed that they received regular queries about health and safety matters, often from safety representatives.

The majority of the workforce, when specifically asked, said that they would refer problems to safety representatives if a problem arose, the others would go direct to their manager or supervisor. Just under half (15/34) of the workforce questioned had already taken a health and safety problem to their safety representative. But when they were asked a rather more general question about who their reference persons would be in the event of a health and safety

---

[5] 71% knew that they had safety representatives, 22% claimed that they did not have safety representation, and 7% did not know (n=45).

[6] Eleven knew the name of their safety representative, 12 claimed to know who she/he was but could not name him/her; and 1 claimed to know nothing.

[7] Twelve of 17 safety representatives interviewed about this firmly believed that staff did know who they were; 2 thought that this was the case; and 3 believed that some staff would know them. One mentioned that there is such a high turnover of staff that it is difficult to keep people informed of his role. Another mentioned difficulties in finding time to travel around the area and become acquainted with staff. Others suspected that staff may confuse them with health and safety officers employed by the company.

[8] This is consistent with other studies. See, for example, Beaumont (1981a: 57); Walters and Gourlay (1990: 27).

problem, safety representatives were not always the first point of reference, especially for civil engineering and signals and telecommunications staff who would be most inclined to go to their supervisors. The interviews also suggest that managers, especially supervisors, accord safety representatives greater responsibility for health and safety than safety representatives perceived themselves to hold. A common comment among those who had complained was that 'it did no good' or it took a long time to achieve action (see also Barrett *et al.*, 1985*a*). This accords with the views of safety representatives themselves and points to some of the frustrations of being a safety representative: 'They expect me to get it changed within five seconds flat, you know for some reason they seem to think that if you are a safety officer or shop representative you can go and get it changed instantly but it is just not like that' (safety representative, interviewee 102).

The Experience of Being a Safety Representative

All of the safety representatives were asked about the *facilities* they had at their disposal, since according to the SRSC regulations they should be provided with essential facilities to do their job. Access to facilities was variable. Most had access to some facilities although two had none at their disposal. Half of those interviewed had access to a room and facilities. Seven had access to use facilities such as a telephone, typewriter, fax, photocopier, or a library but not necessarily all of these. It is difficult to ascertain why there were such wide variations, whether it reflects a reluctance to provide facilities or diffidence in asking for facilities. Some replies did suggest that there may have been some diffidence—or even reluctance—about using facilities:

> I have never been refused anything . . . The last guy had a room and a desk and you know I dare say if I asked for it now I could have it. I know I am entitled to it but as you know that is not really me, all my paperwork is kept in my locker and I know where it is, it is not liable to get chucked about or lost and I am quite happy with that. I have never been refused anything, the use of a telephone or anything, the facilities are there if I want them but I just don't want them. (interviewee 102)

Clearly this was problematic as it highlights the marginal position of safety representatives in the overall organization and the fact that they needed to feel integrated into the system. Generally, however, it was likely that this group of representatives was relatively well provided for as other studies suggest that the facilities available to safety representatives improves according to the size of the company (Walters *et al.* 1993: 65).

The research tried to gain some understanding of what it was like to be a safety representative and found that their experiences were rather varied. They all had differing amounts of contact with other safety representatives. Approximately half of those questioned had either no or very little contact with other safety representatives. Of those who did come into contact with fellow safety representatives, five met them at meetings or seminars, three on safety inspections, and one had written contact with another representative. So we do not get the impression of a community of safety representatives but of lone representatives of the workforce. Where there was contact it was welcomed, but as we can see just under half were isolated in this respect.

The amount of time devoted to safety representative duties also varied, with estimates ranging from 'all the time' to 'little or no time'. This discrepancy was interesting. It was hard to assess whether this was an accurate reflection of the amount of time safety representatives devoted to the job. But it does suggest that there was a division between those who considered that they must always be vigilant and available as safety representatives and those who perceived the job to be tied to much more formal meetings and inspections. The following comments from safety representatives in the same department are illustrative:

> . . . when you are working generally we just have a—if you see anything—just a word about it. So, I'm really watching for things all the time. (interviewee 128)

> . . . it is more monthly, six weekly, monthly. (interviewee 123)

These findings again suggest variability in the extent to which occupational health and safety matters had become constituted as the everyday concern of everyone, for here we have a group who should be especially alert to health and safety issues yet only four of them (21 per cent) regard this as an everyday activity. These findings are consistent with others. Walter and Gourlay (1990), for example, found that 67 per cent of the safety representatives they interviewed spent less than two hours per week on health and safety matters.

The Advantages and Disadvantages of Being a Safety Representative

Although *managers* were not directly questioned about the merits and demerits of being a safety representative, several offered their views. Indeed, five managers mentioned that it was hard to get safety representatives. Some felt that this was explained by apathy, a general reluctance to get involved in anything:

I: Why are there difficulties in recruiting safety representatives?
R: A general apathy, apathy may be too strong a word.
I: Apathy about what?
R: Well . . . apathy may be too strong a word. Apathy seems to imply a 'couldn't care less' attitude to health and safety, or if you like to personal safety. I don't think it's so much—it's just the general reluctance to get too much involved in things. (manager, interviewee 75)

A more important reason seemed to be that these managers felt that there were more disadvantages than advantages attaching to the job. Two advantages were cited by managers, namely that being a safety representative gives a person status and that it gives them knowledge of the law. Four disadvantages were mentioned by managers, namely that being a safety representative involves extra work; that safety representatives are held to account; that they receive nothing in return; and that some managers discourage safety representatives.

The *workforce* were asked a variety of questions designed to discern their views about being a safety representative. First, they were asked if they had ever considered becoming a safety representative. Seventy-nine per cent (33/42) of those asked this question replied that they had not. Their reasons were varied. The most popular responses were that respondents had 'never thought about it'; the view that safety representatives are ' unnecessary'; that being a safety representative involves 'too much work'; that they personally didn't have enough time; that they felt unable to communicate well enough for the job; and that the role is 'too political'. Some respondents lent weight to the view that apathy is relevant: 'I just want to come here and drive trains and go home again'. Some complained that safety representatives have too few powers and others believed that the job necessitated skills they do not possess : 'I'm not much good at reading and writing so really I wouldn't be much good at anything like that'. This explanation should not be underestimated, and one union official explained that such factors could prove a very real obstacle to some of his members. Other studies have also commented that safety representatives are often not skilled in communication (La Trobe, 1990: 318; Walters *et al.*, 1993: 58) and that this is important given their need to communicate with the workforce and also management (Beaumont, 1981*a*: 58).

Two of the workforce respondents had been safety representatives in the past and seven had considered becoming a safety representative. Their reasons for not doing so included a failure to be elected to the local departmental council; a belief that the job should be taken by a younger man; and a fear that it would mean losing money.

The workforce were also questioned directly about whether or not they perceived any advantages or disadvantages attaching to the job of safety representative. Their replies suggest that being a safety representative is not generally perceived as a desirable job. Responses to the question 'Are there any *advantages* to becoming a safety representative?' are shown in Table 7.1.

TABLE 7.1. Proportion of workforce attaching advantages to the job of safety representative

	n	%
Yes	10	26
No/Don't know	25	64
Total	4	10
	39	100

TABLE 7.2. Proportion of workforce attaching
disadvantages to the job of safety representative

	n	%
Yes	21	68
No/Don't know	9	29
Total	1	3
	31	100

Responses to a similar question about the *disadvantages* of being a safety representative were as shown in Table 7.2.

The most obvious *advantage* was that safety representatives acquire a greater knowledge and awareness of health and safety. Apart from this there was no agreement about the advantages. Two respondents thought that there must be some advantages but they couldn't specify any. The *disadvantages* identified with being a safety representative were more numerous. The most frequently cited by the workforce were that it is time consuming; it can lead to unpopularity with colleagues and with management; and that it can position you as 'piggy in the middle'. The following comments are illustrative:

> I've got enough to do without taking on extra work. (worker, interviewee 9)

> . . . you can probably get it in the neck from everyone. (worker, interviewee 88)

> . . . you are the bullet all the time, if anything goes wrong it is your fault because you didn't see to it or you didn't know of it. (worker, interviewee 35)

> . . . you are piggy in the middle so to speak in the system. All the men, lads at work moan at you . . . you go and tell the governor about various discrepancies and then he moans to you . . . as well, so basically you are just there to be moaned at. (worker, interviewee 125)

Beaumont and Leopold's (1984) respondents confirmed these frustrations, claiming that they felt as if they were 'fighting on two fronts', namely management which delayed changes and a workforce who complained but who were not prepared to do anything and would not comply.

When *safety representatives* were asked about the attractions of the job, 11 of 15 said that there was none. Some of these took a pragmatic approach to the job, a typical response being 'It is an unpopular job although it is a necessary one'. Two expressed an interest in safety and another replied that the occasional day out was an attraction. The most cited attraction was that they derived some self-satisfaction from the work:

> You are there to make somebody's safety better and not only our safety, it makes passengers' safety better as well. (interviewee 50)

> Self-satisfaction in getting something done. (interviewee 90)

I believe there is the attraction of doing a job well and seeing that people don't get injured and I believe that does give it some attraction. I believe they think they have done a good job of work because the railways are a dangerous industry, you mustn't run away from it, it is a dangerous industry, the machinery we use is exceptionally heavy. If there are accidents they are usually extremely severe and I believe many safety representatives see that by their action they can first of all avoid accidents happening which is the prime duty . . . If you have a situation where you have avoided an accident you feel good but if one has happened and you are able then by your activity to ensure that compensation is paid then that gives you a feeling of something well done. (union official)

Half (51 per cent) of those responding to Beaumont and Leopold's (1984) postal survey cited an interest in health and safety as an attraction to the job. Beaumont and Leopold's (1984) respondents derived satisfaction from effecting minor changes, improving relations between the workforce and management, and for the authority and status it conferred—few of these were detailed by respondents in this study. Given the inconveniences which could accompany the role, let us turn our attention to the sort of people who were likely to agree to take the job on.

Characteristics of Safety Representatives

Managers, supervisors, and safety representatives were asked what sort of people become safety representatives. The majority of the responses were positive, in fact only 3 of 64 respondents gave a negative response—one manager said that they were people with frustrated ambition, a supervisor referred to them as 'desk thumpers', and another supervisor replied that they were 'people who didn't want to work'. But these were the exceptions: 41 per cent of managers described safety representatives in a positive way and 44 per cent merely stated that they were committed union members or took an interest in union matters. Not surprisingly safety representatives were the most positive in the characteristics they attributed to safety representatives.

'Caring' was the main description of safety representatives, either as a description of safety representatives or as an ideal:[9]

. . . the people at work and at home who take an interest in the welfare of others, they are probably the same people who are on the school governors and all that sort of thing. (manager, interviewee 20)

I would say that I think it is people that care about the people they are working with and care about the workplace and the railway. But maybe

---

[9] Four managers, twelve supervisors, and fifteen safety representatives (a total of 31/64) described safety representatives in this way.

that is not true all the time, but that is certainly the sort of people it should be, the people that actually care about the staff around them and the place they are working in. (manager, interviewee 38)

Quite often it can be people on the local departmental council who have a genuine interest in their working environment and their fellow men if you like, that is not always the case. I have known cases where it has gone the other way and you might find somebody who is looking for a pastime, something other than doing the job he was allocated, but on the whole I think people who have an interest in their environment and their working companions and they feel if they are doing a job for their fellow workers if you like. (supervisor, interviewee 64)

The other striking characteristic attributed to safety representatives is that they are people who are prepared to *do* something rather than just talk about it:

I: What sort of people do you think become safety representatives?
R: I think that is a very, very hard one to answer. I think somebody with a con-
     science, somebody who is a little bit fed up with other people laying things
     about or leaving hazards and anything of this nature where somebody can
     hurt themselves and you think 'God somebody has got to do something
     about this'. And I think that is the type of person that comes along and he
     says to himself 'Well no-one else is going to sort it out, I suppose I had bet-
     ter'. (safety representative, interviewee 90)

Another safety representative explained that this 'sometimes gets classed in other circles as militancy ... I have often said you didn't get an apathetic militant'.

The Usefulness of Safety Representatives

It was extremely difficult to assess what sort of impact, if any, safety represen-
tatives made upon occupational health and safety. While the research was not specifically designed to assess effectiveness, it did include general questions which give some insight into what sort of influence safety representatives were perceived to have.

There was a general feeling that safety representatives did serve a useful role within the industry. Perhaps not surprisingly all except one *safety representative* felt that they were undertaking a useful job. The one dissenter con-
sidered that management frustrated his attempts at being useful. Indeed this criticism was reflected in the remarks of other safety representatives: 'Some-
times I think I am not [doing a useful job], as if you are up against a brick wall, yet at other times everything goes smashing ... It has its ups and downs' (interviewee 28). Undoubtedly the main 'use' of the job according to safety representatives was the channel of communication it offered between the workforce and management:

They [safety representatives] can be very useful sometimes, it is the link you know with the shop floor, they see more sometimes than the front-line supervisors can see. People, the shop-floor people themselves, can approach the safety representatives, whereas they may not go to the supervisor, they can talk more freely with them about problems and they pass these problems on, so they are a useful link in achieving a good standard of health and safety. (interviewee 116)

The large majority (32/39) of the *workforce* also thought that safety representatives were a good idea.[10] They were appreciated for 'keeping an eye on everything' and because they were local. They were also valued for their knowledge of the dangers attaching to the work and for keeping the workforce up to date. Indeed they were credited with keeping the workforce 'on their toes' and for pointing out dangers to management. But regarding safety representatives as a good idea does not necessarily imply that respondents felt that the system was working successfully: 'I think they probably are a good idea. I don't think they function particularly well because I mean normally our [area] is a complete heap, it really is' (worker, interviewee 95).

Safety representatives' lack of authority and lack of powers to enforce were perceived as their main drawbacks: 'I think yes the basic principle is a good idea but in practice it doesn't work because they have not got any authority and they have got no clout' (worker, interviewee 88). When managers and supervisors were asked more specific questions about the impact of safety representatives upon workforce compliance there was a mixed response (see Table 7.3). Supervisors were more inclined to perceive safety representatives as effective than more senior managers. Managers tended to qualify their responses to say that safety representatives could be effective in certain circumstances. This largely depended upon the individual safety representative but it was also relevant, in the view of managers, that managers should use safety representatives successfully and that the company should give safety representatives more time to do their job:

I: Do you think that having safety reps is effective in getting people to comply?

R: Oh definitely yes because it generates things don't they [*sic*]. They are talking to people and some people, some of them might be reluctant to come and speak to me but talk to one of the lads and he will go and look at it and then he will come and see me.

I: So they are helpful in that respect.

R: Definitely I think that they are a must. (supervisor, interviewee 15)

---

[10] Three disagreed, 3 found safety representatives a good idea in some respects only, and 1 did not have a view.

TABLE 7.3. Importance of safety representatives in securing workforce compliance

	Managers		Supervisors		Total	
	n	%	n	%	n	%
Very important	1	4	2	9.5	3	6.5
Do help/can help	5	20	7	33	12	26
Could be effective	4	16	2	9.5	6	13
Sometimes helpful	2	8	1	5	3	6.5
Not helpful	4	16	6	29	10	22
Depends on individual	6	24	3	14	9	19.5
Difficult to say	3	12	—	—	3	6.5
Total	25	100	21	100	46	100

Some managers were keen that they should not rely on safety representatives and regard them as the main means of enforcing compliance. Some acknowledged that it could be very difficult for safety representatives to persuade their colleagues to comply:

> There are very few of them. I think they have enormous difficulties trying to persuade their mates to do things that may be unpopular. I don't think that they see their role as doing that, they see their role mainly as bringing defects to the attention of management and they are very thin on the ground. (manager, interviewee 66)

Safety representatives were asked what they would do if they discovered someone not following the rules. The majority replied that they would have an informal chat with the offender. They also claimed that they regularly did this. Moreover they clearly felt a responsibility to set an example to staff and many of them believed that they had become more compliant since becoming safety representatives (see Ch. 10).

Other research suggests that a key to the effectiveness of safety representatives is working in a culture which is supportive of them. This includes the support of the unions, other employees, and management. The unions can provide crucial information and training (Walters *et al.*, 1993). Safety representatives need to maintain strong links with their constituencies and need to be needed and valued by the workforce (Beaumont, 1981*a*; Walters *et al.*, 1993, 57 ff.). Meanwhile management commitment is vital with respect, for example, to including safety representatives, consulting with them, and responding to their concerns (Beaumont, 1981*b*; Kochan *et al.*, 1977; Walters and Gourlay, 1990; Walters *et al.*, 1990).

But there is no evidence that this support is universally forthcoming. Walters and Gourlay (1990) comment that it can be difficult to find people willing to be safety representatives, and that some safety representatives complain that the support of the workforce is not forthcoming. While this study certainly found respondents very positive towards safety representatives, there was not great effusiveness. Certainly there was not strong evidence of Rees's (1988: 146) finding in the United States that safety representatives commanded the respect of their peers and were more likely to be respected among colleagues. While there was potential for safety representatives to add 'authority and competence to the system', there was evidence of some ambivalence. In this respect the findings accord with those of Dawson *et al.*'s (1988: 87) discussion of the chemical industry, where safety representatives and committees were considered to have increased awareness of health and safety but not proven to be a dominant force for improving health and safety.

Discussion

There was a general feeling that safety representatives played a useful and important role. There was evidence that they broadened the base of social support for occupational health and safety and that there was greater participation and involvement in workplace regulation than there might otherwise have been. But the extent of this participation was perhaps a far cry from that envisaged in Robens and the HSW Act, 1974. In common with other studies, this research did not find evidence of an 'identity of interest' in health and safety which led to accord between everyone in the workplace (Dawson *et al.*, 1988; Genn, 1993). So although legislation had led to the establishment of institutional structures and procedures as part of the company's constitution, it had not yet attained the status of a fully accepted part of everyday life.

Overall, being a safety representative was perceived as an unpopular job. Even within the context of a relatively strongly unionized workplace it was difficult in some areas to persuade anyone to become a safety representative. Moreover all grades of staff, across all departments, could more readily cite the disadvantages rather than the advantages attaching to the job. The major disadvantages mentioned suggest that a great deal of commitment was required in being a safety representative. Not only did the job involve a lot of work and time, it could also make one unpopular with colleagues and management alike. While unpopularity with colleagues seemed to concern the workforce the most, it seemed that the disapproval of management can have long-lasting effects. This became evident in one of my sample areas which was suffering severe difficulties in gaining safety representation. Managers, supervisors, and the workforce all gave the same explanation, namely that reluctance to become a safety representative was the direct result of a previous local manager who was disapproving of any kind of union representative, including safety representatives. His prejudice certainly made an impact, since ten years after his departure from the area his behaviour towards safety representatives was still widely discussed. Against all of this must be weighed the advantages and attractions of being a safety representative, namely an increased awareness of health and safety issues and the satisfaction which may accrue from 'getting something done'. These advantages again seem to lend some support to the view that commitment was essential.

Respondents generally attributed positive characteristics to safety representatives, the most frequently cited description being that safety representatives were caring people or people with an interest in health and safety. The most cynical might observe that only the most caring individuals would be prepared to take the job on given the numerous disadvantages generally associated with it. Certainly there seemed to be a number of obstacles to overcome if the role was to be accorded more general appeal.

None of this suggests that safety representatives held either a clearly defined or powerful role. The variability in even the facilities afforded safety representatives across this one company suggests that there is validity in criticisms that the HSW Act and its associated regulations lacked a clear definition of the role of safety representatives (Dawson *et al.*, 1988). In particular safety representatives emerge as being in a relatively powerless position, not necessarily gaining the support or respect of either their managers or their peers. It is possible that this was exacerbated during the research period because of the decline in union power and also the cutbacks in BR staffing. At such times the power imbalances which may hinder effective worker participation are emphasized. But the evidence of other studies is that this need not be the case. Rees (1988), for example, found that worker participation can be a very effective way of constituting health and safety as the everyday concern of everyone in the workplace. Arguably the position of worker representatives needs to be strengthened (Dalton, 1998; James and Walters, 1999; Nichols, 1999). The evidence from Australia is that safety representatives did not abuse great powers when they were accorded (La Trobe, 1990). But like other studies it was noted that the training and education of worker representatives was very important to their effectiveness. A vital element of this is communication and information about risk and it is to this topic that we now turn.

8

The Communication of Risk:
Information about Health and Safety

Communication emerges as a key issue both in this study and in other studies of risk and the impact of the law. The existing literature emphasizes the importance to corporate compliance of communication. Stone (1975: 201), for example, regards improving a company's internal information process as one of the most effective ways of influencing corporate behaviour. Sigler and Murphy (1988: 50) similarly cite education and awareness of regulation as vital components in achieving corporate compliance and Turner and Pidgeon (1997) underline its significance when they cite information and communication difficulties as a predisposing feature of disasters.

Communication is vital to both a company's relations with the outside world and to its internal relations with its employees. Large companies may be complicated organizations so communication within the company may be difficult. Policies have to be communicated to all areas of the company, some central, some more peripheral. They have to reach different levels of employee, different professions and trades, and in the case of BR, geographically diverse locations. BR was a complicated organization and one which experienced several reorganizations in the 1980s and early 1990s. Dissemination of information was therefore a potential problem. In order to ascertain the impact of health and safety initiatives at an everyday level it is therefore crucial that attention is paid both to differing areas of the company and also to its internal communication.

One of the aims of this research was to ascertain how much was understood about occupational health and safety across different areas of BR.[1] This is of central importance to the extent that if occupational health and safety are to become constitutive parts of everyday working life then it is crucial that they are known about. As we have seen, knowledge of the law, regulatory system, and also company health and safety systems, policies, and procedures was patchy within BR. Accordingly it was important to ask a number of broad-based questions about the sources of information available to BR staff and to include more specific questions about health and safety training and different types of communication.

---

[1] There is a distinction between knowledge of occupational health and safety and knowledge of the regulation of occupational health and safety. The focus in this chapter is upon both.

Sources of Information about Health and Safety

There was a variety of sources of information available to BR staff. There was information from the company, from the unions, and from HSE. There were also professional and trade sources and the general media. Moreover this information could take a number of forms, notably written, verbal, and visual. In addition there was health and safety training. Respondents were asked about their sources of information in three broad areas, namely general health and safety issues and the specific risks associated with their industry; information about the law and legal changes; and information about railway accidents.

The overwhelming majority of employees were aware that there was *general information* available to them about occupational health and safety. The exceptions were a very small minority of staff from the operations and mechanical and electrical engineering departments. The latter is especially surprising given that the problems associated with the dissemination of information might have been expected to have been fewer within the depot environment. The sources of information referred to by staff from across all the regions, departments, and grades of staff interviewed were numerous and varied, ranging from memos and circulars to policy statements, rule books, the law, and the news media.

Different grades of staff referred to different media. The *workforce* referred most frequently to posters and then to noticeboards and leaflets, whereas *safety representatives* were more likely to cite booklets and leaflets and then the local office library. *Managers* referred to a much wider range of sources. The only departmental difference of note was that three-quarters of civil engineering staff referred to the Civil Engineering Safety Manual. This was the only departmental manual to be cited in this way.

The overwhelming majority of sources mentioned by all staff were written sources. Only four of the twenty-two sources mentioned by supervisors, for example, were unwritten, namely training courses, safety personnel, a colleague, and a video. However, as has already mentioned in previous chapters, there were a number of very profound difficulties associated with written sources and the fact that the overwhelming proportion of sources of information were written was identified as a major problem by respondents. A variety of difficulties were referred to. A common complaint from all staff concerned *the volume of paperwork*. Managers and supervisors were most likely to read what was available, although many in these groups admitted that this was an ordeal and they did not necessarily read every word. The workforce was much less likely to read. Managers believed that too much paperwork was generated and that this created the danger that a lot was left unread. One manager commented:

> Like any other organization anything that is laid down in writing generates paperwork which can be a turn off, it can be a positive disincentive. The spirit may be willing to get involved with health and safety but it gets

bogged down in a lot of proforma and questionnaires to a manager, at the front line, at the sharp end, that can be a handicap. (manager, interviewee 45)

Genn (1993: 226) reports similar criticisms in her study of employer responses to health and safety regulation. Indeed she found that while the quantity of information generated posed problems for managers in both large and small companies, the quality and complexity of material 'weighed down' smaller companies, especially those without specialist staff to interpret it for them.

Difficulties of assimilation were mentioned by all grades of staff, especially supervisors. The written information available was considered by some to be unreadable. Indeed the typical workforce descriptions of the information were 'boring' and 'tedious'. Others found it difficult to read: 'I would have to be a lawyer to understand it. It's too complex at the moment, much too complex' (supervisor, interviewee 18). Uncertainty about whether or not the written information was actually read bothered some managers. They felt that a lot of paper was propagated downwards but they had no way of ensuring that it was read. Difficulties in finding time to read everything was mentioned by all staff. Several managers mentioned that they read a lot while travelling or in their own time at home. Members of the workforce complained that they had insufficient time to read the information at work. They perceived that the priority at work was to get the job done and they did not believe that it was legitimate to spend time reading health and safety information.

A fundamental problem for many workers and even some supervisors was their *alienation from the written word*. Managers and safety representatives were particularly aware that their staff were not always comfortable with the written word, perhaps being reluctant or finding it difficult to read, especially if they perceived the information available to be uninterestingly presented. These criticisms led to a preference for more verbal communication about health and safety:

> My health and safety policy statement is quite widely available but I honestly feel that just putting a document out to people, to noticeboards doesn't work, because very often we are dealing with people who are not word-oriented, written word-oriented, so we need to talk to people about it, we need to explain to them because it is word of mouth that makes the impression usually. . . . It has got to be . . . health and safety walkabouts with the safety representatives and general concern for matters which are reported through ordinary channels. I think that gets the message home far better than saying,—there is a copy of the Act, read it; here is a drawing pin on the appropriate noticeboard. People don't read that. (manager, interviewee 25).

Representatives of all of the different grades of staff and departments expressed the need to communicate directly with staff, offering the opportunity for explanation of misunderstood or difficult points. Team briefings, videos, and more training were offered as examples of how communication could be improved.

Comments about *particular forms of communication* were quite revealing of the difficulties of communicating in a large, complex organization. For instance, posters, which were the most frequently cited means of communication by the workforce and supervisors, attracted mixed views about their efficacy as a means of communication. It was explained that the positioning of posters was important. Mess rooms and exits were cited as good situations because it was difficult to avoid posters there. Most importantly, posters needed to be realistic. Staff must be able to relate to the situations portrayed on posters. The most frequently voiced criticism by staff of all grades was that many posters were an 'insult to man's common-sense' and were frequently patronizing. The words 'stupid' and 'belittling' were also common. There were two points here. The first was that the messages were too basic and the second was that the person depicted on the poster was 'too stupid' to identify with. Design was also important. Posters needed to be large and colourful and their message short and to the point. Outdated and wordy posters attracted criticism. The standards of 'pop art' required were high; they expected something commensurate with everyday advertising. Whether or not familiarity could lead to contempt led to a division of opinion. Some believed that the utility of the posters decreased as the number of posters increased. Others were of the opinion that anyone who draws on a poster has at least noticed it. Moreover it may not even be important that staff consciously read posters; the fact that they see them every day may be sufficient to transmit the message subconsciously. Similar criticisms were made about noticeboards, namely that their location matters as did the presentation of notices.

Videos were cited by several respondents as being a useful means of communication, with some potential for future development. But it was emphasized that they need to be well made and not too lengthy. Some observations were made about the content of videos, namely that they should be interesting and either humorous or shocking:

> The method of getting it over is the problem not the subject matter. I think it's got to be done more on the John Cleese-type films on management training—they in effect teach grandmothers to suck eggs but they don't make it seem as though they are . . . they are cleverly done so that you can actually see traits that 'yes maybe I do that'; making it dry, making it stuffy, no matter how simple you make the wording will not get over to people because there is not the interest to read it. (manager, interviewee 27)

The only arguments against videos centred on the use of the television. One respondent believed that the provision of television would encourage staff to watch them when they should be working. Another thought that staff saw far too much television already for a video to be useful. The most praised means of communication were interactive, for example, team briefings. They were not frequently mentioned but this may be because their absence was mentioned more than their presence. They were valued because they involved talking through problems with the staff and responding to their concerns. This was contrasted with a traditional method of relating the rules to staff, namely 'rule-reading' sessions when managers recited the rules aloud to groups of staff, apparently in a fairly perfunctory way.

Explanations of why there was not more verbal interaction with staff about health and safety issues centred on practical issues. For example the railway industry was a twenty-four hour industry where it could be difficult to communicate directly to different shifts, especially those who did not work in a centralized location, such as a workshop. Moreover, sitting staff down in one place to show them a video or talk to them involved taking them off their jobs and it was felt that arranging cover could be costly and difficult. Avoiding these practical difficulties was thought to be one of the only merits of written sources of information such as leaflets, but the criticisms were in themselves revealing of the weighting and priorities of these respondents.

Directors and *departmental safety officers* were well satisfied with the sources of information available to themselves. Directors had very little to say about the sources of information available to staff, although they did express strong views about the problems of communication when discussing the company's internal systems and controls for health and safety (see Ch. 6). They recognized the problems of the comprehensibility of the information available and also with its promulgation. Departmental safety officers expressed some strong views about the information available to staff. They agreed that there was a need to keep information simple and comprehensible. Indeed they considered that some of the information provided was either too legalistic or too technical. They also saw a need for rationalization of the various sources of information. One thought that there should be just one main source, namely a safety manual. Others noted that one of the problems was that the Board, regions, and departments all disseminated information and some co-ordination of effort seemed necessary. They all understood that verbal communication seemed to be more effective than written information. But one problem which concerned them with verbal information was the uniformity of the information being given. They were particularly concerned that managers were accorded a good deal of discretion and there was no obligation to have either team briefings or to purchase the equipment necessary for the use of videos.

While BR was the main source of general information about occupational health and safety, external sources figured most prominently in discussions about *sources of information about the law*. Knowledge of occupational health and safety legislation and any changes to it was strongly related to hierarchical position (see Ch. 4). *Directors* used external sources of information such as the Railway Industry Advisory Group and HSE, and they also relied on their departmental safety officers. In turn these senior safety officers used a variety of external sources ranging from Railway Industry Advisory Group working parties, personal contacts, occupational health and safety magazines, government publications, and Confederation of British Industry information.

Managers also used a variety of sources to keep up to date with legal changes, for instance BR, the HSE, ROSPA, and union publications plus the news media. The majority was confident that they knew of any changes to the law.[2] *Supervisors* used a similar range of sources, the only addition being that they learnt of changes to the law through their managers. They were fairly confident that they did hear about changes to occupational health and safety legislation.[3] *Safety representatives* and the *workforce* also learnt of changes to the legislation from a variety of sources, but unlike those further up the company hierarchy neither of these groups were confident that they heard of changes in the law.

Comments about the accessibility and complexity of the available information on the law very much mirrored comments on general sources of information. Again the large majority of sources were written, leading to the by now familiar complaints that there was insufficient time to read them and that often they were complicated and difficult to read.

The other specific area explored by the interviews was sources of information about *accidents on the railway*.[4] Responses on this subject again revealed strong hierarchical differences. *Directors* and *safety managers* learnt of serious accidents, involving a loss of life and/or widespread disruption, immediately. Their information about other accidents came mainly from the periodic accident statistics collected by the company:

> The practice here is that every accident that involves a loss of life of the member of staff is brought to my attention . . . normally within twenty four hours. If it is a weekend then perhaps it might be a little longer and then it is followed up with a report as to how, what the circumstances were, what are the causes, what is the ongoing action. I would normally be alerted if there is a serious accident that involves widespread disruption or catastrophic failure of a piece of equipment and if someone is very badly injured I would normally be. But it is mandatory over loss of life, it is mandatory over catastrophic equipment failure. . . . Over and above that I look at accident statistics as a routine basis of safety management. (director)

But there was a feeling that the statistics were generally inadequate and there was criticism of the reporting and collating procedures at this level, with one safety officer commenting that he did not hear of accidents either 'often enough or quickly enough'.

Half of the *managers* interviewed were confident that they heard about serious accidents but were less sure that they always heard about less serious

---

[2] 85% of managers (17/20) were confident that they learnt of legal changes.

[3] 63% (12/19) of supervisors were confident that they knew of changes to the law.

[4] The focus here is upon sources of information about accidents. Chapter 9 will consider what respondents knew about accidents and the implications of this.

accidents. Their main medium of communication was company records, either the monthly accident statistics or staff daily logs, otherwise they relied on the 'grapevine':

> Well major ones I find out straight away—I am on call one week in two and even if I am not on call I would expect to hear about a fatality. Major injuries, again I would get to hear straight away. In general small injuries I can only get a feel from the statistics that come around approximately monthly. At one stage one used to sign all the accident forms but that is now delegated to the administrative side . . . it is up to me to go and see the figures and see what is happening and I have a monthly team brief with the managers and we sometimes discuss if there is anything particularly relevant. (manager, interviewee 71)

> I only get to hear about accidents if they stop a person working, I'll hear if a person leaves work, does not report for work, or the supervisor tells me that he thinks it is worthwhile telling me. In other words if he thinks there is a deficiency in something that may reoccur. (manager, interviewee 108)

Supervisors were much less confident that they heard about accidents and were much more reliant than those further up the hierarchy on word of mouth:[5]

I: You only ever hear of accidents in general chit-chat.
R: So word of mouth?
I: Yeah, you are in the office, come in the office Monday, most of the accidents, most of them happen at weekends in overtime . . . my assistant will come in and say you will never guess what so-and-so has done yesterday . . . or a guy comes in to put it in the accident report book in the office and I say what have you done. (supervisor, interviewee 13)

I: How often do you get to hear about accidents?
R: Only when they are done in the depot, unless of course they are in the national press . . . (supervisor, interviewee 101)

The *workforce* and, more surprisingly, *safety representatives* were also heavily reliant upon the grapevine:[6]

I: How often do you get to hear about accidents?
R: Very rare, it is normally through a chain . . . by word of mouth. Occasionally we will get a proper report if it is on a fatality. We had one a little while ago in London, we had the report sent specifically to us . . . in our cabin for all of us to read. . . . That was stuck up for all of us to read

---

[5] Whereas 52% (13/25) of supervisors relied on the grapevine as their main source of information about accidents, 30% (8/27) of managers did so. Half of the managers reported written statistics and reports as their main source of information about railway accidents.

[6] Half of the workforce relied on word of mouth, 26% learnt of accidents through BR (noticeboards, reports, statistics, and the company's in-house magazine), and 20% heard of accidents through the news media (n = 50).

because it was an experienced shunter who had been there 25 years and he got crushed between two wagons and it was a simple mistake. (worker, interviewee 23).

I: How often do you get to hear about accidents?
R: Quite regular.
I: How do you get to hear about them?
R: Grapevine. The last one we heard a fortnight ago, an area movement inspector injured and I believe afterwards died. It was at Sheffield, it happened at the tea time and when we came on night duty at 9 o'clock we were all told about it.
I: So it travels quite fast?
R: Up and down the lines, yes. (worker, interviewee 47)

It was surprising that safety representatives were not better informed, since procedurally they should be informed of accidents. Also, one might have expected that they would be more involved in the investigation of local accidents, but no evidence of this emerged from the interviews.

The interviews therefore suggest that most people on BR learnt of accidents locally through word of mouth or, in the case of serious accidents, through the news media, although it may be observed here that the news media predominantly report passenger accidents rather than accidents involving injuries or loss of life to railway employees. There were apparent differences in *departmental* grapevines with signals and telecommunications staff reportedly using their stock in trade as an efficient means of relaying information and the operations department finding drivers to be a very effective way of spreading gossip through a region. Mechanical and electrical engineering staff wryly commented that it was fairly obvious if anything happened within their depot environment (although this did not mean that they readily learnt of accidents elsewhere):

> In this shop I would probably hear about 99 per cent of accidents . . . if there is an accident within here you hear someone scream or whatever, you hear it and the noise in such a small area. If it is a silly accident, you know someone has hit their thumb or something and cut it and gone up to the hospital then I normally make sure that they have put it in the accident book or I hear about it and see him and make sure that they have put it in the accident book so that they cover themselves for any later date if anything happens and they are not available because of this. (safety representative, interviewee 94)

Railway Inspectorate accident reports did not figure prominently as a source of information about accidents. In response to a general question about sources of information about accidents, three managers and three supervisors spontaneously referred to Railway Inspectorate reports. When more specific questions were asked about these reports the majority of staff said that they had seen copies but this was very much associated with their position in the hierarchy. Indeed there was some uncertainty amongst the workforce about whether these were Railway Inspectorate or BR reports.[7] It is surprising that more safety representatives were not familiar with these reports as one might have expected them to be in automatic receipt of them.

A major rationale for the Railway Inspectorate to keep investigating accidents under the 1871 legislation was the attendant publicity their reports would receive (Hutter, 1992). So respondents were asked if they found the reports useful. Interestingly perception of their usefulness was inversely related to their place in the hierarchy (see Table 8.1). So those staff who were least likely to see the reports considered them to be the most useful. Thus operations and mechanical and electrical engineering staff valued the Reports the most, while signals and telecommunications and especially civil engineering staff found them less useful. This may suggest some confusion about which reports respondents were thinking of when they answered these questions and this may have been partly caused by the circulation of report summaries by safety officers so the source was perceived to have been from within the company. Also, as we saw in Chapter 5, there was confusion about the status of the Railway Inspectorate among some staff. When staff were asked what it was that they valued about the reports they answered in much the way the Railway Inspectorate would have hoped, namely the reports caused them to stop and think about what they were doing, they pointed to the problem areas, and hopefully they would help prevent a recurrence.[8]

Training

Training courses were the most formal sources of information about health and safety provided by BR for its staff. All staff were meant to receive some occupational health and safety training as part of their induction course. Thereafter there were courses, videos, and seminars on specific topics. Staff were questioned about whether or not they had received this health and safety training. If they had, they were asked about how useful they had found it. If they had not received training, they were asked if they would have found it useful.

Table 8.2 details the health and safety training received by respondents. It shows that quite a high proportion of the overall sample did not consider that they had received any health and safety training. It may also be noted that this varied according to grade. Managers were the most likely to have received training and the workforce were the least likely. Of those who received training, the workforce was the most likely to have received specialist health and safety training, usually about specific topics such as first aid training, manual

[7] The following percentages of staff said that they had seen a Railway Inspectorate accident report: managers—97 (28/29); supervisors—87.5 (21/24); safety representatives—68 (13/19); workforce—46 (16/35).

[8] Since the Railway Inspectorate's incorporation into HSE there has been a reduction in the number of 1871 inquiries undertaken and a move to accident investigation under the HSW Act.

Table 8.1. The usefulness of Railway Inspectorate accident reports

Whether or not RI report found useful	Grade of staff								Total	
	Manager		Supervisor		Safety rep.		Workforce			
	n	%	n	%	n	%	n	%	n	%
Yes	13	65	13	72	10	83	8	89	44	75
No	3	15	3	17	—	—	—	—	6	10
Interesting	2	10	1	5.5	—	—	1	11	4	7
Irrelevant	2	10	1	5.5	2	17	—	—	5	8
Total	20	100	18	100	12	100	9	100	59	100

TABLE 8.2. Health and safety training received by BR staff

| Health and safety training received | Grade of staff | | | | | | Total | |
| | Manager | | Supervisor | | Workforce | | | |
	n	%	n	%	n	%	n	%
None	6	19	11	46	30	70	47	47.5
As part of another course	6	19	11	46	1	2	18	18.25
In 1974 only	9	28	1	4	—	—	10	10
Specific health and safety course	11	34	1	4	12	28	24	24.25
Total	32	100	24	100	43	100	99	100

lifting, lookout duties, or working in confined spaces. Of those who had received health and safety training, 80 per cent had found it useful although not always adequate and 10 per cent did not find it useful. Of those who had not received training, 63 per cent felt that it would have been useful if they had received it whereas 33 per cent felt that it would not have been useful.

Respondents identified four main advantages of health and safety training. The first, mentioned by all grades of staff, was the need to know what was expected with respect to health and safety. The second and third advantages were the need to increase awareness of health and safety matters and to bring staff up to date with the legislation and changes in the rules: 'It sharpened up one's awareness of the sort of things that one ought to be looking for and effectively brought up in front of you exactly the size of responsibility you have for that area' (manager, interviewee 136). The fourth reason, mentioned mainly by managers, was as a reminder of priorities and perspectives.

Those who considered health and safety training unnecessary gave two reasons for this. The most popular reason, mentioned by eleven members of the workforce and one supervisor, was that health and safety is 'all common-sense' and not a matter for education. The second argument was that experience is more important than training:

I: Do you think that it would have been useful if you had had some training?
R: No, it is as I say with my job, it's a dangerous job and it is down to common sense, you have to use your head. It is self-preservation, you don't make silly moves, you follow the rule book, you do as you are supposed to and make sure that you don't act in such a way that you are likely to get yourself killed or maimed. (worker, interviewee 23)

I didn't find the training useful. It all seems it was teaching your grandmother to suck eggs because everybody turned around and said well I wouldn't do that anyway. (manager, interviewee 27)

Managers felt particularly disadvantaged by the quantity and quality of training they received, especially when compared with the health and safety training received by safety representatives (see Ch. 6):

I think it is the general comment made by managers that the full-time union-appointed safety representatives get ten days' instruction and managers, if they get anything, get a couple of hours. When the Health and Safety Act was first implemented there were seminars and various things to explain what difference it was going to make but I think that you will find if you spoke to my line manager or any of the other line managers who have been appointed to their post within the last five years, they would say that they have no formal instruction whatsoever in hazard recognition, or even legislation. (manager, interviewee 81)

A knowledgeable safety representative could, in the view of some managers, prove embarrassing because the safety representative would, in all probability, know more than them. More to the point, managers did not necessarily know if the safety representative's demands were legitimate and hence might feel compromised.

Criticisms of training referred to both its quantity and quality. Staff in all departments and at all levels, but particularly managers, felt that refresher courses were essential:

> . . . to remind us all about our priorities and perspectives. (manager, interviewee 44)

> . . . the danger is you only retain so much of it and the longer the period of time I guess, the more you forget it. There is nothing worse than a manager who has one hand tied behind his back and one eye closed because he isn't aware of what has happened. (manager, interviewee 45)

Nine of the thirty-two managers interviewed had not received any training since the introduction of the HSW Act: 'Since the initial rush when the Health and Safety Act first came out and there was a rush to educate people, nothing has happened since.' (manager, interviewee 108).

The quality of training also attracted criticism. *Managers, supervisors,* and some members of the *workforce* considered that the health and safety training available was minimal, insufficient, unsophisticated, and at worst 'boring and patronizing'. A minority of managers added that in their opinion instructors were too low grade and unable to appreciate their problems. Moreover it was remarked that often the surroundings within which the training occurred were dingy and little equipment was available to instructors: 'Everybody's sent on a course and then the place you go . . . it's dirty, dingy, it's no good. It's got no video and the chap who's giving the lecture has to apologize for the room, he's got no equipment to assist him.' (supervisor, interviewee 68). All of these criticisms suggested to some staff that health and safety training was not regarded seriously.

Some suggestions were made about how to improve the content and quality of training. These included a call for practical courses rather than exclusively classroom training and for courses where the language and course content were simple and familiar rather than legalistic or technical. One supervisor exemplified this in his request for a 'version which is more in workshop language than the lawyer version' (interviewee 101).

All of the *directors* and *safety managers* valued training in occupational health and safety. Interestingly only three of the seven directors interviewed had received any training and, more surprisingly, one of the four safety managers had not received any either. All of those who had not received the training felt disadvantaged and even referred to it as a 'gap' in their careers. One in this group also expressed the view that health and safety is secondary to production and not accorded financial priority:

R:	We don't operate any specific health and safety training which you could hold up and say 'this is a three-day manager's course in health and safety'. I think this is one of the big areas that we as a company fall down on because when I first started . . . the region was running a series of seminars, training for managers and supervisors in health and safety as to what their responsibilities were and they were provided by the regional safety organization . . . That has slowly petered out over the years and to the best of my knowledge there is nothing like that available now. So while managers and many of them are young and new, have had no health and safety training whatsoever, and I think that is why you have got these gaps in the system because we are not training them.

I:	Why do you think the training has petered out?

R:	Well, because I don't think that anybody . . . has ever put any money on it. You see we have been very headless in the safety organization . . . it has been treated very lightly by some people on the Board . . . it's pie in the sky because of the current financial climate, the possibilities of being sold off to privatization and one thing and another. I can't see us spending money on a non-productive unit, because that is what it amounts to.

The perception of lack of support from the top of the company could be of central importance. This is a topic which will be examined much more closely in the next part.

Discussion

In her study of the impact of occupational health and safety, Genn (1993) argues that the first step in educating employees about health and safety is access to information, the next step is reading it, and the third step is understanding it. As we have seen, this is a complicated process and the evidence of this study, like Genn's, is that the first step is more readily achieved than the second two.

The overwhelming majority of BR interviewees were aware that information about health and safety was available to them. Numerous sources were cited, but these were mainly written sources and there was a general perception that verbal communication is much more effective. The main source of unwritten health and safety information is training. This was not perceived as being generally available and when it was available it was not regarded as being of a very high quality. Little time was thought to be allocated to health and safety, either for training or to read the information disseminated through the organization and see the videos which were available. Communication thus emerges as one of BR's key areas of difficulty in responding to occupational health and safety regulation.

These findings accord with Nelkin and Brown's (1984) that workers felt poorly informed and felt that they had inadequate knowledge of workplace hazards. Indeed the inequalities in knowledge about health and safety regulation found throughout this study are partly explained by the findings of this chapter namely that information flows reflect organizational style and that style was hierarchical (Turner and Pidgeon, 1997). So those at the top of the organization have more information available to them. This is partly because they have a greater range of sources available to them, because the forms of information available were more accessible to managerial staff, and because the higher one goes up through a hierarchical organization such as BR the greater the personal control there is over time. In other words, inequalities in knowledge relate to other structural inequalities as well as to more specific communication and media issues. It is clearly important that this is understood when considering how communication might be improved and particularly significant given the communitarian aims of the regulation. Regulatory objectives demand that everyone in a company is well informed, most especially so that they understand the risks attaching to the workplace and how to manage those risks. So clearly this is an area demanding attention.

It was undoubtedly the case that BR staff responses were influenced by the fact that they were surrounded in their everyday lives by sophisticated means of communication such as advertising, television, and videos. It seemed that they expected the same high standards at work, which were largely unforthcoming. Attention needed to be given to providing staff with a greater understanding of the broad principles and issues of occupational health and safety in terms of both a basic training and periodic refresher courses. All sources of information needed a great deal of thought about how to increase their availability, accessibility, and interest. Many of those lower down in the organization were ill at ease with written sources of information and access to visual sources of information and training was relatively limited. Staff needed practical, participatory, and interactive communication. Credibility was important to the content of courses, their communication, the person communicating, and the teaching environment. Reiterating the message of other research, it is essential that communication is clear, simple, and disseminated. This means paying attention to design, the language used, and also to rationalizing and co-ordinating health and safety training and information. Simply bombarding with a mass of information without any sense of strategy and direction within an organization could even be counterproductive.

One of the main aims of occupational health and safety regulation was to constitute health and safety as a normal and important part of everyday life. As Sigler and Murphy (1988) comment, the aim is to incorporate regulatory compliance as part of corporate culture. As Rees (1994) elaborates, this involves more than conforming to the law or being competent. Rees refers to this as 'institutionalizing responsibility' and he explains that 'being responsible involves an inner commitment to principles and principled conduct that define and uphold a special competence' (1994: 125). The literature emphasizes that such an objective needs to be fulfilled throughout a organization, from the top to the bottom. Especially important is a strong commitment from the top (Sigler and Murphy, 1988: 103), signalled, for example, in the quality of training provided. Moreover, to be effective, these objectives need to part of the working life of all employees (ibid. 104).

The literature suggests that education and persuasion are the best means of attaining these goals (Rees, 1994: 160), since the reasons for the objective need to be explained and understood. Rees (ibid.) argues that this includes treating staff with dignity, whereas a theme which ran through the BR research findings as a recurring criticism of the existing material was that it was patronizing to the workforce. Sigler and Murphy (1988: 102) stress that compliance programmes need to recognize that corporate cultures vary and thus be tailored to a company's overall culture. Likewise it needs to be recognized that different groups within a company may need addressing in different ways according, for example, to their grade or specialism (Sigler and Murphy, 1988: 102; Stone, 1975).

The literature advocates the broad range of means of education used by BR and stresses the importance of using a variety of methods[9] although on the basis of this research one has to caution that this be done within the context of an overall strategy rather than piecemeal (see above). Sigler and Murphy (1988: 80 ff.) suggest that this effort needs to be continuous. Again this is supported by this research where respondents reiterated the need for refresher courses and specific time put aside for health and safety purposes. The importance of there being specified company personnel charged with promulgating regulatory material is also important. Sigler and Murphy (1988: 140) recommend that natural 'compliance constituencies' are charged with this task, for example, those specialisms which by virtue of their job are interested in compliance. Another suggestion in the literature is that companies could be aided in their task by external bodies. For instance, governments could help in the educative role (Sigler and Murphy, 1988: 139). Alternatively companies could be legally required to disseminate certain types of information within the company (Stone, 1975: 206). The crucial point is that the message gets to all parts of organizations and that it is understood and 'internalized'. Essential here is that those in positions of power in the organization throw their weight, in terms of resources and commitment, behind achieving this. It is also important that information and communication is a two-way process. It is not simply about the dissemination of information throughout an organization but it is also about collecting and collating information from the organization. It is fair to say that these matters were generally not as well understood at the time of data

---

[9] Gricar and Hopkins (1983) used informational responses as one of the factors to gauge organizational responses to health and safety regulation. Their findings were counter-intuitive as they found this factor did not appear to help reduce accidents. They suggest two reasons for this. One is that they used a one-year time lag which was insufficient for the purposes of measuring responses. Secondly, information alone is ineffective unless it is coupled with other safety practices.

collection as they are now.[10] The importance of this research is to enhance our understanding of how communication may be improved and the implications of communicating successfully about risk.

Nelkin and Brown (1984: 74) suggest that better informed workers are more likely to use personal protection and comply with risk management programmes. A repeated explanation in this research for not paying attention to health and safety communications was the opportunity cost of doing so or, put more bluntly, there was always something more pressing to do. The next section will focus more specifically on this in its consideration of understandings of risk and their relationship to the incentives and costs of compliance.

[10] One of the main outputs of the Interdepartmental Liaison Group on Risk Assessment has been guidance on risk communication (ILGRA, 1998).

PART IV

CONSTITUTIVE REGULATION? RISK AND COMPLIANCE

9

Understandings of Risk and Uncertainty

One purpose of regulation, and of the corporate risk management systems it encouraged, was to decrease the health and safety risks to individuals working on the railways. The legislation, associated regulations, and corporate systems and rules were directed to ensuring that the everyday risks to workers were minimized within the context of running a national rail network. So it aimed to manage, rather than eliminate, the everyday risks to the thousands of employees within the industry.

The previous two parts of this book have considered the legal and corporate systems in place and the knowledge of both of these among BR staff. In this part we will concentrate on respondents' understandings of the risks associated with their industry and how these understandings may have influenced their working lives. This chapter will focus on how much was known of the accidents which happened to BR employees at work and will try to discern the impact of these accidents. It will also consider respondents' more general understandings of the risks associated with their working environment and how they react to them. Chapter 10 will examine issues of compliance and non-compliance with risk management systems as they were manifested in state and corporate regulation. How much were individuals prepared to comply? What were their reasons for compliance and non-compliance? And importantly, how did these explanations match up with their understandings of the risks they encountered? The focus of this chapter will therefore be upon the understandings within BR about occupational health and safety risks, whereas Chapter 10 will focus on the propensity to take risks within the structure of the regulatory system.

Knowledge of Accidents

In considering the understandings of risk held by BR staff it is important to appreciate that the research concentrated on involuntary risks respondents were exposed to through work. It also focused on considering crude understandings rather than precise technical calculations, so deals with uncertainty rather than risk. Moreover, the intention of the research was not to be prescriptive but rather to relate 'what it was like for them'. The objective was to find out how company staff perceived the dangers associated with their work. What were their levels of awareness and how did they respond? As Nelkin and Brown cautioned in 1984 (p. ix), 'the perceptions and concerns of workers is a neglected area of risk assessment'. The situation has not changed very much since then so it should be borne in mind that the tools of analysis are relatively unsophisticated. The main aim is to give an impression of how understandings of risk may have contributed to the fulfilment or otherwise of regulatory objectives.

BR employees were asked a number of general questions on the subject of accidents which were followed up with much more specific and detailed questions, the objective being to ascertain employees' understandings of the 'objective risks' associated with their industry and most particularly their company. Generally respondents did identify accidents as one of the major indicators of risk. They differentiated between major and minor accidents, the general consensus being that there were few major and numerous minor accidents. Major accidents were generally taken to mean those resulting in fatalities or serious injury to either members of the public or the workforce. Minor accidents were regarded as more 'routine' and 'everyday' and included such things as cuts, grazes, and sprained ankles. These were categorizations that arose from respondents' experiences and understandings of occupational health and safety accidents and they broadly mirrored the distinctions in the regulations between major and minor accidents (see Ch. 3).

Respondents' main focus seems to have been upon the major accidents and evidently opinions differed about the acceptability of these: 'I suppose it's a lot but there again taking the people they got about I don't suppose it's all that many really' (worker, interviewee 65). Directors and departmental safety managers considered that in absolute terms there were either 'too many' or 'a lot' of accidents on the railway. But this was qualified by two in this group who believed that the numbers were few relative to the size of the workforce, the twenty-four hour nature of the industry, and the environment within which the workforce operated.[1]

Specific questions about the number of occupational safety accidents there had been the year before revealed widespread ignorance. Ability to reply was structured largely according to position in the hierarchy (Chart 9.1). These differences very much reflected the contingencies of work, most particularly receipt of company reports (Ch. 7). Consideration of accident reports and statistics was part of managers' workloads and they were the most confident that they saw accident reports and statistics whereas the workforce, in the context of these questions, did not refer to any accident data. The majority of safety representatives believed that they had access to the relevant accident information but not all supervisors received the accident data. Access to the data did not necessarily mean that it was read or retained. Safety representatives remarked that it could be very difficult to get through the data they received in addition to their other responsibilities. Managers claimed to read the information but

---

[1] 32.5% of all respondents asked about this thought that there were too many accidents; 10% thought that there were quite a lot of accidents; and the majority of 57.5% considered that there were not many accidents (n = 80).

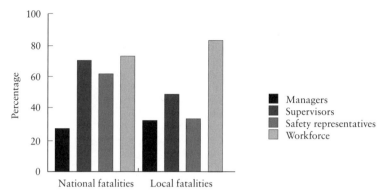

CHART 9.1. Percentage of staff unable to respond to question about worker fatalities according to position in hierarchy

they did not really have a feel for the figures and certainly could not remember them.

Of those attempting to estimate the number of staff fatalities in the previous year, 36 per cent (17/48) replied within the correct range of 11 to 20. Supervisors and safety representatives were most accurate.[2] Managers were most likely to overestimate the figures whereas the workforce were equally inclined to over- as underestimate the figures. At the most senior levels of the company the departmental safety managers were the most knowledgeable, with half of them knowing precise fatality numbers for the company and their department and one knowing how many major accidents there had been. The rest tended to underestimate the number of fatalities but were broadly within the correct range. They had no idea of departmental or major accident figures.

It is perhaps unsurprising that staff were unable to recite specific accident figures.[3] This said, one might expect that they would have a broad idea of the type of accidents and causes of accidents in the industry. When they were asked what sort of accidents happen on the railways, a fairly wide range of responses were offered. The most frequently cited types of accident were as shown in Table 9.1.

There were few departmental differences in the type of accidents mentioned. The only difference of note was predictable, namely that civil engineering staff were more likely, and mechanical and electrical engineering staff were markedly less likely, to refer to track-related injuries than other groups. Nor were there any major differences among the responses of various grades of staff. It was notable that many of the major injuries which feature in the overall accident

---

[2] Only 7 respondents in each group felt able to make an estimate at all. But 57% of these were able to give an accurate response.

[3] Clay (1984: 166) found that almost all of his respondents had difficulty in estimating the percentage of human cancers due to exposure to carcinogens which were used by 15 out of 40 of his sample.

TABLE 9.1. Staff understandings of the types of accidents on the railways

	Percentage of total references
Slipping, tripping, and falling	21
Bangs and trapped fingers	16
Cuts and abrasions	12
Track-related injuries (hit by train/fatalities)	12
Lifting injuries	11
Sprains	6
Electrocution	4
Burns	3
Machinery-inflicted injuries	3

statistics were not mentioned at all except by the most senior staff. These included fractures, amputations, blinded eyes, and serious multiple fractures. This is not entirely unexpected. Given the low number of such injuries, the probability of many respondents in this sample knowing about them was low. The most senior staff would have been most familiar given their focus on company-wide accident data.

The causes of accidents were perceived to be disparate, ranging from being killed by a train (14 per cent of total references) to carelessness (27 per cent of total references) and poor housekeeping (especially poor surfaces) (17 per cent of total references).[4] Perspectives on accidents were very much situationally generated. For example, the only difference between grades of staff was that supervisors were the most ready to attribute carelessness as a major cause of accidents, while senior managers were most likely to refer to non-compliance and poor management. Departmentally there were differences which very much accorded to the nature of work carried out by each department. For example, mechanical and electrical engineering staff most frequently referred to injuries caused by machinery and tools; and signals and telecommunications department and operations staff most frequently referred to poor housekeeping, especially poor surfaces such as oily or icy walking routes and sleepers and loose ballast. Mechanical and electrical engineering and signals and telecommunications department staff were most likely to refer to carelessness. Civil engineering staff were again most likely to refer to fatalities caused by moving trains:

I: What sort of accidents?
R: Get hit by a train I should think. I should think that's the main one, being crushed with things being loaded etc.
I: What sort of accidents?
R: Individuals not paying attention, more often or not.

---

[4] The two other most frequently cited causes were machines and tools—17% of total references and being electrocuted—8% of total references.

I: What happens to them?

R: It could be perhaps get a bang on the leg or if there's a lot of heavy work, moving rails etc. You might catch your foot or something like that. Just for the mere fact that they weren't paying attention, you know they were thinking about their girlfriend the night before or something. (worker, civil engineering department: interviewee 77)

The question of carelessness, of course, points to the issue of whose carelessness and in turn highlights the broader matter of blame. These issues were explored through a variety of questions in the interviews.

Blame and Fault

A very broad question about *fault* was asked, namely 'Whose fault are they [accidents] usually?' Ninety-one per cent of respondents felt able to answer and they offered a variety of answers, many regarding accidents as the consequence of several factors. The most frequently referred to were as shown in Table 9.2.

There were variations in responses according to department and grade. Departmental differences very much reflected variations in working conditions. Mechanical and electrical engineering staff, for example, were the most likely to attribute blame to faulty or noisy equipment, something they may have been particularly aware of in their workshop environment. Signals and telecommunications department staff regarded working conditions, especially poor standards of housekeeping on or about the track, as a major contributory factor to accidents and typically they blamed the civil engineering department for this. Civil engineering staff were much more likely to blame a lack of supervision by supervisors for accidents. Variations according to grade of staff also reflected their different working environments. Safety representatives were, for instance, the most likely to blame management for accidents. Also a greater proportion of supervisors and workforce cited lack of supervision as the cause of accidents,

TABLE 9.2. Staff understandings of whose fault railway accidents are

Cause	Percentage of references
Victim's own fault	39
Carelessness	6
Non-compliance	5
Staff (complacency, 'skylarking')	6
Management	8
Lack of supervision	5
Conditions/Housekeeping	6
Problems with equipment (lack of/faulty/too noisy)	5

both of these groups of course being the ones which experience the most continuous daily supervision at track and workshop levels.

Many of the factors cited by staff did not directly attribute fault to any particular categories of person. It was often a matter of interpretation as to who was held responsible. For example, housekeeping offences were regarded by some as the fault of management, their argument being that management did not allow sufficient time to clear up once a job was completed. Others blamed maintenance staff for these problems, arguing that they did not bother to clear up the site. Non-compliance was also subject to variable interpretation. Some regarded it as the fault of those not complying whereas others considered it to be a supervisory problem, that is, an enforcement problem, whereas another group blamed the rule-makers for impractical rules. It is notable that these accounts blame either the victim or another group of employees within the company. It suggests that there was an abdication of self-blaming for accidents which were regarded as the result of another's actions (or lack of them). It is also noteworthy that blame was apportioned, as this implies that respondents considered that something could be done to prevent accidents; they were not simply the result of 'fate'.

All of this of course serves to highlight the diversified character of blaming and the difficulties in attributing blame and the need for a multi-causal approach to fault attribution. Senior managers certainly took this approach. The majority in this group believed that accidents were the fault of both the victim and management, with a greater emphasis on the responsibilities of the latter. Management were attributed blame for a lack of enforcement, for not ensuring that good working and environmental conditions were maintained, and sometimes for placing too much pressure on staff to complete work quickly. The workforce was considered to be at fault for carelessness and non-compliance whatever its cause:

> . . . it is very easy to talk about categorizing accidents and whose fault it is, there are so many different factors—right tools provided, right materials, right advice, right management guidance. At the end of the day I think we probably glibly attempt to categorize and probably come up with missing the real reason behind it, which may be multi . . . most work situations are fairly complicated. (director)

> A variety of reasons. Why do accidents occur, well that is a good question. I think ignorance, inability, lack of awareness, and I think simply to quickly do something, to bodge something up or something or other where they were unaware maybe of the rules, that is some of the reasons. I would say that the majority of them occur because staff are unaware in some cases of the correct procedure . . . some could well be attributed to bad management or bad supervision. It is not always the person who makes the mistake who is injured, it may be down the chain. It may be a circumstance, you see accidents, a lot of accidents actually occur through a set of

circumstances but how those circumstances existed in the first place could be because of poor management, lack of attention to detail, lack of application of instructions and regulations, or poor supervision of the shop floor. It may not be the person who is injured. (safety officer)

Well it is always over easy an accident being called . . . just purely bad luck. It is an element of bad luck or bad behaviour . . . I would say at least half of the cases, or three-quarters were the person putting themselves in danger, whether it be the painter who puts his scaffolding without proper protection, it is the lookout man working with the gang on the p/way, it is the shunter who has not put out his red lamp before going under the train, or it is the driver who has not looked out for the sign for moving trains, and so, you know, it tends to be somebody not following, not following safety procedures . . . (manager, interviewee 25)

Staff Involvement with Accidents
One measure of the extent to which staff might have come into contact with the actual risks of working on the railways was directly through their own involvement with accidents. The workforce were asked if they had ever experienced an accident and managers, supervisors, and safety representatives were questioned about the extent of their involvement when accidents did occur. The majority of the workforce had experienced an accident, the exception being signals and telecommunications department staff.[5] Only one person considered that they had personally suffered a serious accident, a member of the mechanical and electrical engineering department who had strained his back and had been off work for an initial period of ten weeks and for another seven weeks later.

The types of accidents the workforce had experienced varied, as one might expect, according to department. Civil engineering staff suffered burns, being hit by a bar or rail, or suffering a trolley going over a foot. Mechanical and electrical engineering staff suffered bumped heads, burns, cuts, and sprained ankles caused by slipping. Operations staff cited cuts and bruises and a broken ankle and foot caused by slipping. Signals and telecommunications department staff referred to cuts, burns, and arc eye.

The majority of staff had become involved in the event of an accident.[6] This was especially so for supervisors who were the most likely to be informed immediately an accident occurred. They may have been called upon to administer first aid and would have been expected to fill out accident report forms. Managers tended to be directly involved if they were called upon to lead an inquiry following a serious accident. Other than this their involvement was

[5] The following percentages of workers had personally been involved in an accident: civil engineering—75%; mechanical and electrical engineering—71%; operations—76%; signals and telecommunications department—29%.
[6] 58% of managers, 92% of supervisors, and 53% of safety representatives became involved in the event of accidents; 23% of managers and 10% of safety representatives only became involved if the accident was serious.

usually indirect and concerned them checking and looking through accident books and forms:

> Usually only if it involves the expenditure of money then it will come to me, money in terms of putting right something that may have been found wanting or indeed something that needs improving. It may not have to be inherently unsafe but we could find something that is a bit safer. So I would spend money on there. I have a welfare responsibility as all managers do anyway so you may go and see a member of staff and we have had a couple this week. We have had a couple of incidents where we will probably go and see. . . . I will make a particular point of maybe stopping off and talking to them. (manager, interviewee 45)

Safety representatives became involved if the accident was serious, if there was a dispute about an accident, or if a compensation claim was submitted. Some investigated accidents and submitted reports to their branch and others informed members of their rights and ensured that correct procedures were followed. The involvement of senior managers was indirect. It mainly centred on examining accident statistics and accident reports. From these they identified hazards; checked that the proper procedures had been adhered to; and used the data to direct efforts and resources in the most effective way. Conceptualizations of accidents therefore varied greatly between different groups of employees with workers' views being directly informed by their everyday experiences in the workplace whereas managers experienced accidents indirectly through reading reports.

Non-reporting of accidents was mentioned by all grades of staff from all departments. Minor rather than major accidents were the most likely to go unreported and one respondent estimated that as many as 50 per cent of accidents fell into this category. Two main reasons were forwarded for not reporting accidents. The first was that people did not want to admit how silly they had been. The second and the main reason was that filling in the accident forms was too time consuming and they did not see the point in reporting, for example, a cut thumb:

R: There are many that are not reported.
I: Why might that be?
R: Sometimes I think mainly because the people concerned think they are partially or perhaps wholly to blame. I have always encouraged people over a good many years to report the accidents no matter whose fault and how it occurred, mainly in case there are after-effects of the accident later on, so there is a record of it and since I have understood some years ago that records were compiled of accidents and more serious ones had to be reported to a higher authority this part of it cannot be completed unless people at the ground level where these things occur initially report them . . .
I: What sort of proportion do you think are not reported of the total?
R: Oh, at least 50 per cent. (worker, interviewee 47)

The Impact of Accidents

As we have seen, most of those interviewed had been in contact with accidents at some time in their career, either directly or indirectly. All staff reported broadly similar views about the impact of accidents. Minor accidents were generally regarded as having very little impact. Major accidents were felt to have a salutary effect but usually only in the short term. The majority view was that major accidents could change behaviour temporarily but would have no long-lasting effects:

> Do I know what impact—I find that a difficult one to answer, more than most. It is rather like an accident on the motorway. I think everyone drives more slowly afterwards . . . a driver who just either witnesses or seen an accident, you know gives more care than he perhaps had done previously because it is on his mind and you get these sort of things with level-crossing accidents. Rather like human nature, impact immediate and then tends to dawdle away as time and memory is erased. (director)

> It depends on the scale of this matter, should it be something severe obviously everybody is going to be very very concerned and then we will all get together and see how we can ever stop this sort of thing happening again. And I think minor bumps on the head and things and nails in their feet are taken a little bit lightly and I think sometimes it shouldn't be taken so lightly you know but it is no joking matter . . . somebody got a nail in his foot the other day and somebody had said to him 'well, that wouldn't have happened if you wore a bump cap'. (safety representative, interviewee 90)

> R: If it is a major one then I think, if it was one of us, one of our group, there are only four of us, if one of us had, I think it would hit all of us. But with minor ones we tend to a certain degree treat it as a joke, it is laughed off more as a joke. It is not taken that seriously, especially if it is a bloke like me who have silly accidents, they are laughed at, I mean it was my own fault that I did my face in.
>
> I: You don't think that it would make any of the men you are working with more careful in the future about doing that?
>
> R: No, they just laughed and called me a stupid idiot for doing it. It is like someone the other day had a silly little accident and we have laughed at them. (worker, interviewee 23)

It was only a minority of staff who considered that the impact could be long lasting or even permanent. These exceptions, when the effect lasted longer than the short term, were when a worker had witnessed the death of a close colleague. This could result in a permanent change of behaviour, time off from work, or even cause a worker to leave the railways. Near misses were regarded by some as having a greater impact than news of fatalities:

I think fatalities have quite an important influence, surprisingly sometimes . . . Fatalities I do think have an influence because generally the workforce are fairly cohesive and they do all know each other and they all live together day in day out and if somebody actually gets killed that really does have an impact. And I think really major accidents have an impact as well. I mean when this chap got electrocuted that had quite an impact on everybody. I mean they had all worked quite hard to try and make things safe and it was a really nasty shock. I mean it is somebody that you worked with and so on. I think the problem is the run of the mill things like tripping, falling, and the odd broken ankle and bashed finger and all that, don't have nearly enough effect frankly. (director)

I: What sort of impact does an accident have upon the workforce?
R: It can have a devastating effect, where I was in BREL, when we lost a lad through burns, who died on his way to hospital, and that had a devastating effect on the workforce.
I: Do you think it had a permanent effect?
R: Well it must have done because you lose somebody that you know. I mean a lot of people just have working colleagues, you know the lad, you know you don't have to know his family, and of course a lot of them with working locally you probably know the family anyway. And if he has got really badly done you have got to feel something for the wife, if you see her you know it is difficult. It was bad that one, that broke two hearts I am afraid that one. (supervisor, interviewee 101)

The majority of respondents gave specific examples of major—usually fatal—accidents. These examples were often recalled in detail and were usually local, sometimes happening as much as twenty years previously:

I: When there is an accident what sort of impact does it have upon you and your colleagues?
R: Well if it's fatal very bad.
I: In what sort of way?
R: Well if it's one of your workmates, we all get on together like you know, and somebody goes like that it's very, very upsetting.
I: Does it make everyone more careful?
R: Because my ganger got killed by a train at 'X' and I couldn't eat my dinner for two days.
I: Was that recently?
R: I'm talking about twenty years, over twenty years. I couldn't eat nothing for two days because I was so upset in myself you know.
I: Yes, were you there when it happened?
R: No but I saw the body laid on the platform. You know covered up . . . and that upset me for a week, really upset me because I used to go out and have

a drink with him at night when we finished work and that, you know we finished work. Things like that is upsetting.

I: Do accidents like that make you more careful?

R: On the line, yes.

I: How long would that last for?

R: I got it in my mind all the time. (worker, interviewee 114)

It depends on every instance. Certainly the aftermath of somebody being killed or perhaps having a limb amputated or something like that would literally be in the local folklore for years and you tend to find that they will not repeat the same again, they will teach the new shunter or the new carriage cleaner that's what happened . . . That will, but potentially dangerous incidents which possibly don't actually end up with anybody being hurt or minor grazes or something will probably die after a matter of a few months unfortunately. (manager, interviewee 3)

This suggests that such accidents did make a substantial impact but any possible change in behaviour may be overcome by an underlying feeling that 'life carries on' or 'it won't happen to me':

R: Well initially . . . if a railman gets hit there is always immediate sympathy and they think 'cor make sure it don't happen to us'. But I would say within a couple of hours they have forgotten it.

I: A couple of hours?

R: As quick as that, yes, very quickly. (supervisor, interviewee 13)

R: When I cut my head I've said 'What a silly billy I am'. I wasn't wearing a bump hat, I mean I still in general don't wear a bump hat.

I: Did you wear one next time you went back?

R: No it's just a hazard of the job. You know as long as you're not getting fingers cut off and things like that you just put up with it. The occasional cut on the hand or something like that . . .

I: Why don't you wear your hat?

R: It's just uncomfortable. You end up with a head shaped and hair shaped of the bump hat. (worker, interviewee 84)

In the immediate aftermath of an accident a variety of responses were possible, depending not just upon the severity of the accident but also how close the accident was geographically, departmentally, over time, and personally. The personal make-up of individuals was also considered relevant. The range of emotions described by respondents included anger, sorrow, upset, devastation, and a lowering of morale. The impact upon the family of the injured was cited as being especially upsetting if the accident was local.[7] The behavioural impact ranged from a temporary change of behaviour and increased vigilance to promoting staff curiosity and causing a lot of questions to be asked:

---

[7] Nelkin (1985: 15) suggests that the emotional distress caused by exposure to risks is often ignored, especially in cost-benefit calculations.

I think it depends on what it is. If it is something that you are all probably doing wrong but it is a shortcut to achieving, you know saves time etc, and then somebody comes unstuck doing it. I think maybe people then sort of don't do it for a little while but it soon creeps back in, bad practices do creep back in. Otherwise in a lot of cases I do think that people do tend to think it is bad luck or somebody . . . the idea of somebody being accident prone comes into it quite a lot. (safety representative, interviewee 54)

R: It depends very often whether we have been very close to the people concerned. If we happen to know them of course the impact is a lot greater.
I: Has that happened to you . . . ?
R: It has yes. I have seen it on more than one occasion unfortunately.
I: What, people being seriously injured or killed?
R: Killed. It has not been a very pleasant thing. It has affected me yes. If it has been too bad I have usually had a couple of days off.
I: Would it make you more careful when you did whatever they were doing?
R: Well you try to think it will. You say to yourself I am definitely going to be a bit more careful here, blow it poor old Joe has had it, I'll make sure it don't happen to me.
I: Do you think that works?
R: It does for a time I think.
I: Not long?
R: Not long. I suppose it depends how serious it really was, whether the impact stays longer than what it should do.
I: Were you talking about weeks or months then, or years?
R: Well weeks, yes certainly on very serious things. (worker, interviewee 113)

The organizational impact of accidents was mentioned by a few. This included the internal impact of the introduction of another set of instructions, something that was not necessarily regarded as a good thing to the extent that it may not tackle the root problem. One departmental safety manager explained that it was costly to lose trained staff either permanently or temporarily:

In terms of the impact, one is to decrease the efficiency of the workforce and by that I mean if you, if somebody is hurt various things happen. One is that there is an immediate effect, if you have got the gang stopped for the day or whatever, and particularly if it is a serious accident that can actually have quite a short-term shock effect on people as well. If you actually see somebody badly hurt particularly when it is in your environment, it is different coming across a road accident to actually being part of it. So there is the shock thing . . . which leads to a lack of efficiency, if you lost a person five or six weeks even, sometimes even months. So immediately that has an impact on the gang, they have to reorganize gangs because you can't just bring people in like that, and I think that at the end, or within all that there is a situation where you can actually get to hostility because people have said

'We told the boss about that before and you', all the goodwill that has been generated is suddenly destroyed and it takes a lot of rebuilding because it is their mate that has been hurt. . . . I think it is very costly because you can't measure all of the factors I have just mentioned directly other than the guy is away from work, but the effect can be quite long reaching . . . (director)

Oh yes, accidents affect the workforce in quite a considerable way. There is a morale problem to start, a production problem, there is a certain amount of anger in some cases that accidents have occurred . . . after an accident has occurred which affects a member of the work team . . . it may be weeks before they push it to the back of their minds, particularly if it is an accident that could have happened to them had the same set of circumstances occurred. From a production point of view you can't possibly expect the staff to work at the same output as they did prior to the accident and there will be a tightening in that location where the accident has occurred of health and safety measures which frankly ought to have occurred before the accident happened. (safety officer)

In addition the efficiency of the local workforce may be reduced. Externally the bad publicity which often follows a major accident was perceived to affect adversely the organization's image. Some expressed the view that accidents should be more widely publicized within the organization in order to increase their general impact.

Summary

The most common indicator of risk mentioned by respondents was a generic reference to accident statistics, but when they were questioned about the actual incidence of accidents very little was known. This accords with previous research which suggests that people are not very good at estimating risks (Heimer, 1988: 494). Also in line with the literature is that knowledge of accidents was positively related to hierarchical position. Those in the senior positions tended to know about the more serious accidents and those lower down in the organization had much more locally based knowledge, usually of minor accidents. Understandings of the causes of accidents were departmentally related according to varying working environments. Indeed the very real differences between the work experiences of varying groups doubtless led to the diversities in their knowledge and understandings of accidents.

Generally information about accidents was not retained, even by those at the top of the organization who specialized in health and safety. Not remembering or knowing specific numbers was not in itself important, but the fact that staff did not know the broad numerical range of fatalities and major injuries may indicate that the risks were neither known nor fully appreciated. So let us turn our attention now to how direct questions about risk were understood. How risky was the railway industry considered to be and what did staff consider to be the particular dangers to their health and safety?

Perceptions of Risk

The interviews included a combination of general questions about how risky
the industry was and more specific questions about the particular dangers
encountered in everyday work. While it is important to caution that risk means
different things to different people (Slovic, 1992: 120), it remains the case that
responses to these questions were patterned. In previous chapters and in the first
part of this chapter responses have been markedly patterned according to a
respondent's position in the corporate hierarchy. As one might expect, understandings of risk were also shaped departmentally according to respondents'
particular working environments. More generally the research data suggest that
power and stratification may be crucial to our understandings of risk in the
workplace. Yet, as we will continue to discuss in the rest of this chapter, some
findings are counter-intuitive.

The data imply that the railway industry was generally perceived as a risky
workplace, albeit not unequivocally so. In response to the question 'Is the railway
a risky industry to work in?', *directors* and *departmental safety officers* definitely
regarded the industry as risky. Indeed two safety officers wished that they could
convey this to the staff with greater clarity. The need for this is revealed by the
responses from the rest of the sample. While a majority (55 per cent) did regard
the railways as risky and were prepared to use strong language to emphasize how
risky they considered it to be, a minority (14 per cent) were prepared to reply that
the industry was not at all risky and the rest (31 per cent) either claimed that the
risks varied or qualified their responses. In the case of these qualified responses,
the need to adhere to the rules or to train staff was heavily emphasized:

> Like any industry it is regulated in a way that minimizes the risks and if those
> rules and regulations are adhered to then it is no more and no less risky than
> any other industries it seems to me. For example, an office worker who disre-
> gards the technique of how to put a plug in the wall is likely to be electrocuted.
> . . . The same applies to the railway where hazards are identified and the
> emerging experience is enshrined in rules and regulations, procedures, and so
> on to minimize it. Having said that, there are a lot of people working in an
> environment where there is a lot of moving machinery. (director)

> From a civil engineering point of view, if men don't recognize the safety
> aspects and don't follow them properly, especially working on the live
> line, they could be extremely dangerous. (supervisor, interviewee 64)

Supervisors and *safety representatives* were the most likely to regard the
industry as definitely risky; managers were the most likely to give a qualified
response, and members of the *workforce* were most inclined to fall into the
minority of those who did not perceive the industry as risky.[8] It is difficult to

---

[8] 20.5% of the workforce claimed that the industry was not risky compared to 16% of safety representatives, 8% of supervisors, and 9% of managers.

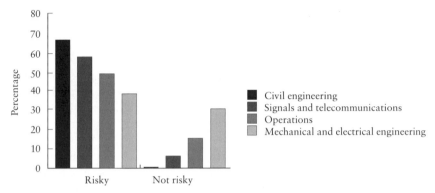

CHART 9.2. Perceptions of the industry as risky according to department

explain this finding but it might be related to the extent to which respondents had direct responsibility for colleagues' health and safety at an everyday 'track level'. Supervisors and safety representatives were both directly and continuously in such a position whereas more senior managers tended to be office based and thus spatially removed from the everyday reality of the risks. The workforce of course were directly exposed to risks but as we will see, they tended to normalize or deny risks, something that was arguably more readily achieved if there was no direct responsibility for others. Also of relevance here are departmental affiliations as there were also strong *departmental differences* which again reveal the situationally generated nature of risk perception. Chart 9.2 reveals that civil engineering staff unequivocally regarded the industry as risky whereas mechanical and electrical engineering staff were much less inclined to regard it as risky. It may be observed that these perceptions of risk very closely mirror the actual risks faced by employees in each department (see Ch. 3).

Comparative Risk

In order to probe further how respondents constructed their notions of risk, they were asked to compare the railways with other industries. Managers quite readily answered the question but supervisors, the workforce, and safety representatives found such a comparison difficult and many were unable to reply.[9]

Managers correctly thought that the railways came in the top ten high-risk industries in the country. It was especially high in their opinion because of the risks associated with those working on or about the track. The same four industries were generally cited as the main points of comparison with the railways, namely the construction, chemicals, and the mining industries and to a lesser extent motorway maintenance. A wide range of miscellaneous industries were mentioned by just a few respondents, ranging from the nuclear industry to

[9] For example, half of the supervisors questioned were unable to answer this question and just over half of the workforce.

farming. *Senior managers* disagreed about the comparative risks between the railways, mining, and construction[10] but unanimously agreed that the nuclear and fishing industries were more dangerous. With the exception of mining they were in fact inaccurate in their comparisons. For example, according to injury rates and absolute injury numbers, the chemicals industry and motorway maintenance are less risky than the railway industry. The construction industry, however, ranks fifth to the railway industry's fourth by injury rate, and the absolute number of injuries in the construction industry is greater than that on the railways (Ch. 3).

Responses to this question are of particular interest as they give us some idea of how those in the industry constructed their notions of risk. Managers took the potential for accidents, especially fatal accidents, as their main indicator of risk. The actual accident statistics plus the degree of risk associated with the daily activities of the workforce combined to determine the comparative risk associated with the railways. Very few other respondents could articulate how they perceived risk. Their main criterion was accidents, in particular the potential risk of injury and especially fatalities. Some mentioned accident statistics or insurance ratings but only to the extent that they thought that the railways figured quite high in these but not at the very top:

> . . . It must be a risky industry, it's fairly high up on the . . . fatalities and injuries and that in general league manufacturing and associated industries so it must be a risk industry. I mean it depends what you mean by is it a risky industry. Statistics say it's a risk industry but what's a risk industry really? I mean it does look good as your safety procedures and so on . . . I've tended to answer that question in terms of accident statistics. I meant the building industry is worse and we know it's worse and can understand that. And you could argue that the building industry is a less risky industry than the railway industry given the trains hurtle up and down the track at 125 m.p.h. and you've got high voltage equipment up there. All of those issues you could argue that, for example, mining industries are more risky industry but in practice of course it isn't . . . so I tend to answer that question in terms of the statistics. (director)

> I have to say that it is a risky industry to work in because the statistics say it is. If you look at the rate per thousand deaths, if I remember rightly it is fourth in the hierarchy with North Sea oil, construction, agriculture being the three above it and not I think because the statistics say it is. Yes I think it is and I don't think that is sufficiently realized either. (safety officer)

As with other studies, these responses suggest that estimates of annual fatalities were but one factor contributing to judgements of risk. Other factors such as *catastrophic potential* and *controllability* were also significant (Slovic, 1992:

---

[10] Mining, chemicals, and motorway maintenance were generally considered to be more dangerous than the railways by 10 respondents and on a par with it by 7 respondents.

120). Comparisons with the mining, chemical, and nuclear industries under-lined this as they were seen as more risky than the railways because they had a greater potential for catastrophe. This said, the risks were also seen to be greater when members of the public could be affected and in this respect the railways were seen to be particularly vulnerable.

Another indicator of risk was the *continual presence of danger*, in particular the presence of moving parts of machinery which demanded continual alert-ness: 'Very risky. As soon as you step out of the office it is a very risky environment but then I think that is by the nature of the transport systems and high speed objects, heavy objects moving at high speed and very silently are a high risk' (supervisor, interviewee 58). It was for this reason that motorway mainte-nance was perceived as dangerous. An interesting observation regarding the continual presence of risk was made by one departmental safety manager. He cited the third rail[11] on the Southern Region as one of the major dangers of the railway yet he continued to explain that its potential for danger was greater than its actual danger in terms of accidents. This he explained in terms of it being such an obvious and ever present hazard that everyone treated it with respect. This line of reasoning perhaps throws light on why the trains were perceived as so hazardous. While they were an obvious risk, they were not continually pres-ent in the way that the third rail was. Hence it seemed to be their unpre-dictability, especially given their speed, quiet approach, and inability to stop quickly or take evading action, which was regarded as a fundamental element of their risk.

The importance of *certainty* to perceptions of risk was again highlighted by those factors which one director considered to decrease the risk factors of the railway as compared to the nuclear industry. The railways, he argued, had an advantage to the extent that the dangers were well known so at least the com-pany knew what the problems to be tackled were. The nuclear industry he regarded as more worrying because the hazards were hidden and even unknown. In line with these arguments, health problems were considered to be potentially more worrying than those relating to safety by two respondents in this group. Indeed it was interesting that stress and an emphasis upon human behaviour figured prominently in senior managers' lists of major problems to be tackled by the railways. The tangibility of the risks thus emerges as an important factor in constructing notions of risk. But again this was likely to be structured according to hierarchical position to the extent that intangible risks are the most difficult to manage. And prominent here was the fact that intangi-ble risks are often the most difficult to communicate about, especially if their effects are long term (Hutter, 1997).

The other main criterion informing perceptions of risk was the *attitude of the industry* to health and safety. Relevant factors here included whether or not

---

[11] The third rail provided the electric current, via a ground-level rail running parallel to the track, to trains on Southern Region.

the industry was safety conscious, whether it followed good procedures for health and safety and whether it was seen to care. Deficiencies in these areas were seen to make the construction industry so risky. Indeed it is worth commenting that the importance of complying with the rules was again highlighted in this respect. Let us now turn our attention to how respondents handled more specific questions about the risks associated with their work.

Specific Risks Associated with the Railways

As we have seen, there was not total unanimity that there were hazards or dangers associated with working on the railways. Moreover different grades of staff and those from various departments identified distinct hazards and dangers. *Working on or about the track* was unhesitatingly referred to by senior managers as the most dangerous activity undertaken on the railway. It was also regarded as a hazard by the overwhelming majority of staff working on or about the track (see Chart 9.3). In the civil engineering department it was identified as the primary danger by managers and supervisors but not by the workforce. The dangers associated with the track were perhaps obvious, namely the presence of moving trains. In particular the speed and quietness of modern trains were perceived as most worrying especially as they required constant vigilance:

> With this job it is a split second, that is all it takes where with a lot of jobs outside you can generally move, you can do all sorts to avoid an accident or to get out of it. But with this, I mean, you have only got a split second and you are under a train and you are not going to stop a train on a sixpence. (worker, interviewee 23)

> It is the track-side, on track condition, with trains getting quieter and faster. This is the difficulty we are having with these quiet trains doing 125, on the other regions they are even quieter. We have got electrics[12] . . . we do have trouble with high speed trains because they do tend to whisper along. That's something we've got to be prepared to look at . . . When you have got a good sight with a headlight working on the front and plenty of yellow on the trains then there is no reason why you shouldn't give adequate warning. (manager, interviewee 100)

The *volume* of traffic was also mentioned by several respondents, especially with reference to Southern Region which served busy commuter routes into south London. The *shunting* of trains in depots, sidings, and stations was cited as one of the great dangers for operations staff. Indeed it was the second most frequently referred to hazard by operations staff, although it was more likely to be perceived this way by managers rather than the workforce.

The movement of traffic was not the only concern relating to the track. The *third rail* (which is electrified) on the Southern Region was identified as one of the most risky features of the workplace by signals and telecommunications department staff and was also a concern for civil engineering employees:

---

[12] Electric-powered trains.

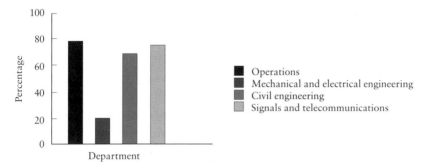

CHART 9.3. Working on or about the track: percentage of respondents citing as a risk according to department

It depends what job you are doing. If you are working on the track yes, you have got to say it is risky. You have got trains going at 100 m.p.h. and you have got a 750 volt juice rail, so yes you have got problems. But if you are a clerk and sitting in an office all day then probably the biggest danger is somebody smoking next to you. (manager, interviewee 38)

Obstacles around the track and *poor housekeeping* were regarded as another complicating factor which could increase the likelihood of falling in front of a train. Signals and telecommunications department staff expressed concern that they were often in danger of becoming so absorbed in their work that they did not hear trains approaching:

It has got to be a high risk, it must be a high risk. We are a protected industry in the sense that we have systems that are designed to protect us, it is when those systems are down that we become extremely vulnerable because we are working in what I think is a dangerous place. It is moving machinery, very quiet moving machinery, it is moving at very high speed, there is the risk that if you are dealing with something that has gone wrong you are engrossed in what has gone wrong. Therefore your awareness of what is going on around you becomes dented, dimmed, ineffective, and a lot of our accidents are in fact involved out on the track. (manager, interviewee 45)

A minority of staff from different departments referred to lookout protection as problematic, either because they did not fully trust others to look out for them or because they were sometimes tempted not to use lookouts to increase the speed of the job. In combination these factors could lead to great risks:

We are in a moving business, working in an outside environment, we are also working at things like high speed and in all sorts of weathers, the nature of the . . . goods that we convey also have hazards. We are also basically an engineering industry at heart and therefore there are all sorts of hazards that are natural within an engineering environment. So altogether I see the railways being a very hazardous occupation both for our workforce and potentially if we were not to keep it under very very close review for our customers. (director)

The main hazard is being hit by a train, associated with the third or fourth most dangerous industry in the country which is construction. So if you put the two together you have a recipe for disaster unless you are very very careful. (safety officer)

There's the problem, there are people getting killed. They've got a construction site which goes from Victoria to Brighton and on that construction site uneven floors, they've got a rail with 750 volts going down the middle of it unprotected and people are walking round it. They've got trains coming at them at 100 m.p.h. Now that's a problem, that's a problem isn't it? (union safety official)

Well railways are inherently dangerous or can inherently be dangerous, a dangerous activity. Trains move very fast, they are very heavy, and they are no respecter of life or limb. We also of course operate a lot of heavy equipment, cranes etc. in the maintenance and repair locomotives, all of which can be potentially very, very dangerous, moving heavy loads around, tools, equipment, you name it we have got it. (manager, interviewee 91)

The only other hazard cited by a significant number in the operations department was *passengers*. The particular concerns here related to drunk and aggressive passengers and those who opened train doors as a train was moving into or away from stations. Equipment and lifting were the other main concerns of civil engineering, mechanical and electrical engineering, and signals and telecommunications department staff. Indeed, lifting was identified as by far the most risky activity undertaken by mechanical and electrical engineering staff. The heavy weight of machinery, especially lifting machinery, was the main worry of these staff, plus of course the weight of the objects to be moved. Cranes were frequently cited as a source of concern. Other aspects of machinery which were considered to pose a danger were their moving parts, and, a less frequently voiced concern, their noise levels. Electricity was a concern of staff from all departments, but especially the workforce of the civil engineering department. Working under trains was referred to as a danger by several members of the mechanical and electrical engineering workforce, their most pressing concern being that trains might move while they were underneath them.

Numerous other risks were also mentioned, partly department specific but not exclusively so. In the operations department, for example, stress and vandalism were mentioned by some respondents, whereas civil engineering staff were more concerned by working at heights and the conditions of walkways. Slippery floors were a problem mentioned by a minority of staff from all departments:

Flooring, lighting . . . the lighting is very poor, the floor is very slippery . . . especially when it is wet and oily and it is supposed to be a non-slip floor. The fork-lift is dangerous because that slips and slides all over the place.

And there are lots of things you can catch your hand on and I know we are supposed to wear bump hats when we go underneath the train but the bump hat has got a peak on it and you can't always see what you are doing . . . it is impractical . . . (worker, interviewee 84)

Two broader issues were raised in the context of these questions. First were the dangers of familiarity, namely the dangers of overfamiliarity or complacency and the reverse of this, unfamiliarity with a working environment. Mechanical and electrical engineering managers, for instance, were concerned that their staff only went to the running line in the case of derailments and breakdowns; consequently they were far less aware of the potential dangers than, for example, civil engineering and signals and telecommunications department staff. There was also concern about new, young staff who needed educating about the dangers of the industry:

. . . getting it across to the men . . . I would definitely like to see that, especially the boys that work on the track and to get youngsters to comply with the rules and regulations and health and safety is very hard. (supervisor, interviewee 18)

New blokes, they're the people you've got to watch. (worker, interviewee 69)

The second issue concerned the pressure of time, namely the danger that the pressure of work could lead to shortcuts being taken and the risk that overtime working, especially when it was excessive, could lead to tiredness and a lack of attention and alertness:

. . . on the work site we are getting slimmer, we are getting slimmer with supervisors, we are slimming down managers, we've tried to slim down. Even the workforce is getting slimmer and they perceive they are under threat because the threat is that if they don't work productively we shall cut contracts. So I suppose that there is a great incentive to take risks, they see contractors taking risks, they are not stopping them very effectively because in contract supervision we are very slim, we do not fully supervise all our contract work. So I suppose there is an incentive on our own staff to take risks. (manager, interviewee 66)

Productivity pressures such as these figure prominently in accounts of risk-taking (Carson, 1982; Heimer, 1988; Nelkin and Brown, 1984). Familiarity also emerges from the literature as an important factor in risk perception. Familiar risks are more easily accepted (Nelkin, 1985: 16). Moreover there is a documented tendency to underestimate the risks associated with familiar activities (ibid. 83). This can lead to complacency or the view that 'it can't happen to me' (Cutter, 1993):

I don't think it is risky. I mean I have been on the railway twenty-seven years and I have never seen anybody hit by a train or injured. But at the same time I have seen near misses . . . I have had a near miss. Usually when you haven't, usually in the first couple of years, you go on the railway and you are cautious and gentle and then you get blasé and you have a near miss. I have had a near miss and I don't know anybody who hasn't had a near miss and after that you change. (supervisor, interviewee 15)

These findings corroborate other research which suggests that risks are viewed as more acceptable if they are familiar and have a low catastrophic potential (Slovic, 1992: 124 ff.). It also accords with the findings of Pollnac *et al.* (1995) who suggest that workers in high-risk industries may trivialize or totally deny the dangers associated with their work. Indeed their denial may well become part of a subculture of denial. Writing with reference to oceanic fishermen they write:

Constant exposure to the dangers of fishing probably habituates one to their presence and reinforces attitudes of denial, further reducing their salience . . . Habituation appears to be part of the 'denial of danger syndrome', where denial of danger is reinforced by the reduction of salience caused by extended exposure. It is simply too costly in psychic energy to maintain a state of heightened concern for extended periods of time. Even in the most stressful conditions, such as combat, habituation occurs (1995: 158).

This accords with a suggestion in some of the literature that a fatalistic approach to risk can develop alongside a view that accidents are inevitable and cannot be completely eradicated. Moreover Slovic (1992) suggests that the social impact of accidents in familiar, well-known systems, such as rail accidents, is low. These issues also emerge in response to questions about *accident prevention*. The majority (76 per cent: 85/112) did believe that accidents in general could be prevented[13] and 74 per cent thought that something more could be done to reduce staff accidents but responses varied, apparently in inverse relationship to the actual risks faced by respondents. Mechanical and electrical engineering and signals and telecommunications department staff were the most inclined to the view that accidents were preventable and civil engineering staff, who were the most likely to suffer fatal accidents, were the most inclined to consider prevention as either not possible or difficult. Managers and especially supervisors were more inclined to the view that accidents could be prevented than either safety representatives or the workforce. Some observed that whereas fatalities and major accidents were preventable, minor accidents were more difficult to do anything about. Senior managers were divided on these issues. While the majority of them believed that more could be done to reduce accidents, there was a divergence of views about the inevitability of accidents. On the one hand there were those who felt that accidents should not have happened and nothing should be taken for granted. On the other hand, some subscribed to the view that some accidents were inevitable; some referred to such accidents as 'acts of God'; others were unspecific.

---

[13] 11% thought that the possibility of accident prevention varies; 4% thought that it is difficult to prevent accidents; and 9% did not think it possible to prevent accidents.

These views, of course, have important implications for the possibilities and limitations attaching to organizational action to prevent accidents. Fatalistic views can quickly become a rationale for not acting. Indeed, some might regard fatalistic views as partially the result of organizational inaction. On the other hand, there are likely to be pragmatic and financial limits to risk reduction. What is interesting in this research was that respondents had plenty of suggestions about what could be done to prevent accidents. This was important as it suggests that they believed that there were ways in which they could take control over their working lives. The most frequently mentioned suggestions for preventing general and staff accidents are documented in Table 9.3.

Different grades of staff favoured different methods of improvement.[14] The emphasis of the *workforce* was very much upon changing behaviour, thus they were the most likely to suggest that more care was needed.[15] Compliance with the rules was almost exclusively a workforce suggestion. Education was considered important by all grades except supervisors:

I: Do you feel that more could be done to reduce staff accidents in your industry?

R: Yes I think if people were made more aware perhaps of their responsibilities of what they are supposed to do and what the end results could be if they don't do what they are supposed to then yes, I think it would cut it down a bit.

I: How do you think you could achieve that?

R: By better training, by more literature, or literature put out in simple language instead of some of these complicated terms they use instead of putting straightforward simple language for the layman, can understand that he has got to do his job right otherwise he can endanger someone else, then I think perhaps yes something would get through. (worker, interviewee 23)

Education was seen by some respondents to be complicated by the fact that there was, on some parts of the railway, a high turnover of staff. Hence it could be difficult to provide all of the necessary training.[16] *Safety representatives* were the most likely of all grades of staff to suggest that more accidents could be prevented by improved working environment and improved equipment, namely issues of workplace design. This also emerged as a workforce and safety officer concern (Nelkin and Brown, 1984: 51):

Mostly they [accidents] are tripping, slipping, falling, like so many I mean something in the order of about 45 per cent of all accidents on BR . . . and

---

[14] There were no departmental differences in these responses.

[15] 44% of the workforce recommended this compared to 11% of safety representatives, 35% of supervisors, and 22% of managers.

[16] There is some evidence that education campaigns and information programmes do not necessarily lead to targeted changes in perception and behaviour. See Adler and Prittle (1984); Green (1995). There is also evidence that when information is available there is patchy understanding of it. See Renn (1992).

TABLE 9.3. The prevention of accidents: staff suggestions

Suggestion for improvement	General accidents: % of total suggestions	Staff accidents: % of total suggestions
More care	30	4
Better education	14.5	29
Improved working conditions	13.5	17
Improved management support and supervision: greater emphasis on health and safety	6	11
Improved working methods	4	—
Improved and properly maintained equipment	—	6
Compliance with the rules	5	4

that is caused often by environmental conditions are poor. You see it is not just that we are a hazardous industry from the point of view that you can be run over by a train, in the course of trying to get away from being run over by a train and stepping into your position of safety you have to cover a lot of ground and a lot of rubbish and lot of oil and bits of rail and things like this and therefore we do get a lot of problems, some of which could be solved by perhaps insisting on the right sort of footwear. We do endeavour to do that, the fact still remains the people turn up for work in trainers and things like this for engineering work which is ridiculous, although we do have a subsidized footwear scheme that whilst it is not perfect is a lot better than it was. (safety officer)

Some staff did believe that accidents were inevitable but the majority view was that attempts should be made to try to minimize the risks:

. . . across the railways, you start to think well even if you did everything that is humanly possible and put all the money to it and all the equipment, how much you have to reduce that number by and I think you get to an irreducible number, the very nature of the thing is that one year you might get none, another year you might get half a dozen and that is why it is difficult to say whether you should invest because there will be an irreducible number I am sure. (director)

Some considered that the only way to prevent accidents was to stop trains running, but others spoke of the need to balance health and safety with costs. The cost of reducing accidents was perceived by some to be fewer trains and slower trains, something they regarded as disruptive and financially costly:

If the trains ran slower where the men were working, men would have more time to get out of the way so the dangers of being hit by trains would be far fewer. Therefore the fatalities would be reduced, but we carry passengers to get from A to B in the shortest possible time generally. So there is a cost element that comes in there that could be priced but it would make a hash of the timetabling system in that one day there may be lots of jobs on, reducing train speeds and another day there may be nothing going on, so that is one element of costs. The other one is completely automatic warning systems. (manager, interviewee 75)

. . . we break a lot of rules by carrying items across the live rail which is purely to get the job done . . . last year we were working at Waterloo and we were in the middle there and they were running trains literally around us and if you stepped the wrong way you could easily walk into it. It is the same old thing, the railway has to make money and the will to keep them running no matter what and they will go round you. So it's a thing they just can't shut down even though it would be a lot safer for us but I believe we are just a number, they will always carry on, there will always be someone to take our place. (worker, interviewee 135)

A minority view was that greater investment in health and safety would help. Insufficient financial investment was regarded as a product of the drive to increase profits and a feeling that health and safety was non-productive. At a more everyday level, lack of money was also seen to prevent attention being paid to less serious issues such as the improvement of staff accommodation and the provision of lights at crossings and sidings. Some also felt that there was insufficient investment in staff, leading to excessive hours being worked and minor problems being left unattended to:

Shortage of staff, that is what it is. They have cut back and cut back on the staff safety side in a lot of areas I think has gone to the wall. There are not enough staff on there to maintain proper safety standards. (worker, interviewee 23)

I accept that there is a limit as to how much money you can throw at a problem but I do think it is a useful part of health and safety is training and training not just on health and safety matters but on communication. Communication with supervisors and communication with local managers because quite often staff might see something that is dangerous and are scared and I think scared to describe them, to actually say something to their supervisors to their managers and I think more money could be spent training people in that way. (worker, interviewee 53)

Discussions of staff accidents—rather than accidents in general—led to an emphasis less upon individuals changing and more upon organizational change. Again a multi-factor approach was called for and again this was reflected in the responses of senior managers. Indeed this group took a much broader systematic view of risk management. They suggested, for example, that more attention should be paid to the identification and minimization of hazards through such means as improved reporting systems and statistics and the initiation of improved systems of work. The most popular view was that there should be better monitoring and enforcement to ensure good and safe standards were maintained. They recognized a need to increase awareness of the risks involved through more training and publicity. They also argued that there was a pressing need for everyone to take health and safety seriously and to be accountable for their work according to these criteria:

> First of all by trying to take a long objective look at every work process so as to identify hazards and to identify the means of avoiding that hazard or minimizing that hazard and then of trying to systematize a working practice and, if you like, a safe practice which may be the basis of training or whatever that will render that operation safe, to all intents and purposes safe . . . Point two is that one needs very good systems of monitoring and reporting to see in fact that those systems work and that part of that is statistical reporting . . . secondly there is this process of audit. (director)

> The answer to that is that there is always more could be done . . . it doesn't always have to be a large sum of money you have to spend either. It is the dedication of a certain amount of time and thinking and input of detail at all levels from the employee to the supervisor, to the manager. I think a lot more could be done with very little extra effort actually, it is an attitude of mind to health and safety which does vary in different European countries even. (director)

Senior company officials viewed the health and safety problems facing the railways in much more generic terms than other grades of staff. The general problem was identified as combining the needs of operating the railway with the needs for track maintenance and ensuring safety. In order to increase and maintain the safety element of this, a number of factors needed examining. Those identified by directors and safety managers were the 'human element', in particular minimizing reliance on human judgement, especially in the areas of lookout protection and signalling[17] and passing signals at danger. They also emphasized the need to know what goes wrong and why, to find out why rules are broken, and to collate basic accident statistics centrally to identify risks. They wanted to increase awareness of the whole workforce to the risks involved in their work through training and ensuring that managers knew what they should be doing.

Health Risks

Staff almost exclusively identified safety risks rather than health risks.[18] Just 15 of 116 respondents referred to health risks when asked if there were any dangers associated with their work. They referred to one of five perceived risks, namely asbestos, chemicals, noise, stress, and visual display units.

---

[17] Some railway inspectors were concerned about the overreliance on automated systems, especially in the lack of 'human' skills in the event of a technological breakdown.

[18] The literature suggests that there is an increasing awareness of risks to health (Nelkin and Brown, 1984: p. xv). This is difficult to discern in this study, although a longitudinal study would be necessary to establish this more certainly.

Staff were asked if they distinguished between health and safety and if there were any health as opposed to safety problems which concerned them in their job. Just over half of the sample (65 per cent) did not distinguish between health and safety and the majority (over 70 per cent) were unable to identify a health as opposed to a safety problem. Managers and safety representatives were most likely to see the distinction between health and safety. While the majority of directors and safety managers were aware of health problems and could cite examples, not all regarded health and safety as separate. Two directors and three departmental safety managers thought that health and safety were really the same thing and most certainly they were treated as such by the railway, that is, as a totality. Others emphasized that while health and safety might be regarded as distinct, the greater concerns of the railway were safety rather than health related. The fact that this seemed to be the case was identified as a problem in itself by one safety manager and one director:

I: Do you distinguish between health and safety at all or do you regard them as the same thing?

R: Good question. I have never thought about that, we always bracket them together. I do treat them as the same thing. I recognize the differentiation, that safety is something where somebody gets an electrical shock, health is somebody who has got an overdose of radiation from a piece of faulty equipment or something over a long period of time, or dust, over a long period of time. And that is why I differentiate it, one is a kind of physical injury and one is the deterioration over time. (manager, interviewee 25)

A wide range of health hazards were referred to by all grades of staff who felt able to identify such problems. The risks posed by chemicals, such as cleaning agents and weed-killers, were the most frequently referred to. Mechanical and electrical engineering safety representatives and workers were most concerned about fumes. AIDS concerned staff from all departments and stress was identified by operations staff, especially drivers.[19] Some respondents recognized that health problems may be more difficult to detect:

> . . . noise . . . gradually you go deaf and you don't realize it. Though I must admit once again we are told that you should use such things as ear protection and I am afraid being a human being people tend to neglect these or they have left them in their locker and they are one end of the depot and somebody starts and revs engines and things. Well, over time as I say you go deaf, you don't notice it but other people do. (safety representative, interviewee 90)

This response points to the importance of tangibility in risk perception. Risks where the harms are manifested at some future date are more difficult to comprehend than those where the harms are immediately effected. This is part of

---

[19] Stress is identified in the literature as one consequence of the lack of control over risks (Nelkin and Brown, 1984: 38).

the reason why safety matters were more readily understood than health concerns.

Senior company officials identified stress as a major problem. One director explained that some managers were placed under great personal stress by the demands placed upon them by, for example, the demands for cost-cutting, getting the job done, and fulfilling health and safety requirements. Stress was identified as detrimental to individuals and the company. Maintaining an awareness of health and safety issues and ensuring constant vigilance was perhaps one of the major problems faced by the company:

> I am beginning to become concerned in the area of health and safety about a range of issues about working environment relative to stress, cost pressures perhaps . . . For instance, there is growing evidence that stress, personal stress, not managerial stress, personal stress amongst quite large parts of the workforce brought on by a variety of factors actually is detrimental to performance and is positively detrimental to some aspects of safety. (director)

> I think we ought to be . . . drawing out on a clearly objective basis where our priorities should lie in keeping a healthy workforce through safe working and all that within the environment of safe operation of the railway for the customer. We can do that by looking at an analysis of where the failures are . . . (director)

Activism and Risk

Nelkin and Brown (1984: 83) describe a range of adaptations to workplace risks, ranging from carelessness to caution, denial to protest, resignation to activism. In order to gain some idea of how perceptions of risk translated into personal concern and action within BR, the workforce were asked if there was anything at work which was a risk to their health or safety and, if so, had they done anything about it. The majority (55 per cent) replied that there was nothing which they presently considered a risk to their health and safety, with those in the civil engineering and operations departments being the least worried. Those who did identify problems mentioned a wide range of concerns. The most frequently cited problem in the operations department was noise, this being a particular concern of drivers referring to the noise in cabs. Fumes in the workshop environment were mentioned by mechanical and electrical engineering staff. In addition there was a wide range of problems each referred to by just a few respondents. These included asbestos, stress, complacency about health and safety, oil and grease on platforms, and a lack of equipment. It was interesting that this question—which came towards the end of the interviews—elicited concern about both health and safety problems. Yet a question asking 'What are the major health and safety problems now facing the railways?' revealed that although the large majority identified problems, this did not mean that there was great dissatisfaction with the company. Many staff prefaced their replies by saying that they were generally satisfied with standards of health and safety.

Those who identified risks to their health or safety were almost equally divided in their propensity to do anything about the problem in terms of complaining or simply raising the problem with someone else. Those who did complain were equally as likely to approach their safety representative as their manager. Only one respondent said that his problem had been resolved. Those who did not complain explained this either in terms of accepting risk as part of the job or because they saw no point—either because they felt that nothing would be done or because they believed that the management already knew about the problem. So there was no suggestion in this study that risks to worker health and safety were the source of great conflict (cf. Nelkin, 1985: 13).

Discussion

In modern societies there are many everyday risks known to individuals in their personal lives, as consumers and as workers. There is a growing awareness of existing risks, the recognition of new risks, and paradoxically in the face of this a greater appreciation and fear of risk. As Manning (1992c: 101) observes, our ability to make sense of risk is limited: 'In practice, individuals are left to weigh, deny, finesse or otherwise juggle everyday risks, some of which are invisible, irreversible and increasing in effect, and arising from multiple and often unknown sources'. This research highlights the fact that the ways in which we do make sense of risk are situationally generated. More particularly it underlines how workers' knowledge and understandings of occupational health and safety risks are pragmatically informed. Perceptions of risk were thus related to social location, particularly to hierarchical position. This affected the levels of danger perceived and also what seemed dangerous (Douglas and Wildavsky, 1982; Heimer, 1988).

While the risks on BR were theoretically calculable, they were not necessarily calculated 'on the job' (Hutter and Lloyd-Bostock, 1992: 190). Very few BR employees had a detailed knowledge of the risks they encountered but they did have a broadly accurate view of the types of fatal accidents that happen and why. Minor accidents were not treated as seriously as other types of accident but the reasons for these types of accident were broadly comprehended, albeit simplistically, by many respondents. The large majority of those interviewed had come into contact with an accident at some time or another but their reaction to it very much depended upon the outcome and their own personal sensibilities. The impact of accidents seemed to be structured by the exigencies of the job and important here were organizational goals and routines. Many spoke of an imperative to keep the trains running: some regarded this as a production pressure, others spoke of it in terms of a railway culture. More generally it was very striking that occupational health risks were rarely understood except by those at the top of the organization who had, as part of their job, access to data about the longer-term and more insidious dangers to health in the occupational environment.

Corporate knowledge of accidents was patchy. Indeed the availability of accident information within the company emerged as problematic. Information about accidents seemed to depend upon the sophistication of local grapevines (see Ch. 7). Not even senior managers received easily accessible accident information. The data they received often comprised lists of fatalities and injuries, typically on a regional or departmental basis rather than collated summaries accompanied by company-wide analyses. Decentralization seemed to be part of the problem, again since information collected regionally was not necessarily centrally collated in a form which could be used by the organization as a whole. Arguably a centralized, standardized,properly designed system would have facilitated the reporting of accidents and the collation and effective analysis of data. The main purpose of centralized organizational data is to know better what the risks are. But there were also important symbolic aspects to data collection, for the fact that the data were being collected and used, and in some cases followed up by senior staff, indicated interest and concern from the 'top'. Moreover, as Rees (1988: 111) explains, statistics such as these influence powers of self-perception, for example, notions of 'good' and 'bad' safety performance.

As we know, there are serious difficulties in the collation of any statistics. Certainly, for example, non-reporting of accidents was confirmed as a real problem within BR, especially the non-reporting of minor accidents. Explanations of the non-reporting of accidents suggested that the way in which data were collected is important. Simple improvements such as the design of simple accident reporting forms were called for (Ch. 7). Moreover the reporting procedures needed to be open to the identification of new problems. It also needs to be recognized that there is an uneasy balance to be maintained between the reporting of accidents and disciplinary procedures for non-compliance. If there was a serious possibility of disciplinary procedures following an accident, then staff would be unlikely to report any accidents they thought that they could cover up.

There was very little evidence of activism about occupational health and safety risks among BR employees. This does not necessarily imply that risks are accepted but it may suggest that they are related to in a very pragmatic way. Pollak (1995: 187) introduces the notion of heuristics (rule of thumb) to describe how risk is routinely coped with in everyday situations, a notion that concurs with the finding that employees worked with broad understandings of risk and uncertainty. Perceptions of risk are the product of many different influences such as training, experience, and culture (Cutter, 1993; Hutter and Lloyd-Bostock, 1992: 197). They are structured according to social factors. Nelkin and Brown (1984) argue that responses reflect specific experiences at work such as personal economics and constraints, perceptions of occupational choice, trust in the system, and identification with the goals of the organization. BR workers' inactivism may well be explained by their lack of occupational choice and poor pay, in other words, they may have felt unable to be more choosy about their employment given their low skill levels and the general lack of work at the time of the research (Carson, 1982). It may therefore be that attitudes to risk were shaped by the choices available (Nelkin and Brown, 1984: 84 ff.) so risks were normalized and accommodated to because employees felt that there was little that could be done to change things. But it may be more complicated than this.

Wildavsky and Drake (1990), for example, suggest that individuals perceive risks in a manner that supports their way of life and a central finding of this research was that understandings of occupational risks were inextricably related to respondents' social distance from the workplace. Thus occupational status has emerged as especially significant, in particular the differences found between different grades of staff, so replies reflected respondents' position within the company. Senior managers took a broad overview of occupational health and safety issues. They regarded regulation as risk management and focused on systems and general trends. Further down the organization, concerns tended to be more specific and focused but were ones which had generic implications, for example, communication and education. Those at most risk were sometimes the least likely to perceive the risks in their working environment. There were a number of explanations for this. One is that those further up the corporate hierarchy had more information available to them and thus had a broader view of the risks associated with the workplace. For example, they knew more about accident trends than those lower down whose knowledge tended to be more locally based, but knowledge of accidents was systematically transformed as it was processed from 'blood on the tracks' to accident reports and eventually to corporate and regulatory statistical data.

Another explanation was that understandings of risk were linked to a sense of autonomy and agency. Nelkin and Brown (1984: 4) argue that exposure to risks is related to social status, with production and maintenance workers being the most exposed to risk. The effects of these social influences are reflected in adaptations to risk (Cutter, 1993). But there was also a degree of trust in the system which was regarded to some extent at least as paternalistic. This said, respondents did come up with a variety of suggestions about how risks could be reduced so clearly this implies that they felt that they did have some control over risks.

In considering how understandings of risk could be improved, it is important to appreciate that risk perceptions were influenced not just by 'hard data' but by what information and how much information was conveyed throughout the organization and how it was conveyed (Heimer, 1992: 187). This said, there is a need to be cautious about over-emphasizing the effects of disseminating information as this was but one way of reducing risks. Moreover it was one which placed the emphasis very much upon individuals. Arguably risks should be reduced as much as possible at source or by engineering cuts (Nelkin and Brown, 1984: 69). But zero risk was not a universal expectation within BR. There was more a notion of tolerable risk operating at societal, corporate, and individual levels. But this tolerability was of course structured and the vital role of regulation was ordering this balance and helping to structure the choices workers were presented with. The evidence of this study was that risks were to some extent normalized, even denied—they were typically seen as a fact of life. Regulation potentially has a vital role in helping to ensure that risk is more actively and continuously managed. As Reiss (1992) reminds us, risk assessment—and we might add risk management—are continuing activities. Whether or not they can constitutively effect a change in attitudes and ultimately behaviour, remains to be seen. The next chapter will examine these issues in greater detail by paying attention to risk-taking and compliance with risk management systems of the law and company systems.

10

Risk-Taking and Compliance

In Chapter 9 we saw that the majority of respondents had a broadly accurate understanding of where, why, and how accidents happened within their working environment. There was a suggestion that everyday risks were often coped with through normalization and even denial. Indeed the evidence of the last chapter seems to suggest that when accidents did occur their effects were more often than not short-lived. This chapter will push further the issue of how risk may or may not influence lives by considering how understandings of risk may be related to the propensity to take risks. In particular the focus is on issues of compliance and non-compliance with state regulation, and on the resulting company risk-management systems.

Compliance and Non-compliance

Compliance and non-compliance are complex concepts. In the regulatory context their definition and implementation may be subject to various interpretations and situational constraints; moreover these may change over time (Di Mento, 1986; Edelman *et al.*, 1991; Hutter, 1997). This has led to the view that compliance may best be regarded as a process involving interaction, negotiation, and renegotiation among the numerous actors in the regulatory process (ibid.). Di Mento remarks: 'Compliance has no one definition. Non-compliance has no one explanation . . . Recommendations aimed at achieving compliance must recognize the varying and at times contradictory perceptions of rule violations and must take into account the complex processes that make for non-compliance' (1986: 163). Indeed it is perhaps because of these difficulties that compliance theory is so underdeveloped. We have little knowledge of what leads to either compliance or non-compliance in the regulatory context.

At one level the extent of regulatory non-compliance is unknowable, since reporting procedures present a very distorted view of the extent of non-compliance and violation (Nichols, 1999). It is well documented, for example, that enforcement agency statistics reflect only a very small proportion of the violations detected by inspectors (Grabosky and Braithwaite, 1986; Hawkins, 1984; Hutter, 1997). We do know, however, that the range of potential regulatory violations is considerable and the reasons for compliance and non-compliance are various (Di Mento, 1986, 2 ff.). It is important when discussing regulation to distinguish between the compliance of the organization and the compliance of individuals within the organization. It is also important not to simplify explanations of regulatory compliance and non-compliance. Decisions may be made on a case-by-case basis rather than according to abstract principles. There is no simple explanation of workplace deviance. Businesses vary in their ability and motivation to comply and they also differ over time and across issues. Explanations of compliance and non-compliance therefore involve a complex of factors (Clay, 1984; Di Mento, 1989; Massey, 1979; Sigler and Murphy, 1988).

Our understandings of regulatory compliance are further complicated by the fact that much regulation involves corporations. Assigning responsibility and blame for corporate behaviour is laden with difficulties, especially in a legal system premised on individual culpable wrongdoing. Arguably the problems are exaggerated when corporations are anthropomorphized into rational thinking beings (Stone, 1975; Wells, 1993). This raises all sorts of questions about 'who' it is who acts 'officially' (Selznick, 1980: 12). This question is not fully resolved in British regulatory law. There are numerous examples of tensions between the punishment of individuals and corporate sanctioning which are reflected in the penalties available—fines only for corporations and fines and imprisonment for individuals. This has led corporate offending to be regarded differently from individual wrongdoing. Indeed this partly fuels the debate about the criminality of regulatory offences, for example, the argument that corporations are less likely to be stigmatized as criminal than individuals (Baucus and Dworkin, 1991; Richardson *et al.*, 1983; Snider, 1987; Yeager, 1991). It certainly leads to concern that individuals may be scapegoated in the face of impotence to target the wider organization.[1]

The HSW Act, 1974, has tried to tackle the problem of assigning responsibility within organizations by the introduction of safety policies which identify responsible individuals (see Ch. 6). But as we have seen this has not removed the controversy about the extent to which individuals can be held responsible for what some regard as a lack of systemic safeguards.[2]

One of the themes that emerges from the limited literature on the subject of workplace understandings of, and responses to, occupational health and safety regulation is that there is great variation between workplaces with respect to their motivation to comply (Genn, 1993). Dawson *et al.* (1988) found that the size of a firm and the size of the site were the key variables in indicating how responsive a site may be to occupational health and safety regulation, with the large sites and those belonging to larger firms being the most responsive to

---

[1] Attempts to prosecute Great Western Trains following the 1997 Southall train crash in which 7 people died failed because of the difficulties in identifying negligence by any individual within the company. The judge supported calls for a change in law to ease the prosecution of large corporations for manslaughter. Manslaughter charges were also brought against the train driver but were dropped because he had been psychologically damaged by the accident.

[2] These controversies emerge in other regulatory domains. For example, the case of the Barings Bank trader Nick Leeson raises questions not just about his own wrongdoing but the system which allowed him—even encouraged him—to behave in the way he did. Depending upon perspective this is a case of either white-collar crime (if Leeson is held to be at fault) or corporate crime (if Barings Bank is held to be at fault) or both.

occupational health and safety regulation (see also Brittan, 1984; GMB, 1986; Gricar, 1983).

According to these findings, BR could be expected to be generally compliant. But large companies pose problems of their own because their potential for deviance is much greater. As Di Mento observes, 'size correlates with differentiation in a firm and the greater the differentiation the greater the possibility of non-compliance' (1986: 156; see also Vaughan, 1982). So the risk management problems encountered by large companies may be both complex and complicated. This was fully understood by regulatory officials in Britain who were sensitive to differences between areas, both across sites and within sites (Hutter, 1997; cf. Bardach and Kagan, 1982).

Consideration of corporate compliance therefore has to take into account the compliance of the company and also the complexity of individuals within them. It also needs to recognize that 'Corporations are collective entities lacking a single set of desires and motivations' (Sigler and Murphy, 1988: 195). It is important not to regard corporations as homogeneous. There are variations *between* companies and also *within* companies (see Ch. 1). The concern of this study is the everyday compliance of people within BR, including the company's efforts to secure the compliance of their employees in furtherance of their management of occupational health and safety risks. The focus as always is upon the extent to which occupational health and safety requirements may have become constitutive at an everyday level. This chapter will pay particular attention to factors in the workplace which may have either encouraged or obstructed the fulfilment of regulatory objectives.

Explanation of Compliance and Non-compliance

Different theoretical traditions have identified different reasons for compliance (Olsen, 1992). Let us begin by considering the literature on corporate compliance.

Corporate Compliance

There are a number of explanations of corporate compliance and non-compliance which to varying extents relate to the classical model of business in its assumption that businesses will pursue their self-interest above all else.[3] The most clearly related explanation is that profitability is a pressure against compliance (Sigler and Murphy, 1988: 56). In its most extreme forms, this argument holds that profitability is the dominant overriding concern of business to the

---

[3] See Stone (1975: 37 ff.) for a critique of this model. Braithwaite (1981) argues that an economistic view of compliance and non-compliance may even weaken the moral force of the law. See also Makkai and Braithwaite (1993).

exclusion of much else (Pearce and Tombs, 1990). Kagan and Scholz (1984) differentiate between types of business and refer to this type as 'amoral calculators' who are motivated by profit-seeking and who calculate the economic costs of compliance.[4] Cost is a much-cited reason for non-compliance (Chelius and Smith, 1987), yet few authors would simply relate compliance and non-compliance to cost. Wilson (1980: 359) notes that profit maximization is 'an incomplete statement of corporate goals'. Likewise, Di Mento (1986: 137) emphasizes that financial resources alone are an insufficient explanation of compliance—and one might add, non-compliance.

It is important to understand that cost does not refer only to the capital costs of compliance, for example, the costs of safety equipment and safety officers. It also embraces more indirect costs which may actually be a pressure to comply (Sigler and Murphy, 1988: 69). These include the threat of private lawsuits, increased insurance premiums, the prospect of compensation payments and claims, and avoiding the indirect costs of accidents, including 'downtime' and labour dissatisfaction (Bardach and Kagan, 1982: 60 ff.). Self-interest thus emerges in a variety of guises as a major explanation of corporate compliance. The most striking example of this involves sites where strict compliance is necessary to the viability of the works (Genn, 1993). In such cases there is much more than profitability at stake for the whole site of production could be in danger. The most obvious example is a chemical works where, for example, safety considerations may be paramount as the risks of non-compliance could be catastrophic. In these cases the corporate and regulatory concerns coincide.

Some explanations of corporate compliance approximate more closely to models of corporate responsibility. Thus they emphasize considerations other than the pursuit of profit, although it is important to appreciate that these accounts do not deny the importance of the profit motive, regarding it as one of several considerations. There are, of course, a variety of interpretations of corporate social responsibility (see Stone, 1975: chs. 8 and 9) and these are reflected in compliance theory, albeit in a rudimentary way. The most clear-cut explanation of this type is that companies comply because of adherence to moral principles (Sigler and Murphy, 1988: 51), for example, a genuine concern for the environment or the health and safety of the workforce (Hutter, 1997). This suggests a commitment both to the spirit and the letter of the law. Other companies may comply not because they believe in the law but because they feel that they have an obligation to comply out of 'good citizenship'. Kagan and Scholz (1984) explain that in this type of firm decisions are principled. But this, of course, does not mean that compliance is inevitable. As Kagan and Scholz (1984: 68) point out, there is the possibility of principled non-compliance (see Ch. 4).

---

[4] See Braithwaite *et al.* (1994) for an empirical examination of the Kagan and Scholz typology. Arguing against rational choice approaches, they contend that greater attention be paid to the social context and to understanding how to incorporate all regulatees into the regulatory system.

Where commitment is absent, enforcement of the regulations could itself be a motivation to comply (Gunningham, 1984). Some authors adopt a classical deterrence approach to the importance of enforcement and argue that penalties will only deter if sufficiently high to have an impact on profitability (Carson, 1982; Clinard *et al.*, 1980; Pearce, 1976). Others can find no evidence that higher penalties provide more deterrence than lower penalties and emphasize instead the damaging symbolic effects of being punished at all (Gray and Scholz, 1991). This relates directly to another central motivation identified in compliance theory, namely compliance motivated by a concern to protect corporate reputation (Miller and Sturdivant, 1977; Olsen, 1992). Large companies are seen as particularly concerned to protect their image and so are those whose relationships with the public were already or potentially strained. Business is clearly perceived to be susceptible to external pressures from a variety of sources, ranging from consumers to peer-group pressure (Di Mento, 1986: 86). Indeed it is precisely these pressures which lead Fisse and Braithwaite (1983) to identify publicity as an important form of social control for corporations (see also Clinard *et al.*, 1980; Braithwaite, 1989). An explanation of non-compliance which directly contradicts the classical model is non-compliance resulting from organizational incompetence where, whatever the goals of the organization, there is an inability on the part of its managers to achieve them (Kagan and Scholz, 1984: 68).[5]

Employee Compliance and Non-compliance

Explanations of the compliance and non-compliance of those within organizations mirror to some extent accounts of corporate compliance and non-compliance. For example, self-interest arguments emerge as explanations of individual non-compliance (Becker, 1989). It is argued that there are a variety of pressures upon employees and that non-compliance may be caused where it appears more 'rational' to fulfil other more highly prized objectives such as getting the job finished as quickly as possible (Dawson *et al.*, 1988). Lack of enforcement is another variant of this argument, which approximates to deterrence theory in criminology (Sigler and Murphy, 1988: 80 ff.). There is contradictory evidence about the importance of these arguments, arising, for example, in accounts of compliance with tax laws. Some argue that the likelihood of detection through audit is significant in explaining compliance (Witte and Woodbury, 1985), whereas others have not found this to be the case and argue for a more complex explanation (Brooks and Doob, 1990). These types of argument essentially claim that there is a trade-off between risk-taking and other objectives. A variant of this explanation is that non-compliance is the result of laziness, such as the failure of employees to use safety equipment and clothing because it is alleged that they hinder work (Hutter, 1997).

---

[5] Each different theory has its own limitations and each leads to different control strategies. See Kagan and Scholz (1984); Lofquist *et al.* (1997).

The most common explanation of workplace deviance is ignorance or a lack of awareness of the law (Brittan, 1984; Clay, 1984; Dawson *et al.*, 1988; Genn, 1993). Sigler and Murphy (1988: 139) claim that ignorance is widespread. A related explanation of non-compliance is a lack of awareness of the risks associated with non-compliance (Sigler and Murphy, 1988:80; ch. 8 this volume).

Some explanations of non-compliance focus on the workplace. For instance, non-compliance may be associated with a negative corporate culture where compliance is not encouraged and where there may be peer pressure not to comply (Massey, 1979; Sigler and Murphy, 1988; Whitehurst, 1977). Low worker morale was a major reason for non-compliance identified by occupational health and safety inspectors in Britain (Hutter, 1997). Low morale could result for a variety of reasons. For instance, it could be a consequence of low pay or industrial action such as a work to rule or strike. Often, of course, these factors were related. A positive corporate culture, however, could encourage compliance and lead to intra-organizational pressures to comply (Bardach and Kagan, 1982).

The more principled arguments which approximate the corporate social responsibility arguments also appear in relation to employee compliance, for example, arguments that compliance derives from a moral stance or because someone feels that they should be a 'good citizen'. Brittan's (1984) study of the impact of water pollution control on industry found that a 'moral obligation' to comply was the major explanation of compliance. By contrast, legal obligation played little role in employee compliance (cf. Makkai and Braithwaite, 1994).

It is of course important to underline again that in reality compliance and non-compliance need multi-causal explanation. Companies vary and so do the personnel within them. There will be what Bardach and Kagan (1982) refer to as 'good apples' and 'bad apples' and a range in between in any regulated population and within any company. It is also important to recognize that different regulatory objectives lead to varying notions of effectiveness. As Sigler and Murphy (1988: 130) point out, the criminal law is directed primarily to deterrence rather than compliance, whereas regulatory law is oriented primarily to compliance. Thus regulatory laws are essentially proactive rather than reactive. Moreover regulatory laws have a constitutive as well as a controlling objective. So knowing the requirements and understanding the reasons for their existence may be more important indicators of compliance than maximizing the costs of non-compliance and deterring non-compliance through threats. This should be borne in mind when considering compliance and non-compliance at BR.

Compliance and Non-compliance Within BR

The research concentrated most specifically upon the degree to which employees within BR complied with health and safety regulations. It thus considered the willingness of staff to comply and tried to discover what activities and circumstances were likely to lead to compliance and non-compliance, and why. In addition, it examined the trade-offs between compliance and other factors at both workforce and managerial levels. Levels of corporate compliance were gauged through the responses of senior personnel and employees' perceptions of company attitudes to health and safety. These indicate, for example, employees' understandings of corporate attitudes to health and safety, especially in relation to other objectives, and their preparedness to invoke internal systems to enforce health and safety regulations.[6]

Levels of Compliance and Willingness to Comply

Respondents were asked about their own compliance with occupational health and safety regulations; and managers, supervisors, and safety representatives were asked additional questions about the propensity of the workforce to comply.

The *workforce* were asked several questions about their willingness to comply. First they were asked specific questions about the availability of special health and safety equipment and their propensity to use it. Secondly, they were asked some more general questions about their compliance. All except one of those interviewed said that they were provided with safety equipment and clothing, thus indicating corporate compliance in its provision. The majority also claimed that they 'always' or 'usually' used the equipment.[7]

When the workforce were asked the more general question 'Have you ever ignored a health and safety regulation or the rule book?' higher levels of non-compliance were admitted to. Seventy-six per cent of those interviewed admitted that they had ignored a health and safety regulation or the rule book.[8]

The majority of *senior managers*, *managers*, and *supervisors* tried to comply but acknowledged that they might not always succeed.[9] Indeed there was a presumption among many respondents that full compliance was an impossibility, in particular that people cannot possibly stay alert to risks all of the time:

I: Do you yourself always comply with health and safety requirements?
R: Wouldn't think so, no. I would be naïve and totally stupid if I said I did. (director)

---

[6] Another indicator of corporate compliance is the establishment of internal systems discussed in Part III.

[7] There were departmental differences, with a majority of signals and telecommunications staff and especially civil engineering staff claiming to be compliant and all of the mechanical and electrical engineering workers responding that they did not always use the equipment at their disposal.

[8] Mechanical and electrical engineering staff were again the most likely to admit to non-compliance and signals and telecommunications and civil engineering workers the least likely. However, even in these groups the majority admitted to non-compliance.

[9] When managers and supervisors were asked whether they personally complied with the regulations, they responded thus: yes—33%; try to—41%; no—26% (n=54). All of the directors and one of the four departmental safety officers interviewed also doubted that they always complied with health and safety regulations but all emphasized that they tried to. The other three safety officers claimed that they always complied.

> I suspect I probably fail in the human terms as much as anybody else does. Perhaps I place myself in positions that I shouldn't do, so in the sense of being a human being I am sure I do err. (manager, interviewee 36)

Supervisors were altogether more cautious and qualified in their responses than other managers were. For example, whereas 45 per cent of managers said that they definitely complied only 17 per cent of supervisors replied in this way.[10] The majority of *safety representatives* claimed that they usually complied with health and safety rules and regulations, although they admitted to occasional non-compliance:

> I: Do you always comply with health and safety demands?
> R: If you are absolutely honest probably not, no. (safety representative, interviewee 90)

Managers, supervisors, and safety representatives were also asked for their views on *workforce compliance*. Just over half (53 per cent) thought that there was workforce non-compliance. There were some minor departmental differences in responses and also variations in responses according to grade of staff. Most marked here was that managers were the most cynical about the likelihood of workforce compliance and supervisors the least cynical. Signals and telecommunications managers were the most inclined to regard their staff as compliant and civil engineering managers were the least inclined to this view.

Managers, supervisors, and safety representatives were also asked a more specific question, namely whether the workforce always used the safety equipment available. The overwhelming majority (88 per cent) replied that they did not. Supervisors were again the least inclined to perceive non-compliance, but even then 75 per cent of respondents in this group thought that the workforce did not always used the safety equipment at their disposal.[11]

These responses do not imply that non-compliance was the norm. Rather they indicate the popularity of the notion that full compliance is a human impossibility, a theme which is reflected in some of the various responses to the question 'Do you think there is a lot of concern amongst the workforce about health and safety?'

> I'd have to say no that I don't. Much less than I would have hoped. (director)
>
> Generally, grudgingly. (manager, interviewee 110)
>
> Overall I would say yes, but then like with any bunch of people you always get those who are the exception and want shortcuts to getting the work

---

[10] Departmentally, civil engineers were by far the most likely to admit that they did not always comply whereas operations staff were the most likely to claim that they did comply.

[11] Signals and telecommunications responses to this question were interesting as they were a complete reversal of their replies to the general question. In response to this specific question signals and telecommunications staff were the most inclined to perceive non-compliance and operations staff the least inclined. Only 19% of operations managers, supervisors, and safety representatives perceived that the workforce used their safety equipment 'most' of the time.

done. But overall yes I would say—but it does require reminders from time to time of their personal responsibility. (manager, interviewee 20)

I don't think any of them understand that they are actually complying with any rules and regulations for health and safety, they are doing things out of common sense. (manager, interviewee 27)

On the whole yes they do. There's some you got to keep on to. (supervisor, interviewee 112)

I don't think that there is a lot of concern. (safety representative, interviewee 41)

It's a fairly don't care less attitude. (safety representative, interviewee 85)

In the main yes, but there are some problems. (union official)

When questioned about their own levels of compliance the workforce admitted to greater non-compliance than was perceived to be the case by managers, supervisors, and safety representatives. But the opposite was true with respect to replies to the specific questions about the use of safety equipment. The majority of the workforce claimed that they tended to use the equipment available, but the majority of those responsible for or representing them disagreed.

Examples of Non-compliance

All grades of staff cited similar examples of non-compliance. These included failing to wear safety clothing and not complying with rules about working on or about the track (the area where most fatalities occur). Managers were aware that they took short-cuts although they tried hard not to. The most frequently mentioned instances of non-compliance were failing to wear a hard hat and non-compliance on or about the track, for example, going on to the track without lookout protection; walking in the wrong direction; and not using walking routes. A miscellaneous range of other examples was offered, including asking staff to work excessive hours and failing to wear goggles. Supervisors and safety representatives referred to a similar range of examples to managers, and in addition cited not wearing high visibility vests and driving trains from the wrong end. The large majority of the workforce referred to a failure to wear protective safety clothing. The most frequently referred to were hard hats/bump caps; goggles/visors; and high visibility vests.[12] The second largest category referred to by the workforce related to the track. Not using walking routes and lookout protection were the most frequently referred to. Not wearing high visibility vests is also, of course, track-related non-compliance.

There were few differences between staff from various departments. Not surprisingly, the differences which were apparent reflected varying working

---

[12] This is of course interesting in light of workforce claims that they use the safety equipment provided. This suggests that managerial and safety representative reports of non-compliance are likely to be accurate.

environments. For example, mechanical and electrical engineering staff most frequently referred to not wearing bump caps (hard hats); mechanical and electrical engineering and signals and telecommunications staff most often referred to not wearing goggles; signals and telecommunications staff were most likely to refer to not using lookout protection; and operations staff most frequently referred to not using walking routes and not wearing high visibility vests.

Managers, supervisors, and safety representatives' perceptions of workforce non-compliance were in line with workforce self-reports. The two most prominent responses centred on failure to wear protective clothing and use safety equipment and track related non-compliance. Departmental differences mirrored those of the workforce, the only refinement worthy of note being that respondents from all departments in the managers, supervisors, and safety representatives' group cited drivers, and to some extent guards, as the primary offenders for non-compliance with the rules about wearing high visibility vests. This was the source of much contention as it was felt that drivers should be the most aware of the risks of not wearing high visibility clothes when on or about the track.

Explanations of Compliance and Non-compliance

Explanations of compliance and non-compliance can be deduced from a number of the answers given in response to general questions about respondents' own compliance and non-compliance and from managers, supervisors, and safety representatives' understandings of workforce behaviour. There were a number of more focused questions such as those to the workforce about their use of health and safety equipment and their opinions about how health and safety considerations related to more general working patterns and habits. In addition, separate questions were asked about areas which appear as significant in the existing literature, namely disciplinary procedures in the face of non-compliance and the relative importance of health and safety at work.

The main focus of this discussion is upon respondents' accounts of their own and their colleagues' compliance and non-compliance. The next section will consider the company's compliance and non-compliance.

Non-compliance

Respondents offered a wide range of reasons for their own occasional non-compliance. Interestingly, the most common explanation of non-compliance to be found in the literature, namely *ignorance* or a lack of awareness of the law (see above), did not emerge as a major explanation offered by the railways respondents. However, supervisors did cite ignorance of the rules as an explanation of their own non-compliance and general levels of understanding of the law and company policies do suggest that it is an area that has some explanatory value (see Ch. 6). Respondents' central explanation of workplace deviance was a *lack of awareness of the risks* involved in not complying. Yet this explanation does not withstand scrutiny. For example, it is striking that the most fully understood risk on the railways was track-side work (see Ch. 9) and the most frequently cited examples of non-compliance were a failure to comply with track-side regulations. The examples of lack of awareness offered in the interviews suggest that alternative explanations should be considered. But let us first consider the examples offered in the interviews.

A lack of awareness of the risks was said by respondents to be reflected in a common explanation of non-compliance, namely 'taking the easiest and most convenient' option. This emerged as a major explanation of both managerial and safety representative explanations of workforce non-compliance:

> I think it is human nature to try and gain a few minutes to go home or whatever. (safety representative, interviewee 33)

I: How important is health and safety ?

R: Not very high. You see a lot of the jobs here are time work and although you have got to stay here for eight hours . . . you could probably get finished in four if you just chuck everything out of the way and just really get stuck in.

I: But what do you do once you have finished?

R: You just keep out of the way, you sit out in the carriage or something, you maybe just keep out of the way of foremen or management. (safety representative, interviewee 102)

> . . . it is very difficult to tell a bloke that he is not quite working safely if he knows he can do it a bit faster and you know, have five minutes extra at the end of the day for a rest. (supervisor, interviewee 101)

Managers explained that non-compliance occurred both when it was easier or more convenient not to comply and as a result of carelessness or forgetfulness. Indeed the most senior personnel interviewed attributed their own occasional non-compliance to thoughtlessness and forgetfulness. Similarly the workforce's main explanation of their non-compliance was their own tendency to take the easier and more convenient options:

R: . . . wearing a high visibility vest, the rule book says that you should wear it when on or about the running line. We've all crossed the running line before without wearing it, yes I've done it . . . I've nipped across without it and I've walked across without it.

I: Can you spell out for me why?

R: Mainly because I'd left it behind and I was trying to do it a bit quicker—nine times out of ten I've used it, it's because I was going home and I never had it on me and I was taking a short-cut. (worker, interviewee 12)

Another worker explained that he and his colleagues do not always wear the special trousers which they should wear when using a chainsaw: 'it's human nature again isn't it. You know what I mean, it's a short cut . . . If it's only you know, a small job that I could do with a saw I wouldn't go putting it on. We do many things in between. But we do it a lot, we are using the saw a lot' (interviewee 69). Managers, supervisors, and safety representatives shared this understanding of worker non-compliance. Some interpreted it as laziness, some to the fact that it was easier or more convenient not to comply, and others directly to a lack of awareness or understanding of the risks involved in non-compliance:

> I think that very often it is sheer laziness on the person's part, can't be bothered to walk to the stores counter to say look can I have a pair of gloves or a pair of goggles or whatever, to probably considering that the wearing of them is perhaps inconvenient to them. The wearing of goggles, they can mist up. The wearing of a hat restricts your head room when you are in a confined space anyway, the wearing of gloves can make the handling of an item a bit more difficult. There is a lot of that about it as well. (manager, interviewee 86)

> A lot of them just don't think they are necessary, like the earmuffs, things like that, don't understand the dangers that it can be. (safety representative, interviewee 123)

It is not at all clear that a lack of awareness of the risks involved is the dominant explanation of non-compliance in these examples. In some cases respondents did not appear to connect the reasons for the regulations with the risks they encountered. But in other cases locally, pragmatic notions of the need for compliance appeared to be displacing organizationally generated regulation. The suggestion that risks are either normalized or denied is reinforced by explanations forwarded by a minority of safety representatives, namely that non-compliance was the result of an 'it will never happen to me' attitude and over-familiarity with the working environment. It was observed, for example, that drivers were most inclined to non-compliance with the wearing of high visibility vests:

> . . . one of the great difficulties we had surprisingly—and I couldn't always appreciate the mentality of this—was getting drivers to wear . . . high visibility clothing if they had to get off the train. I can never understand why drivers were reluctant to wear them because as they drove the trains it must have been perfectly obvious to them how important they were but we have won the battle on that now, they are more willing to wear them. (departmental safety officer)

This last point was explained in terms of their belief that they knew the track better than anyone and a feeling that this could lead to a stubbornness about complying.

Another strong message from these explanations of non-compliance is that employees balanced immediate comfort against distant risk. There did not seem to be any suggestion among this group of respondents that these matters were systematically calculated but rather that they appeared to be the result of pragmatic inclinations. This resonates with suggestions in the medical literature on risk-taking that individuals engage in some form of *cost-benefit analysis* in deciding whether to comply with treatment. Notions of 'cost' and 'benefit' are socially constructed on the basis of previous experience, their understanding of the risks of non-compliance, information from a variety of sources including professional advice and colleagues, as well as their own beliefs (Donovan and Blake, 1992; Emcke, 1992). Similar explanations emerge from my data: 'I think sometimes they [workforce] think it [compliance] is unnecessary. The reason they don't do it is because they don't see the risk as high enough to make the effort necessary and worthwhile' (manager). A director makes a similar argument when explaining workplace deviance: 'it really is just too much effort. They are either thinking or unthinkingly, probably the latter, making some sort of personal assessment about the value of the precaution against the risk involved'.

A variant of the cost-benefit theme is that the *discomfort of safety clothing* or *impracticality of rules* explains workplace deviance. For instance 59 per cent of the workforce believed that safety equipment and occupational health and safety regulations made a difference to the way they worked, with 31 per cent regarding them as a hindrance:

R: I know tonight I will break the rule book.
I: How will you be breaking the rule book tonight?
R: By making the system work.
I: In order to do your job?
R: To do my job. Now if I make the system work, or I make a cock-up somewhere, the rule book will come back up to me, so the rule book only works in one direction. (safety representative, interviewee 22)

> I walk down tunnels by myself, often I go on the track, you should have a lookout man but I don't take him. I would never get my job done which goes back to my saying that you have to break the rules to do the job. (manager, interviewee 74)

Twenty-one per cent regarded the regulations as a help; and 7 per cent regarded them as both a hindrance and a help. The positive aspects of health and safety were that they offered protection and made staff feel safer. The negative aspects referred to were threefold. First, the health and safety considerations slowed up work; secondly, health and safety clothing was uncomfortable; and thirdly, health and safety clothing could be impractical, for example, hard hats fall off when you bend over; goggles mist up; and gloves make jobs less manoeuvrable.

These explanations also figure in other studies. Genn (1993: 230) concluded that employees do not play a major role in promoting better safety standards partly because they do not understand occupational health and safety regulation and partly because of workforce resistance to the use of protective clothing, guards, and safety procedures. Many managers, supervisors, and safety representatives sympathized with the workforce and volunteered that they too found many items of safety clothing very uncomfortable, especially in the hot weather. Indeed we should not be dismissive of the idea that regulation may actually be dysfunctional. Moreover there may be circumstances in which the workforce have a better understanding of how to avoid risk than their superiors (see Ch. 8). Nevertheless, there is one inescapable thread running through these explanations of non-compliance, namely that organizational goals and routines did not necessarily imply that health and safety issues were dominant. This point is crystallized in discussions of safety concerns being subservient to *other pressures*, such as a broader pressure to complete the job.[13]

Supervisors argued that other pressures forced them to take short-cuts. Four of the six safety representatives who responded to questions about non-compliance attributed their own deviation from the rules to other pressures. Sometimes this was spoken of positively in terms of the dedication (*sic*) of staff who overlooked the rules to get the job finished quickly:

R: ... at certain times I have staff who are working longer hours than possibly I would reasonably think they should. I would never deliberately put someone in a very key position but there are times when I have an emergency when, let's say, a bridge has caved in ... and I will allow people to work more than twelve hours to keep the railway running ...

I: Why does this happen?

R: I think there's two main reasons and the first one is something that is built into all railway people, some of the staff will argue it's not but I believe it is, that there's pride in the job. That you actually never see the job stop and you will keep going to any degree to keep the people moving to get them home or the traffic ... For all that people say about the modern day railway men, they will not leave the job unattended ... (manager, interviewee 5)

I should imagine that like in most industries the job's to be done, what is to be done as quickly as possible, and that will tend to put pressure on health and safety in corners being cut. (supervisor, interviewee 92)

I think they [managers] are being pushed to the limit just to keep the railways running. (safety representative, interviewee 8, referring to the pressures on managers)

---

[13] See for example, Dawson *et al.* (1988); Nelkin and Brown (1984: 97). The dominant focus of discussion are work pressures. But some staff referred to alternative, non-work, pressures, for instance, they did not regard safety clothing and procedures as conforming with a 'macho' image. So the pressure could come from a variety of sources such as managers, peers, and general working culture. Moreover the nature of the pressure could also vary.

All the walking routes they're supposed to be made sure they are all right, just don't have time to do it. Cut down on the staff and you're expected to do the same things. Ladder inspections—haven't got the time to go round and do those. Cut down on supervisors, who's going to do it? . . . I have to honestly say I can't be possibly following them all because there's insufficient time. The intention is there but there is so much else to do nowadays, the pressures are enormous, financial as well as everything else, this just has to take its place. (manager, interviewee 110)

All respondents, but especially managers, were asked about the priority they personally gave to *health and safety relative to other concerns*. In response to the question 'What priority do you give to health and safety?' the clear majority of managers (60 per cent) and supervisors (68 per cent) said that health and safety had prime or fairly high priority:

I give it high priority. I wouldn't say it was my highest to be fair, if I have got a heavy workload, actually meeting that workload is our main priority. But it's definitely the one under that, sort of A2 priority. (manager, interviewee 38)

It is number one, it is at the back of everything that I do. If you looked at the kind of problems that come across my desk . . . health and safety have to be in the background. (manager, interviewee 81)

I don't give it a priority. It is part of it and it is wrapped up in everything we do. I feel strongly about it, it is not a priority item. Other items are optional, some have priority, but safety is there all the time. (manager, interviewee 107)

On a scale 1 to 100 I suppose about 80 per cent, the reasons being is I suppose, health and safety one must admit can be a drawback in many ways because some safe working practices it takes longer to do. (supervisor, interviewee 87)

What priority? Well I should think that comes second to the job actually, it has to. (supervisor, interviewee 119)

This broadly accords with the views of senior personnel. No director or departmental safety officer accorded health and safety top priority—five felt that it had 'very high priority' and six considered that it had 'fairly high priority'.

In answering the more specific question about how important health and safety was in relation to other responsibilities, the priority accorded to health and safety lessened. Only 9 per cent of respondents (three managers and three supervisors) regarded health and safety as either most or very important. The majority of managers (64 per cent) regarded health and safety to be of equal importance to other concerns while a majority of supervisors (54 per cent) viewed it as subservient or of low importance. Meanwhile the workforce claimed that health and safety was either important relative to other jobs (55 per cent) or equal to other concerns (18.5 per cent). Safety representatives' perceptions of the importance attached to health and safety broadly accorded with those of managers and supervisors. However, their perceptions of the importance attached by the workforce were the reverse of the workforce's own perceptions, that is, the majority of safety representatives thought that the workforce attached low importance to health and safety: 'The majority of people you employ are interested in one thing and that is how much money you are giving them at the end of the week and a lot of them don't worry about the company's rules, regulations, health and safety' (supervisor, interviewee 82).

A theme running through these accounts is that there are competing organizational objectives to health and safety and primary here is the production pressure. This is a dominant theme in the literature on risk-taking (see Ch. 9; Carson, 1982; Heimer, 1988; Nelkin and Brown, 1984) and one which is reflected in more detailed questions to managers, supervisors, and safety representatives about which aspects of the job took higher priority than health and safety. This question throws the focus away from personal reasons for compliance and non-compliance towards broader company-related explanations. The majority (28) claimed that nothing else took priority. The 21 respondents who did cite other aspects of their job which took priority over health and safety referred to three specific aspects, namely 'getting the job done', 'keeping the trains running', and 'the budget':

> I perceive my responsibility to the passengers much more than my responsibilities to my people . . . that doesn't mean I would willingly let my people get killed. (manager, interviewee 66)

> . . . perhaps the main thing against our management is that they don't like any delays on the trains but . . . the problems I encounter with health and safety is not usually due to the trains running, it is normally what happens when they are off the train, walking and forward . . . (safety representative, interviewee 33)

Senior personnel specifically referred to 'production', that is, keeping the trains running, as carrying more importance than occupational health and safety. They also referred to 'safety of the line', in particular passenger safety:

> You can't have complete safety, you have got to balance the risk . . . we are operating in a financial situation and there are times when we have to say well we could provide this safeguard but we have to balance them to what degree of risk is involved . . . If we decide that money needs to be spent on factors to improve safety, we have to put a case forward to the businesses for that money to be spent. There is no pot of gold on the desk that you can dip into . . . We have got to go through the motions of making a financial case for it. (director)

> Priority 1 is getting the job done irrespective . . . Priority 2 is getting the job done efficiently and effectively and priority 3 is incorporating safety, health, and welfare into that, rather than integrating it. (director)

> I think they give it high priority … the whole thing is fail safe … the whole thing is bound together. If you are going to operate in a safe manner such that you don't cause a dreadful accident to trains at the same time, you must act in a safe manner to yourself. (director)

These views were also reiterated by a national union official: 'Safety can be put in two ways. If it is operational safety, that is a high priority. If it is safety of the workforce, that is not in the same category.'

Another indication that worker non-compliance has organizational explanations is the identification of a *lack of enforcement* as a major explanation of workplace non-compliance:

I: Do your workforce comply willingly with health and safety regulations?

R: When we enforce them, yes. We did have problems with things like high visibility vests initially, perhaps with 1 per cent of the workforce or even a lower percentage than 1 per cent with hard hats. Again, I think that if we enforced rigidly we would get acceptance, we haven't and we don't.

I: Why do you think that is?

R: Actually because of our lack of enforcement.

I: But why do you think they don't do it themselves?

R: Because they don't know it exists until we enforce it. (manager, interviewee 66)

Managers, supervisors, and safety representatives were asked what they would do if they discovered someone not following the rules. The first option for managers and supervisors would be to go through laid-down procedures. Their second and most likely response, and safety representatives' most preferred response, would be to have an informal chat with the offender:

> It depends on how dangerous it is, immediately if it could result in injury or fatality we would stop them there and then. If it was a minor infringement of something that wasn't potentially dangerous we might not stop them but go around and tell their supervisor. But there's always a reluctance to bypass the hierarchical system. (manager, interviewee 66)

In the case of managers and supervisors an informal chat seemed to comprise a 'telling off', whereas safety representatives preferred the description 'point out the non-compliance'. All directors and safety officers expected something to be done if non-compliance was witnessed. This group would first adopt an informal persuasive approach and talk personally to the offender. In the event of persistent non-compliance they would escalate their disciplinary response. Some pointed out that their response would vary according to the severity of the non-compliance. If it was serious then they would talk to the offender and contact his line manager too:

> I think you go through a procedure like with many other things, that you try and persuade people, talking with them and wanting to find out why

they have got resistance, that is the first thing. Secondly, you try and persuade them, thirdly, you might get to a stage where you actually have to formally warn them that they are being silly and therefore they face discipline and ultimately you might actually have to sack somebody ... but ultimately we will actually dismiss somebody. (director)

This accorded with workforce expectations:

I think that there is a difference between rules because of lack of knowledge and breaking rules persistently and persistent rule breakers should be punished. (worker, interviewee 53)

Well obviously if you break the rules they do take, they give you a verbal warning and sometimes they can suspend you, it all depends on if you are going to cut corners where it could involve people losing their lives or yourself then therefore they should take it seriously. (worker, interviewee)

When respondents were asked how often they had pursued the course of action they had described, managers and supervisors admitted that they had rarely if ever actually proceeded in the ways they described. Safety representatives, however, replied that they regularly pointed out non-compliance. Asked what they would do if they saw someone not following health and safety rules, they unequivocally said that they would intervene: 'I would feel duty bound to tell him so' (interviewee 41).They also made it clear it could lead to unpopularity: 'Very often and it is very unpopular you know, it has to be done' (interviewee 90).

Six of the senior personnel interviewed said that they had had cause to respond to non-compliance among the workforce, although this was not a frequent occurrence.

Workforce understandings of disciplinary procedures very much accorded with managerial and safety representative accounts. The majority understood that their supervisor or boss would be most likely to adopt an informal approach if they discovered that someone had not followed health and safety rules.[14] Only 9 respondents had ever been reprimanded for non-compliance with health and safety rules. So there was a general understanding that non-compliance was unlikely to result in disciplinary action:

I: If your supervisor or boss discovered you weren't doing something you should be doing to do with health and safety what would he do?
R: I would get a reprimand.
I: Has that ever happened?
R: It has happened, yes.
I: Did it make a difference to you?
R: Yes.

---

[14] The majority (20/38) responded that they would give a verbal warning; the rest would either take more formal action (6/38); do nothing (6/38); vary their response according to circumstances (3/38); and the remainder (3/38) did not know what they would do.

I: For how long?

R: For as long as it takes to forget it. (worker, interviewee 14)

I: Does it worry you that you could be subject to disciplinary action if you don't follow the rules?

R: Well yes and no. Yes, it is always there at the back of your mind that if you do something wrong and you break one of the rules and someone sees you and you could get raked over the coals or a number 1 or a severe warning. But on the other hand sometimes you think oh well, you have only got one job to do and it makes life just that little bit easier to do this one move, it is a technicality that is something you shouldn't do but you do it . . . (worker, interviewee 23)

The majority thought that more formal procedures should be followed. Yet the threat of disciplinary action did not have a positive influence upon staff because it was not seen as a credible threat. This said there was no suggestion of ideological resistance to compliance (cf. Whitehurst, 1977) or of a normative culture which encouraged deviance (cf. Massey, 1979).

Responsibility for non-compliance is variously attributed. Managers blamed themselves for their own non-compliance. A few managers tried to explain that the nature of their work contributed to their non-compliance. In particular, they explained that their visits to the work site were often short and unplanned. Hence they may not have had the required safety clothing with them or may have been tempted to take short-cuts to save time. Supervisors tended to distance the reasons for non-compliance from themselves. They argued either that they were ignorant of the rules or that other pressures forced them to take short-cuts, thus laying responsibility with the company. Clearly a mix of company and individual responsibility explains non-compliance. Ignorance of the requirements, the perceived low prioritization of health and safety, and a lack of enforcement may all be laid with the company: 'We all know that jobs are in danger of not being done safely by people who take short-cuts . . . it is up to management to be vigilant of that kind of practice to stamp it out. It is up to management to make sure that whatever we suggest as alternative is right' (manager, interviewee 25). Individuals also make choices and take risks, but the problem is deciding how much responsibility they can reasonably take and the parameters within which they take them:

Accidents happen because they ignore policies, what is expected of them. And then somebody loses an eye or gets a bad cut . . . purely and simply because they are not wearing goggles and they regret what they have done. (manager, interviewee 63)

The workforce are probably their own worst enemy 50 per cent of the time. (safety representative, interviewee 102)

The regulatory ideal would of course be that safe ways of working would have been internalized and automatic, but clearly this was far from the case.

Compliance

It is as important to detect reasons for compliance as for non-compliance, not least because it may offer some constructive ideas about how to improve levels of compliance. Managers, supervisors, and safety representatives were asked why they tried to comply with health and safety rules and regulations. Table 10.1 documents their replies.

The most pressing reason for the compliance of this group was 'to set an example' to staff. Safety representatives exemplified this most as the majority of respondents in this category commented that they had become much more compliant since becoming a safety representative. When they were asked if they complied with health and safety regulations typical responses were:

> I do because I have to set an example. (safety representative, interviewee 90)

> I do as far as I could see I do. I wouldn't knowingly openly expose myself to a thing which I feel is unsafe and therefore it is within the management's requirements of my safety. So I wouldn't expose myself really as I said earlier on as a matter of leadership to other men. (safety representative, interviewee 41)

Managers felt that they had a moral duty to promote health and safety:[15]

> Well as a manager you are the example. I mean if a manager knowingly breaks regulations or fails to observe laid-down instructions, I mean if I start using the short-cut, or endeavour to use the short-cut, then my staff say what is good enough for the boss is good enough for me. (manager, interviewee 45)

> I am conscious all the time because I am a safety engineer amongst other things that I have got to set an example I suppose . . . I have to be seen to comply with the rules in total. I simply cannot take short cuts and then expect others to do things right, it simply isn't good enough to work on the basis of do as I say not what as I do. (safety officer)

Twenty-two members of the workforce were asked about their reasons for compliance. The most frequently offered response (13 respondents) was that they complied because they were aware of the risks involved in not complying. Among the examples offered were those who had seen accidents involving non-compliance; those who wore masks because they understood that inhaling asbestos fibres or lead fumes was dangerous; those who wore goggles to avoid dust and dangerous particles flying into their eyes; and those who were concerned about the impact on their families if anything were to happen to them (see also Clay, 1984: 325). These examples reinforced the views of those managers who considered that safety measures were accepted when the risks were known. This involved knowledge of the rule and an understanding of the need

---

[15] 35% of managers asked about factors weighing in favour of health and safety cited a moral imperative to promote health and safety.

Table 10.1. Reasons for compliance

Reasons for compliance	Grade of staff						Total	
	Manager		Supervisor		Safety reps.			
	n	%	n	%	n	%	n	%
Own safety	5	25	3	23	2	33	10	26
To set an example	14	70	5	38	4	67	23	59
To protect others	—	—	4	31	—	—	4	10
'No reason not to'	1	5	—	—	—	—	1	2.5
To avoid prosecution	—	—	1	8	—	—	1	2.5
Total	20	100	13	100	6	100	39	100

for the rule: 'Firstly I don't want to see anybody injured and it is in the interests of the man's own welfare and also I don't want to be prosecuted either so obviously I have a big stick over me . . . but my main concern is the welfare of my staff' (supervisor, interviewee 64). Indeed one of the main factors identified by managers as encouraging safety within the industry was that the railways, especially the track, is a dangerous environment:

> The things that are most pro—it is a dangerous place to be. So there is a very strong sense of a need for safety. It is an industry that has prided itself on its safe carrying record, so purely on publicity grounds it doesn't do us much good whatsoever. The staff are brought up fairly strong with this safety of the customer and therefore if it is good enough for them it is good enough for me type of attitude brings about safety. Most people are in tight-knit groups which tend to form a community and therefore self-preservation. They all look after one another in that sense. (manager, interviewee 108)

Managers also felt that compliance was most likely when the rules were enforced, a view shared by seven members of the workforce who explained their compliance in terms of enforcement. Two respondents offered pragmatic reasons for their compliance, namely that they wore their overalls to keep clean. Generally therefore the reasons for compliance mirror explanations of non-compliance and thus reinforce our understanding of the factors both encouraging and obstructing the attainment of regulatory objectives.

Most of this discussion has, of course, concentrated on employee compliance. Let us return briefly to focus more particularly on understandings of corporate compliance.

Views of Corporate Compliance

Various questions were asked about the levels of concern about health and safety that exist within the company and managers, supervisors, and safety representatives were directly asked for their opinions about BR's attitude to health and safety. Their responses, detailed in Table 10.2, reveal that on balance, BR was perceived as having a good attitude to health and safety, with supervisors, and especially managers, being the most satisfied and safety representatives the least. Minor differences did emerge according to department. Mechanical and electrical engineering staff were the most satisfied and civil engineering and signals and telecommunications staff the least satisfied.

Senior personnel considered that BR as a corporate body had a concerned, caring, and responsible attitude and a duty to protect the health and safety of its employees. Explanations of corporate compliance mirrored those for individual compliance, namely compliance driven by moral imperatives and a dangerous working environment:

Table 10.2. British Railways' attitude to health and safety: the views of managers, supervisors, and safety representatives

Attitude of British Railways	Grade of staff						Total	
	Manager		Supervisor		Safety reps.			
	n	%	n	%	n	%	n	%
Very good	—	—	—	—	2	17	2	4
Good	—	—	11	58	—	—	11	22.5
Satisfactory	14	78	—	—	2	17	16	33
Improving	1	5.5	—	—	—	—	1	2
Average	1	5.5	—	—	—	—	1	2
Varies	—	—	1	5	—	—	1	2
Needs improving	1	5.5	2	10.5	1	8	4	8
Unsatisfactory	1	5.5	5	26.5	4	33	10	20.5
Minimal	—	—	—	—	3	25	3	6
Total	18	100	19	100	12	100	49	100

> British Railways Board are very keen and very interested in a safe environment for all of its staff for a variety of reasons, (a) the social implications because of the individual members and (b) at the end of the day—and this is probably [how] the railway are actually looking at it—but if you have somebody injured or killed it is an awful lot of money to retrain or replace that person so at the end of the day it is in our interest to look after our men and staff. (manager, interviewee 26)

> I think that as a major employer of people, as an industry that has inherent risks in it and as an industry that views it . . . as a fact of life, we have got to be responsible employers. (manager, interviewee 43)

Some had reservations that complacency may have crept in and a concern that there was a need for greater commitment to action, especially to improve the practices and procedures for health and safety:

> It is firmly expressed, I would hope with commitment. I would like to see some more of that commitment in practice after ten years. (director)

> Formally I think very good. Informally I think it's been done far too much by a series of bits of paper. We haven't really aimed at getting the message properly into peoples' heads. (manager, interviewee 66)

Other respondents identified problems in gaining commitment further down the hierarchy:

> British Railways itself, the people who make it right at the top, do a good job. But getting it home to various managers is quite a hard point . . . I have had a manager get up and say he doesn't give two hoots about it, he gets jobs done otherwise. (safety representative, interviewee 94)

Finally there were those who were more cynical of the company's intentions:

> Cosmetic, they will dish out a lot of propaganda, they'll dish out posters, there is no check to see if they are exhibited, there is no check to see if anybody reads anything, there is no feedback communication whatsoever . . . it is as if someone said 'ah, I must do that, send it out. Yes I have sent it out, thank you, I have done my bit and that is the end of it.' (supervisor, interviewee 15)

> . . . their other responsibilities come first and then health and safety as far as I am concerned . . . if they could keep trains going is more important than anything else. (safety representative, interviewee 85)

> I still feel that they are more concerned with saving costs than spending money. (safety representative, interviewee 123)

Senior personnel were also asked a much more direct question about what sort of factors they took into account when considering whether or not to implement particular health and safety proposals. Cost was most frequently referred to by the directors, whereas the primary concern of the departmental safety officers was the practicality of any proposal. The two other main factors mentioned as meriting consideration were the risks and benefits associated with the proposal. The identification of financial and business pressures as significant is not surprising. They take on a central position in the risk/regulation literature and also run through the responses of less senior managers. For example, while the majority of managers (including supervisors) claimed that nothing weighed against health and safety, the cost and time involved in health and safety emerged as the two main reasons cited by the minority as weighing against health and safety: 'Pressures not to comply would be purely time and, if you like, cash flow . . . There are certain limits on cash flow. Yes we can have that but you can have it next month rather than this' (manager, interviewee 108).

The importance of these was highlighted by the other most frequently cited factor regarded as weighing against health and safety, namely 'business pressures'. Senior personnel spelt out that the financial costs of health and safety were a negative influence, especially in the face of business pressures to reduce costs and increase productivity. They also felt that cumbersome health and safety procedures could increase the difficulty of the job for employees and lead to non-compliance:

> Well the pressures against it obviously are financial pressures and I can't think of any other pressures . . . well I suppose there are certain procedures that can be cumbersome, time consuming, and therefore in the end it is costly. The pressures for it are that one wants to grow an image as a responsible employer making a proposition in the labour market, particularly that we are looking for good responsible employees which is particularly important . . . (director)

More specific questions about the *cost* of health and safety were asked of senior personnel, managers, supervisors, and safety representatives. They were asked general questions about the cost of complying with health and safety demands, and managers and supervisors were asked about expenditure budgets. The majority (67 per cent) considered compliance to be costly. Supervisors were more likely than managers or safety representatives to regard it as costly. Departmental safety officers felt unable to assess the absolute costs of health and safety. Five directors considered these costs to be within the range 'very, very costly' to 'relatively costly', whereas two believed the costs to be low.[16] Respondents from each of the categories questioned about this qualified their response to emphasize that costly did not in their view mean too costly. The cost of life was also regarded as great and any money spent on health and safety was both valued and seen as necessary:

> Financially it must cost millions but the cost in human suffering etc. you know, obviously it costs more in human suffering not to provide it but financially it must cost millions. (manager, interviewee 38)

---

[16] Operations and mechanical and electrical engineering staff were most likely to regard it as costly and civil engineering and especially signals and telecommunications staff were the least likely to regard it as such.

There are times when it is costly yes, but what price is a human life? (manager, interviewee 136)

. . . it is easier to keep something safer, cheaper to keep something safer than wait for the big accident and then change everything because of this accident which has been caused in the first place by not adhering to health and safety, so I think it is reasonably safe compared to other projects on British Rail. (safety representative, interviewee 33)

It's more costly not to comply. (safety representative, interviewee 98)

The two directors who regarded the costs as low expressed the opinion that it was cost effective to be safe:

I think it's an investment. (director)

It cannot be costly, it must be more cost effective to actually do the sensible thing, the right-first-time things because people, an injury to a person . . . it is an investment of £0.5 million. If you have got that investment of £0.5 million you . . . take precautions to protect the investment and therefore against that backcloth I don't think that it is costly. (director)

Twenty-four of the 30 managers interviewed had expenditure budgets, as did 1 supervisor. Health and safety did not figure as a separate item in these budgets, except for one signals and telecommunications manager who had a small proportion of his budget specifically allocated to health and safety. It follows from this that the overwhelming majority could not with any accuracy assess what proportion of their budget health and safety represented: the estimates made ranged from an 'insignificant proportion' to 25 per cent of expenditure budgets:

I: So you don't know what proportion of your budget you spend on health and safety?

R: It would not be costed that way, tools would be on tools, clothing, safety signs on maintenance. (manager, interviewee 108)

It is minuscule compared with the total cost of the budget. The total budget is £43 million a year for our department and I would have thought the amount spent on depots, tools, test equipment—I would be surprised if it totalled more than £150,000. (manager, interviewee 117)

Well I have never really analysed the cost, obviously there must be a cost involved but in terms of the equipment I should think that it is not over expensive if you compare it, in my department, to the sort of budgets we are using for the actual work. I mean we are talking hundreds of thousands of pounds and perhaps a couple of thousand pounds worth for safety equipment. (supervisor, interviewee 64)

Interestingly, those at the top of the company could not estimate the costs of health and safety. Opinion was divided as to the merits of itemizing separately the cost of health and safety. Certainly there was a suspicion expressed at other levels that costs were used as a reason for not implementing some health and safety proposals and that it was amongst the first area to suffer when cost pressures were increased (see Nelkin and Brown, 1984: 63). Clay's (1984) survey of employers revealed that just below half of his respondents felt that compliance costs would have a significant impact upon a company's broader investment plans, the majority believing that it contributed to inflation. Clay's respondents also argued that small businesses were especially vulnerable to compliance costs and a loss of competitive advantage. But BR was, of course, a large company, albeit one under serious financial constraints (see Ch. 2).

When senior personnel were asked specifically about the costs of health and safety, they differentiated between the marginal costs imposed by new health and safety legislation and the absolute costs of health and safety. The extra costs incurred by legislative changes were considered to be minimal because it was believed that the railways already voluntarily met minimum legislative standards. But they did admit that while they complied with most Railway Inspectorate requirements, they did not always do so because of their costs. In such cases cost-benefit calculations came into prominence:

I: Do you find what RI ask for reasonable?

R: Ninety-nine per cent of the time.

I: What constitutes the 1 per cent where you may disagree?

R: Usually because I think in any item you buy an element of insurance and there must be a point where we think the last 1 per cent is sufficiently remote that it doesn't justify the means . . .

I: So, you are saying that in that 1 per cent what you are really weighing up is the risk against the cost?

R: Yes. (senior manager)

As we will discuss in the next chapter, such a perspective on health and safety was to move increasingly into vogue in subsequent years.

Discussion

From the discussion in this chapter we learn that the risk management systems BR had in place were not fully effective. BR provided safety equipment and safety clothing but these were not always used. It had in place rules and systems for health and safety but these were not always enforced. It also had health and safety education, but the risks were not always understood by its staff. Its provision of health and safety hardware and systems would place it as highly motivated in the broad spectrum of employers (Genn, 1993). But clearly this is insufficient for the attainment of regulatory objectives and it seems that much more is demanded of companies if regulatory objectives are to be met and risk is to be managed more effectively.

The findings remind us that regulation is not always and self-evidently pragmatic for those it is trying to protect. They may use their own agency to interpret local situations in ways that contradict the regulations. For example, the discomfort of clothing and inconvenience of safety equipment emerged as an explanation for non-compliance. It is easy to dismiss this as an 'excuse' for non-compliance, but it is clear from the interviews that managers and supervisors sympathized with these reasons for non-compliance (see also Nelkin and Brown, 1984). This suggests that there would be some benefit in the organization spending more time and even money on the design of these items and looking for more 'user friendly' items. This is further suggested by the reasons forwarded for complying with the rules, where some said that they wore protective clothing because of its usefulness, for example, in keeping clean. Other examples included wearing high visibility clothing because it offered protection from the rain and cold. More research could lead to improved designs and a choice of clothing could be helpful to take account of the fact that not everyone is the same:

> I think we can do a lot . . . I believe we have got clothing that is bulky then we may be able to get better clothing, we may be able to get walking routes better. It is no good having a perfectly safe walk route that nobody uses so we have got a responsibility there. This is going to cost but nevertheless even within that, even if something has got no money we can help, but yes health and safety, real safe practices can hinder [work]. (national union official)

The findings of Chapter 9 are reinforced in highlighting the need for more extensive training and education to promote understanding of the health and safety risks on the railways. However, it should not be assumed that awareness of the risks guarantees compliance. Non-compliance on or about the track was one of the areas most frequently cited, even though it was well understood that this was the most risky area of the railways. Also two of the most popular explanations of non-compliance were that it could be more convenient not to comply and that carelessness and forgetfulness were contributory factors. The non-compliance discussed by respondents typically comprised 'small-scale lapses' such as 'just nipping across the tracks' or 'forgetting' to put on safety clothing. But this was an industry in which one small lapse could lead to serious—even fatal—injury. It also seemed to be the case that the 'small lapses' were often established as the 'norm'. This suggests that organizational scripts were not successfully countering non-compliance nor were organizational routines placing health and safety issues as paramount. This was partly reflected in a lack of enforcement. It was clear that formal disciplinary procedures for non-compliance were regarded as rare. So managerial staff failed to discipline for lapses which they could readily understand. From one perspective this could be interpreted as empathy from managers who understood the irritations of, for example, safety equipment, but from another perspective it could be seen as indicative of a lack of support for regulatory objectives. Thus the constitutive objectives of regulation were undermined. Indeed one US study of the effectiveness of safety systems found that a reliable measure of safety programme effectiveness was the quality of management systems. The role of supervisory staff was identified as especially important (Bailey and Peterson, 1989).

There were also perceived to be broader pressures on employees which could result in a reordering of health and safety as priorities. Some of these pressures were self-inflicted and others were perceived as organizational. BR's attitude to health and safety was generally perceived to be good, yet health and safety were not felt to be accorded top priority. The major pressures against health and safety were perceived to be costs and time. Cost referred mainly to business production pressures to keep the trains running and complete jobs quickly rather than to the capital cost of health and safety initiatives. The large majority felt that money spent on health and safety was money well spent but it was nevertheless repeatedly cited as a limiting factor upon achieving regulatory objectives. But these broader company-related problems were not overriding. There is also evidence that senior BR personnel wanted the company to be regarded as a caring, socially responsible employer and that this was also an important factor in the compliance debate. There was evidence from the research that many employees regarded them in this way. Indeed there was evidence from all sectors of the company that compliance with health and safety regulation was regarded as morally important.

It is perhaps a measure of the honesty accorded to the research interviews that the large majority of staff were prepared to admit to at least occasional non-compliance with health and safety rules and regulations. Some even reported regular non-compliance. It would of course have been extraordinary and suspicious to have full compliance reported by a majority of respondents. Indeed they were articulate about their non-compliance.

The findings support a multi-causal explanation of compliance. Respondents explained their compliance with reference to one broad set of factors, namely their awareness of the risks involved in their working environment. Yet the areas where they most readily admitted to non-compliance were the areas they recognized as the most risky (Ch. 9). Accounting for this discrepancy suggests that connections are not necessarily made between regulation, risk management systems, and everyday risks. And this adds further weight to the suggestion that risks may be normalized and denied in everyday working situations. This is important because these are major obstacles to the constitutive objectives of regulation. On a more positive note what also emerges as important for compliance are feelings of social responsibility at the individual as well as corporate levels. Those vested with responsibility—notably managers and safety representatives—felt a duty to set an example, a factor which contributes to our understandings of patterns of compliance and non-compliance. This is an area which demands much more extensive examination.

An underlying message on the subject of compliance is that staff of all grades were not clear how much priority they should accord to health and safety. The messages from the top of the organization were perceived as ambiguous and even contradictory. This, it might be added, is not unique to the railways, but is an ambiguity that characterizes regulatory debates and takes one directly to the essence of regulation as a form of risk management rather than as a means of eradicating risk (Hutter, 1988). Organizational scripts, routines, and goals all need to consistently support regulatory objectives. At the time of this research production pressures could counter and change individual assessments of risk-taking. So the gains of non-compliance could be seen to outweigh the costs. For instance, taking short-cuts was not countered by enforcement but may even have been rewarded by increasing productivity.

While it is possible to point to the political economy for explanation of these findings, it is not a sufficient source of explanation. We need to pay attention to what is relevant and feasible and as Heimer (1988) indicates this should not necessarily lead us to be too pessimistic about regulation; on the contrary it points to its central importance in trying to effect a reordering of corporate priorities. In short, it is essential that we do learn more about the issues of risk and compliance and develop our practical and theoretical understandings of these and how they relate to regulation and other risk management regimes and strategies.

PART V
POSTSCRIPT

11

Privatization and the Safety Cascade

The years immediately after the main data collection for this research witnessed an acceleration of trends already in evidence during the research period. The privatization process came to a climax in 1993 with the Railways Act, which paved the way for the full privatization of BR. The model of enforced self-regulation brought in by the HSW Act was greatly extended and the systematization of approaches to regulation continued. Privatization actually exacerbated the very conditions identified by the research reported in this book as problematic to the success of enforced self-regulation. And it did so as a more extreme version of the enforced self-regulation model was introduced, one in which an industry regulator was established. In the fullness of time, the system demonstrably failed, thus raising serious questions about the limits of self-regulatory regimes. This chapter will describe the changes which occurred in the post-research period, consider their effects, and then discuss some of the lessons to be learnt from the experience.

Privatization

The privatization of BR was part of a broader programme instituted by the 1980s Conservative government (Foreman-Peck and Millward, 1994; Graham and Prosser, 1991; Veljanovski, 1987). Its purpose was to replace public sector support for the railways with private sector investment and management (Department of Transport, 1994), the intention being that the privatized companies would recover all of their own costs. As we have seen, the privatization process began in the early 1980s with the selling-off of subsidiary parts of the company. There was little doubt that full privatization was the ultimate goal. The privatization of the railways was discussed at the 1988 Conservative Party Conference and plans for its implementation discussed in a 1992 White Paper *New Opportunities for the Railways* (Bradshaw and Mason, 1994: 34). The 1993 Railways Act saw the fulfilment of these ambitions. It paved the way for the privatization of BR, an industry which had since 1948 been unified and nationalized (Department of Transport, 1994). The changes proposed by the Act were radical and one prominent railway commentator referred to it as 'a revolutionary and controversial piece of legislation' (Bradshaw and Mason, 1994).

Institutionally, privatization replaced a unified vertical command structure with a complicated structure of some sixty independent businesses contracting with each other.[1] Some of these had previous railway experience, others had none. The new structure separated the operation and the maintenance of the infrastructure from the operation of train services. At the centre of the new structure are the infrastructure controllers, the only widespread element in the new system (HSE, 1996: 129) and important because they have been allocated central safety responsibilities (see below). Railtrack, which was set up in April 1994,[2] is so far the only infrastructure controller and as such it owns and manages the track, signalling, and other operational infrastructure of the railways.[3] The company is devolved geographically into ten zones. BR remains in operation to control those parts of the industry not yet privatized, so the company is effectively being slowly run down.

Privatization was accompanied by a complex new *regulatory structure*, much of it concerned with the commercial aspects of the business and the protection of passenger interests. For example, a franchising director is responsible for overseeing the franchising of passenger services; ten rail users consultative committees have been established; and a rail regulator has been appointed to promote competition and protect consumer interests. An important part of the regulator's remit is to approve access agreements between Railtrack and the train operators. In addition, the Monopolies and Mergers Commission, the Director of Fair Trading, and the Secretary of State for Trade and Industry have regulatory authority with respect to differing aspects of the new organization. *State* regulation of health and safety at work remains much the same as before at an organizational level, namely it is the responsibility of HSE, and most specifically the Railway Inspectorate. And the HSW Act is still the central legislation.[4] But of most relevance to this study are the complex new arrangements for the health and safety of the workforce within the newly structured railway which were outlined both within the 1993 legislation and the discussions preceding it. These arrangements impose extended health and safety responsibilities upon the industry itself.

---

[1] This was the initial estimate. *The Railway Safety Annual Report 1995/96*, however, estimated that at this stage they were dealing with some 107 separate units.

[2] Railtrack is not specifically mentioned in the 1993 Railways Act. In law there is provision for more than one infrastructure controller.

[3] Railtrack was originally set up as a separate government-owned company but in 1996 it too was privatized. It owns property (stations, depots, and track); co-ordinates train services; and serves as a leaseholder for train operating companies which operate passenger rail services, freightliner services, rolling stock lease companies which lease trains to the operators, and infrastructure services companies which provide, maintain, and renew the track and signalling.

[4] New regulations have also been made under the HSW Act, namely the Railways (Safety Case) Regulations, 1994 (see below), the Railways (Safety Critical Work) Regulations, 1994, and the Carriage of Dangerous Goods by Rail Regulations, 1996.

The Safety Cascade

The new arrangements for health and safety which accompanied privatization were referred to by those in the industry as a 'safety cascade'. This describes a system which greatly extends previous notions of self-regulation, by making the infrastructure controllers responsible for overseeing 'the safety of the operational network under the supervision of HSE'. These controllers thus have responsibilities for their own activities under the HSW Act and for the entire operational network under the 1993 Railways Act. The key to this system is the *Railway Safety Case* (RSC).

The Safety Case

The safety case approach to health and safety was advocated by the Cullen Inquiry into the Piper Alpha explosion in 1988 (Cullen, 1990). Since then it has been promoted by HSE as a major tool of inspection and self-regulation. This approach requires companies to carry out formal safety assessments of serious hazards and risks in the workplace and to explain how these are being managed. The application of this approach to the railway industry is enshrined in the Railways (Safety Case) Regulations 1994. They outline the requirements and status of a safety case and the schedules to these regulations explain what they should cover. These particulars are quite specific and directional, and they clearly aim to constitute systems, policies, and procedures which will become part of the everyday life of the railways. They include consideration of safety policy, risk assessment, safety management systems, safety standards, accident investigation, the design of premises and plant, and provision for audit. The regulations also require provision for the active participation of employees through consultation procedures and they require the recording of audits and action taken in consequence of them.

Infrastructure controllers, train operators, and station operations must prepare safety cases. The infrastructure controllers' safety cases must be accepted by HSE. But the infrastructure controllers then hold responsibilities for validating the safety case of anyone using the infrastructure, hence the imagery of a cascade. At the moment Railtrack—as the only infrastructure controller—takes sole responsibility for this. It is responsible for ensuring that franchisees, the track renewal and infrastructure maintenance companies, and the rolling stock lease companies have a properly validated safety case before issuing them with a licence. This involves Railtrack in examining lengthy documented safety cases from potential leaseholders and the safety cases that leaseholders have agreed with their suppliers and contractors. Safety cases should be reviewed every three years and revised whenever necessary. Beyond this the regulations specify a duty to conform to the safety case and all employees have a duty to co-operate with their employers to enable this compliance. Non-compliance is deemed a criminal offence. If the infrastructure controller rejects a leaseholder's safety case, which in effect would refuse them access to the rail network, then there is a right of appeal to the Secretary of State for Transport who will take advice from HSE.

The Railways (Safety Case) Regulations reinforce the constitutive ambitions of earlier occupational health and safety legislation.[5] The safety case approach requires that safety becomes an active and integral part of everyday working life. This is reflected in Railtrack's *A Guide for Operators of Independent Passenger Services* which explains its expectations of safety cases: 'It is vital that your safety case, like Railtrack's, is a "living document". You will have a duty to follow the procedures and arrangements described in it at all times. Railtrack will carry out formal safety audits of your compliance with your safety case . . .' (Railtrack, 1993: 4).

The regulations also reinforce the communitarian aspirations of Robens and the HSW Act and in particular the Management of Health and Safety at Work Regulations 1992 'which require employers who share a workplace to co-operate with each other and co-ordinate their safety procedures' (HSE, 1996: 128). They also allocate vital safety responsibilities to the infrastructure controllers, who regulate market entry through the validation of safety cases and who have a monitoring role through the expectation that they will periodically audit compliance. Thus the infrastructure controllers become part of the enforcement machinery of 'enforced self-regulation', with the Railway Inspectorate having an overseeing role. The 1993 Railways Act effectively extends the principle of self-regulation.

The Railway Inspectorate

The period of fieldwork for the BR study also witnessed the beginning of a period of institutional and cultural change for the Railway Inspectorate, changes which again progressed further during the rest of the 1990s.

In December 1990 the Railway Inspectorate became part of HSE and thus one of its constituent inspectorates. Railway Inspectors were moved out of the Department of Transport to HSE buildings in another part of London (Bradshaw and Mason, 1994: 32–3). Prior to this there had been a movement towards appointing non-railway personnel as chief inspecting officers of railway for the first time in the Railway Inspectorate's history. These developments have resulted in a number of changes. For example, they led to the reorganization of the Inspectorate; greater formalization in management style; a move to team work; and greater management of staff. One inspector remarked, 'One of

---

[5] The Railways (Safety Critical Work) Regulations, 1994, identify critical work on the railways and specify that those undertaking that work should be competent and fit. Again the companies employing these persons have responsibility to enforce this. So we see an extension of the constitutive ambitions of occupational health and safety regulation as the legislation endeavours to penetrate corporate life and specify safe working practices.

the objectives was to try to create within the Railway Inspectorate a feeling that we are all playing with the same harmony and we are not a series of virtuoso performers'. The management changes were emphasized dramatically when the Inspectorate joined HSE in 1990:

> The most significant change in the move to HSE was the increase in the management of us and the increased call on the one hand to account for what we're doing and why—justify ourselves . . . as an Inspectorate. What are its projections? What are its objectives, output measures, and how have you achieved them? Demonstrate, prove, discuss . . . much greater management pressure to prove you are producing value for money. (railway inspector)

This was partly attributed to an increase in interest in railway safety and also to a change in staff. Not only were there changes at the top of the Inspectorate but there were changes throughout the organization. This was as a result of a rapid expansion of the Inspectorate following the King's Cross incident.[6] Many of the new entrants came from other areas of HSE and brought with them different ideas about policy, strategy, and prioritizing work. As one inspector remarked, 'RI is now managed by civilians who have a different culture and outlook'. The changes referred to here are changes which also influenced the industry, namely the development of a more systematic approach to occupational health and safety.

The Systematization of Health and Safety

Moves towards an apparently systematic and rigorous approach to health and safety had already begun during the data collection period for this research. This approach emerged in response to a variety of influences, some of which were specific to the industry and others of which were general and extended beyond the railway industry. The specific events were the aftermath of the King's Cross and Clapham Junction accidents, which caused the whole railway industry to reappraise completely its approach to health and safety (see Ch. 3).

The Clapham Inquiry Report is especially relevant for BR as the company was the main subject of this report. The recommendations emphasized the importance of not just setting targets but achieving them and auditing them (Hidden 1989, paras. 13.2, 13.16, 13.53) and the sheer volume of recommendations in the report led to the development of a methodology to prioritize using cost-benefit and risk assessment schemes:

---

[6] In 1974 the Railway Inspectorate had a field force of 15 Railway Employment Inspectors, by 1988 this had dropped to 8, largely because of retirements. More money became available to both attract more inspectors and to increase their pay. In 1989 7 extra inspectors joined and by 1995 25 officers were working at field-level. Privatization increased the demands on the Inspectorate and this led to further recruitment in the 1990s.

... we couldn't afford all we were being asked to do post-Clapham so we had to identify and prioritize. (industry representative)

The famous question is 'where do you draw the line?' So we went to costs of life figures and looked at diminishing return areas. Software came out as worthwhile whereas hardware schemes were not. A lot of consultation was involved. (industry representative)

Management consultants with expertise in the chemicals industry were hired by BR. They were largely responsible for the introduction of risk assessment and cost-benefit analyses to the industry,[7] an approach which resonated with the more business oriented culture dominating the company, a culture in which cost issues were much more prominent than in previous decades (Dent, 1991).

These changes manifested themselves in a variety of ways in the industry, including the production of annual safety plans containing safety objectives and safety performance indicators. Prior to privatization BR had started producing such a plan, the first one being published in 1991. Post-privatization, as a much diminished company, they continued to produce a plan but probably of more importance now are the plans produced by Railtrack and by the Railway Group.[8] *Risk management* figures very prominently and explicitly in the new regime. Five of the six strategic objectives in Railtrack's *1994/95 Safety Plan* are risk related, namely:

- organizational change risk;
- passenger individual risk;
- public risk;
- workforce risk;
- passenger multi-fatality risk.

More generally, risk assessment has become increasingly weighty both at the level of national policy decisions and also locally. Local managers are expected to think in terms of risk assessment. Health and safety auditing has also emerged as a key tool in the management of occupational health and safety risks.

The systematization of approaches to occupational health and safety can also be seen as part of a broader societal/governmental trend, in particular the emphasis upon performance indicators such as safety targets, safety plans, and safety audits (Hood and Jones, 1996; Power, 1997). This was, for example, reflected in governmental approaches to regulation. In 1996, for instance, the Interdepartmental Liaison Group on Risk Assessment (ILGRA) was set up so that senior policy-makers could consider 'more efficient and effective ways for

---

[7] Arguably cost-benefit analysis has always been an integral part of health and safety regulation. In the HSW Act, for example, it is inherent in the term 'reasonably practicable' (Dalton, 1998; Dawson *et al.*, 1988; Horlick-Jones, 1996). What is new in the 1990s is the systematic and widespread use of cost-benefit tools.

[8] The Railway Group is defined as 'all organisations operating on or associated with Railtrack's railway infrastructure' (Railtrack, 1995: 4).

regulating and managing risks' (ILGRA 1998: 2). HSE promoted a range of risk management techniques, such as total quality management techniques (TQM) which were popularized in the early 1990s (Dalton, 1998). Thus the Railway Inspectorate was influenced by some of the trends in the regulation of occupational health and safety towards a more risk-based approach to inspection work (HSE, 1997: 116). Indeed, the Inspectorate increasingly characterized its work as risk based, for example: 'As well as effectively targeting its efforts to address risk on the railway and its methods of control, HMRI strives to understand and meet public expectations' (HSE, 1996: 11). This is a reflection of HSC's mission statement which is outlined, for instance, at the start of the *1997/98 Annual Report and Accounts*: 'To ensure that risks to people's health and safety from work activities are properly controlled' (HSC, 1998). Risk assessment was also key in the requirement to produce safety cases: 'The Railways (Safety Case) Regulations 1994 have the primary purpose of requiring railway operators to put into place management systems that will adequately control all risks' (HSE, 1997 p. ix). Indeed the Railway Inspectorate emphasized the importance of risk assessment later in this Report: 'The railways, in common with many other industries, are increasingly using a risk-based approach to the management of safety. Assessment of risks is widely used to support the development of standards, inform decisions on investment, prioritise maintenance and guide working practices' (ibid. 112).

The safety case is regarded as an increasingly important audit tool and of greater potential value than off-the-shelf safety audit schemes. Local managers are expected to undertake regular safety audits and are externally audited every three years. Railtrack's safety case is audited by its own auditors and also by the Railway Inspectorate, who assess Railtrack's procedures for auditing the train operating companies' compliance with their safety cases (HSE, 1997: 13 ff.).

How successful these new risk management techniques are is the subject of a critical literature. The trend to the greater quantification of risk[9], for example, is hotly debated. The mathematical basis of the quantified risk assessments (QRAs) is disputed, especially where there are small numbers involved or where there are no reliable data to work from (Cohen, 1996; Toft, 1996). The interpretation of the data may prove difficult in a variety of ways. For example, the causes of a risk may not be clear, and even where they are clear the decision about what is an acceptable risk needs to be taken and that is essentially a political decision. Indeed some claim that the procedures themselves are value laden (Hood and Jones, 1996). A more extreme position negates the whole attempt to produce an objective measure of risk, arguing that all assessments are inherently subjective (Slovic, 1992). Difficulties with these measures and approaches were recognized by industry representatives and regulators alike. One of the

---

[9] This involves, for example, applying a numerical target to strategic objectives, for instance: 'The risk to passengers will be controlled so that on average no individual passenger is exposed to a risk of fatality greater than 1 in 50 million per journey' (Railtrack, 1995: 5).

inspectors I interviewed worried about the practicalities of risk assessment: 'What is a risk—HSE doctrine is that we should drive the risk down as far as to be reasonably practicable and the argument really becomes "how low is low and what is the cost?" If we are into the region of "only just" why spend any more driving it down lower still . . . .'

Interaction between the industry and regulators reveals the contentious and negotiable nature of these measures. For example, in the Railway Group's *Safety Plan 1995/96* the industry appealed to the HSW Act and its requirement of 'reasonable practicability' and to HSE guidance in support of its interpretation and use of risk assessments:

The guidance suggests upper and lower levels of risk for individual employees or members of the public affected by the activity, i.e. those that are beyond the 'upper limit of tolerability', and those that are 'broadly acceptable'. Between these boundaries lies a region of risk known as 'ALARP' (As Low As Reasonably Practicable) where the costs of risk control measures may be evaluated against the benefits of those measures . . . there is an obligation on any organisation to seek all means to reduce risk towards the 'broadly acceptable' level as long as the costs are not grossly disproportionate to the benefits gained. A policy of using cost benefit analysis in conjunction with risk assessment is appropriate. (Railtrack 1996: 5)

These sorts of arguments were thus taken into account in the weighting system used by the industry. The HSE's *Annual Safety Report 1996/97* picked up these arguments. It stated that the elimination of risk was not a possibility, especially within the limits of the law (HSE, 1997: 12 ff.). But it emphasized that quantified risk assessment (QRA) and cost-benefit analyses should be seen as 'aids to decision-making' and it criticized some employers for: 'tending to present QRAs as a precise justification for their position either for taking no action to improve safety or, worse still, *as a justification for reducing the level of safety already provided*' (HSE, 1997, p. ix).

In his Foreword to the *Annual Report* the Chief Inspector of Railways commented: 'I will expect operators to go that extra step in the pursuit of safety rather than stop as soon as the figures indicate that they appear justified in doing so. When in doubt decisions should, in my opinion, always be on the safe side' (ibid.). The *1997/98 Annual Report* followed up on these criticisms. In particular it supported the QRA Forum, a cross-industry body, and drawing upon the experiences of the forum commented upon the disparities in the values different companies gave to common risks (HSE, 1998: 105).

Despite these very real problems with the new risk management techniques, their symbolism is not wasted on either the industry or the regulator. They both understand that it is one way of publicly demonstrating that they are addressing risk (Clarke, 1999; Hood and Jones, 1996: 86), and this is felt by both to be especially important given that the railway industry is much more in the public view than many other industries and this may well affect public perceptions of risk. But at the same time that more systematic approaches to health and safety were used to boost public confidence in railways safety, they were also leading to increasingly acrimonious relations between the industry and the state regulator.

Relations between the Industry and the Railway Inspectorate

Relations between the Inspectorate and industry have undoubtedly become more distant and formal during the 1990s. Inspectors have encountered an increasingly adversarial tone in their relations with the industry:

> We [the Railway Inspectorate] are now increasingly beginning to see challenges. In the past it was rather a case of the inspector says 'jump' and they [industry] say 'how high'. Now the question is 'Why?' and 'Are you going to make me?' They are getting more business like and saying, do we have to spend this money? . . . because we have been challenged—or foresee that we will be challenged—we perhaps do more soul searching ourselves before making recommendations and reaching conclusions of what should be done. (railway inspector)

The systematization of approaches to occupational health and safety has led to a greater readiness to challenge regulatory demands and the tools of systematization have emerged as tools of adversarial relations. The Inspectorate's *Annual Report 1996/97* makes specific reference to this:

> The days when what an Inspector said was done regardless of cost are gone—and it is no bad thing for Inspectors' judgements to be occasionally challenged, so that it is assured that enforcement is 'proportionate' to the risk. However such challenges by risk assessment (seemingly more often designed to *justify avoiding additional work* rather than supporting the need for it) will continue to put Inspectors on their mettle and will occupy more time and effort to counter them as necessary. (HSE, 1997: 13, emphasis added)

These changes led to a more formal relationship: 'They [railway companies] are more questioning about suggestions and recommendations and we [railway inspectors] are more careful we have the evidence, but having got the evidence we are probably more assertive in saying 'That's what we want'' ' (railway inspector). Another railway inspector made a similar observation:

> We are trying to flex our muscles a bit more . . . In the old days we would have trusted them to fix it, now there is an attitude 'Well I don't see why we should. We have done a risk assessment, or we have looked at it and we're disputing what you are doing and no we won't do it.' Now plainly if that is going to be the attitude then we shall have to use what particular powers are open to us to say in this particular case 'I'm sorry, you will'. (railway inspector)

As this quotation suggests, attitudes towards *legal action* have changed. Inspectors now use legal action more readily. They started to take their own cases, whereas traditionally solicitors had been employed to do this.[10] Moreover they are more prepared to prosecute for health and safety offences such as 'failing to maintain a safe system in the running of trains', cases where there had been no fatality and cases which were often more difficult to prove than those where there is hard, tangible evidence of non-compliance (Hawkins, 1992*a*; Hutter and Lloyd-Bostock, 1992).

Industry attitudes towards legal action have also changed. Apart from being more prepared to challenge the Inspectorate, the industry is also discerned to be paying more systematic attention to notices and legal action. There is now a system where those at the highest level of the companies are informed of legal action against them and where managers are called to account for this. This, of course, contrasts with the situation uncovered by the earlier fieldwork for this study (see Ch. 5). Interestingly the perception in industry is of less legal activity than implied in the interviews with railway inspectors: 'there was an initial flurry of prosecutions, but their preference is still to work with us rather than rush to the statute book' (industry representative). This view is borne out by internal HSE documentation (HSE, 2000*a*) and by the statistics (see Table 11.1), although it is difficult to make any firm claims on the basis of such a short period. If we compare these figures with those for 1980–92 (Ch. 5), then we find that there have not been any significant changes in the number of prosecutions and improvement notices compared to the early 1990s. There were slightly more prohibition notices in the latter years of the 1990s. This suggests that inspectors' claims that increased pressure is now being exercised refers not so much to legal action as such, but to the more general toughening up across all enforcement methods which they referred to in interviews. Moreover it seems that this shift in approach predated privatization and is more associated with the increasing influence of HSE and the King's Cross and Clapham Junction accidents.

There are a number of related reasons for these changes. There has been subtle pressure to do things differently. Largely this came from within the Inspectorate, from the new staff, especially those in charge of the Inspectorate. It is also a result of the increased scrutiny to which the Inspectorate is subject, and the fact that the greater numbers of inspectors have made higher levels of action possible. The changes to the industry have also played a role, especially the increasingly commercial environment and the fragmentation which has led the Inspectorate to have less confidence in parts of the industry and thus to rely less on trust and more on formality than was the case with BR (HSE, 2000*a*). In some cases standards are seen by the Inspectorate to have deteriorated.

Another indicator of more acrimonious relations between the industry and the regulator is reflected in the fact that the Railway Inspectorate has become increasingly vocal in their censure of the industry. They are much more prepared

---

[10] Typically inspectors only take undefended cases; they still use solicitors for defended cases.

TABLE 11.1. Legal action by the Railway Inspectorate, 1995/6–1998/9

Action	1995/6	1996/7	1997/8	1998/9
Prosecution	3	6	8	10
Prohibition notice	8	4	19	6
Improvement notice	15	20	14	15

Source: Annual Reports (HSE, 1996, 1997, 1998, 1999).

than previously to issue critical press statements about the industry[11] and they have used their Annual Reports much more aggressively as a vehicle of complaint (Hutter, 1997). These changes are well illustrated by the case of automatic train protection (ATP). This case exemplifies how BR, Railtrack, and the privatized companies became more confident in challenging regulatory demands on them and also illustrates how a new systematic approach to risk management has been used as a tool of regulatory resistance. It is also a case which is central to two major train accidents which have brought the whole safety cascade system into serious doubt, and which are discussed in more detail later in this chapter.

Automatic Train Protection (ATP)

ATP is defined in the Hidden Report into the accident at Clapham Junction (1989: para. 15.8) as . . . 'a term used to cover a wide range of systems in use on the Continent which are provided to stop a driver passing a signal at danger and in the most recent applications exceeding a safe speed for the line and if he does so the train is automatically brought to a stop'. The Railway Inspectorate first called for BR to consider ATP in 1985 and in 1988 BRB accepted the scheme and established a ten-year plan for its introduction (Hidden Report, 1989, paras. 14.27–14.31). But in 1989 the Hidden Report injected some urgency into the matter when one of the Inquiry's main recommendations was the installation of ATP over a five-year period (1989, para. 15.6). At this time BR was still nationalized and BRB had assured the Court of Inquiry that it had 'adequate funds to ensure the safe running of the railway' (para. 14.13). Nevertheless there were, even at this stage, signs of resistance to the scheme. Hidden (para. 14.21–2) reports a letter sent in 1988 from the then Director of Operations to the Joint Managing Director, Railways in which he had warned that there was a 'change

---

[11] In March 1998, for example, the *Guardian* reported concern over Railtrack's safety powers (17 Mar. 1998). Later that month HSE publicly threatened to prosecute Railtrack for not completing repairs (*Guardian*, 27 Mar. 1998). In December of the same year the same newspaper carried a headline 'Angry watchdog tells Railtrack to install £152m. safety scheme' (7 Dec.). In 1999 HSE put notices on 102 signal boxes and the Inspectorate publicly warned Railtrack to improve the condition of its track, threatening enforcement action in the face of non-compliance.

of railway culture' brought about by the introduction of business sectors and business managers who may not be sympathetic to 'non-commercial proposals'. It resulted in greater scrutiny of these projects and delays in the investment in ATP (and other safety projects). Hidden thus made a number of recommendations about ATP and the relationship between safety and cost:

48. The Department of Transport and British Railways Board shall make a thorough study of appraisal procedure of safety elements of investment proposals so that the cost-effectiveness of safe operation of the railway occupies its proper place in a business-led operation.
49. British Railways shall develop an adequate system of allocating priority to projects to ensure that safety standards are not compromised by delay.
50. British Railways shall ensure that the organisational framework exists to prevent commercial considerations of a business-led railway from compromising safety.

Two trial sections of track were fitted with ATP immediately after the publication of the Hidden Report. But the industry's commitment to ATP dwindled and one of the railway inspectors I interviewed post-privatization cited the failure to install ATP as evidence of the industry's resistance to regulatory demands.[12] BR representatives made public moves to distance themselves from ATP. For instance, in July 1994 the Joint Managing Director (Safety) gave a conference paper entitled 'Value for Money in Transport Safety Measures' in which he made the case against ATP, explaining the basis upon which the judgement was made:

The cost per life is only one element in the decision making process which also takes into account general economic, commercial and political factors and public reaction.

Whenever a decision is made on safety spending, an implicit valuation of life has been made. There is now a broad consensus that society's willingness to pay for safety equates to it putting a valuation of around £1M–£2M on a life.

For road schemes, the figure used is £700,000. For railway investment, the figure generally used is £2M. There are a variety of reasons for this, e.g. unlike the motorist who can make choices about the way he drives, the rail passenger is not in control of the risks involved.

The present national economic priorities mean that the level of investment on the existing railway remains below the £1bn annual figure needed to keep the system in good running order . . . Existing orders for new commuter trains will be completed, but the priority must then be to renew track and signalling. The alternative would be an increasing number of speed restrictions due to track conditions and temporary line closures . . . Against this background of limited resources a programme to install ATP on a network-wide basis must be weighed alongside necessary investment in modernisation.

---

[12] The Hidden Report also recommended the introduction of on-train data recorders; the introduction of cab radios as a matter of priority; research into the structural integrity of Mark 1 stock; and the introduction of total quality management (TQM) and external safety audits. The introduction of cab radios had not been fully implemented five years after the report and neither had the Mark 1 rolling stock been either improved or withdrawn from service.

A judgement also has to be made on the problem that if prices for rail travel are pushed too high, for safety purposes, the result may well be to divert more people to the roads, where the risks are much higher. (Raynor, 1994: 12, 18, 19)

ATP thus fell foul of the risk assessments used to prioritize work. The arguments centred on cost and prioritization. As one of my interviewees explained: 'We must prioritize the most effective things. If we put our money in ATP we are taking it away from more effective schemes . . . We can't eliminate risk but we are directing funds to where it's needed most' (industry representative). The Uff Report into the Southall crash observes that the industry's distancing from ATP occurred 'just before Railtrack took over as infrastructure controller' (2000: 153).[13] The controversy about ATP continued through the mid to late 1990s. The Uff Report documents 'a lack of commitment to ATP, if not outright hostility' (2000: 164) and notes that by 1997 the position of ATP lay in the balance. During this period the Inspectorate kept on the pressure for Railtrack to act on the problem, including a chapter in the annual *Railway Safety Reports* devoted to 'Train Protection Strategy'. The number of signals passed at danger was reported annually to Railtrack and the train operating companies were urged to develop new technologies to deal with the problem. The regulators also canvassed public opinion.[14] The debate was also fuelled by a number of accidents. For example, accident inquiry reports following rail accidents at Newton in 1991 and Cowden in 1994 both endorsed the Hidden Report proposals about ATP (Uff, 2000: 150). But the most prominent accidents raising concerns about ATP were the Southall crash in west London in 1997, when 7 were killed and 150 were injured, and the collision of two trains two miles outside Paddington Station at Ladbroke Grove Junction in October 1999 in which 31 people were killed and over 400 were injured, some critically.

One of the ironies of the Southall and Ladbroke Grove accidents is that they occurred on track which was part of the ATP pilot scheme. But in the Southall case the system was not fully operational in one of the power cars involved in the crash. Following the accident the train operating company involved, Great Western Trains, put a great deal of effort into bringing its pilot scheme into operation but it did not lead to national fitment. Rather it was one of the technologies developed as an alternative to ATP, the train protection warning system (TPWS), that Railtrack and the train operating companies were eventually ordered to install by August 1999. They were given four years to install the system across the rail network. This system is not as fail-safe as ATP but is considerably cheaper. Yet, within two months of this announcement, it appears that another signal passed at danger contributed to the Ladbroke Grove accident, one of Britain's worst rail crashes in recent railway history. In its First Interim Report following the accident, HSE noted :

---

[13] Later in the report it is argued that the downgrading of ATP would have occurred regardless of privatization, on grounds of cost effectiveness (Uff, 2000: 167).

[14] See, for example, HSE (1997: 101) where the concerns of the House of Commons Transport Select Committee at the failure to implement train protection systems was reported.

The immediate cause of the accident appears to be that the Thames train passed a red signal (a 'signal at danger') some 700m before the collision point . . .

Early evidence suggests that the accident would have been prevented by the installation and correct operation of a Train Protection Warning System (TPWS) . . .

As part of a pilot scheme, Automatic Train Protection (ATP) equipment was fitted to the Great Western train. However, experience has shown the ATP to suffer from reliability problems and the equipment was switched off because it was not operational. However, on the evidence gained so far, this was unlikely to have had a bearing on the accident . . . (HSC, 1999*a*).

These findings led HSE to write to Great Western about keeping ATP working and to all train operating companies telling them to re-brief their drivers on signals passed at danger. There is no doubt that the failure to introduce more sophisticated train warning systems following the Hidden Report was very much in the spotlight following the Southall and Paddington accidents. The Southall Inquiry found that the accident would not have happened if ATP had been operational (Uff, 2000: 80). It is possible—but not yet conclusively proven—that the absence of an operational train warning system contributed to the Ladbroke Grove accident and the great loss of life it incurred.

Health and Safety on the Railways in the Mid to Late 1990s

Assessing the impact of privatization on occupational health and safety is very difficult, largely because of the difficulties in unravelling the complexity of influences on the accident statistics (see Ch. 1). Moreover there are insufficient data to make any firm deductions. Caution therefore needs to be exercised in considering the data we do have. What we do know is that HSC data for accidents to railway employees and contractors since the privatization of the railways (see Tables 11.2 and 11.3) are very much in line with earlier accident trends.[15] While the fatalities figures suggest improvements, the overall injuries figures are not so encouraging. Moreover the indications are that the problem areas for the occupational health and safety of railway staff have not changed very much since the BR study. For example, track safety continues to be a major problem. This led the Inspectorate to initiate the Track Safety Initiative in 1995. This involved a review of the rule book and other documents that affected track workers, and the introduction of new arrangements to protect these staff (HSE

---

[15] These data reveal that the number of fatal accidents to railway staff and contractors has continued to fall while the accident rate for major and minor injuries rose in 1995/96; fell, for the first time in nine years, in 1996/97; and increased by 13% in 1997/98. There is a difficulty in interpreting these figures as changes to the reporting arrangements were introduced in 1996. The Reporting of Injuries, Diseases and Dangerous Occurrences Regulations 1995 (RIDDOR 95) came into force on 1 April 1996. These revised the definition of major injuries and replaced the monthly bulk reporting of certain minor injuries with individual reporting of minor injuries. Despite these changes the Railway Inspectorate was of the opinion that the 1996/97 figures did represent a real fall in the underlying accident rate (HSE, 1997).

TABLE 11.2. Worker fatalities, 1995/6–1997/8

1995/6	1996/7	1997/8
5	2	3

Source: Annual Reports (HSC, 1996, 1997, 1998)

TABLE 11.3. Major and minor injuries to railway staff and contractors, 1995/6–1997/8

Rate per 100,000 employees	1995/6	1996/7*	1997/8*
Major injuries	184	337	456
Minor injuries	3,397	1,842	2,088

Note: * Change in reporting procedures under RIDDOR, 1995.
Source: Annual Reports (HSC, 1996, 1997, 1998).

1996, 84 ff.). The management of contract staff remains of particular concern (HSE, 1998: 13), as does the communication of health and safety information. The communication issue has led to the establishment of a Railway Industry Advisory Committee (RIAC) working group to investigate the subject. One area that was, in many respects, ignored at the time of my data collection was occupational health and safety. During the mid to late 1990s this has become increasingly prominent. For example, the *1995/96 Annual Report* was the first to include a specific chapter on the topic and this is now a regular feature of the annual reports. Moreover, occupational health and safety is also the focus of a RIAC working group (HSE, 1998: 98).

HSC and the Railway Inspectorate appear keen to stress the continuity of the trends in the statistics and to avoid concerns about privatization. In 1999 the Chief Inspector of Railways, commenting on the latest railway statistics, stated 'There is no evidence in these figures that the railways are less safe than they were before privatization, indeed many of the trends remain downwards' (press release E154: 99, 12 Aug. 1999).[16] Yet there is no doubting that the regulators have been uneasy about health and safety in the industry, as is demonstrated by their public criticism and increasingly adversarial relations with the industry (see above). So how can we explain this? Part of the explanation must be a wish to side-step the political controversy surrounding privatization. But it must also be relevant that the figures are very sensitive to major incidents involving multiple fatalities and other injuries.[17] And while the so-called underlying trends

[16] A year earlier the Chairman of HSC stated 'We have no evidence from these figures that most matters under the direct control of railway operators are less safe than they were before privatization. Railways remain the safest mode of land transport' (press release E187: 98).

[17] This is exemplified by a table in the 1997/98 Annual Report on Railway Safety (HSE, 1998: 25) which maps out train accident fatalities and notes how much of the total figure is accounted for by specific major accidents. The fatality figures for 1987–1998 are illustrative: 1987—10; 1988—40 (35—Clapham Junction); 1989—18 (5—Purley accident); 1990—4; 1991/92—11; 1992/93—5; 1993/94—6; 1994/95—12 (5—Cowden accident); 1995/96—7; 1996/97—1; 1997/98—10 (7—Southall accident).

appeared to be stable during the 1990s, at the end of the decade two major accidents resulted in serious loss of life and injuries. According to many commentators these were 'accidents waiting to happen' as the safety systems of the industry became increasingly unstable and unreliable, and as ultimately the model of enforced self-regulation accompanying privatization dramatically failed.

The Southall and Ladbroke Grove Accidents

The Southall and Ladbroke Grove accidents share a number of features in common. They both involved collisions outside London on a major commuter route. They both resulted in multiple fatalities to passengers and in both cases there was a suggestion that a major contributing factor was the passing of signals at danger (see above). In any event, the coincidence of these factors would have created the conditions for a great deal of public concern and the institution of public inquiries (Hutter, 1992). But these accidents took on a particular significance as they crystallized and focused a growing concern with privatization and most particularly with health and safety arrangements on the railways. Both accidents elicited the 'classic' response to railway accidents, namely the immediate announcement of a public inquiry by the Secretary of State for the Environment, Transport, and the Regions. Such proclamations follow a well-trodden institutionalized path of handling social and political concern about major railway accidents and other disasters with a public and political dimension (Hutter, 1992; Reiss, 1989). The declaration of a public inquiry underlines governmental concern about the accident and evidence that something is being done in response to it. It is a public acknowledgement of the accident's severity and a demonstration that it will be thoroughly investigated.

The Ladbroke Grove accident prompted a more far-reaching inquiry than Southall.[18] The terms of the inquiry for the Ladbroke Grove accident extend well beyond the specific accident, namely:

1. To inquire into, and draw lessons from, the accident near Paddington station on 5.10.99, taking account of the findings of the HSE's investigations into immediate causes.
2. To consider general experience derived from relevant accidents on the railway since the Hidden Inquiry [see below], with a view to drawing conclusions about:
   a. factors which affect safety management
   b. the appropriateness of the current regulatory regime

---

[18] Both inquiries were held under the HSW Act, 1974, rather than the 1871 Regulation of Railways Act which was for so long the authorizing legislation for railway accident investigation. This represents a general shift in favour of this legislation as the Railway Inspectorate has come more and more under the influence of the HSE. While the HSW Act, section 20 places constraints on publication these inquiries are exceptionally being held under section 14(2)(b) of the Act which directs that the inquiry proceedings be held in public and the inquiry report be made public.

c. in the light of the above, to make recommendations for improving safety on the future railway.

In the accompanying letter to Lord Cullen, who was appointed to undertake the Ladbroke Grove Inquiry, the Chair of the Health and Safety Commission also noted: 'We should not want you to feel constrained by . . . your broader terms of reference if you consider that other issues emerge which should be fully examined . . . (HSC press release CO44: 99).[19]

The Ladbroke Grove accident also prompted a number of additional inquiries. One day after the Ladbroke Grove accident the Secretary of State for the Environment, Transport, and the Regions ordered a further independent assessment of rail safety systems; a review of general safety management arrangements within Railtrack; and a review of Railtrack's safety and standards directorate. In addition HSE undertook two internal reviews of the Railway Inspectorate and the events leading up to the Ladbroke Grove accident. The apparent reason for all of this additional attention appears to be that this accident happened just two years after the Southall accident, on the same area of track, and with the suspicion of similar causes. Moreover the Ladbroke Grove accident incurred a particularly high number of fatalities (31) and over 400 other injured persons, which place it as one of the worst railway accidents in Britain in recent years.

The Southall collision was the first major rail accident to occur since the full privatization of BR. This—in combination with the Ladbroke Grove accident and the far-reaching inquiries they have provoked—has focused a good deal of attention on rail safety in the mid to late 1990s. I will therefore take data from this research and the findings of the Southall Inquiry and those Ladbroke Grove inquiries which will have reported by the time this book goes to press, to examine some of the trends which led to the growing unease with health and safety on the railways in the mid to late 1990s, some of which may have contributed to these accidents.[20]

Themes and Trends Influencing Occupational Health and Safety on the Railways in 1990s

A number of themes run through the 1990s story of occupational health and safety on Britain's railways. They explain the increasingly adversarial relationship

---

[19] The remit of the Southall Inquiry was much more limited to investigating the causes of the particular accident. In some senses the Ladbroke Grove Inquiry overshadowed the Southall Inquiry, and this was certainly a complaint of the victims of the Southall accident. This was partly because the Southall Inquiry was delayed because of legal action (see below). However, the importance of the Southall accident should not be underestimated. The inquiry is important in its own right and it is possible that Ladbroke Grove would have prompted a less extensive response had Southall not preceded it.

[20] This section will draw, where relevant, on reports resulting from the Southall and Ladbroke Grove accidents, in particular those published before May 2000.

between the industry and the regulator and, more significantly, they are symptomatic of the very real problems underlying the 'safety cascade' system of enforced self-regulation accompanying the privatization of BR. Some of these themes are very specific to the particular context but we should be mindful that they also convey broader messages. Indeed many of the factors emerging as significant on the fully privatized railways are continuations of processes apparent in the previous decade and thus transcend institutional change.

Institutional Changes

The institutional changes resulting from the full privatization of BR created very real difficulties. The *speed and scale of the change* caused massive problems for the industry and the regulator alike. In order to meet its health and safety obligations Railtrack set up a safety and standards directorate to deal with safety standards, the preparation and revision of Railtrack's own safety case, and the validation and auditing of leaseholder safety cases. A director, Safety and Standards, was also appointed, reporting directly to the chairman of the company. An indication of the task facing this directorate appears in *Railway Safety 1995/96* where it is estimated that over a three- to four-year period Railtrack will have developed some 4,000 standards for the Railway Group (HSE, 1996: 130).

The Railway Inspectorate was similarly affected. HSE's internal inquiry following the Ladbroke Grove accident identified a Railway Inspectorate under very heavy pressure. It was explained that Railtrack sought to revise many of the 6,000 Railway Group Standards it inherited from BR; and that privatization was accompanied by a dramatic increase in approvals of new work, a rise from 275 in 1993 to 6,000 in 1999 (HSE, 2000b). Moreover the level of complaints also increased, thus posing additional burdens on the Inspectorate. This led the Inspectorate to adopt a more selective approach to its approval procedures than it would normally have adopted (ibid.).

The sheer volume of new companies in the industry caused further problems. The *1995/96 Annual Report* reported that there were 'more companies active in the operation of the railway than at any stage since the early 1920s' (HSE, 1996, p. vii). It continued 'change, particularly rapid change, carries its own risk' (ibid.). This was particularly so as privatization led to an influx of newcomers to the industry, many of whom were unfamiliar with the railways environment. This led to a variety of consequential difficulties. For instance Railtrack and the Railway Inspectorate both encountered difficulties in recruiting suitably qualified personnel. And clearly the need for such personnel has been acute, partly to handle the volume of work created by the privatization but also to cope with the additional work caused by those companies and personnel unfamiliar with the railway environment.[21] The HSE Inquiry docu-

---

[21] HSE Annual Reports expressed concern about the under-reporting of accidents in a fragmented industry (HSE, 1997: 89) and also the ability of companies to control contractors (ibid. 115).

ments a shortfall of 24 staff in the Railway Inspectorate in 1999, and the report notes a specific problem in recruiting staff with technical knowledge and experience of the railway industry (HSE, 2000*a*).

Privatization also exacerbated a number of difficulties identified in the BR study, most particularly those related to *fragmentation* and *communication*. One of the major findings of the BR study was that co-ordinating and communicating between the various parts of one large geographically dispersed company caused major difficulties for the enforced self-regulatory regime then in place. One might therefore expect that the dramatic break-up of the industry into so many separate companies might exacerbate these difficulties, especially given the short period of time within which this occurred and the simultaneous introduction of the safety cascade system of regulating health and safety.

Fragmentation led the Inspectorate to have less confidence in parts of the industry. This partly relates to the levels of inexperience they encountered in some areas. This point was raised by the Environment and Regional Affairs Committee in 1998:

When public policy is to attract travellers off roads, the safety of rail travel must be firmly based on robust and impartial regulatory systems. This is particularly important when the fragmentation of the railway has led to a host of new companies, contractors, sub-contractors and individuals working on the railway, some of whom have little or no railway experience. (quoted in Uff, 2000: 169)

The Railway Inspectorate has found itself having to adopt the co-ordination role previously undertaken by BR. For example, some inspectors identify a greater number of problems attaching to the submission of new plans as there is now, apparently, less consultation between different parts of the industry concerning the feasibility of schemes. Obviously this has placed greater burdens upon their ability to process applications for the approval of new works, especially as the Railway Inspectorate itself suffered communication problems as a result of its growth in numbers and its separation into three independent divisions. This apparently resulted in ineffective information exchange, which in turn increased the Inspectorate's difficulties in responding to the changing industry (HSE, 2000*a*).

Fragmentation is identified as a problem in the Southall Report, as are difficulties of co-ordination and communication. For example, delays in resolving problems with ATP are partly attributed to the absence of any co-ordinating authority (Uff, 2000: 168). A lack of co-ordination was also evident in the post-accident investigation of the Southall crash (ibid.). Another persisting feature of the industry is problems with communication. The Southall Report reiterates some of the problems identified in the BR research reported earlier in this book:

The railway industry is overburdened with paperwork, such that it is to be doubted that many individuals can have a proper grasp of all the documents for which they bear nominal responsibility. The stock answer to any problem which is identified is to produce yet more paperwork in the form of risk assessments, Group Standards and the like . . . the problem of effective communication persists and there were many examples of recently generated paperwork which has the capacity to confuse and obfuscate in just the same way as the old system did. The lesson to be learned, yet again, is that ineffective communication is no communication. (2000: 208)

Difficulties of communication, the associated problems of co-ordination, and the influx of newcomers to the industry, all heighten the significance of health and safety training and education, factors which the findings of the research into BR identified as crucially important. Many of the post-Clapham changes were directed to increasing awareness of health and safety issues throughout the industry and involving everyone in health and safety. Whether or not these efforts have been effective is difficult to tell, but the evidence of the Southall Report suggests that they have not. Clearly there are difficulties: 'There's much more general awareness at all levels but I wouldn't claim that it's consistent. In an industry like the railways which is so dispersed communications is the single biggest problem' (industry representative).

While privatization and the preparation, validation and audit of safety cases have focused the minds of senior management, the effects lower down are felt to be patchy. An industry representative explained:

> Middle and junior management, they've been well subjected to all the propaganda, they're all meant to be doing monthly safety meetings . . . they've got different degrees of priority . . . the attitude of the local supervisors and junior managers is the single major thing that impacts on the effectiveness of safety awareness being picked by people at the grass roots level. (industry representative)

Another major difficulty arising from both the fragmentation of the industry and the new regulatory system is the allocation of *responsibility* for health and safety. The new system raises complex questions about responsibilities for health and safety, and the place of health and safety requirements in the contractual relations between the different parts of the railway. The contractual relations are especially important given that each contract may be separately negotiated. HSE's principal relationship is with Railtrack since Railtrack's railway safety case is subject to validation by HSE, while Railtrack must validate the railway safety cases of train and station operators. These difficulties have affected the introduction of safety systems. The Uff Report into the Southall accident cites the ATP project as exposing major difficulties in the management of cross-company projects because of a lack of a contractual framework between Railtrack, operators, and equipment owners for the sharing of costs for projects (2000: 190).

As the number of firms involved increases, so do disputes about responsibility. Inspectors explained, for example, that they feel a greater need now to undertake accident investigations: 'confidence is diminishing under the new regime because, of course, the various parties all want to show that they are not to blame because there is big money flowing now . . . So we have less confidence that we will get truthful and unbiased reports on the circumstances and causes of accidents'. A Railway Inspector explained: 'The situation is intensely complicated, particularly in respect of who is responsible for this issue. It is going to become extremely difficult to decide who is responsible, therefore who deserves the notice, who gets prosecuted, which manager' (railway inspector).

The situation is especially acute with respect to accident investigation, where the new companies have incentives to deny liability. Inspectors commented that more lawyers are now involved in accident investigations. It is becoming increasingly apparent that different interests have different viewpoints about responsibility. There are now several players, all of whom have a vested interest in blaming the others. Also the unions are involved—an added perspective here as they are also anti-privatization. Moreover increasing emphasis has been placed on the enforcement of accident investigation recommendations because companies are no longer automatically accepting these recommendations.

Industry representatives also acknowledged that accident investigation has been complicated by privatization. Railtrack is responsible for accident investigation and operators are required to co-operate with these investigations. However, issues of financial liability can undermine this process, since admitting liability could generate claims from victims and also from other companies for delays and loss of business. It was acknowledged that some small railway companies could be closed down by a large accident. One industry representative summed up the general situation thus: 'everyone is fighting like hell to deny liability . . . it will be more like a law court and it's bad for safety'.

Issues of responsibility are also inextricably tied up with issues of *blame*. Increasingly multi-causal theories are being subscribed to, as demonstrated by HSE's First Interim Report into the Paddington accident which stated:

The immediate cause of the accident appears to be that the Thames Train passed a red signal [a 'signal at danger'] some 700m before the collision point. The reasons why the train passed at the red light are likely to be complex. RI will be looking at the underlying causes as well as any more obvious ones. Our belief is that it is a systems failure and that any action or omission on the part of the driver was only one factor (HSC, 1999a: para. 5)

The Southall Inquiry reached a similar conclusion, attributing primary blame to one of the train drivers and secondary blame to the train operating company and to Railtrack for various failures (2000: 88). The whole issue of accident investigation has been subject to difficulties as there has been increasing pressure to invoke the criminal law. It seems that the public is looking for more scapegoats, looking for someone to blame and prosecute.

During the late 1980s and early 1990s witnesses were increasingly fearful of prosecution and some were refusing to give evidence to Railway Inspectorate accident inquiries in case they incriminated themselves prior to criminal trial (Hutter, 1992). Following the Purley train crash in 1989 a train driver was convicted of manslaughter for going through a red signal, the conviction happening some nine years later in 1998. Another driver was convicted of manslaughter after the 1996 crash at Watford Junction, although he successfully appealed to the Court of Appeal for a reduction in his sentence. This trend has continued and there has been growing pressure to call the body corporate to account in the criminal courts. This is epitomized by the Southall case, which led the Crown Prosecution Service to charge the Great Western Train Company with seven charges of manslaughter through gross negligence. The driver of the high-speed train was also charged with manslaughter and the company was charged with offences under the HSW Act. The case is an interesting one. No convictions resulted from any of the manslaughter charges because of the difficulty in identifying negligence by any individual within the company (the charges against the driver were dismissed because he was psychologically damaged by the accident). The judge in the case supported a change in the law to ease the prosecution of large companies for manslaughter. The company pleaded guilty to charges under the HSW Act, so successful legal action was brought against the company under regulatory legislation, but this was clearly viewed by the press, the families of those killed in the crash, and the judge to be separate from the opprobrium which attached to more traditional criminal charges.

These accusatorial trends have had implications for the inquisitorial-style accident investigation. The Southall prosecutions affected the conduct of the public inquiry as they held up the hearing of evidence by some two years, a matter which much exercised the Southall Inquiry team who questioned the assumption that 'the interests of enforcing the criminal law should take precedence over the needs of safety' (Uff 2000: 30).[22] In effect tensions between the need for confidentiality in the criminal proceedings clashed with the investigation of rail safety. HSE delayed its inquiries so as not to compromise the criminal investigation being conducted by the British Transport Police (BTP) (whose investigation led to the manslaughter charges). The Railway Inspectorate offered guidance to the police but it refrained from collecting its own evidence for any possible charges under the HSW Act 'in order firstly to avoid both repeated interviewing of witnesses and any doubts as to collection of evidence and, secondly, to avoid prejudicing enquiries BTP may wish to make' (letter from Deputy Chief Inspector of Railways to the Southall Inquiry Secretary on 15 Jan. 1998).

There are clearly difficulties here as the public inquiry waits upon the criminal proceedings before commencing with the public hearing of evidence, and as the Railway Inspectorate waits upon the police before considering its case under HSW legislation. In the case of the Ladbroke Grove accident, unprecedented action was taken in the immediate aftermath of the accident, with HSE releasing an interim report on the accident (HSC, 1999a) just three days after the accident. In addition the Railway Inspectorate stated that as 'significant findings'

---

[22] The Uff Report devotes a chapter to delays to the progress of the inquiry. See chapter 8 of the report.

came to light it would make them public where appropriate. A second interim report was published at the end of October 1999 (HSC, 1999*b*) and a third in April 2000 (HSE, 2000*e*). Yet problems were highlighted in the early days of the Ladbroke Grove Inquiry when it emerged that individual copies of documents presented to the inquiry would be barred from use in a prosecution for corporate manslaughter. The intention was to try to avoid the delays to the investigation process which occurred in the case of the Southall Inquiry.[23] Such issues focus attention on the very real tensions which exist between the constitutive and control aspects of using the criminal law to regulate risks, a topic to which we will return in the final chapter.

Cultural Changes

The institutional changes arising from privatization raise serious questions about the ability of the industry and regulators to cope with both the speed of change and the new regulatory regime. This has been exacerbated by cultural changes, many of which were in evidence prior to privatization, notably the growth of the business culture and the systematization of health and safety regulation.

The tensions between *commercial* and safety concerns have undoubtedly been heightened by privatization. Costs are increasingly visible as commercial interests become more prominent and tendering is important. The Inspectorate's *Plan of Work 1996–97* noted:

Securing safety in such a dramatically different industrial and commercial environment will be a major project in itself. . . . This present lack of stability and the prospect of continuing change within the industry, has other important implications for the Inspectorate. As the industry becomes more commercially oriented, many staff without traditional railway backgrounds are being attracted to it. Their inexperience places greater calls on the time of Inspectorate staff . . . (1996: 4).

There are profound financial concerns raised by the effects of privatization and in turn the implications for safety.[24] Some commentators do not believe that the rail network in Britain can be operated without substantive state subsidy, particularly given the relative lack of investment it was deemed to have suffered in previous decades. There is concern about the prospects for private investment in the infrastructure and rolling stock and about the possibility of asset stripping. In turn this leads to anxiety about consumer service with respect to the maintenance of the network, timetabling, and costs. More generally there is a worry that safety considerations will become very much more

---

[23] The Attorney-General stated that copies of these documents could be used by the police in any prosecution they initiated but the copies presented to the inquiry could not be used. In the event, there was deemed to be insufficient evidence to put together a prosecution for corporate manslaughter.

[24] Not surprisingly the privatization of BR proved controversial. See Bradshaw and Mason (1994) for a review of these criticisms.

secondary as the privatized companies struggle to make profits. Railtrack has been explicit in its recognition that there is the potential for tension between health and safety and commercial objectives: 'The validation of your safety case and the consequential periodic auditing of your compliance with your safety case will be carried out by Railtrack's Safety and Standards Directorate which will be kept, as far as possible, separate from Railtrack's commercial arm' (Railtrack, 1993). This is also discussed in a *Railway Gazette International* (1994: 219) account of an interview with the chairman of Railtrack:

> In addition to managing the infrastructure as a commercial business, Railtrack is also charged with acting as safety regulator for train operators, and the operators of stations and light maintenance depots. This clearly creates problems for Horton [chairman of Railtrack]. He is trying to resolve it by creating 'a Chinese wall, which also has to exist in my head' between his Director, Safety & Standards . . . and the commercial part of the organisation under the Chief Executive . . .

Of course this tension has always characterized regulation, which is why regulation is a form of risk management rather than risk elimination. But arguably the new institutional arrangements for the railway industry heighten these pressures.

Railtrack itself encounters potentially conflicting objectives. According to its safety remit Railtrack has to validate the safety case of all operators using the rail network. It also has to check that the safety case is being complied with. The system provides for a revocation of licence in the event of a failure to comply with a safety case. Railtrack staff explained that if one of their audits discovered non-compliance then senior Railtrack staff would meet with senior representatives of the company concerned and persuade them that corrective action was necessary. Their approach would be incremental and if necessary they would involve the Railway Inspectorate. The rail regulator would eventually be informed and the licence withdrawn and the company forced out of business. But whether or not this would actually happen is the million-dollar question, especially if a major passenger company is involved in an important rail area. The indications are that Railtrack may have experienced difficulties in this. HSE's internal inquiry into the events leading up the Ladbroke Grove accident notes that during 1998 the Inspectorate became aware that Railtrack was not acting as the Inspectorate would have expected when it found that train operating companies were not complying with their safety cases. The Report explained this in terms of a contractual reluctance to force the issue, partly because it could raise questions of financial liability (HSE, 2000a). The Southall Report also raises questions about whether regulation policy applied by signallers was changed to take greater account of commercial considerations. In particular it noted that Railtrack and the train operating companies were under commercial pressures to run to timetable because of the possibility of penalty payments (Uff, 2000: 46). HSE's evidence to the Ladbroke Grove Inquiry pointed to other sources of economic difficulty, namely the pressures exercised by the rail regulator and by shareholders to keep commercial interests in sharp focus (HSE, 2000*d*).

The other major cultural change is an apparently much more rigorous and *systematic* approach to health and safety. This has proved to be double-edged. On the one hand it forces a much more serious and sustained focus on health and safety through such things as audits and performance indicators. But on the other hand it also leads to resistance to accept some regulatory demands. Meanwhile regulatory officials are changing their orientation, prompted partly by their institutional move to HSE and partly by changes in the industry. Some view this increased systematization and prioritization positively and a crucial part of effective risk management. But viewed from a different perspective this is yet another rationale for large corporations not to prioritize regulatory objectives. Certainly there is a danger that too much faith can be placed in the success of audits (Power, 1997). Depending upon circumstances, audits and cost-benefit analyses can become as much a form of mystification as an analytical tool. Indeed one US study into safety performance of the American railroads found a counter-intuitive negative correlation between safety performance and audits and inspections (Bailey and Peterson, 1989).

Unease with the risk management techniques used by the railway industry were apparent in the Southall and Ladbroke Grove inquiries. The Southall Inquiry is blunt in its criticism: 'risk assessment procedures have been shown to produce variable results, which are seldom rigorous and sometimes questionable. No primary or secondary paper-based system is a substitute for common sense and commitment to the job' (Uff 2000: 208). The evidence given by the Director of HSE to the Ladbroke Grove Inquiry concentrates more specifically on problems in the methods and perspectives used:

The industry culture appears to look at *outcomes*, with insufficient attention to *potential for harm*, and at *frequencies* rather than *consequences*: the approach of SPADS [signals passed at danger] is an example of this. Assessment of risks is also dominated by 'hardware' issues and a rigid use of quantified appreciation of human factors: risk assessment of signalling systems exemplifies this incomplete perspective. The concern is that HSE should have done more to challenge the industry effectively (HSE, 2000*d*, para. 18).

The Railway Inspectorate has also been criticized for its use of risk assessment. The main criticism was an insufficient emphasis upon risk assessment procedures, for example, in its data collection and analysis and also in its approach to safety cases (HSE, 2000*a*). The validity of this criticism is borne out by recent events. The Southall and Ladbroke Grove accidents demonstrate how cautiously we should approach railway statistics because of their vulnerability to major disasters. Related to this should be some caution in basing future predictions on past performance and most particularly in using this as a basis for arguing against effecting improvements. So it is important that these analyses are contextualized. Determining what is an acceptable risk or acceptable cost is difficult and negotiated and it raises a host of issues. For example, from whose point of view should one view risk, cost, and benefit? There is a long tradition in the environmental field, for example, which suggests that such analyses favour business as the costs are always much easier to calculate than the benefits (Bugler, 1972; Gunningham, 1974; Owens, 1990; Yeager, 1991). This is partly because indirect costs and benefits are rarely considered. Moreover we need to decide how to choose between competing analyses and how much weight to give to public fears and complacency. None of these are fixed since they are shifting calculations which depend upon time, place, and perspective. Arguably, for instance, concerns about ATP and safety on the railways will have increased dramatically in the period following the Southall and Ladbroke Grove accidents. But will this concern be sustained? And how much notice should we take of it? These issues are increasingly the stuff of debate between the industry and the state regulators. And increasingly it seems that the approach of the state regulators is itself subject to challenge.

The extent to which the state regulators were keeping pace with institutional changes in the railway industry is a theme running through the mid to late 1990s. As we have seen, the Railway Inspectorate was itself subject to institutional and cultural changes and doubts have been raised about its ability to adjust to these. Many of these relate to the constitutive role of the law, for example, the endeavour to put into place safer systems and procedures and to increase the formal risk assessment procedures in this task. Where these fail the law provides for a more controlling enforcement role. The *enforcement approaches* of health and safety inspectors (and indeed other regulatory agencies) in Britain remains controversial (see Ch. 1). Criticisms of the Inspectorate's approach (described above) became more evident following the Ladbroke Grove accident when HSE served Railtrack with three enforcement notices related to signalling.[25] This action prompted questions about why such action was taken reactively rather than proactively. Certainly Railway Inspectorate enforcement approaches are the subject of critical attention in the internal HSE inquiries following the Ladbroke Grove accident. These acknowledged the increasingly distant relationship between the industry and the Inspectorate, as described above, but nevertheless thought that the Inspectorate's approach had not kept pace with the speed and extent of change within the industry, most particularly with its complexity and increased commercial orientation (HSE, 2000*a*). Yet it also acknowledged that the Railway Inspectorate encountered difficulties in its enforcement role as its actions were increasingly challenged by the industry. Apart from problems in adapting culturally to a more legalistic enforcement

---

[25] These were one improvement notice requiring the company to put into place additional controls at the twenty-two signals leading to the signals most frequently passed at danger (SPADs); one improvement notice requiring the company to produce a plan to reduce the risk to all remaining signals with a recent history of repeated SPADs; and one prohibition notice on the signal passed at danger in the Paddington accident.

style, resources also proved problematic as protracted legal disputes are resource intensive,[26] thus raising questions about *regulatory capacity*.

As noted above, both the industry regulator and the state regulator have experienced serious difficulties in recruiting experienced staff and in coping with the very high volume of work generated by privatization. The regulatory capacity of the company holding regulatory responsibilities is thus seriously compromised, but so is the ability of the regulatory agency to oversee the self-regulatory system. Questions of *accountability* thus come into prominence, most particularly the Inspectorate's record of overseeing Railtrack's role as the industry regulator. This of course relates to resource capacity and to the Inspectorate's accommodative enforcement approach. It also relates to the Inspectorate's apparent failure to come to terms with the safety case approach. HSE's internal reports criticized the Inspectorate for inadequate monitoring and auditing of Railtrack's activities with regard to both Railtrack's own safety case and its monitoring of the safety cases of companies using the rail network and concluded that some inspectors did not appear comfortable with the cultural changes effected by the safety case approach (HSE, 2000*a*).

Issues of regulatory capacity and accountability have significance beyond this particular case study as they are both central to successful self-regulatory regimes. Accordingly difficulties in these areas are symptomatic of much deeper problems, so let us turn our attention to these and what the future prospects for railway safety seem to be.

Future Prospects

The most serious doubts raised by the BR research and subsequent developments on Britain's railways centre on enforced self-regulation and the extent to which this regime should be adopted. In particular the safety cascade system raises a variety of worries. Prominent here are concerns about the independence of the industry-based regulator. This is especially so when the company vested with major regulatory responsibilities is in a contractual relationship with the regulated concerning access to the industry (in this case via the rail network) and the financial arrangements for this.

Railtrack has become the focus of increasing concern in debates about Britain's railways. The Railway Inspectorate and the trade unions have indicated their anxiety about the role of the company and so has the Commons Select Committee on the Environment, Transport, and Regional Affairs. This committee had been worried for some years by the safety arrangements on the privatized railway. It recommended in 1998 that transport safety regulation should

---

[26] Railtrack did actually appeal against the prohibition notice and two improvement notices issued after the Ladbroke Grove accident. HSE's internal inquiry noted that fighting such actions was resource intensive but did not necessarily accept that this is a good reason not to proceed with legal action otherwise considered justified (HSE, 2000*a*).

be undertaken by a single, independent regulator and that Railtrack should be relieved of its role in safety regulation and a separate and independent safety authority established. It also commissioned HSE to review arrangements for standard setting, mainly the responsibility of Railtrack's Safety Directorate. Shortly after the Ladbroke Grove accident HSC published its *Interim Report of the Review of Arrangements for Standard Setting and Application on the Main Railway Network* (1999c). The document itself is essentially inconclusive to the extent that it recommends further consultations with the industry before making a decision. Almost immediately, however, the Minister for Environment, Transport, and the Regions (also the Deputy Prime Minister) requested HSE to appoint a specialist team to investigate the concerns raised by the interim report.[27]

This additional report commissioned by the Deputy Prime Minister expressed concern that the safety and standards directorate of Railtrack was insufficiently distinct from the company's commercial interests and it recommended separation of the safety departments from commercial interests in the company (HSE, 2000c). This report was also critical of accountability in the new system and recommended that HSE should oversee Railtrack's safety operations much more rigorously and should take a much more active role in checking Railtrack's audits of network users. But beyond this it also recommended that HSE should take over some of the safety responsibilities currently held by Railtrack, in particular its responsibilities for accepting and auditing the safety cases of one group of network users, namely the train operating companies.

At a minimum an erosion of Railtrack's regulatory role seems inevitable, with a corresponding increase in the role of the state regulator. It seems likely that the Railway Inspectorate will become more integrated into the central organization of HSE. In response to HSE's internal inquiry into the Railway Inspectorate, following the Ladbroke Grove accident, the Director-General of HSE promised more support for the Inspectorate, more direction in its use of risk assessment tools, especially the safety case approach, and a strengthening of its enforcement approach (HSE, 2000d). How far the state regulator is able to go in developing a stronger enforcement line remains to be seen, but it is clear that they do not have an entirely free rein. For example, the law dictates that costs must be taken into account in determining what are reasonable regulatory demands. So again we are confronted with more fundamental questions about the role of the law as a regulatory tool, questions which we will revisit in Chapter 12.

It is difficult to anticipate how the difficulties surrounding rail safety will be resolved. Clearly there is a widespread view that the existing system is not

---

[27] He hinted that he was considering moving responsibility for safety from Railtrack, but he was mindful that any alternative arrangements should be superior to those they were replacing: '. . . one which ensures greater coherence on safety . . .' and did not result in an increase in risk (Department of the Environment, Transport, and the Regions, statement, House of Commons, 19 Oct. 1999). It remains to be seen whether this will be the eventual outcome of the post-Ladbroke Grove inquiries or whether it is just political, post-accident, rhetoric.

working in the best interests of safety. Indeed it is for this reason that so many different inquiries were established following the Ladbroke Grove accident, but it remains to be seen how far these inquiries do actually extend. In the past the scope of inquiries and the implementation of their recommendations have proved problematic. The King's Cross (Fennell, 1988) and Clapham Junction (Hidden, 1989) Inquiries attracted some controversy for not extending their investigatory nets sufficiently wide. Both of these inquiries considered the immediate circumstances of the accidents and to varying extents the railway companies involved. But neither inquiry considered the wider pressures on the railway industry, in particular government policy towards the railways. There have, of course, been major changes since these inquiries, namely the privatization of the railway industry. The Southall Report explicitly distances itself from privatization. In his preface, for example, Professor Uff argues that the industry is still heavily influenced by BR procedures and structures but also accepts that 'the new structure of the industry has inevitably affected the events under consideration' (2000: p. *b*). The report also confines itself to matters of relevance to Southall and explicitly avoids more general safety issues. This was because the inquiry was overtaken by the Cullen Inquiry into Ladbroke Grove which, as we have seen above, has been given a broader remit regarding railway safety. In addition, a Joint Inquiry involving Professor Uff and Lord Cullen has been set up to consider the future of train protection and warning systems, the future application of ATP and SPAD prevention (Uff, 2000: 125 and appendix 21).

But we need to be mindful that once inquiry reports have been published their recommendations may not be implemented. Professor Uff rejects suggestions that the industry will not feel obliged to comply with the Southall Inquiry's recommendations, arguing that there are 'obvious moral and political pressures to comply' (Uff, 2000: 210). Although it may appear unthinkable in the wake of a major accident, and in the midst of the public and political protestations surrounding them, that inquiry recommendations will not be followed, it is nevertheless the case that the Southall and Ladbroke Grove accidents may in part have been the result of a failure to implement the recommendations of the Hidden Report on the Clapham Junction accident in 1988. While many of the safety measures and rules of the modern railway have been developed in response to accident inquiries, the fact remains that the attitudes of the industry have changed. It is no longer so willing to comply with regulatory demands and increasingly prepared to challenge them. For these reasons the outcome of these accidents and the subsequent inquiries seems far from clear-cut, although one can only remain optimistic that fundamental changes to railway safety will result, including responses to the lessons learnt about the limits of self-regulation. Indeed developments post-King's Cross, post-Clapham, and post-privatization suggest that many of the difficulties in regulating risk identified in this research transcend institutional structures and industry organization— although these can clearly influence the difficulties attaching to the regulation of risk. The introduction of the safety cascade at the same time as privatization is illustrative of this. It introduced an extreme version of enforced self-regulation in circumstances which the BR study would suggest were precisely the conditions in which it could not work successfully. This case study therefore draws attention to the difficulties which need to be addressed if the enforced self-regulation model is to have a chance of success in the ordering of industry priorities in favour of health and safety. It is to these broader regulatory issues that we turn in our next and final chapter.

PART VI

CONCLUSION

12

Constituting and Controlling Risk Management: The Regulation of Economic Life

Questions about the influence that the law can have in managing risks in modern society have been considered in this research through an in-depth study of occupational health and safety on the railways. It is a study of one company in one industry in one country at one moment in time. But it offers us a partial glimpse into other areas of social and economic life. It also raises important issues about the influence of risk in our lives and the possibilities of controlling corporate deviance. In this chapter I will draw together the main conclusions arising from the empirical study and consider the theoretical and policy implications arising from these.

Regulating Risks on BR

Regulation is one way in which risks are managed in modern societies. It is thus one method of trying to effect a particular ordering within corporate and economic life. In the case of occupational health and safety regulation, it is an important way of ordering priorities so that the risks associated with the workplace are taken into account and their management given prominence within organizations. Occupational health and safety regulation thereby aims to harness the regulatory powers of the company and become an integral part of corporate life. State regulation not only constitutes the legitimate railway market but it also attempts to structure the relations between different groups within companies and the systems and procedures they adopt in pursuit of regulatory objectives. So regulatory law guides the industry's risk management task by requiring regulatory texts, the production and distribution of knowledge about risk, and a general system of communication to identify and manage risk (Ericson and Haggerty, 1997).

The constitutive objectives of occupational health and safety regulation in Britain are ambitious. The ideal is that regulatory objectives are so well internalized and incorporated into organizational scripts and everyday life that they are normalized and taken for granted. Crucially the law must be translated into the daily operation of the organization. Moreover this regulation has communitarian ambitions to empower employees and to realize them as stakeholders in health and safety. This seems to imply a diminishing importance of hierarchy and regulation yet, as we have seen, organizational and hierarchical safety nets of discipline and control remain in place in case of non-compliance. In the event of these constitutive efforts failing, then regulatory law also provides for controls and sanctions to be applied. Issues are thus raised about controlling corporate deviance and apportioning responsibility and blame in organizational life.

Research Findings: The Constitutive Objectives of Regulatory Law

Analysis of the research data reveals that occupational health and safety regulation did have an institutional impact on BR. The company had responded to the constitutive demands of regulatory law and had put in place fairly elaborate systems for the promotion of health and safety in the workplace. But the systems were in many respects too elaborate and counterproductive as they proved difficult to communicate. So while health and safety had been incorporated into organizational scripts, the evidence is that understanding of these scripts was variable (Ch. 6).

Levels of participation and empowerment also varied. Despite the intention that occupational health and safety should be the concern of everyone in the workplace, understandings of occupational health and safety issues were strongly patterned hierarchically. Those in the most senior positions had the greatest understanding of health and safety risks and the strategies for managing these risks, while those further down the hierarchy often knew relatively little. Safety representatives, who might have been expected to know much more by virtue of their position and additional health and safety training, were often poorly informed (Ch. 7).

Regulation shaped what the company did, but not as fundamentally as regulatory objectives intended. The major evidence for this is the extent to which regulation appears to have influenced everyday activities. BR had risk management systems in place and they complied with the letter of the law, but there were crucial gaps in corporate understandings of risk. In particular there was no central collation of 'bad news' in the form of readily accessible accident data or data about legal action. Instead collation of this type of information was ad hoc and compartmentalized at a departmental level. Even here it was typically the province of safety departments. So there were problems in accessing the information at the lower levels of the organization—including safety representatives. There were also no centralized understandings of these data, with important implications for the company's central ability to manage risk where these data could have served as bases of risk assessment (Ch. 9).

Fragmentation of the company emerged as a major obstacle to the constitutive objectives of occupational health and safety. At the time of this research BR had very different traditions and cultures in each department. Indeed these departments operated semi-autonomously. They had their own organizations and policies, and each embraced different professional skills. This led to a great source of variation. Likewise so did the geographical spread of the company, which covered the entire rail network in Britain, thus necessitating good communication within and between departments.

All of these factors are identified by the research literature as significant in the control of—or indeed failure to control—risk in organizational settings. Complexity, for example, is a key variable in studies of disaster. Perrow's (1984) work on normal accidents identified system complexity as a predisposing factor to unforeseen interactions occurring and accidents resulting. Turner and Pidgeon (1997) also identify complex systems as being prone to the interaction of unanticipated errors and misunderstandings which can lead to disaster. Vaughan's (1996) analysis of the Challenger accident picks up similar themes. These studies all underline the difficulties of controlling risk in complex and especially technical settings. And Turner and Pidgeon, in particular, point to the centrality of communication in these systems. Indeed there is great resonance between the findings of this research into Britain's railways and Turner and Pidgeon's general explanation of why people do not act upon information, which exists and which could warn of accidents, namely that: 'the relevant information is not available to them at the appropriate time in a form which it is possible for them to use' (1997: 162). The research findings on risk exemplify this.

Research Findings: Risk

BR and the individuals working within it typically operated with notions of uncertainty rather than risk. So no one did the 'calculations', but operated instead according to 'rules of thumb'. This happened at the corporate level to the extent that accident data were not centrally understood. Consistent with Turner and Pidgeon's analysis we find that 'information was noted but not fully appreciated', either because of other work pressures or because of a false sense of security engendered by incomplete or biased risk management techniques (Ch. 11). Also 'information was not correctly assembled' (Turner and Pidgeon, 1997). This was for a variety of reasons including it being buried amongst other material and being distributed among several departments rather than centrally collated. On occasions, such information was even wilfully withheld, through non-reporting by individuals to the company, or since privatization non-reporting by companies to the regulatory authorities, or more recently because of the fear of legal liability (Ch. 11). Beyond this we can identify another theme, namely that the data suggest that risks tend to be normalized or denied, and regarded as 'facts of life'. The evidence from this study is that this happened at both the organizational level and at the level of the individual worker (Ch. 10).

There are structural explanations for this approach to risk, centring on the broader employment market and also upon organizational explanations, most notably the culture of production which is crystallized in the so-called railway 'ethos' that 'keeping the trains running' is of primary importance (Vaughan, 1996). The implication is that keeping the railways operational takes priority in the ordering of the company, and it also appears to take priority in the ordering of preferences by individual employees. Indeed the suggestion coming out of the data is that there was a tendency to take short-cuts. In so doing there is a denial of the known risk, most typically reflected in the sentiment 'it will never happen to me'. Arguably employees should not have a great deal of space in which to make such decisions, since the structures and pressures should minimize employees' ability to take risks. But as Vaughan (1996) illustrates, the normalization of deviance, and we can add risk, can quickly permeate a company, influencing individuals, groups of workers, and the organization itself.

The evidence of this research is also that perceptions of risk are situationally generated, with social distance from the workplace emerging as especially important. Thus we can discern strong occupational and hierarchical dimensions to the social distribution of knowledge about risk (Turner and Pidgeon, 1997). Those in senior managerial positions learnt about risk through reports and statistical data read in their offices. This gave them a broad overview of occupational health and safety risks and contributed to their thinking about risks in terms of risk management systems, rules, and trends. This contrasted with those who were much more proximate to the everyday risks of the railways, who had little idea of the bigger picture, and viewed risks according to their own personal knowledge. Accidents were often regarded as unique and they were explained in terms of individual carelessness or 'luck' rather than systemic or structural reasons. Thus perceptions of risk influenced perceptions of responsibility and compliance. An important theme is that knowledge is pragmatically received and is interpreted and acted upon according to situational constraints. As other studies have demonstrated, patterns of communication tend to be structured by authority and reflect the division of labour in an organization (Turner and Pidgeon, 1997: 103).

Research Findings: Regulation and Control

Knowledge within the railway industry of the control aspects of regulatory law followed a similar hierarchical pattern as the constitutive aspects of regulation. So they were better understood by senior personnel, largely again for situational reasons, namely that they have the most contact with regulatory officials.

No great fear of the criminal sanction emerged from this study, which may partially be explained by the fact that it was seldom invoked. But it also appears that attitudes to legal action were grounded in notions of 'fairness' and 'justice'. There was no evidence of the company strategically avoiding legal action. This study questions even the fundamental assumption that information about legal action against the company was regarded as 'bad news'. There was no evidence that information was not collated and transmitted because of a reluctance to transmit 'bad news' up through an organization. Rather each legal case was judged on its own merits and this determined whether or not it was regarded as 'bad news' at all. Moreover subsequent action or inaction by the company was dependent on this judgement. In cases where the legal action was regarded as 'unfair', those involved in and implicated by the case would not be adversely affected, for example, in terms of their careers. Disciplinary action would, however, be likely if the legal action was deemed to be justified. It is of course within this social and managerial context that daily practices developed. Certainly there was evidence that internal company control systems were not always rigorously enforced.

Interestingly, however, the industry view was that policing and control are necessary to keep health and safety high on company agendas. This of course resonates with the academic literature, where the much-criticized 'command and control' regulation is regarded as far from redundant. It is increasingly seen to work in concert with other sources of regulation and other regulatory methods and appears to be especially important in underpinning them (Aalders, 1993; Boyer and Meidinger, 1985; Gunningham, 1995; Hutter, 1999).

Research Findings: The Legitimacy of Regulatory Objectives

Perceptions of the legitimacy of regulatory objectives both within the company and between the company and the regulatory agency are important to our understandings of corporate responses to regulation.

In this study employees' views about the legitimacy of regulatory objectives within the company derived from a number of sources, including the robustness and responsiveness of the systems in place to regulate health and safety in the company. Employee responses on these topics were finely tuned and considered. So, for example, the amount of paperwork available actually bred suspicion because it was so voluminous. Employees did not regard the plethora of rulebooks and policy statements as indicative of the lengths to which the company was going to put sophisticated risk management systems into place. Rather they suspected that the company was 'passing the buck' for occupational health and safety to them. More tangible signals of the legitimacy accorded to regulation by the company were seen to reside in the time staff were given to read risk-related texts, by the clarity of these texts, and by the quantity and quality of training which accompanied them. At the time of this research these activities were not accorded much priority; indeed even managers complained about how little training they received, especially compared to the training offered to safety representatives.

Another signal of the legitimacy accorded to regulatory objectives by the company was the responsiveness of the systems in place to deal with problems. This embraced the speed and readiness with which problems taken to managers, safety representatives, and joint consultative committees were remedied. It also included the enforcement of company occupational health and safety systems, procedures, and rules. The credibility of the disciplinary system in place was very much related in the minds of staff to the company's readiness to invoke disciplinary procedures in the face of non-compliance. Also important was the time allocated to 'do the job' and most particularly the pressure to finish jobs. This was taken as symbolic of the support given to regulatory objectives. Of crucial importance was the visible and substantive support given to regulatory messages by senior staff (Heimer, 1996). Decoupling regulatory activity into a separate part of the organization, namely a safety department, was regarded as insufficient, but not having a specialist department at all was also taken as a sign of lack of investment in regulatory objectives. The signal of full legitimacy was a specialist safety department, full backing and commitment from the top of the organization, and the internalization of responsibility throughout the company. These matters are often referred to as the 'safety culture' of an organization. The presence of a 'good' safety culture in which resources, commitment, norms, and practice fall in behind regulatory objectives, is identified in the broader literature as significant to risk management in organizational contexts (Turner and Pidgeon, 1997: 187 ff.; Vaughan, 1996).

At the corporate level the railways research identified shifting perspectives on the legitimacy of regulatory objectives. While there was little evidence of BR challenging Railway Inspectorate demands, it should be remembered that company directors and senior members of the Railway Inspectorate did engage in regular negotiations over how compliance was defined and managed (Hutter, 1997). Employee perceptions during the research period seemed to be that regulatory objectives were not accorded top priority within the company, although it is certainly the case that greater notice was taken of them towards the end of the data collection period as the full effects of the King's Cross and particularly Clapham Junction accidents began to be felt. These railway disasters prompted a complete review of the system. Indeed this is resonant of so much railway and general regulatory history, namely safer practices and more regulation emerging from disaster. The company began to put in place much more systematic and formalized review systems involving risk assessment, cost-benefit analyses, and prioritization of work. But it also started to challenge what it was being asked to do by the regulatory authorities, a process that has been accentuated by privatization. Indeed it is important to appreciate the dynamic nature of regulation, as cultures are created and recreated according to a variety of characteristics, some endogenous to the company and others exogenous to it. The outcomes of changes are of course not always predictable.

Before moving beyond the case study of BR, the main points arising from the research data warrant summary:

- Risk management systems and procedures had been instituted but they were not fully operationalized.
- Everyday awareness and understanding of both the legal and corporate risk management systems was sketchy.
- There were no centralized corporate understandings of risk.

- At the individual level employees did have a broad understanding of the risks associated with their work.
- Most of the time employees complied, but situational and structural imperatives did lead to non-compliance.
- The empowerment of employees was variable and the communitarian objectives of regulation remained largely unfulfilled.
- Respondents saw the control aspects of regulation as necessary, but there was no evidence of fear of the criminal sanction.
- Legal action was judged on its merits on a case-by-case level, and where it was regarded as 'unfair' it had less impact on the corporation.
- The research period saw an increasing inclination to challenge regulatory agency decisions.

Where regulatory ambitions were not being met the main obstacles emerged as:

- the fragmentation of the company, both organizationally and geographically;
- serious communication difficulties;
- inequalities in knowledge of regulation and risk;
- difficulties in the perceived legitimacy of state regulation and corporate risk management efforts.

The significance of these factors has been highlighted by events subsequent to the research. As the privatization process progressed so did the fragmentation of the industry, thus exacerbating the potential for both communication difficulties and inequalities in knowledge. Moreover the entry into the industry of companies and personnel who were unfamiliar with the railways may intensify these inequalities further. The experience since privatization appears to underline the salience of the findings and the central messages of the BR study reported in this book (Ch. 11).

Modelling Corporate Responsiveness to Regulation

One way of conceptualizing the findings of the BR study and relating them to broader regulatory objectives is to map out different levels of corporate response to a system of enforced self-regulation. Figure 12.1 presents a three-phase model of corporate responsiveness to the constitutive objectives of regulation. The first phase involves the design and establishment of organizational structures and systems which are concerned with promoting, monitoring, and taking responsibility for risk management within the company. This typically involves establishing a committee structure to consider risk management and regulatory compliance, and the appointment of specialist personnel and departments. It also involves setting up procedures and rules for managing risks and ensuring compliance. The main corporate players in this phase are likely to be senior management and specialist risk managers. Outside advisers may also be

Normalization phase ↑	Compliance with risk management procedures and rules are part of normal, everyday life; awareness of risk is internalized. There is corporate understanding of risks and individual awareness throughout the organization.	Everyone in the company is involved.
Operational phase	Risk management systems, procedures, and rules are operationalized/implemented. Committees meet; audits are undertaken; rules are enforced. Safety culture established.	Main players at corporate level are all levels of management; worker/community representatives.
Design and establishment phase	Risk management systems, procedures, and rules are established. Committees are set up and specialist personnel appointed. Risk management becomes part of organizational scripts.	Main players at corporate level are senior management and specialist personnel.

FIG. 12.1. Corporate responsiveness to regulation

involved. These may be from a variety of sources, for example, from the state regulatory agency or possibly external consultants. In this phase there may be extensive borrowing of ideas from outside the company (DiMaggio and Powell, 1991).

The second phase is termed the operational phase. It comprises the formal implementation of the structures and procedures established in phase 1. So the committee structure is operational, audits are taking place, and the rules are being enforced. During this phase an increasing proportion of staff would be expected to know about corporate risk management structures and the procedures, rules, and personnel in place to promote and monitor them. At this phase it is expected that everyone in the organization is becoming involved in implementing and complying with the management of risks.

The third phase represents what we might take to be the regulatory ideal, namely that risk management and regulatory compliance are fully integrated parts of corporate culture (Sigler and Murphy, 1988). Thus regulatory objectives have been constituted as 'normal' and taken-for-granted aspects of both organizational and individual working life. In other words the regulatory objectives and corporate risk management systems are perfectly aligned and everyone in the company has internalized regulatory messages and complies with them. Whereas the first and second phases are involved primarily with the institutionalization of responsibility (Rees, 1994; Stone, 1975), the third phase is signified by real internalized behavioural change.

An important aspect of the model is that it is dynamic. As one moves from the first to the third phase, the importance of hierarchy diminishes as participation and stake-holding increase. So risk management moves from being the preserve of senior managers and specialist personnel to involving everyone. Awareness of risks increases; responsiveness to risk increases; and compliance with regulation grows. Moreover compliance in the third phase is 'normalized' and emanates from a deep understanding of the risks of non-compliance. Risk management may also change organizationally. Whereas risk management systems may be regarded as organizationally and culturally distinct 'add-ons' in phase 1, they are regarded as fully integrated and a normal and necessary part of corporate life in phase 3. Likewise, regulatory compliance may move from being regarded as 'optional' and a 'bonus' in phase 1 to being normal and expected in phase 3.

Questions of legitimacy also vary between the three phases. In phase 1 regulatory and corporate risk management systems may not be regarded as fully legitimate. But part of the rationale for the establishment and operational phases is that legitimacy will increase as the regulatory and risk management systems take effect. Accordingly a feature of the normalization phase is that the legitimacy of these objectives and systems is taken for granted.

A crucial point about the model is that it is not unilinear and that it is possible to move both forwards and backwards through the different phases. The perfect objective would be movement from the first to third phases but this is not inevitable. In its most ideal form, phase 3 may in reality be a rarity, even an impossibility. Even if it is attained it is likely to be only temporary, as one of the major problems encountered in managing risks is maintaining full compliance once it has been achieved and maintaining regulatory objectives as a priority within the company. Backward movement from phase 3 to 2 is therefore likely, but movement from phase 2 to phase 1 is also possible for very similar reasons, namely the difficulties of maintaining compliance and preventing complacency from dampening regulatory objectives.

Each of these phases of course encompasses a wide range of conditions. The design and establishment phase, for instance, involves potentially lengthy and complex organizational change involving the identification of risks, consultations with experts, and the design, development, and eventually establishment of institutional structures, systems, and procedures for the promotion and fulfilment of regulatory objectives. Some of these are identified in Figure 12.2. These refinements need to be taken into account, both in using the model to sharpen our awareness of corporate behaviour and in developing and refining the model.

Perhaps the most significant move is that from phase 1 to phase 2. Given the very real difficulties in reaching phase 3, it is likely that the move from phase 1 to phase 2 is statistically the most common move and the one which regulators are most concerned to achieve (see below). Figure 12.3 outlines the features of the operational phase. It also indicates the range of characteristics which would denote a move into phase 3.

The BR research suggests that this company was, at the time of main data collection, early in the second phase of corporate responsiveness. The features

Consultations with regulatory agency; other companies; unions
Employment of in-house or external risk management consultants

Risk identification
Prioritization of risks
Development of risk management and compliance objectives
Development of risk management and compliance programmes of action

Design and development of an institutional structure:
Specialist regulatory departments and personnel
Committee structure

Design and development of systems and procedures:
Policies, rules, and procedures for managing risk compliance
Training and education programmes
Internal communication systems
Disciplinary procedures
Monitoring procedures

Establishment of:
Regulatory responsibilities within the company
Communication of objectives, policies, structures, and procedures throughout the organization

FIG. 12.2. Characteristics of the design/establishment phase

Operational phase
Risk management systems, rules, and procedures become embedded in the organization
Committee meetings, audits, reviews become a routine part of corporate life
Organizational scripts increasingly take account of regulatory objectives
Training and education programmes are updated and become an established and regular part of corporate life
Funding budgets are regularly reviewed

Self-regulatory systems become much more developed and sophisticated
Rules are enforced and disciplinary procedures instituted when necessary
Monitoring procedures are improved and reviews and audits are acted upon
Safety culture emerges and becomes established

Normalization phase
Compliance and risk management systems, rules, and procedures are seen as a normal and necessary part of routine corporate life
Responsibility for regulating risks increasingly institutionalized
Safety culture fully embedded
Regulatory objectives prioritized
Legitimacy of regulatory objectives unquestioned
Awareness of risk internalized throughout the organization

Corporate risk and compliance systems fully reviewed and continue to be improved
Regulatory messages sustained
Self-regulation fully operational
A two-way flow of information about risk and compliance operational throughout the corporate hierarchy

FIG. 12.3. Indicators of the operational and normalization phases

of the establishment phase were well in place and the focus needed to be upon operationalizing the systems and structures and embracing a wider constituency of corporate personnel within the system. The post-research period underlines that it is possible to move 'backwards': the railway industry in Britain moved 'back' to the establishment phase post-privatization as the industry was restructured and new systems had to be established afresh.

The BR research indicates some of the variables which influence movement between the three phases of corporate responsiveness. Thus issues, by now familiar, which emerge as particularly significant are the ability of an organization to collate and disseminate knowledge of risks, to manage these risks, and to introduce an effective compliance policy (see also Turner and Pidgeon, 1997; Vaughan, 1996). In organizations which are fragmented or where communication is difficult, upward transition between phases is problematic, whereas the constitutive ambitions of regulation are more readily met in organizations which are more tightly coupled and which have good communication systems in place.

Corporate culture is also significant. Where there is a corporate culture sympathetic to regulatory objectives then transition from phase 1 towards phase 3 is more likely than in companies where this commitment is lacking. Particularly important are perceptions of real commitment to regulatory compliance and risk management from those at the top of the organization; the allocation of proper funds and time for risk management and compliance; and the prioritization of regulatory objectives compared to other corporate objectives. As the railways case illustrates, the balance between commercial and regulatory interests changes over time. Moreover there is no simple equation between cost and safety, since other considerations also play their role. The literature suggests that we need to take into account a variety of factors (see Ch. 10). These include the nature of the business involved (Genn, 1993); corporate commitment to regulatory objectives (Hutter, 1997); and issues relating to corporate reputation (Di Mento, 1986; Fisse and Braithwaite, 1983; Olsen, 1992). The external regulatory environment is also important (Carson, 1982; Gunningham, 1984; Hutter, 1997). Key here is the state regulator.

In systems of enforced self-regulation, the regulatory agency is cast into the role of overseer of the company's own efforts to regulate. However, differential levels of self-regulation and compliance are inherent in the model of corporate responsiveness. We might therefore expect the regulatory agency's role and approach to vary accordingly. Figure 12.4 extends the model of corporate responsiveness and sets out what we might expect the relationship between the company and the state regulator to be. Essentially it is anticipated that as a company moves from phases 1 to 3, the involvement of the state regulator decreases and by the time phase 3 is reached, state regulatory involvement with the company is minimal. This model also anticipates that the strategy of the regulatory agency changes between phases. So in the establishment phase the emphasis is upon constitutive regulation, putting structures and systems into

Normalization phase	State regulatory involvement minimal Reliance on corporate self-regulation Strategy: distance monitoring and overseeing
Operational phase	State regulatory involvement medium to high Emphasis: constitutive/controlling Strategy: insistent to sanctioning
Establishment phase	State regulatory involvement high Emphasis: constitutive Strategy: educative and persuasive strategy likely

FIG. 12.4. Corporate responsiveness and the state regulatory involvement

place. And the most likely enforcement strategy is likely to be persuasive and educational.[1] This is because it is likely to be judged that a company's regulatory capacity is limited and relatively rudimentary at this point. For example, it may not be fully aware of what needs to be done to comply and how to approach compliance. The reasons for this may range from ignorance of risk identification and assessment procedures to ignorance of regulatory requirements. Substantial costs may also be incurred during this phase, for example, considerable time and effort may be expended in designing and developing systems. It is also likely that there will be the financial costs of putting compliant hardware into place, for example, pollution control or health and safety equipment, computer software, and so on. Inspectors may well take a pragmatic approach to this, recognizing that a programme of compliance needs to be established which prioritizes work according to risk. So long as the company appears willing to make progress then a persuasive strategy is likely. But once the initial development stages of this phase have been passed through, the strategy may become more insistent, especially in the face of any apparent unwillingness to progress forward to phase 2.

In the operational phase the regulatory emphasis is upon pursuing the constitutive objectives, but with a greater preparedness to adopt a controlling role should the company not make progress voluntarily. The enforcement strategy in phase 2 is thus likely to be a mixture of the insistent and sanctioning strategies depending upon corporate capacity and willingness to comply. Early in this phase the concern will be to ensure that regulatory risk management systems and procedures are embedded in the company and are working. But later in this

---

[1] The predicted responses of the state regulators are derived from the existing literature. See Chapter 1. The terms persuasive, insistent, and sanctioning strategies are also discussed in Chapter 1 and in Hutter (1988; 1997).

phase regulatory officials will press for the introduction of reflexive monitoring and the refinement of existing systems and procedures in the light of new information. They will press for a more inclusive and expanding system and focus on the fine-tuning of the company's self-regulation. It is at this point that companies may become aware that compliance is a continually creative process and that in many important respects full compliance may be elusive (Hutter, 1997).

Regulators will judge what phase an organization is at according to criteria such as those presented in Figures 12.2 and 12.3. But they rarely act on this information alone. They make judgements about how much confidence they have in a company, in its personnel, hardware, systems, and processes. They also assess how far they can push a company towards higher levels of compliance and greater levels of self-regulation. And crucially these are not one-off judgements, they are continually assessed and reassessed in the light of new information and changing circumstances. In the normalization phase it is expected that a company will do these things for itself. So it will know what needs improving and how to effect this and most importantly it will do so voluntarily without external pressure. The emphasis is therefore very much upon corporate self-regulation, with the state agency playing a minimal, arm's length overseeing role.

It must be recognized that there are wide variations between businesses. Studies of regulation teach us a number of things, not least that regulators and the regulated are in an interactive relationship. They can be mutually constraining on the one hand and may actively thrash out the boundaries of regulation and compliance on the other. The relationship between regulatory agencies and companies is rarely a simple tit-for-tat relationship but is rather complex. These relationships have histories, involving different personalities, shifting regulatory parameters, changing commercial environments, and fluid political agendas (Hutter, 1997). In some circumstances the company will be in a stronger position to resist regulation than the regulator is to enforce it. This depends on a variety of factors such as the framing of the legislation, the evidential requirements of the law, access to information, and so on. But one determining factor is generally thought to be the size and regulatory capacity of the company involved.

As we saw in Chapter 1, it is generally supposed that larger companies have greater regulatory capacity than smaller companies. Likewise they have a greater capacity to resist regulation. According to the classical model, resistance from companies is to be expected. But the data from this study support the view that large companies have problems of their own and that resistance may be too simplistic an explanation of non-compliance (see also Di Mento, 1986). This research questions the extent to which even large companies are able to set up their own risk management systems. So, non-compliance may be the result of incompetence or a lack of communication. Indeed large organizations may be extremely difficult to control precisely because of their size; thus communication emerges as a key factor in the ability of companies to self-regulate and

manage risk. The complexity of large companies may in itself lead to conflicting goals, misunderstood messages, and unintended consequences. It cannot
simply be assumed that everyone in the same company shares the same objectives and has similar regulatory capacity, or that there are shared understandings of regulation and its merits.

We have so far operated with a fairly simple model of the company. We
should be cautious about simplifying too much. We need to heed the structural
models of corporations which regard the company as complex, differentiated,
and not necessarily operating as one unit. It is clear that we cannot understand
more fully the impact of regulation and corporate responses to it until we focus
more critically upon corporations as complex organizations with varying professional constituencies, hierarchies, norms, and cultures. So the corporate
responsiveness model may need to be applied to consider different sectors of a
company as well as the overall company position.

Developing the Model

Figures 12.5 and 12.6 summarize some of the features of the three-phase model
of corporate responsiveness we are developing. Figure 12.5 pulls together the
changing dynamics between the three phases. It highlights, for instance, the
increasing participation in risk management as the company moves from phase
1 to phase 3. So regulation moves from being the province of senior managers
and specialist personnel in phase 1 to include everyone in phase 3. This is
accompanied by the increasing legitimacy within the company of regulatory
systems and objectives. So there may be initial scepticism among all levels of
staff in phase 1, but by phase 3 these systems and objectives should be accepted
as normal, integral, and necessary to the company's well-being. If phase 3 is to
be achieved at all, then the move from phase 1 to phase 3 must involve an awareness and understanding of risks among everyone in the company and more than
this, a corresponding behavioural change which is reflected in increasing levels
of compliance. By phase 3 corporate self-regulatory systems are fully operational, thus necessitating less state regulatory involvement.

Movement within and between phases is no easy matter and Figure 12.6
starts to map out the conditions which may foster or hinder progression
between phases. It postulates that the three phases are broadly characterized by
low/medium/high levels of co-ordination of the regulatory effort across the
organization; of dissemination of regulatory messages within the company; of
commitment to regulatory compliance; of stake-holding in corporate regulatory regimes; and of the equality of knowledge about risks and their management. It seems likely that these factors will be correlated. It is also possible that
the phase a company has reached in achieving regulatory objectives parallels its
achievements in other areas of corporate life, since the conditions influencing
movement between phases 1 to 3 are largely generic characteristics of organizations. For example, it is unlikely that a poorly co-ordinated company will have

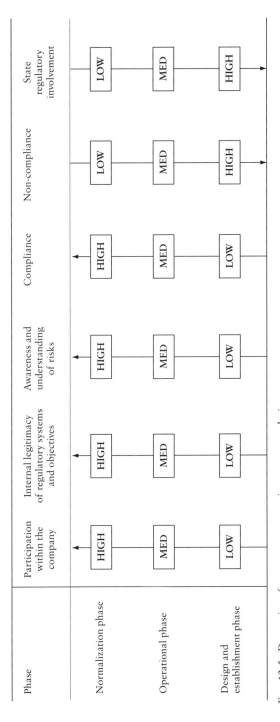

Fig. 12.5. Dynamics of corporate responsiveness to regulation

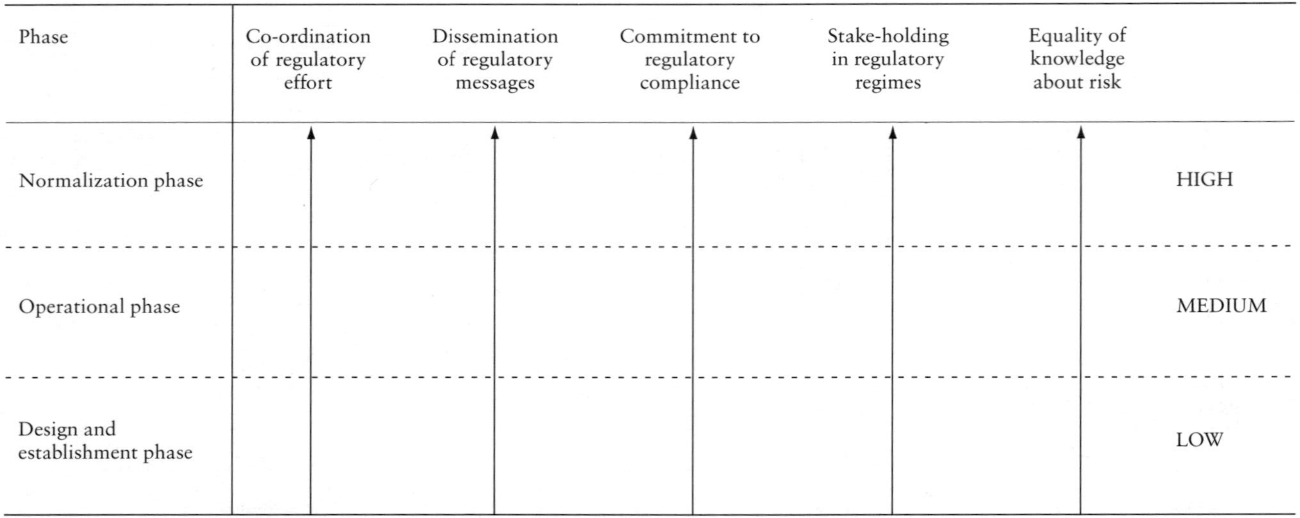

Phase	Co-ordination of regulatory effort	Dissemination of regulatory messages	Commitment to regulatory compliance	Stake-holding in regulatory regimes	Equality of knowledge about risk	
Normalization phase						HIGH
Operational phase						MEDIUM
Design and establishment phase						LOW

Fig. 12.6. Conditions influencing movement between phases 1–3

excellent co-ordination of its regulatory effort, since its risk management systems are much more likely to reflect its ability to co-ordinate in other areas of corporate life. But such matters are questions for research. This is a model which is derived from a combination of one in-depth case study and the existing, albeit limited, literature on corporate responses to regulation. It is, however, a model which could be applied to other companies, to other domains, and also to consider the responsiveness of different parts of one company. Indeed the hope is that it is one tool which may lead to a deeper appreciation of the ways in which regulation can operate as one way of managing risks in modern society. Inextricably related to this is the development of compliance theory, and as Vaughan argues strongly: 'What matters is that the research is designed to explore systematically how the known correlates of organizational misconduct—competition for scarce resources, institutionalized norms, organization characteristics and the regulatory environment, in combination—affect decisions to violate'(1998: 53). This necessarily involves a focus on organizations. Indeed Clarke (1989: 182) argues that 'Organizations, not individual members of our society, are the most important risk assessors in our society'.

This research maps out a number of key areas which may be specifically pursued in the future. These include examining more extensively and systematically the dynamics in Figure 12.6. This involves developing a deeper understanding of what conditions favour or inhibit the movement between different phases of corporate responsiveness to regulation and thus influence the fulfilment of constitutive regulatory objectives. We know that businesses are not driven simply by material concerns, but we need to discern what other factors may be relevant. Economic action is socially situated and we need more sophisticated understandings of how relationships within companies might reflect broader social patterns. The sociology of economic life literature, for example, suggests that morality, culture, and politics are influential as well as goodwill, reciprocity, and trust (see generally Granovetter and Swedberg, 1992; Smelser and Swedberg, 1994). The findings of this study suggest that some of these factors may be exploited to some effect in the regulatory context but we do not have a great evidence of how this might work. These issues are all worthy of further systematic exploration. In addition, a deeper appreciation of the relationship between broader social inequalities and economic life may enable us to understand better some of the difficulties in effecting regulatory mandates.

Another key area for development is shown in Figure 12.4. While there is now a substantial literature on regulatory agencies and their enforcement approaches, we still need more detailed work on how corporations view their relationship with the external regulatory environment. This includes more about their perceptions of state regulators and what they are trying to achieve. But it also includes much more work on the other players in regulatory space. It is important, however, that we work with a broad conceptualization of regulation and its role in managing risk in society. Regulation is pervasive, it is not simply about external control. Regulatory space may be occupied by competing demands, influences, and objectives, some of which are internal to the company and some external. So, as we have outlined above, there will be corporate imperatives to regulate and maybe state ones too. Indeed, as the railways example demonstrates, a company may be subject to multiple state regulators who may not always be pulling in the same direction (Ch. 11). And beyond the individual company and the state, there are other potential players in regulatory space. These may include insurance companies, non-governmental organizations, and industry and trade organizations (Grabosky, 1994, 1995a). A significant feature of regulation is the trend to regulatory mix (Gunningham and Sinclair, 1999; Hutter, 1999). Rarely do we see only one regulator occupying regulatory space; in reality it is usually occupied by several players. The model of enforced self-regulation is one of the state actively trying to harness the efforts of the company to occupy regulatory space and direct its own risk management systems. We can see a similar pattern in some cases of third party enforcement where the state requires third parties, such as professional organizations, to undertake a regulatory role (Cheit, 1990; Gilboy, 1998; Grabosky, 1995a). Alternatively such a role may be voluntarily assumed by other parties, for example, interest groups (Cable and Benson, 1993).

It is of course important that the development of a model such as the one outlined here will draw upon and contribute to broader academic theories and policy debates and it is to these that we now turn.

Lessons from BR

Occupational health and safety regulation in Britain is based upon the deeply ambitious ideals propounded by the Robens Committee (Ch. 2). It rests upon an acknowledgement that regulation involves a variety of interest groups which should ideally be drawn into the regulatory process. It also holds out as an explicit ideal the notion that regulation should become an everyday part of everyday life rather than being seen as a bolt-on 'extra'. In these respects Robens and the system advocated by this committee were advanced and aimed to move regulation beyond simplistic models of cajoling businesses to do something they might not otherwise want to do. Indeed it is this more sophisticated model of regulation which informs our model of corporate responsiveness.

But the Robens Committee was idealistic in many of its assumptions. For example, it presumed an identity of interests between everyone in the workplace to promote health and safety above other workplace pressures. Arguably this led to an underestimation of the difficulties in achieving regulatory objectives. Most particularly, the structural inequalities which may hinder successful self-regulation were ignored, especially the power differences in the workplace. This was highlighted during the research period when the power of the unions was in serious decline, the position of unskilled and semi-skilled workers was weakened by high unemployment, and the company itself was being rationalized as the privatization process started. This was all very different from the political climate which saw the introduction of the Safety Representatives and Safety Committees Regulations, and it challenged further the assumption that regulatory objectives over occupational health and safety would 'naturally' and commonly be prioritized. At times such as the research period, other objectives are experienced as more immediate and pressing at both the corporate and the individual levels and the need for stronger law is underlined. This is not to argue that the Robens objectives were all misplaced or misguided, but it is to purport that if we are too idealistic in our views of the regulated we may take risks with our regulatory regimes. Indeed the experience of BR must cause us to ask serious questions about the ability of companies to self-regulate. Even if we assume a great willingness to comply, there may remain serious difficulties in managing risks in a large and diverse company. Moreover there may be problems of regulatory capacity. This is not simply a matter of the ability to finance regulatory demands but also the availability of knowledge about how to comply and the ability to implement this.

We should not forget that relative to many companies and small businesses in Britain, BR was quite highly motivated to regulate occupational health and safety and also well resourced. Indeed it was probably one of the better motivated and able companies to implement occupational health and safety regulation in the late 1980s and early 1990s. So we can speculate that if this company was having serious difficulties in self-regulating, then many other companies were experiencing more serious difficulties, especially smaller, less well-resourced companies.

The regulatory ideal is a perfect alignment between regulatory compliance and corporate risk management systems and in our model of corporate responsiveness to regulation this is represented by the third normalization phase. For a variety of reasons this alignment is not always forthcoming and it is for this reason that the controlling aspects of regulation exist. The Robens Committee did recognize that compliance is not necessarily automatic from all companies and advocated an enforcement approach akin to Ayres and Braithwaite's (1992) notion of 'responsive regulation' in which regulatory agency enforcement approaches are tailored to the willingness and ability of a company to self-regulate. So regulation will be with a light touch where self-regulation is working and with a heavier hand where this fails. Moreover regulatory officials are encouraged to use the full range of enforcement tools in order to encourage corporate self-regulation. This approach is also built into our model of corporate responsiveness to regulation (see above and Figure 12.3).

Responsive Regulation

A key ingredient of responsive regulation is flexibility, namely the flexibility to adapt different methods to individual circumstances (Ayres and Braithwaite, 1992; Bardach and Kagan, 1982; Grabosky, 1995*a*: 363; 1995*b*: 272). The crucial point here is that this is a dynamic approach to regulation, one in which the regulators and regulatees interact across time and space and in which the complexities of corporate structures, groupings, and personalities are recognized. Also important is the harnessing of other non-state and non-legal sources of regulation (Ayres and Braithwaite, 1992). The importance of a regulatory mix—or 'instrumental combinations'—is central to the design of smart regulation as discussed by Gunningham and Sinclair (1998). They argue for a policy mix and recommend core design principles, but are also careful to emphasize that instruments need to be matched to particular circumstances.[2] While it is important to harness multiple regulatory sources, the cautionary message of this research is that we should not become too reliant on any one source such as company systems, or on any one set of enforcement methods. Responsive regulation should signal a willingness to use the full range of methods when necessary and this means that we should on occasions pay more attention to the 'enforced' part of enforced self-regulation. We should also be ready to use alternative sources of regulation, as experience suggests that the criminal law is not always an effective way to regulate economic life.

It is important to appreciate that command and control regulation has put the criminal law to different uses than are traditionally understood. The different objectives of traditional criminal law and regulatory law are not widely understood. But clearly there are differences and one key to understanding this is the recognition that the purpose of regulation is to manage rather than to eliminate risks. The very use of the word 'regulation' signals a toleration of the activity subject to control, as opposed to much criminal law which attempts to prohibit certain activities and behaviours. The notion of regulation immediately raises a host of perhaps unanswerable questions about what is acceptable. These are unanswerable questions to the extent that what constitutes regulatory compliance is changing and shifting according to a range of variables including technology, scientific knowledge, public opinion, local circumstances, and so on (Hutter, 1997).

It is also important to reiterate that regulatory law is geared primarily to remedy rather than punishment so the control aspects appear to be secondary to the constitutive objectives (see Ch. 4). Nevertheless, whatever the prioritization of regulatory objectives, it remains the case that regulatory law has a dual role, namely constitutive and controlling (Ch. 1). At key moments this dual use of the criminal law leads to a clash of legal purpose, notably when there are calls for the law to be used punitively and symbolically for regulatory breaches (see below). Moreover the difficulties in dealing with corporate misconduct continue to compound the issue.

---

[2] These regulatory developments resonate with the broader visions of social control analysed by Cohen (1985; see below).

Corporate Behaviour

The message from this study and the general research literature is that it is important to acknowledge that there is considerable variability between companies and also within companies. Businesses are not internally monolithic, homogeneous, and rational and this may affect their ability to operate effectively across a range of corporate activities. Indeed our study of BR suggests that the organizational problems BR encountered may have affected their ability to meet financial targets and posed difficulties in meeting occupational health and safety requirements. For example, the company had variable fortunes in meeting its financial obligations. In 1986 and 1989 it met its financial targets (set in 1983 and 1986 respectively) but thereafter it struggled, partly because of the recession. So BR clearly had difficulties in complying with the demands placed upon it in other areas of corporate life, including the financial area, which some theories suggest would be most highly—even exclusively—prioritized.

The tensions between the culture of production and the safety culture are undeniable and some companies are undoubtedly powerful and exploitative. It is for such reasons that companies breed suspicion in themselves with respect to the extent of their power locally, nationally, and globally and in relation to less powerful groups who may be harmed by corporate activities, for example, consumers and employers (see Ch. 1). It also leads some commentators to speculate that companies use their power and influence to escape regulation, most especially criminal sanctions. But even when they are prosecuted, taken to court, and sanctioned, the fact is that regulatory offenders are not necessarily regarded as criminal (Hutter, 1997; Tappan, 1947). There are a variety of potential explanations for this, some relating to the class position of offenders, some to the difficulties in assigning responsibility within corporations, and some to the fact that the technicalities of the breaches make it difficult to appreciate the potential effects of non-compliance (Baucus and Dworkin, 1991).

The example of Britain's railways clearly highlights the difficulties associated with attributing responsibility and blame to corporate activities. Since full privatization, there appear to have been an increasing number of reasons why companies will deny corporate liability for non-compliance and most especially for accidents. Most salient is the potential financial liability to victims and to other rail users.[3] The increasingly adversarial climate has also led individuals within companies to be less ready to admit liability for fear of a criminal prosecution (see Ch. 11).

Questions of blame have increasingly been recognized as multi-faceted, being typically a combination of individual, systemic, and corporate failures.

---

[3] BR used to insure for disaster only. Fragmentation of the railways means that compensation has to be from the company responsible for any mishap to all other companies affected. This has led to a growing role for insurance companies within this industry.

But issues of 'fairness' remain, the most fundamental question being who in an organization can be held to blame for corporate failure? And is it fair to hold individual misdemeanours to account without also holding corporate failures to account? It is on this issue that the law as it presently stands in Britain offers few solutions. While both individuals and organizations may be prosecuted under many regulatory regimes, for example, health and safety, corporations cannot be so readily held to account under criminal legislation, as the Southall and Ladbroke Grove cases have revealed (see Ch. 11). A key difficulty here is to identify an individual within a company who can be held responsible for corporate failure.[4] It seems likely, in Britain at least, that this legal anomaly may now be tackled by new legislation. In May 2000 the Home Office published a consultative paper on *Reforming the Law on Involuntary Manslaughter* (Home Office, 2000). Part 3 of this document proposes a new offence of 'corporate killing' specifically to cover cases such as King's Cross, Clapham Junction, and Southall. It is proposed that the investigation and prosecution of these offences should be undertaken by health and safety enforcing authorities in addition to the police and Crown Prosecution Authority. The paper also tables for consideration proposals for enforcement activity against directors or other company officials, who may be disqualified from acting in a management role in Britain if found guilty.

But there are no guarantees that this will radically change normative views on regulatory offences, the majority of which do not necessarily lead to tangible injury and many of which appear to many commentators to be 'merely technical' (Justice, 1980). There have been attempts to overcome the problems accompanying the dual use of the criminal sanction as both remedial and punitive in the regulatory context. One device has been to introduce both criminal and civil penalties in regulatory regimes.[5] The regulators favour this because of the difficulties they encounter in controlling corporate offenders, the argument being that civil injunctions are more efficient and effective than the available criminal remedies. For example, civil sanctions require a lower burden of proof than criminal law. But the anti-business lobby is not satisfied with this development. Cable and Benson argue, for instance, that there are potential negative consequences of this for society: 'Unlike criminal penalties, civil injunctions do not stigmatize offenders. They lack the punitive and deterrent effects of criminal sanctions, making corporate environmental crimes less costly for corporations and hence more likely to occur' (Cable and Benson, 1993: 467).

At one level this reflects what Ayres and Braithwaite (1992) refer to as a 'barren dispute' over whether or not regulatory offenders are criminal. This is a debate which is partially fuelled by different perspectives and paradigms

---

[4] See Wells (1993) for a thorough discussion of the legal issues involved.

[5] A move to expand the range of enforcement tools has been proposed, for example, in the context of market abuse in the Financial Services and Markets Bill in Britain. There is evidence from the United States that federal regulators have been using civil injunctions against corporate violators.

of understanding about corporate activities which, as Ayres and Braithwaite indicate, are in many senses irreconcilable. More than this, the challenge is to reconcile the tension between the constitutive and controlling aspects of regulatory law. Responsive regulation seems to offer the optimal solution here, most particularly if used in conjunction with other sources of regulation and risk management. If we move to the broader social control literature, it also becomes apparent that many of the characteristics of regulation are not so unique to the regulatory setting. And it is with this literature that we will conclude this study. While the social control literature is typically associated with the control of individual deviant behaviour, it is, as we will see, a literature which can usefully be developed to embrace and inform our understanding of the regulation of risk in organizations.

Social Control and the Regulation of Risk in Organizations

The broadly accommodative control framework associated with occupational health and safety on Britain's railways characterizes much regulatory control and is identified by some authors as a form of control characteristic of modern societies (Hutter, 1997; Reiss, 1984; Rock, 1995). It is contended that new strategies and forms of social control have emerged in response to broader social changes. These include increasing heterogeneity and fragmentation (Horwitz, 1990) and, of particular relevance to this study, the growth of organizations and the complexity of organizational life. Reiss (1984) argues that the emergence of large-scale organizations creates problems of detection and proof as organizations have greater capacity to avoid detection and the power to bargain. This, argues Reiss, is one reason why modern societies turn increasingly to compliance-based systems of control, which mobilize resources proactively, rather than deterrence-based systems, which are reactive and punitive. But compliance-based systems are not unique to organizational control, they also characterize other areas of social control including, for example, policing (Hutter, 1997; Rock, 1995), family disputes (Ingleby, 1992), personal injury claims (Genn, 1987), and lawyer–client interactions (Felstiner and Sarat, 1995). Indeed changes in regulation mirror broader shifts in social control in modern societies.

Cohen (1985) maps out the ways in which patterns of control have developed in his book *Visions of Social Control* in which he discusses a number of 'Master Patterns' in deviancy control. He identifies three phases of control, of which phase 3, which emerges in 'the mid-twentieth century', is of most concern to this study. It is characterized by a number of features, notably increasing ideological attacks on the state apparatus, running alongside an actual strengthening of control systems. So, the state apparatus stays in place and new, diverse forms of control are added to the repertoire; the focus of control is thus dispersed and diffused; the boundaries blur; professional dominance is ideologically attacked but is nevertheless strengthened and further extended; and the methods of control stress inclusion and integration (Cohen, 1985: 16–17).

Although Cohen's focus is largely upon deviant behaviour and deviant people rather than the social control of organizational deviance, his theory illuminates regulatory developments on the railways and also more generally over the past thirty years. State regulatory systems (command and control systems) have, as Cohen suggests, witnessed ideological attack. Occupational health and safety regulation, like other forms of regulation, has suffered a two-pronged attack from two very divergent political positions. On the one hand, command and control regulation has been criticized by pro-regulation groups for being ineffective, while on the other hand pro-business groups (notably the Thatcher government in Britain and the Reagan presidency in the United States) have called for deregulation because regulation is seen to overburden the economic sector. Yet intervention has intensified through reregulation and the growth of alternative sources of regulation, such as supranational regulation.

The place of regulatory control has experienced net widening similar to that described by Cohen, as new and diverse forms and sources of regulation have been marshalled. In the case of BR, for example, it was subject to a system of enforced self-regulation introduced by the Robens Report and encapsulated in the HSW Act. This, as we have seen, sought not only to co-opt corporate efforts to manage risk and promote regulatory objectives but moved the focus of control away from corporate hierarchy to encompass everyone in the workplace. Thus the focus of control became dispersed and diffuse and, crucially, increasingly inclusive. Regulation now attempts to penetrate deep into the corporation and boundaries have become blurred as public and private controls have merged. This was particularly the case when the legislation fully privatizing the railways created the safety cascade involving the state regulator overseeing industry self-regulation.

This has been accompanied by a massive growth in the risk and regulation professions. For instance, there has been a proliferation of safety officers, safety departments, and consultancy firms. Some of these have emerged from the regulated industries, while others are a diversification of mainstream consultancy agencies (Power, 1997). Management consultants were involved in the post-Clapham review of health and safety arrangements on BR. Moreover specialist risk managers and health and safety personnel have played an important role within the industry, most especially the post-privatization industry when their skills have been in high demand (Ch. 11). The running debate on this topic has been on the extent to which these professionals should be decoupled from the rest of the organization since decoupling can run counter to the constitutive objectives of regulation, where ideally responsibility for regulation would be internalized throughout the organization.

There is also a coincidence between regulatory modes of control and more general patterns of social control. So reparation, restitution, reintegration, and inclusionary modes of control are characteristic of both individual and organizational control. Arguably they are vital in regulation given the constitutive ambitions of regulation and given the nature of the activities being controlled, namely continuing economic activity and above all risk management. Constitutive regulation aims to be inclusive and the action taken by regulatory agencies is typically reparative and restitutive in its intent. The overriding regulatory objective is to constitute risk management systems as an integral and important part of corporate activity and beyond this to engender a deep understanding of these amongst all parts of, and all individuals within, the company.

Crucially of course risk management is not just the subject of control in the regulatory context but it is also a form of control in its own right. It aims to bring risk under control through systems, procedures, and training which maximize the areas where the company has control and minimize the areas where it does not (Bernstein, 1996). This involves risk identification and assessment, the prioritization of risks, and the development of control systems. Regulation tries to ensure that these systems are in place and that they are given priority. Regulation guides corporate risk management decisions but it is companies which have to ensure that the systems they put into place are durable, practicable, and capable of maintaining and enhancing regulatory objectives. In some cases this is easily achieved as the company already has sophisticated and effective risk management systems in place, while in other cases a business's management of risks may be very rudimentary and its systems ineffective, or even non-existent. But in all cases a degree of control is likely, as sustaining basic messages can pose major difficulties.

Corporate Risk Management

In many respects corporate risk management parallels regulation. Within the company and outside it there are social, political, economic, legal, and organizational parameters to regulation, especially since the endeavour pivots on risk management rather than risk elimination. There is a fine balance to be struck here between competing pressures and this has to be maintained in the face of shifting boundaries of knowledge, public and political tolerance, economic 'realities', social attitudes, legal possibilities, and organizational constraints and opportunities.

Within companies there are likely to be cross-business effects of risk. There are varying areas of risk, such as business risk, market risk, operational risk, and reputational risk and there are likely to be multiple domains of compliance risk. For example, there may be environmental, health and safety, tax, consumer, planning, and competition regulations to meet. Moreover these may cut across each other and in so doing create more complex sources of risk. Indeed, regulatory authorities themselves may have individual requirements which create risk management problems in other domains. It is for reasons such as these that integrated control systems are becoming increasingly popular. Indeed there is an apparent regulatory trend in this direction. In environmental regulation, for example, there has been a move to a broader holistic conception of the environment and its protection. Increasingly it has been recognized that environmental problems are interrelated and more far-reaching and long term than previously understood. This has led to a wider view of how to regulate and protect the environment which is reflected in the emergence of integrated pollution control (Hutter, 1999). Other areas have witnessed similar trends, for example, occupational health and safety and financial regulation.[6] And similar trends are advocated for corporate risk management (Jorian, 2000; Meulbroek, 2000).

Regulation and Risk

Regulating risk in modern societies clearly demands that greater attention be paid to the inner workings of the corporation and its relationship with the external world. It is also vital that we focus on how routine everyday risks are managed throughout an organization, rather than focus too much on disasters and life at the top of an organization. Clearly both are important but not to the exclusion of the apparently mundane, taken-for-granted activities of organizational and corporate life. Indeed one of the important messages of disaster studies is that disasters can often be traced back to mundane routines at seemingly unimportant levels of organizational life. As Vaughan (1996) explains, deviance can readily be normalized. The aim of regulation is in many respects the mirror image of this, namely the normalization of risk management.

It is important that we broaden our understandings of regulatory and economic life. We need to understand the role of different forms of regulatory control and how they interact. It is increasingly recognized that far from being a negative externality, regulation is an integral and endemic part of economic life, just as it is in other areas of social life. Moreover it has positive benefits, not just for those it protects but also for business itself, which benefits from the 'order', as opposed to chaos, that social control engenders. Regarding regulation as risk management emphasizes its beneficial aspects, but it also highlights once again the need for balance, since risk can also have positive effects. As with all forms of social control, 'too much' can be a 'bad thing' but 'too little' can lead to anarchy (Cohen, 1985).

Regulation is essentially about order—order in economic life and order in corporate life. It is also increasingly about the co-existence and complementarity of public and private sources of order, the relationship between state and market control, and the connections between individual, corporate, and social

---

[6] There has, for instance, been a growth in integrated regulatory agencies. In Britain these include HSE, the Environment Agency, and the Financial Services Authority.

responsibility. And increasingly these are global questions as risks come to be recognized as transnational and issues of regulation extend beyond geopolitical borders. The need to understand the relationship between regulation and corporate risk management is thus even more pressing and must come to occupy a more central part of our intellectual agendas. This is particularly important as regulation and risk management illuminate broader areas of economic and social life and, most important of all, because these are issues that influence the everyday well-being of us all.

APPENDIX 1: DATA COLLECTION

I entered this research project with experience of the railway industry. My previous research with the Railway Inspectorate (Hutter, 1997) meant that I was very familiar with the industry and its working environment. I knew the structure of the industry, the occupational health and safety risks associated with the work, and how these were regulated. Of particular importance was that in my previous research I had employed ethnographic techniques and so had been out and about on the track, visited depots, and so on. this was important in gaining credibility, as was my association with the Railway Inspectorate.

Most of the data for this study were collected in the period from late 1988 to early 1992. This comprised 134 in-depth interviews with BR staff and the representatives of the railway trade unions. A wide cross-section of staff was interviewed from the four main functional departments, namely the civil engineering, mechanical and electrical engineering, operations, and signals and telecommunications departments. Access to the company was secured through the directors of these four departments and the Director of Employee Relations. They were approached in late 1987 and early 1988 by letter and access to the company was fairly readily achieved. This can partially be attributed to my familiarity with the industry and by the associated support I was able to call on from key people known to the company.[1] It was also recognized within the comapny that the research was potentially important and of value to the industry.

The interview sample was selected in consultation with senior BR staff and the railway unions. Respondents were drawn from three different regions of the national rail network and also from different grades in the company's hierarchy of staff, notably directors and departmental safety officers, managers, supervisors, and the workforce. Safety representatives and regional union officials were also interviewed. Whereas there is a balance between the number of managerial staff and members of the workforce interviewed within each department, there is an imbalance across departments. This is because each department had different views about the numbers of staff it felt should be interviewed so as to be representative. Thus while the operations department clearly felt that they employed a very wide range of different skills which should be included in the sample, the civil engineers did not regard it as necessary to interview such large numbers of its staff.

The interview schedules used in data collection are reproduced in Appendix 2. They were designed to encourage open-ended discussion of questions and to avoid asking questions which would restrict interviewees in their replies and could even suggest answers to them.[2] The emphasis was on discerning how respondents interpreted issues and perceived

---

[1] I am grateful to Professor Bill Bradshaw, a former senior manager with BR and a colleague at the Centre for Socio-Legal Studies, who wrote a supporting letter to the directors I approached.

[2] A great deal of work went into these schedules and I am grateful to colleagues at the Centre for Socio-Legal Studies, representatives of the Railway Inspectorate, the trades unions, and British Railways staff for their help in preparing these schedules which were so vital to the research.

health and safety. Interviews lasted from forty minutes to two hours, usually varying according to the grade and specialism of the staff involved. All of the interviews were taped and most were undertaken by myself, although I was fortunate enough to have a few months' research assistance in mid-1988. It was not always possible to ask interviewees all of the questions on the schedule, usually because of limitations on the length of the interview. Interviews all took place on railway premises and in every case a private space was provided; the quality varied from plush London offices to 'sheds' in railway sidings. It should be appreciated that the interviews took staff away from their normal jobs, sometimes for several hours. This caused more disruption for those interviewees who were part of a work gang and may indeed be one reason why fewer civil engineering staff were interviewed, as the removal of one person for a few hours could disable the entire gang from particular tasks for that period of time. Senior officials of the main railway unions were also interviewed, at their respective headquarters in London.

A second, much briefer, phase of interviews took place in late 1995 and 1996 with key individuals in the railway industry and the Railway Inspectorate. The intention of these interviews was to gain some impression of the impact of privatization upon occupational health and safety within the industry and also the impact of the changes instituted post-Clapham.

All of the interviews were transcribed and the main academic analysis of the data took place once the interviewing was completed. The one exception to this was the result of the safety division of the civil engineering department requesting an analysis of the data I had collected on trackside safety. These data were used in the development of a major trackside safety campaign in 1989/90. The main data analysis took place once all of the transcripts were ready. The data were analysed according to department and position in the hierarchy. The main patterns arising from the data were identified and, where relevant, quantified. Particular attention was paid to the spontaneity of responses, for example, how respondents could volunteer topics without prompting. And of central relevance to the research were the interpretations respondents offered and their explanations of occupational health and safety regulation within the industry.

Following the main phase of interviewing, reports arising out of the reserach were submitted to BR and the railway unions. Agreement was reached concerning the usual assurances of confidentiality and anonymity, and at no point did either the unions or BR seek to influence the research findings or pose any constraints on publication. The research generated a lot of interest. Apart from the reports, I was approached by a stream of people from the railway industry, ranging from members of the Board who wanted to discuss the findings, safety officers, local managers interested in raising awareness in their areas, and commercial film units who were tendering for safety campaign films for the industry.

RESEARCH ENVIRONMENT

The general environment of BR during the research period is outlined in Chapter 2. The company was in a period of unsettling change. The privatization process was under way, there were company reorganizations, staff cuts, and a generally bleak economic climate. A few months into data collection the Clapham Junction accident occurred. This reverberated through the higher echelons of the company and added significance to the research which was already under way.

Like most organizational research settings, this company had relatively efficient grapevines and news about my work typically travelled ahead of me. As always, this highlighted the need to maintain confidentiality between interviews and to appear credible and legitimate. The fact that directors were included in the interview sample certainly enhanced the willingness of more junior staff to be interviewed. This partially reflected the hierarchical structure of the company. But it also signalled that senior managers were taking the study very seriously. So not only were they willing to allow me to interview more junior staff and give them time off to be interviewed, but importantly they were also going through the process themselves. But this would not on its own have secured their full co-operation, especially given some of the more sensitive questions included in the interviews. Hence the importance of questions of researcher credibility and legitimacy. The fact that I had spent many months accompanying staff from the Railway Inspectorate on their inspection of stations, depots, and trackside working was important. It gave me personal credibility and also meant that I was familiar with the working conditions, working practices, and also the jargon of the railways.

Another important factor in legitimating the research was the support of the unions. The National Union of Railwaymen (NUR) included an item on my research in its Safety Bulletin which explained what the research was about, who I was, and significantly gave the research its backing: 'Her approach has been considered by the Health and Safety Sub-Committee who have recommended that the Union participate at all levels in the project'. An item also appeared in British Railways' national newsletter explaining the research and lending its support.

The contacts secured during the main phase of interviews and in my previous research with the Railway Inspectorate enabled my return to key individuals in the early 1990s to discuss the impact of privatization.

In addition to the interviews, documentary sources were also consulted. For example, corporate safety policies, rule books, and training materials were examined and where possible I was given access to statistical data such as they were. But the main source of data remained the interview transcripts which provided such a rich source of information and a testament to the time and honesty accorded to the research by BR and most importantly by its staff and also the unions.

APPENDIX 2: THE INTERVIEW SCHEDULES

Basic Facts
1. What is the official title of your job?
2. What does your job involve?
3. How long have you been in your present job?
4. [If applicable] What did you do before?
5. What are the geographical boundaries you are responsible for?
6. How many members of the workforce are you responsible for?
7. What types of activities are undertaken by this workforce?
8. Are there any hazards or dangers associated with the activities of this workforce?
9. What are the most dangerous activities you oversee?
10. Do you distinguish between health and safety or do you regard them as the same thing?
11. Are there any particular health, as opposed to safety, matters which concern you in your job?

The Board's Policies for the Health and Safety of the Workforce
12. Does the Board have official policies regarding the health and safety of staff? [Probe]
13. Do you think that your staff know what these policies are? [Probe]
14. Are there checks to ensure policy is followed? [Probe: what are they?]
15. What do you think about these policies?
16. Does anyone in the company have special responsibility for health and safety?
17. If so, who are they?
18. Do you undertake workplace inspections?
19. How often?
20. Are these joint inspections with the workforce?
21. Have you received any training in health and safety?
21. If no, would you have found it useful if you had?
22. If yes, what sort of training did you receive?
23. Who from?
24. Was it helpful when you first started work?
25. Now that you have been in your job for a while do you still consider the training to be adequate?
26. Do many people bring health and safety problems to you?
27. If so, what sort of problems?
28. What do they expect you to do?

Safety Representatives
29. How many unions are there in the area you are responsible for?
30. How many safety reps. are there?

31. Do you have as many as you should have?
32. What sort of people become safety reps.? [Probe: do they share similar characteristics?]
33. Are the safety reps. also LDC representatives?
34. If yes, do you have any views about this?
35. Do you have joint union/management safety committees?
36. If yes, how often do they meet?
37. Who chairs them?
38. What sort of issues do you discuss?
39. What action follows from safety committees and inspections?

The Risks Involved with the Railways
40. Is the railway a risky industry to work in?
41. Is it possible for you to compare it with other industries, to say it is more dangerous than one industry or less dangerous than another?
42. Are there many accidents amongst the workforce?
43. Do you know how many fatalities there were amongst the workforce in BR last year?
44. Do you know how many (a) major staff accidents, (b) staff fatalities there were in your department last year? your region last year? your area last year?
45. What sort of accidents were they? [Probe]
46. What sort of less serious accidents happen in your department?
47. How do they happen?
48. Whose fault are they usually?
49. Are they often accidents that should not have happened, or are they accidents that could not be prevented?
50. How could they be prevented?
51. Do you feel more could be done to reduce staff accidents in your industry?
52. How often do you get to hear about accidents?
53. Do you get involved as a manager?
54. In what ways?
55. What sort of impact does an accident have upon the workforce?
56. How long does the impact last for?

The Law
57. What health and safety regulations do you have to observe? [If don't know, probe: have you heard of the Health and Safety at Work Act?]
58. What do these laws and regulations require you to do?
59. What duties does the law put upon the workforce regarding health and safety?
60. What duties does the law place upon you as a manager?
61. What do you think about these rules and regulations?
62. What are your sources of information *re* health and safety matters? [Probe]
63. Do you get to hear about changes in the law or new regulations?
64. Is this information usually written down or does someone tell you?
65. [If written down] How much do you manage to read?

The Railway Inspectorate

66. You have told me about the railway's checks upon health and safety, is there anyone else responsible for checking health and safety on the railways? [If no, prompt with government agency for air pollution control. If still no, ask if they have ever heard of the Railway Inspectorate.]
67. Do you know the name of your local inspector?
68. Do you know what he looks like?
69. Where are the local offices of the Inspectorate?
70. Would you approach these inspectors for advice on health and safety matters? If not, why not?
    If yes, what sort of matters?
71. When did you last receive a visit from an inspector?
72. Who did he speak to during his visit?
73. How long did the inspector stay?
74. What did he do during the visit?
75. How frequently are your premises/area/activities inspected?
76. Do you see the same inspector each time?
77. How frequently do you think they should be inspected by an inspector?
78. How useful do you find inspectors' visits? [Probe: in what sort of ways?]
79. Do you take a lot of notice of inspectors' comments? Always? Why?
80. What sort of things do you do, that they ask of you?
81. What sort of things would you ignore—if any?
82. Are you asked to do anything which you find irritating or unnecessary?
83. Do you find what they say reasonable?
84. How do you get along with the different inspectorates you deal with?
85. How important do you think inspectors are in bringing about higher standards of health and safety (a) on your site, (b) generally?
86. Have you ever seen Railway Inspectorate accident reports?
87. Have you found them useful? [Probe]

Legal Action

88. What legal action can inspectors take?
89. How frequently do you think inspectors (a) serve notices, (b) prosecute?
90. Has your firm been (a) served with a notice, (b) prosecuted?
91. Who do they prosecute?
92. What for?
93. Do you know what sort of penalties can be imposed by the courts if someone is taken to court and found guilty?
94. When the Railway Inspectorate does prosecute, it could prosecute individuals or it could prosecute the Board. Have you any views about who it should prosecute?
95. Is legal action something that worries you when an inspector visits?

The Workforce and Compliance

96. Do the workforce comply willingly with health and safety rules and regulations? [Probe]
97. Do they, for example, always use the safety equipment you provide?
98. Do they have an interest in not complying?
99. If you discover someone not following health and safety rules what do you do?

100. Have you ever done this? If yes, how often?
101. How effective do you consider safety representatives are in terms of getting the workforce to comply?
102. How much concern is there amongst the workforce about health and safety?
103. What do you think about BR's attitude to health and safety?
104. Do you yourself comply with health and safety demands, if so why [not]?
105. Do you always comply?
106. Completely?
107. Why bother?
108. What sort of factors do you take into account when considering whether or not to implement particular health and safety proposals? [e.g. policy changes]
109. When a new health and safety initiative or proposal comes about, what sort of thing gives rise to it?
110. Who usually suggests changes?
111. What priority do you give to health and safety?
112. How important is health and safety in relation to your other responsibilities?
113. Which aspects of your job take priority over health and safety matters?
114. And, which take less priority?
115. Do you think that complying with health and safety demands is costly? [If yes, probe: how costly?]
116. Do you have an expenditure budget? If yes: does health and safety figure in that budget?
117. What proportion is this of your total expenditure budget?
118. What other demands do you have on your expenditure budget?
119. Is there anything the inspectorate has asked you to do which has been too costly?
120. What factors weigh for and against health and safety?
121. Finally, what are the major health and safety problems now facing the railways?

Thank you very much.

INTERVIEW SCHEDULE FOR SAFETY REPRESENTATIVES

Basic Facts
1. Which staff do you represent and over which areas?
2. How many members of the workforce do you represent?
3. What types of activities do they undertake?
4. Are there any hazards or dangers associated with the activities of your members?
5. Do you distinguish between health and safety or do you regard them as the same thing?
6. Are there any particular health, as opposed to safety, matters which concern you in your job?

Safety Representatives
7. How many unions are there on site?
8. How many safety reps. are there?
9. Do you have as many as you should have?

10. What contact do you have with other safety reps.?
11. How long have you been a safety rep.?
12. What do you think your main job is as a safety rep.?
13. How much time do you spend on health and safety at work?
14. How did you become a safety rep.?
15. What sort of people become safety reps.?
16. Are the safety reps. also LDC representatives?
17. How long will you be a safety rep.?
18. What were the attractions of the job?
19. What sort of training did you receive for the post? [Probe]
20. Who from?
21. Was it helpful for getting you started?
22. Now that you have been a safety rep. for a while, do you now consider the training to be adequate?
23. Do people know you are the safety rep.?
24. Do many people bring health and safety problems to you?
25. How many approaches would you get in a month?
26. What sort of health and safety problems are brought to you?
27. What do they expect you to do?
28. How do you communicate and consult with your members about health and safety matters?

The Board's Policy for Health and Safety
29. Does the Board have official policies regarding the health and safety of staff? [Probe: what are they? Where would you find them written down?]
30. Do people know what they are?
31. Are there checks to ensure policy is followed? [Probe: what are they?]
32. What do you think about these policies?
33. Does anyone in the company have special responsibility for health and safety?
34. If so, who are they?
35. Do you have joint union/management safety committees?
36. How often do they meet?
37. Who chairs them?
38. Who represents the unions in them?
39. Do you have copies of the minutes?
40. What sort of issues do you discuss?
41. Do you undertake workplace inspections?
42. How often?
43. Are these joint inspections with management?
44. What action follows from safety committees and inspections?
45. What sort of facilities do you have provided for you as a safety representative? [e.g. telephone or room]

The Risks involved with the Railways
46. Is the railways a risky industry to work in?
47. Is it possible for you to compare it with other industries, to say that it is more dangerous than one industry or less dangerous than another?

48. Are there many accidents amongst the workforce?
49. Do you know how many fatalities there were amongst the workforce in BR last year?
50. Do you know how many (a) major staff accidents, (b) staff fatalities there were in your department last year? your region last year? your area last year?
51. What sort of accidents were these? [Probe]
52. What sort of less serious accidents happen in your department?
53. How do they happen?
54. Whose fault are they usually?
55. Are they often accidents that should not have happened, or are they accidents that could not be prevented?
56. How could they be prevented?
57. Do you feel more could be done to reduce staff accidents in your industry? [If yes, what?]
58. How often do you get to hear about accidents?
59. Do you get involved as a safety rep.?
60. In what ways?
61. What sort of impact does an accident have on the workforce?
62. Is there a long-lasting effect?

The Law
63. What health and safety laws and regulations do you have to observe?
64. What do these laws and regulations require you to do? [If don't know, probe: have you heard of the Health and Safety at Work Act?]
65. If yes, what duties does the law put upon your employers regarding health and safety?
66. What duties does the law put upon the workforce regarding health and safety?
67. What do you think about these rules and regulations?
    If no, continue here.
68. What are your sources of information *re* health and safety matters? [Probe: do you get leaflets, magazines, notice boards?
69. Do you get to hear about changes in the law or new regulations?
70. Where from?
71. Is this information usually written down or does someone tell you?

Railway Inspectorate
72. You have told me about the railway's checks upon health and safety, is there anyone else responsible for checking health and safety on the railways? [If no, prompt with government agency responsible for air pollution control. If still no, ask: have you heard of the Railway Inspectorate?]
73. Do you know the name of your local inspector?
74. Do you know what he looks like?
75. Where are the local offices of the Inspectorate?
76. Would you approach these inspectors for advice on health and safety matters?
    If not, why not?
    If yes, what sort of matters?
77. Do you know when an inspector last visited your area?
78. Were you informed of the visit beforehand?

79. Do you think/know if management knew of the visit in advance?
80. What do you think about this?
81. If relevant: who did he speak to during his visit?
82. Did he speak to you or another safety rep?
83. What did he do during the visit?
84. How long did the inspector stay?
85. How frequently are your premises/area inspected?
86. Do you see the same inspector each time?
87. How frequently do you think they should be inspected by an inspector?
88. Did the inspector pass on any information to you (a) during, (b) after the visit?
89. Did you have any problems you wanted to discuss with the inspector?
90. What sort of problems would you discuss with inspectors?
91. Do you take a lot of notice of inspectors' comments? Why?
92. What sort of things do you do, that they ask of you?
93. What sort of things would you ignore—if any?
94. Do inspectors ask you to do anything which you find irritating or unnecessary?
95. Do you find what they say reasonable?
96. How do you get along with the different inspectorates you deal with?
97. How important do you think inspectors are in bringing about higher standards of health and safety in your area of work?
98. Have you ever seen Railway Inspectorate accident reports?
99. Have you found them useful? [Probe]

Legal Action
100. What legal action can inspectors take?
101. How frequently do you think inspectors (a) serve notices, (b) prosecute?
102. Do you know of any prosecutions or notices served? [If yes, probe]
103. Who do they prosecute?
104. What for?
105. Do you know what sort of penalties can be imposed by the courts if someone is found guilty?
106. When the Railway Inspectorate does prosecute, it could prosecute individuals or it could prosecute the Board. Have you any views about who it should prosecute?

Health and Safety Matters: How they affect the Workforce and Management
107. Do the workforce comply willingly with health and safety rules and regulations?
108. Do they, for example, always use the safety equipment provided? [If no, probe]
109. Do they have an interest in *not* complying?
110. How much concern is there amongst the workforce about health and safety? If yes: about what? What have you done about it?
111. What do you think about BR's attitude to health and safety?
112. Do you think that management comply willingly with health and safety rules and regulations?
113. Do you think there is a lot of concern amongst the management about health and safety?
114. If you saw someone not following health and safety rules, what would you do?
115. Have you ever done this? If yes, how often?
116. Do you yourself comply with health and safety demands; if so why [not]?

117. What sort of factors do you take into account when considering whether or not to accept particular health and safety proposals? [e.g. policy changes]
118. When a new health and safety initiative or proposal comes about, what sort of thing gives rise to it?
119. Who usually suggests the changes?
120. Which aspects of your job take priority over health and safety?
121. And which takes less priority?
122. How costly do you think compliance is for your employers?
123. How important do you think health and safety are to your employers in relation to their other responsibilities?
124. How important is it in relation to the workers' other responsibilities?
125. Can you think of any circumstances where health and safety rules may hinder the workforce?
126. What other factors weigh for and against health and safety?
127. What are the major health and safety problems now facing the railways?
128. Finally, do you think that as a safety rep. you are doing something useful?

Thank you very much for your help.

INTERVIEW SCHEDULE FOR WORKFORCE

Basic Facts
1. What is the official title of your job?
2. What does your job involve? [i.e. what are your main activities?]
3. How long have you been in your present job?
4. [If applicable] What did you do before?
5. Are there are hazards/dangers associated with the work you do?
6. What are they?
7. What are the most dangerous activities you undertake?
8. And what do you think are the least dangerous?
9. Do you distinguish between health and safety or do you regard them as the same thing?
10. Are there any particular health, as opposed to safety, matters which concern you in your job?

The Board's Policies for Health and Safety
11. Does the Board have official policies regarding the health and safety of staff? [Probe: What are they? Where would you find them written down?]
12. Do people know what they are?
13. Are there checks to ensure this policy is followed? [Probe: What are they?]
14. What do you think about these policies?
15. Does anyone in the company have special responsibility for health and safety?
16. Who are they?
17. Have you every received any health and safety training for your job?
18. If no, would you have found it useful if you had?
    If yes, when?
19. Who from?

20. Was it helpful when you first started your job?
21. Now you have been in your job for a while, do you still consider the training to be adequate?
22. If you were worried about your health or safety at work who would you talk to?
23. Is there any information about health or safety available to you? Where?
24. Have you ever looked at such information?
25. Was it useful?

Safety Representatives

26. Do you have a safety rep.?
27. If no, ask why and whether they have ever had a safety rep.?
28. If yes, who is it?
29. How often do you see him?
30. How would you contact him?
31. Does he pass on much information about health and safety to you?
32. Is this information useful?
33. Have you ever taken a health or safety problem to your safety rep.? [If yes, probe]
34. If a problem arose would you take it to your safety rep.?
35. What would you expect him to do?
36. Do you think that safety representatives are a good idea?
37. Why?
38. Have you ever thought about becoming a safety rep. yourself?
39. If not, why not?
40. Are there any advantages in becoming a safety rep.?
41. If yes, what are they?
42. Are there any disadvantages?
43. If so, what are they?

The Risks involved with the Railways

44. Is the railways a risky industry to work in?
45. Is it possible for you to compare it with other industries, to say it is more dangerous than one industry, or less dangerous than another?
46. Are there many accidents amongst the workforce?
47. Do you know how many fatalities there were amongst the workforce in BR last year?
48. Do you know how many (a) major staff accidents, (b) staff fatalities there were in your department last year? your region last year? your area last year?
49. What sort of accidents were these? [Probe]
50. How do they happen?
51. Whose fault are they usually?
52. Are they often accidents that should not have happened, or are they accidents that could not be prevented?
53. How could they be prevented?
54. Do you feel more could be done to reduce staff accidents in your industry?
55. How often do you get to hear about accidents?
56. Who/where from?
57. Have you ever been involved in an accident on the railways?

58. If yes, could you tell me about it?
59. What sort of impact does an accident have upon you and your colleagues?
60. Is this a lasting effect?

The Law

61. What health and safety laws do you have to observe?
    [If don't know, probe: have you heard of the Health and Safety at Work Act?]
62. If yes, what do these laws and regulations require you to do?
63. What duties does the law put upon your employers regarding health and safety?
64. What duties do you have?
65. What do you think about these rules and regulations?
66. If no, continue from here.
67. Where does your information about health and safety matters come from?
68. Do you get to hear of changes in the laws or new regulations?
69. Where from?
70. Is this information usually written down or does someone tell you?
71. You have told me about the railway's checks upon health and safety, is there anyone else responsible for checking health and safety on the railways? [If no, prompt with government agency responsible for air pollution control. If still no, ask: have you heard of the Railway Inspectorate?]
72. Do you know the name of your local inspector?
73. Do you know what he looks like?
74. Where are the local offices of the Inspectorate?
75. Do you know when a health and safety inspector last visited your site/area?
76. Did you know about the visit beforehand?
77. Do you think/know if management knew of the visit in advance?
78. What do you think about this?
79. If relevant: who did the inspector speak to when he visited?
80. Did he speak to you?
81. What did he do during his visit?
82. How long did the inspector stay?
83. Did anyone let you know if the inspector found any problems during his visit?
84. If so, who? And how?
85. How frequently is your area inspected by an inspector?
86. Do you see the same inspector each time?
87. How frequently do you think inspectors should visit your area?
88. Do you take a lot of notice of inspectors' comments?
89. Why?
90. What sort of things do you do, that they ask of you?
91. What sort of things would you ignore—if any?
92. Do inspectors ask you to do anything which you find irritating or unnecessary?
93. Do you find what they say reasonable?
94. How important do you think inspectors are in bringing about higher standards of health and safety in your area of work?
95. Have you ever seen Railway Inspectorate accident reports?
96. Have you found them useful? [Probe]
97. What legal action can inspectors take?
98. How frequently do you think inspectors (a) serve notices, (b) prosecute?

99. Do you know of any prosecutions or notices served? [If yes, ask for details]
100. Who do they prosecute?
101. What for?
102. When the Railway Inspectorate does prosecute, it could prosecute individuals or it could prosecute the Board. Have you any views about who it should prosecute? I now want to ask you some questions about how health and safety matters affect you personally.
103. Are you provided with any special health and safety equipment? [Probe: such as a high visibility vest or bump cap?]
104. How often do you use it?
105. Does this equipment help or hinder your work or does it make no difference?
106. Have you ever ignored a health and safety regulation or the rule book?
107. If no, can you think of any circumstance when you might ignore a health and safety precaution?
    If yes, can you give me an example?
108. Do health and safety considerations make any differences to the way in which you do your work? [e.g. speed, ease].
109. What do you think about this?
110. If your supervisor/boss discovered that you had not followed the health and safety rules what would he do?
111. Has he ever done this?
112. What should happen to you if you break the rules?
113. Does this worry you?
114. How important do you think health and safety matters are in relation to your other jobs?
115. Is there anything at work which you think is a risk to your health or safety?
116. If yes, what do you think should be done about this?
117. Have you raised the problem with anyone?
118. Finally, what do you think are the major health and safety problems now facing the railways?

Thank you very much for your help.

REFERENCES

AALDERS, M. (1993) 'Regulation and In-Company Environmental Management in the Netherlands', *Law and Policy* 15/2: 75–94.

ABOLAFIA, M. Y. (1985) 'Self-Regulation as Market Maintenance', in R. Noll (ed.), *Regulatory Policy and the Social Sciences*, Berkeley: University of California Press.

ADLER, R., and PRITTLE, D. (1984) 'Cajolery or Command: Are Education Campaigns an Adequate Substitute for Regulation?' *Yale Journal of Regulation* 1/2.

ALDERMAN, G. (1973) *The Railway Interest*, Leicester: Leicester University Press.

ATHERLEY, G. R. C., BOOTH, R. T., and KELLY, M. J. (1975) 'Workers' Involvement in Occupational Health and Safety in Britain', *International Labour Review* 2: 469–82.

AYRES, I., and BRAITHWAITE, J. (1992) *Responsive Regulation*, New York: Oxford University Press.

BAGWELL, P. S. (1963) *The Railwaymen: The History of the National Union of Railwaymen*, London: George Allen & Unwin Ltd.

—— (1984) *End of the Line? The Fate of British Railways Under Thatcher*, London: Verso.

—— (1996) *The Transport Crisis in Britain*, Nottingham: Spokesman, for European Labour Forum.

BAILEY, C. W., and PETERSON, D. (1989) 'Using Perception Surveys to Assess Safety System Effectiveness', *Professional Safety* (Feb.): 22–6.

BALDWIN, R. (1995) *Rules and Government*, Oxford: Clarendon Press.

—— (1997) 'Regulation: After "Command and Control" ', in K. Hawkins (ed.), *The Human Face of the Law*, Oxford: Clarendon Press.

—— and HAWKINS, K. H. (1984) 'Discretionary Justice: Davis Reconsidered', *Public Law*: 570–99.

BALL, H., and FRIEDMAN, L. (1965) 'The Use of the Criminal Sanctions in The Enforcement of Economic Legislation: A Sociological View', *Stanford Law Preview* 17: 197–223.

BARDACH, E., and KAGAN, R. (1982) *Going by the Book: The Problem of Regulatory Unreasonableness*, Philadelphia: Temple University Press.

BARRETT, B. (1977) 'Safety Representatives, Industrial Relations and Hard Times', *Industrial Law Journal* 63 (Sept.): 165–78.

—— HOWELLS, R., and JAMES , P. (1985a) 'Employee Participation in Health and Safety: The Impact of the Legislative Provisions: First Report of a Survey of Thirty Organisations', London: Middlesex Polytechnic Business School.

—— —— —— (1985b) *Employee Participation in Health and Safety: The Impact of the Legislative Provision*, London: Middlesex Polytechnic Business School.

BARRILE, L. (1995) 'Why Not Lock 'em Up? A Humanist Realist Strategy for Combating Corporate Violence', *Quarterly Journal of Ideology* 18/3–4 (Dec.): 67–106.

BARTRIP, P. W. J., and BURMAN, S. (1983) *The Wounded Soldiers of Industry*, Oxford: Clarendon Press.

BAUCUS, M., and DWORKIN, T. M. (1991) 'What is Corporate Crime? It is Not Illegal Corporate Behaviour', *Law and Policy* 13/3: 231–44.

BEAUMONT, P. B. (1981*a*) 'The Nature of the Relationship between Safety Representatives and Their Workforce Constituencies', *Industrial Relations Journal* 12/2: 53–60.

—— (1981*b*) 'Explaining Variation in the Enterprise Response to Industrial Relations Legislation: the Case of the Safety Representative Regulations', *Personnel Review* 10/1: 11–15.

—— and LEOPOLD, J. W. (1984) 'The Motivation, Activities and Turnover of Union Safety Representatives: Some Evidence from Britain', *Work and People* 10/2: 25–9.

—— —— and COYLE, J. R. (1982) 'The Safety Officer: An Emerging Management Role?' *Personnel Review* 11/2: 35–8.

BECK, U. (1992) *Risk Society: Towards a New Modernity*, London: Sage.

BECKER, G. S. (1989) 'Political Competition among Interest Groups', in J. F. Shogren (ed.), *The Political Economy of Government Regulation*, Boston: Kluwer.

BERNSTEIN, P. L. (1996) *Against the Gods: the Remarkable Story of Risk*, New York: John Wiley & Sons.

BLACK, J. (1997) *Rules and Regulators*, Oxford: Clarendon Press.

BOYER, B., and MEIDINGER, E. (1985) 'Privatizing Regulatory Enforcement: A Preliminary Assessment of Citizen Suits under Federal Environmental Laws', *Buffalo Law Review* 34: 833–964.

BRADSHAW, B., and MASON, L. (1994) 'Rail Privatisation: Facts, Issues and Opportunities', Oxford: Oxford Economic Research Associates Ltd.

BRAITHWAITE, J. (1981) 'The Limits of Economism in Controlling Harmful Corporate Conduct', *Law and Society Review* 16/3: 481–504.

—— (1984) *Corporate Crime in the Pharmaceutical Industry*, London: Routledge & Kegan Paul.

—— (1985) *To Punish or Persuade: Enforcement of Coal Mine Safety*, Albany, NY: New York Press.

—— (1989) *Crime, Shame and Reintegration*, 226 edn., Cambridge: Cambridge University Press.

—— GRABOSKY, P., and WALKER, J. (1987) 'An Enforcement Taxonomy of Regulatory Agencies', *Law & Policy* 9: 323–51.

BRAITHWAITE, V., BRIATHWAITE, J., GIBSON, D., and MAKKAI, T. (1994) 'Regulatory Styles, Motivational Postures and Nursing Home Compliance', *Law & Policy* 16/4 (Oct.): 363–94.

BRICKMAN, R., JASANOFF, S., and IILGEN, T. (1985) *Controlling Chemicals: The Politics of Regulation in Europe and the United States*, Ithaca, NY and London: Cornell University Press.

BRITISH RAILWAYS BOARD (1963) *The Reshaping of British Railways*, Great Britain: Central Office of Information.

—— (1988) *Statement of Safety Policy*, London: British Railways Board.

—— (1991) *Safety Plan 1991*, London: British Railways Board.

BRITTAN, Y. (1984) *The Impact of Water Pollution Control on Industry*, Oxford: Centre for Socio-Legal Studies.

BROADBENT, D. E., REASON, J., and BADDELEY, A. (1989) 'Human Factors in Hazardous Situations', *Royal Society Discussion Meeting*, London: Royal Society of London.

BROOKS, N., and DOOB, A. N. (1990) 'Tax Evasion; Searching for a Theory of Compliant Behaviour', in M. L. Friendland (ed.), *Securing Compliance*, Toronto: University of Toronto Press.

BUGLER, J. (1972) *Polluting Britain*, Harmondsworth: Penguin.

BUREAU OF LABOR STATISTICS (1993) 'Occupational Injuries and Illnesses in the United States by Industry 1991', Washington: US Department of Labor.

BURK, J. (1988) *Values in the Market Place: the American Stock Market Under Federal Securities Law*, Berlin: de Gruyter.

CABLE, S., and BENSON, M. (1993) 'Acting Locally: Environmental Injustice and the Emergence of Grass-Roots Environmental Organizations', *Social Problems* 40/4: 464–77.

CAPRIO, G. J., and KLINGEBIEL, D. (1996) 'Bank Insolvencies: Cross Country Experience', Washington: World Bank.

CARSON, W. G. (1970) 'Some Sociological Aspects of Strict Liability and the Enforcement of Factory Legislation', *Modern Law Review*: 396–412.

—— (1974) 'Symbolic and Instrumental Dimensions of Early Factory Legislation: A Case Study in the Social Origins of Criminal Law', in R. Hood (ed.), *Crime, Criminology and Public Policy*, London: Heinemann.

—— (1980) 'The Institutionalisation of Ambiguity: Early British Factory Acts', in G. Geis and E. Stotland (eds.), *White Collar Crime: Theory and Research*, Beverly Hills, Calif.: Sage.

—— (1982) *The Other Price of Britain's Oil*, Oxford: Martin Robertson.

CHANNON, G. (1996) 'A. D. Chandler's "Visible Hand" in Transport History: A Review Article', in Gourvish (1996).

CHEIT, R. E. (1990) *Setting Safety Standards: Regulation in the Public and Private Sectors*, Berkeley: University of California Press.

CHELIUS, J., and SMITH, R. (1987) 'Firm Size and Regulatory Costs: The Case of Workers' Compensation Insurance', *Journal of Policy Analysis and Management* 6/2.

CLARKE, L. (1989) *Acceptable Risk? Making Decisions in a Toxic Environment*, Berkeley: University of California Press.

—— (1999) *Mission Improbable: Using Fantasy Documents to Tame Disaster*, Chicago: University of Chicago Press.

CLAY, T. R. (1984) 'Combating Cancer in the Workplace: Implementation of the California Occupational Carcinogens Control Act', University of California.

CLINARD, M., YEAGER, P., and CLINARD, R. (1980) *Corporate Crime*, London: Collier Macmillan.

COHEN, A. V. (1996) 'Quantitive Risk Assessment and Decisions about Risk', in Hood and Jones (1996).

COHEN, S. (1985) *Visions of Social Control: Crime, Punishment and Classification*, Cambridge: Polity.

COLEBATCH, H. K. (1989) 'The Concept of Regulation in the Analysis of the Organised World', *Law and Policy* 11/1: 71–237.

COMMITTEE OF INQUIRY (1986) *Outbreak of Food Poisoning at Stanley Royal Hospital: Report of the Committee of Inquiry*, London: HMSO.

COMMITTEE ON THE REVIEW OF RAILWAY FINANCES (1983) *Railway Finances: Report of a Committee Chaired by Sir David Serpell*, London: HMSO.

CRANSTON, R. (1978) *Consumers and the Law*, London: Weidenfeld & Nicolson.

—— (1979) *Regulatory Business: Law and Consumer Agencies*, London: Macmillan.

CROALL, H. (1992) *White Collar Crime*, Buckingham: Open University Press.

CULLEN (1990) 'The Public Inquiry into the Piper Alpha Disaster', London: HMSO.

CUTTER, S. L. (1993) *Living with Risk*, Sevenoaks: Edward Arnold.

DALTON, A. (1998) *Safety, Health and Environmental Hazards in the Workplace*: London: Continuum Publishing Group.

DAVIS, K. C. (1969) *Discretionary Justice*, Baton Rouge, La.: Louisiana State University Press.

DAWSON, S., WILLMAN, P., BAMFORD, M., and CLINTON, A. (1988) *Safety at Work: The Limits of Self-Regulation*, Cambridge: Cambridge University Press.

DENT, J. F. (1991) 'Accounting and Organizational Cultures: A Field Study of the Emergence of a New Organizational Reality', *Accounting, Organizations and Society* 16/8: 705–32.

DEPARTMENT OF TRANSPORT (1981) *Requirements for Level Crossings*, London: HMSO.

—— (1984) *Britain during the year 1983*, London: HMSO.

—— (1987) *Report on the Safety Record of the Railways in Great Britain during 1986*, London: HMSO.

—— (1992) *New Opportunities for the Railways: The Privatisation of British Rail*, London: HMSO.

—— (1994) *Britain's Railways: A New Era*, London: HMSO.

DIMAGGIO, P. J., and POWELL, W. W. (1991) *The New Institutionalism in Organizational Analysis*, Chicago: University of Chicago Press.

DI MENTO, J. F. (1986) *Environmental Law and American Business: Dilemmas of Compliance*, New York: Plenum Press.

—— (1989) 'Can Social Science Explain Organisational Non-Compliance with Environmental Law?', *Journal of Social Issues* 45/1: 109–32.

DODD, N., and HUTTER, B. M. (2000) 'Geopolitics and the Regulation of Economic Life', *Law & Policy* 22/2: 1–24.

DONOVAN, J., and BLAKE, D. (1992) 'Patient Non-Compliance: Deviance or Reasoned Decision-Making?' *Social Science and Medicine* 34/5 (Mar.): 507–13.

DOUGLAS, M., and WILDAVSKY, A. (1982) *Risk and Culture*, Berkeley: University of California Press.

DRAKE, K., and WILDAVSKY, A. (1990) 'Theories of Risk Perception: Who Fears What and Why?' *Daedalus* 119/4.

DWYER, J. P. (1990) 'The Pathology of Symbolic Legislation', *Ecology Law Quarterly* 17: 233–316.

—— (1993) 'The Use of Market Incentives in Controlling Air Pollution: California's Marketable Permits Program', *Ecology Law Quarterly* 20: 103–17.

EDELMAN, L. B., PETTERSON, S., CHAMBLISS, E., and ERLANGER, H. S. (1991) 'Legal Ambiguity and the Politics of Compliance: Affirmative Action Officers' Dilemma', *Law & Policy* 13/1 (Jan.): 74–97.

EMCKE, I. (1992) 'Medical Authority and its Discontents: A Case of Organised Non-Compliance', *Critical Sociology* 17/3.

ERICSON, R. V. and HAGGERTY, K. D. (1997) *Policing the Risk Society*, Toronto and Buffalo: University of Toronto Press.

FEDERAL RAILROAD ADMINISTRATION (1998) *Railroad Statistics: Annual Report 1997*, Washington: US Department of Transportation.

FELSTINER, W. L. F., and SARAT, A. (1995) *The Process of Negotiation*, New York: Oxford University Press.

FENNELL, P. (1988) *Investigation into the King's Cross Underground Fire*, London: HMSO.

FISSE, B., and BRAITHWAITE, J. (1983) *The Impact of Publicity on Corporate Offenders*, Albany, NY: State University of New York Press.

FOREMAN-PECK, J., and MILLWARD, A. (1994) *Public and Private Ownership of British Industry*, Milton Keynes: Open University Press.

FROUD, J., and OGUS, A. (1996) ' "Rational Social Regulation and Compliance Cost Assessment" ', *Public Administration* 74: 221–37.

GABE, J. (ed.) (1995) *Medicine, Health and Risk: Sociological Approaches*, Oxford: Blackwell.

GARLAND, D. (ed.) (1990) *Justice, Guilt and Forgiveness in the Penal System*, xviii, Edinburgh: University of Edinburgh Centre for Theology and Public Issues.

GENERAL, MUNICIPAL, BOILERMAKERS AND ALLIED TRADES UNION (1986) 'The Freedom to Kill?' GMB Health & Safety Policy Paper.

GENN, H. (1987) *Hard Bargaining: Out of Court Settlement in Personal Injury Actions*, Oxford: Clarendon Press.

—— (1993) 'Business Responses to the Regulation of Health and Safety in England', *Law and Policy* 15: 219.

GIDDENS, A. (1990) *The Consequences of Modernity*, Cambridge: Polity Press.

—— (1994) *Beyond Left and Right: The Future of Radical Politics*, Cambridge: Polity.

GILBOY, J. (1998) 'Compelled Third-Party Participation in the Regulatory Process: Legal Duties, Culture and Non-Compliance', *Law and Policy* 20/2: 135–55.

GLENDON, A. I. (1977a) 'The Role and Training of Safety Representatives', *Occupational Safety and Health* 7/11: 35–6.

—— (1977b) 'The Role and Training of Safety Representatives (part 2)', *Occupational Safety and Health* 7/12: 37–9.

—— and BOOTH, R. T. (1982) 'Worker Participation in Occupational Health and Safety in Britain', *International Labour Review* 12/4 (July–Aug.): 399–416.

GOURVISH, T. (1980) *Railways and the British Economy 1830–1914*, London: Macmillan.

—— (1986) *British Railways 1948–73: A Business History*, Cambridge: Cambridge University Press.

—— (1990) 'British Rail's Business-Led Organisation, 1977–1990: Government–Industry Relations', *Britain's Public Sector—Business History Review* (Review 64): 109–49.

—— (ed.) (1996) *Railways*, Brookfield, Vt.: Scolar Press.

—— (1997) 'The Regulation of Britain's Railways', in J. McConville (ed.), *Transport Regulation Matters*, London: Pinter.

GRÄBE, S. (1991) 'Regulatory Agencies and Interest Groups in Occupational Health and Safety in Great Britain and West Germany: A Perspective from West Germany', *Law & Policy* 13/1 (Jan.): 55–72.

GRABOSKY, P. (1994) 'Green Markets: Environmental Regulation by the Private Sector', *Law and Policy* 16(4): 419–48.

—— (1995a) 'Using Non-Governmental Resources to Foster Regulatory Compliance', *Governance* 8/4: 527–50.

—— (1995b) 'Counterproductive Regulation', *International Journal of the Sociology of Law* 23: 347–69.

——(1995c) 'Regulation by Reward: On the Use of Incentives as Regulatory Instruments', *Law and Policy* 17/3: 257–82.

—— and BRAITHWAITE, J. (1986) *Of Manners Gentle*, Melbourne: Open University Press.

GRAHAM, C., and PROSSER, T. (1991) *Privatising Public Enterprises*, Milton Keynes: Open University Press.

GRANOVETTER, M., and SWEDBERG, R. (1992) *The Sociology of Economic Life*, Boulder, Colo.: Westview Press.

GRAY, W. B., and SCHOLZ, J. T. (1991) 'Analyzing the Equity and Efficiency of OSHA Enforcement', *Law & Policy* 13/3: 185–214.

GREEN, J. (1995) 'Accidents and the Risk Society: Some Problems with Prevention', in R. Bunton, S. Nettleton, and R. Burrows (eds.), *The Sociology of Health Promotion: Critical Analyses of Consumption, Lifestyle and Risk*, London: Routledge.

GRICAR, B. (1983) 'A Preliminary Theory of Compliance with OSHA Regulation', *Research in Corporate Social Performance and Policy* 5: 121–41.

—— and HOPKINS, H. (1983) 'How does Your Company Respond to OSHA', *Personnel Administrator* (Apr.): 53–7.

GUNNINGHAM, N. (1974) *Pollution, Social Interest and the Law*, London: Martin Robertson.

—— (1984) *Safeguarding the Worker*, Sydney: The Law Book Company.

—— (1995) 'Enforcement, Self-Regulation, and the Chemical Industry: Assessing Responsible Care', *Law & Policy* 17/1: 57–109.

—— and SINCLAIR, D. (1999) 'Designing Smart Regulation', in Hutter (1999).

HAHN, R. W. (1989) 'The Political Economy of Environmental Regulation: Towards a Unifying Framework', *Public Choice* 65: 21–47.

HANCHER, L., and MORAN, M. (1989) *Capitalism, Culture and Regulation*, Oxford: Clarendon Press.

HARDY, H.N. (1989) *Beeching—Champion of the Railways?* Shepperton: Ian Allan.

HASSELDINE, J. (1993) 'How do Revenue Audits Affect Taxpayer Compliance?', *Bulletin for International Fiscal Documentation* 47/7–8.

HAWKINS, K. (1983) 'Bargain and Bluff: Compliance Strategy and Deterrence in the Enforcement of Regulation', *Law and Policy Quarterly* 95: 35–73.

—— (1989*a*) ' "Fatcats" and Prosecution in a Regulatory Agency: A Footnote on the Social Construction of Risk', *Law and Policy* 11/3: 370–91.

—— (1989*b*) 'Rule and Discretion in Comparative Perspective: The Case of Social Regulation', *Ohio State Law Journal* 50/3: 663–79.

—— (1992*a*) 'The Regulation of Occupational Health and Safety: A Socio-Legal Perspective', London: Health and Safety Executive.

—— (ed.) (1992*b*) *The Uses of Discretion*, Oxford: Clarendon Press.

——, and THOMAS, J. (1984) *Environment and Enforcement: Regulation and Social Definition of Pollution*, Oxford: Clarendon Press.

——, and THOMAS, J. (1984) (eds.) (1984) *Enforcing Regulation*, Boston: Kluwer-Nijhoff.

HEIMER, C. A. (1988) 'Social Structure, Psychology and the Estimation of Risk', *Annual Review of Sociology* 14: 491–519.

—— (1992) 'Your Baby's Just Fine: Certification Procedures, Meetings and the Supply of Information in Neonatal Intensive Care Units', in Short and Clarke (1992).

—— (1996) 'Explaining Variation in the Impact of Law: Organisations, Institutions and Professions', *Studies in Law, Politics and Society* 15: 29–59.

HENSHAW, D. (1991) *The Great Railway Conspiracy: The Rise and Fall of Britain's Railways since the 1950s*, Burtersett: Leading Edge Press.

HIDDEN, A. (1989) *Investigation into the Clapham Junction Railway Accident*, London: HMSO.

HOME OFFICE (2000) *Reforming the Law on Involuntary Manslaughter: The Government's Proposals*, London: Home Office.

HOOD, C., and JONES, D. K. C. (1996) *Accident and Design*, London: UCL Press.

HORLICK-JONES, T. (1996) 'Is Safety a By-Product of Quality Management?', in Hood and Jones (1996).

HORWITZ, A. V. (1990) *The Logic of Social Control*, New York and London: Plenum Press.

HOWELLS, R. W. L. (1974) 'Worker Participation in Safety: The Development of Legal Rights', *Industrial Law Journal* 3/2: 87–95.

HSC (1988) *Annual Report 1987–88*, London: HMSO.

—— (1990) *Annual Report 1988–89*, London: HMSO.

—— (1991) *Annual Report 1990–91*, London: HMSO.

—— (1992) *Annual Report 1991–92*, London: HMSO.

—— (1998) *Annual Report and Accounts 1997/1998*, London: HSE Books.

—— (1999*a*) *Train Accident at Ladbroke Grove Junction, 5 October 1999: First HSE Interim Report, October 1999*, London: HMSO.

—— (1999*b*) *Second Interim Report on the Ladbroke Grove Railway Accident, 29 October 1999*, London: HMSO.

—— (1999*c*) *The Interim Report of the Review of Arrangements for Standard Setting and Application on the Main Railway Network*, London: HMRI.

—— (2000) *Levels and Trends in Workplace Injury: Reported Injuries and the Labour Force Survey*, www.hse.gov.uk/hsestats

HSE (1995*a*) *Railway Safety: HM Chief Inspecting Officer of Railways' Annual Report on the Safety Record of the Railways in Great Britain during 1994/95*, London: HMSO.

—— (1995*b*) *Railway Safety: HM Chief Inspecting Officer of Railways' Annual Report on the Safety Record of the Railways in Great Britain during 1993/94*, London: HSE Books.

—— (1996) *Railway Safety: HM Chief Inspecting Officer of Railways' Annual Report on the Safety Record of the Railways in Great Britain during 1995/96*, London: HSE Books.

—— (1997) *Railway Safety: HM Chief Inspecting Officer of Railways' Annual Report on the Safety Record of the Railways in Great Britain during 1996/97*, London: HSE Books.

—— (1998) *Railway Safety: HM Chief Inspecting Officer of Railways' Annual Report on the Safety Record of the Railways in Great Britain during 1997/98*, London: HSE Books.

—— (1999) *Railway Safety: HM Chief Inspecting Office of Railways' Annual Report on the Safety Record of the Railways in Great Britain during 1998/99*, London: HSE Books.

—— (2000*a*) *A Report on Some General Issues Arising from the Internal Inquiry into Events Leading up to the Ladbroke Grove Rail Accident*, London: HSE.

—— (2000*b*) *Internal Inquiry Report: Events Leading up to the Ladbroke Grove Rail Accident*, London: HSE.

—— (2000*c*) *Railtrack's Safety and Standards Directorate Review of Main Functions and their Locations*, London: HSE.

—— (2000*d*) *Statement of Witness: Ladbroke Grove Rail Inquiry Part 1*, www.hse.gov.uk/railway/paddrail/witness.htm.

—— (2000*e*) *Third Interim Report: Train Accident at Ladbroke Grove Junction, 5 October 1999*, London: HSE.

HUTTER, B. M. (1988) *The Reasonable Arm of the Law? The Law Enforcement Procedures of Environmental Health Officers*, Oxford: Clarendon Press.

—— (1992) 'Public Accident Inquiries: The Case of the Railway Inspectorate', *Public Administration* 70: 177–92.

—— (1993) 'Regulating Employers and Employees: Health and Safety in the Workplace', *Journal of Law and Society* 20/4: 452–70.

—— (1997) *Compliance: Regulation and Environment*, Oxford: Clarendon Press.

—— (1999) *A Reader in Environmental Law*, Oxford: Clarendon Press.

—— and LLOYD-BOSTOCK, S. (1990) 'The Power of Accidents: The Social and Psychological Impact of Accidents and the Enforcement of Safety Regulations', *British Journal of Criminology* 30: 453–65.

—— ——(1992) 'Field Level Perceptions of Risk in Regulatory Agencies', in J. Short and L. Clarke (eds.), *Risky Decision Making: Complexity and Context*, Boulder, Colo: Westview Press.

—— and MANNING, P. K. (1990) 'The Contexts of Regulation: Impact on the Health and Safety Inspectorate in Britain', *Law and Policy* 12/2: 103–36.

—— and SORENSON, P. (1993) 'Business Adaptation to Legal Regulation', *Law and Policy* 15/3: 169–78.

ILGRA (1998) *Risk Assessment and Risk Management: Improving Policy and Practices within Government Departments: Second Report Prepared by the Interdepartmental Liaison Group on Risk Assessment*, London: www.hse.gov.uk.

INGLEBY, R. (1992) *Solicitors and Divorce*, Oxford: Clarendon Press.

JAMES, C. (1993) 'Social Processes and Reporting or Non-Reporting', in M. Quinlan (ed.), *Work and Health*, South Melbourne: Macmillan.

JAMES, P., and WALTERS, D. (1999) *Regulating Health and Safety at Work: The Way Forward*, London: The Institute of Employment Rights.

JASANOFF, S. (1991) 'Cross-National Differences in Policy Implementation', *Evaluation Review* 15/1: 103–19.

—— MARKLE, G. E., PETERSON, J. C., and PINCH, T. (eds.) (1995) *Handbook of Science and Technology Studies*, London: Sage.

JASPER, J. W. (1992) 'Three Nuclear Energy Controversies', in D. Nelkin (ed.), *Controversy: Politics of Technical Decisions*, 3rd Edn., London: Sage.

JORIAN, P. (2000) 'Value, Risk and Control: the call for Integration', *The Financial Times (Mastering Risk)* (16 May).

JUSTICE (1980) *Breaking the Rules*, London: Justice.

KADISH, M., and KADISH, S. (1973) *Discretion to Disobey: A Study of Lawful Departures from Legal Rules*, Stanford, Calif.: Stanford University Press.

KAGAN, R. A. (1978) *Regulatory Justice*, New York: Russell Sage Foundation.

—— (1994) 'Regulatory Enforcement', in D. H. Rosenbloom and R. D. Schwartz (eds.), *Handbook of Regulation and Administrative Law*, New York: Marcel Dekker.

—— and SCHOLZ, J. T. (1984) 'The "Criminology of the Corporation" and Regulatory Enforcement Strategies', in Hawkins and Thomas (1984*b*).

KELMAN, S. (1981) *Regulating America, Regulating Sweden: A Comparative Study of Occupational Safety and Health Policy*, Cambridge, Mass.: MIT Press.

KOCHAN, T. A., DYER, L., and LIPSKY, D. B. (1977) *The Effectiveness of Union-Management Safety and Health Committees*, Kalamazoo, Mich.: W. E. Upjohn Institute for Employment Research.

KOLKO, G. (1965) *Railroads and Regulation, 1877–1916*, Princeton, NJ: Princeton University Press.

KOSTAL, R. W. (1994) *Law and English Railway Capitalism*, Oxford: Clarendon Press.

KRIMSKY, S., and GOLDING, D. (eds.) (1992) *Social Theories of Risk*, Westport, Conn.: Praeger.

LA TROBE (1990) *Occupational Health and Safety Project*, Melbourne: La Trobe.

LEOPOLD, J. W., and BEAUMONT, P. B. (1982) 'Safety Policies—How Effective are they?' *Occupational Safety and Health* 12/10: 24–6.

LEVY, D. (1994) 'Talking a Green Game: Corporate Environmentalism Shows its True Colors', *Dollars and Sense* 193/14–17: 40–1.

LEWIS, D. (1974) 'An Industrial Relations Approach', *The Industrial Law Journal* 3/2: 96–104.

LINDGREN, C., GARCIA, G., and SAAL, M. (1996) *Bank Soundness and Macroeconomic Policy*, Washington: IMF.

LLEWELLYN, D. (1999) 'The Economic Rationale for Financial Regulation', *FSA Occasional Paper* (Series 1).

LLOYD-BOSTOCK, S. (1992) 'The Psychology of Routine Discretion: Accident Screening by British Factory Inspectors', *Law and Policy* 14: 45–76.

LOFQUIST, W. S., COHEN, M. A., and RABE, M. A. (eds.) (1997) *Debating Corporate Crime*, Highland Heights, Ky: Academy of Criminal Justice Sciences, Northern Kentucky University.

MAJONE, G. (ed.) (1989) *Deregulation or Reregulation*, London: Pinter.

MAKKAI, T., and BRAITHWAITE, J. (1993) 'The Limits of the Economic Analysis of Regulation: An Empirical Case and a Case for Empiricism', *Law and Policy* 15/4: 271–325.

—— —— (1994) 'The Dialectics of Corporate Deterrence', *Journal of Research in Crime and Delinquency* 31(4): 347–73.

MANNING, P. K. (1977) *Police Work: The Social Organisation of Policing*, Cambridge, Mass.: MIT Press.

—— (1992*a*) 'Big Bang Decisions: Notes on a Naturalistic Approach', in Hawkins (1992*b*).

—— (1992*b*) 'Technological Dramas and the Police: Statement and Counterstatement in Organisational Analysis', *Criminology* 30/3: 327–46.

—— (1992*c*) 'Nuclear Incidents: Accidents, Violations of the Status Quo or Crimes?' *Industrial Crisis Quarterly* 6: 99–113.

MASSEY, J. (1979) 'Deterrence: A Social Learning Approach', Midwest Sociological Association Paper.

MEULBROEK, L. (2000) 'Total Strategies for Company-Wide Risk Control', *The Financial Times (Mastering Risk)* (9 May).

MILLER, K., and STURDIVANT, F. (1977) 'Consumer Responses to Socially Corporate Behaviour: An Empirical Test', *Journal of Consumer Research* 4/1.

MILLWARD, N. E. A. *et al.* (1992) *First Findings from the (1990) Workplace Industrial Relations Survey*, London: Department of Employment.

MINISTRY OF TRANSPORT (1968) *Report of the Public Inquiry into the Accident at Hixon Level Crossing on January 6th (1968)*, London: HMSO.

MITNICK, B. (1980) *The Political Economy of Regulation*, New York: Columbia University Press.

NATIONAL OCCUPATIONAL HEALTH AND SAFETY COMMISSION (1998) *Compendium of Workers' Compensation Statistics Australia 1996/97*, Canberra: National Occupational Health and Safety Commission.

NELKIN, D. (ed.) (1985) *The Language of Risk: Conflicting Perspectives on Occupational Health*, Beverly Hills, Calif.: Sage Publications.

—— (ed.) (1992) *Controversy: Politics of Technical Divisions*, 3rd edn., London: Sage.

—— and BROWN, M. S. (1984) *Workers at Risk: Voices from the Workplace*, Chicago: University of Chicago Press.

NICHOLS, T. (1999) *The Sociology of Industrial Injury*, London: Mansell.

NOLL, R. (ed.) (1985) *Regulatory Policy and the Social Sciences*, Berkeley: University of California Press.

NOVAK, W. J. (1996) *The People's Welfare: Law & Regulation in Nineteenth Century America*, Chapel Hill, NC: University of North Carolina Press.

OGUS, A. (1994) *Regulation: Legal Form and Economic Theory*, Oxford: Clarendon Press.

OLSEN, M. (1982) *The Rise and Decline of Nations: Economic Growth, Stagflation and Social Rigidities*, New Haven: Yale University Press.

OLSEN, P. (1992) *Six Cultures of Regulation*, Copenhagen: Copenhagen Business School.

OWENS, S. (1990) 'The Unified Pollution Inspectorate and Best Practicable Environmental Option in the United Kingdom', in N. Haigh and E. Irwin (eds.), *Integrated Pollution Policy Control in Europe and North America*, Washington: The Conservation Foundation.

PARRIS, H. (1965) *Government and the Railways in the Nineteenth Century*, London: Routledge & Kegan Paul.

PAULUS, I. (1974) *The Search for Pure Food*, London: Martin Robertson.

PEARCE, F. (1976) *Crimes of the Powerful*, London: Pluto Press.

—— and TOMBS, S. (1990) 'Ideology, Hegemony, and Empiricism', *British Journal of Criminology* 30/4: 423–43.

PERROW, C. (1984) *Normal Accidents*, New York: Basic Books.

POLANYI, K. (1975) *The Great Transformation*, New York: Octagon Books.

POLLAK, R. A. (1995) 'Regulating Risks', *Journal of Economic Literature* 33: 179–91.

POLLNAC, R., POGGIE, J., and others (1995) 'Cultural Adaptation to Danger and the Safety of Commercial Oceanic Fisherman', *Human Organisation* 54/2.

PORTER, M. E. (1990) *The Competitive Advantage of Nations*, London: Collier Macmillan.

POWER, M. (1997) *The Audit Society: Rituals of Verification*, Oxford: Clarendon Press.

RAILTRACK (1993) *Railtrack: A Guide for Operators of Independent Passenger Services*, London: Railtrack.

—— (1995) *Railway Group Safety Plan 1994/95*, London: Railtrack plc.

—— (1996) *Railway Group Safety Plan 1995/1996*, London: Railtrack plc.

RAILWAY GAZETTE INTERNATIONAL (1994), *Railway Gazette International*.

RAILWAY INSPECTORATE (1996) *Plan of Work 1996–97*, London: HMSO.

RAYNER, S. (1991) 'A Cultural Perspective on the Structure and Implementation of Global Environmental Agreements', *Evaluation Review* 15/1: 75–102.

RAYNOR, D. (1994) 'Automatic Train Protection', *Value for Money in Transport Safety Measures*, The Royal Society of Medicine.

REES, J. (1988) *Reforming the Workplace: A Study of Self-Regulation in Occupational Safety*, Philadelphia: University of Pennsylvania Press.

—— (1994) *Hostages of Each Other: The Transformation of Nuclear Safety since Three Mile Island*, Chicago: Chicago University Press.

REISS, A. (1984) 'Selecting Strategies of Social Control over Organisational Life', in Hawkins and Thomas (1984a).

—— (1992) 'The Institutionalisation of Risk', in Short and Clarke (1992).

RENN, O. (1992) 'Concepts of Risk: A Classification', in Krimsky and Golding (1992).

REPORT OF THE HOUSE OF REPRESENTATIVES STANDING COMMITTEE ON ABORIGINAL AFFAIRS (1964) 'The Effects of Asbestos Mining on the Baryugil Community', Canberra: Australian Government Publishing Service.

RICHARDSON, G. M., OGUS, A. I., and BURROWS, P. (1983) *Policing Pollution: a Study of Regulation and Enforcement*, Oxford: Clarendon Press.

RIMINGTON, J. (1992) 'Overview of Risk Assessment', *Risk Assessment Conference*, Queen Elizabeth II Conference Centre, London.

ROBENS (1972) *Safety and Health at Work—Report of the Committee*, London: HMSO.

ROCK, P. (1973) *Making People Pay*, London: Routledge & Kegan Paul.

—— (1995) 'Sociology and the Stereotype of the Police', *Journal of Law & Society* 22/1: 17–25.

ROSE-ACKERMAN, S. (1992) *Rethinking the Progressive Agenda: The Reform of the American Regulatory State*, New York: Free Press.

SELZNICK, P. (1980) *Law, Society, and Industrial Justice*, New Brunswick, NJ: Transaction Books.

SHEARING, C. (1993) 'A Constitutive Conception of Regulation', in P. Grabosky and J. Braithwaite (eds.), *Business Regulation and Australia's Future*, Canberra: Australian Institute of Criminology.

SHORT, J. F., and CLARKE, L. (eds.) (1992) *Organisations, Uncertainties and Risk*, Boulder, Colo.: Westview Press.

SIGLER, J. A., and MURPHY, J. E. (1988) *Interactive Corporate Compliance: An Alternative to Regulatory Compulsion*, New York: Quorum Books.

SITKIN, S. B., and BIES, R. J. (1994) *The Legalistic Organization*, Thousand Oaks, Calif.: Sage.

SLOVIC, P. (1992) 'Perception of Risk: Reflections on the Psychometric Paradigm', in Krimsky and Golding (1992).

SMELSER, N. J., and SWEDBERG, R. (1994) *The Handbook of Economic Sociology*, New York: Princeton University Press.

SMITH, N. (1990) *Morality and the Market: Consumer Pressure for Corporate Accountability*, London: Routledge.

SMITH, R., and WYNNE, B. (eds.) (1989) *Expert Evidence: Interpreting Science in the Law*, London: Routledge.

SNIDER, L. (1987) 'Towards a Political Economy of Reform, Regulation and Corporate Crime', *Law and Policy* 9/1: 37–68.

STENNING, P. C., SHEARING, C. D., ADDARIO, S. M., and CONDON, M. G. (1990) 'Controlling Interests: Two Conceptions of Order in Regulating a Financial Market', in M. L. Friedland (ed.), *Securing Compliance*, Toronto: University of Toronto Press.

STIGLER, G. J. (1971) 'The Theory of Economic Regulation', *Bell Journal of Economics* 2: 3–21.

STONE, C. (1975) *Where the Law Ends: The Social Control of Corporate Behaviour*, Prospect Heights: Waveland Press.

SUNSTEIN, C. R. (1990) *After the Rights Revolution: Reconcieving the Regulatory State*, Cambridge, Mass.: Harvard University Press.

TAPPAN, P. (1947) 'Who is the Criminal?' *American Sociological Review* 12/1: 96–102.

TOFT, B. (1996) 'Limits to Mathematical Modelling of Disasters', in Hood and Jones (1996).

TURNER, B. A. (1994) 'Causes of Disaster: Sloppy Management', *British Journal of Management* 5/3: 215–20.

—— and PIDGEON, N. F. (1997) *Man-Made Disasters*, Oxford: Butterworth-Heinemann.

UFF, J. (2000) *The Southall Accident Inquiry Report*, London: HSC.

UNGER, R. M. (1975) *Knowledge and Politics*, New York and London: Free Press/Collier Macmillan.

VAUGHAN, D. (1982) 'Transaction Systems and Unlawful Organisational Behaviour', *Social Problems* 29/4: 373–9.

—— (1996) *The Challenger Launch Decision: Risky Technology, Culture and Deviance at NASA*, Chicago: University of Chicago Press.

—— (1998) 'Rational Choice, Situated Action, and the Social Control of Organisations', *Law and Society Review* 32/1: 23–61.

VELJANOVSKI, C. (1987) *Selling the State*, London: Weidenfeld & Nicolson.

VISCUSI, W. K. (1983) 'Alternative Approaches to Valuing the Health Impacts of Accidents: Liability Law and Prospective Evaluations', *Law and Contemporary Problems* 46: 49.

WALTERS, D., and GOURLAY, S. (1990) *Statutory Employee Involvement in Health and Safety at the Workplace: A Report of The Implementation and Effectiveness of the Safety Representatives and Safety Committees Regulations 1977*, London: HSE.

—— DALTON, A., and GEE, D. (1993) *Worker Representation on Health and Safety in Europe*, Brussels: European Trade Union Technical Bureau for Health and Safety.

WEAIT, M. J. (1989) 'The Letter of the Law? An Enquiry into Reasoning and Formal Enforcement in the Industrial Air Pollution Inspectorate', *British Journal of Criminology* 29/1: 57–70.

WELLS, C. (1993) *Corporations and Criminal Responsibility*, Oxford: Clarendon Press.

WHITEHURST, W. (1977) 'Suffocation by Regulation', *Journal of Social and Political Studies* 2/1.

WILDAVSKY, A., and DRAKE, K. (1990) 'Theories of Risk Perception: Who Fears What and Why?' *Daedalus* 119/4.

WILLIAMS, J. L. (1960) *Accidents and Ill-Health at Work*, London: Staples Press.

WILSON, G. K. (1985) *The Politics of Safety and Health*, Oxford: Clarendon Press.

WILSON, J. Q. (1980) *The Politics of Regulation*, New York: Basic Books.

WILTHAGEN, T. (1993) 'Reflexive Rationality in the Regulation of Occupational Health and Safety', in R. Rogowski and T. Wilthagen (eds.), *Reflexive Labour Law*, Boston: Kluwer-Nijhoff.

WITTE, A. D., and WOODBURY, D. F. (1985) 'The Effect of Tax Laws and Tax Administration on Tax Compliance', *National Tax Journal* 38.

WYNNE, B. (1989) 'Establishing the Rules of Laws: Constructing Expert Authority', in R. Smith and B. Wynne (eds.), *Expert Evidence: Interpreting Science in the Law*, London: Routledge.

YEAGER, P. C. (1991) *The Limits of the Law: The Public Regulation of Private Pollution*, Cambridge: Cambridge University Press.

INDEX